ANNE SEBBA

Enid Bagnold

THE AUTHORIZED BIOGRAPHY

Weidenfeld and Nicolson

LONDON

First published in paperback in Great Britain in 1988 by
George Weidenfeld & Nicolson Limited
91 Clapham High Street, London sw4 7TA

ISBN 0 297 79363 2

Printed in Great Britain at
The Bath Press, Avon

Enid Bagnold

For My Parents

Contents

Illustrations

Acknowledgements

My first debt is to the children and executors of Enid Bagnold: Laurian d'Harcourt (Comtesse Anne-Pierre d'Harcourt), Timothy Jones, Richard Bagnold Jones and Dominick Jones. I thank them most warmly for allowing me to examine and quote from the papers of Enid Bagnold, for entrusting me with many of these in my own home over a period of years, for offering me generous hospitality, for never failing to answer even my most trivial questions and, above all, for sharing with me their understanding and memories of a most remarkable and original woman and mother. To Denys Lambert too, in his capacity as Enid Bagnold's executor and friend of the Jones family, I extend thanks for help and cooperation.

This book is an authorized biography. However, the selection of material, the narrative of events and the points of view expressed are the results of my own judgement and are therefore my own responsibility entirely.

Many other people have generously given me their time, searched on my behalf for letters or photographs, permitted me to quote from copyright material or helped me in myriad ways to see this book to fruition. I know the following list cannot adequately convey my gratitude to them but I hope they will understand if I do not thank them all individually. They are: Anthony Alpers, Barbara Anderman, Perry and Joseph Anthony, Dame Peggy Ashcroft, the Viscountess Astor, the Hon. David Astor, Michael Asquith, Gladys Atkins, Brigadier and Mrs R. A. Bagnold, Dr Wendy Baron, Nicola Beauman, Sybille Bedford, Anne Olivier Bell, Nora Beloff, Eliot Bliss, Doris Blum, Mark Bonham Carter, Mrs Basil Boothby, the late Carol Brandt, Lord Briggs, Pat Brown, Janet Burroway, Vivienne Byerley, Arthur Calder-Marshall, Judy Campbell, Christine Carpenter, Mirabel Cecil, Lady Chancellor, Ludi Claire, Caroline Coombes, the late Lady Diana Cooper, Cecilia Cussans, Elizabeth Dacre, Dr David Davidson, Andrew Davies, Allan Davis, the Duchess of Devonshire, Elaine Dundy, E. Edbrooke, H. S. Ede, Sumner Locke Elliott, Peter Eyre, Robert Feld, Gwen Ffrangcon-Davies, Geraldine Fitzgerald, Robert Flemyng, Bryan Forbes, Edward Fox, Robert Freedman, Lord and Lady Freyberg, Christopher Fry, the Hon. Clive and Mrs Gibson, Sir John Gielgud, Penelope Gilliatt, Lady Gladwyn, Lady

Glenconner, Victoria Glendinning, Peter Glenville, Lady Glock, Jean Goodman, the late Ruth Gordon, Graham Greene, Richard Green-Wilkinson, Joan Greenwood, Miron Grindea, Donald Hall, Selina Hastings, Jack Henry, Gavin Henderson, Katharine Hepburn, Tara Heinemann, Priscilla Hodgson, Michael Holroyd, R. Nesbitt Horne, John Houseman, Eileen Hose, Cecile Howard, Angela Jones, Penny Jones, Garson Kanin, Felix Kelly, Robert Lantz, Pandora Lebon, James Lees-Milne, Deirdre Levi, Kathleen Levy, Kenneth Lindsay, Joan Ling, Richard Lister, Paula Long (Gellibrand), Prince Jean-Louis de Faucigny-Lucinge, Mary Lutyens, Mary Lynn, Christopher MacKane, Henry Manisty, Lady Mansergh, Albert Marre, Vivian Matalon, Douglas Matthews, Winnie Maxwell, Alec McCowen, Siobhan McKenna, Isabelle McHardy, Hayley Mills, Lord Monk Bretton, Sabrina Montfort Bebb, Elaine Moss, Eileen Neale, Nigel Nicolson, the Marquess of Northampton, the Viscount Norwich, M. Abbot van Nostrand, Dr John O'Hara, John Osborne, George Painter, Michael Parkin, Trekkie Parsons, Frances Partridge, John Perry, Rosemary Peto, Charles Pick, George Pinker, Fred Pritchard, Philippa Pullar, Mark Ramage, Margaret Ramsay, John and Rosalind Randle, Esther Rantzen, Julia Read, Bryan Robertson, Patience Ross, the Hon. Mrs Keith Rous, Joan and Eric Rubinstein, Victor Samrock, Rosalie and Sam Sebba, Pat Shute (Royal Society of Literature), Martin E. Segal, Irene M. Selznick, Amanda Smith (Samuel French), Henry Smith, Oliver Smith, Hilary Spurling, the Rev. Noel Staines, Mary Talbot, Dorothy Taylor, Elizabeth Taylor, Michael Thornton, Myfanwy Thomas, Edward Thompson, John Trewin, Peter Ustinov, Keith Vartan, Mrs William Vestey, Hugo Vickers, Martin and Linda Walls, Elizabeth Wansbrough, Erich Warburg, Georgina Ward, Daphne Webb, Dame Veronica Wedgwood, Noel Willman, Peter Willes, Irene Worth, Noel Woolf, Frances Young.

I would also like to acknowledge the help provided by the following libraries and institutions and their staff: the Ben Uri Art Gallery, London; the Henry W. and Albert A. Berg Collection of English and American Literature, New York Public Library, Astor, Lenox and Tilden Foundations; the Beinecke Rare Book and Manuscript Library, Yale University Connecticut; the Brighton *Argus*; Department of Special Collections, the University of California, Los Angeles; Harry Ransom Humanities Research Center, University of Texas at Austin; Kettle's Yard, University of Cambridge; the London Library; Mercury Gallery, London; Department of Special Collections McFarlin Library, University of Tulsa, Oklahoma; Reuters, London; Richmond-upon-Thames Library; The Society of Authors on behalf of the Bernard Shaw Estate; the *Sunday Times*; Manuscript Section, University of Sussex Library; Michael

Sissons on behalf of the Literary Estate of Rebecca West; the Author's Literary Estate and the Hogarth Press for permission to quote from passages in the edited volumes of Virginia Woolf's Diaries and Letters.

My agent Gill Coleridge and my editors at Weidenfeld & Nicolson, John Curtis and Alex MacCormick, deserve special thanks.

To my husband, Mark Sebba, my partner in this as in everything, go my most loving thanks. His enthusiasm, practical support and stimulating criticism (although not always accepted) have sustained me over five years. Without him...

Anne Sebba
Richmond, 1986.

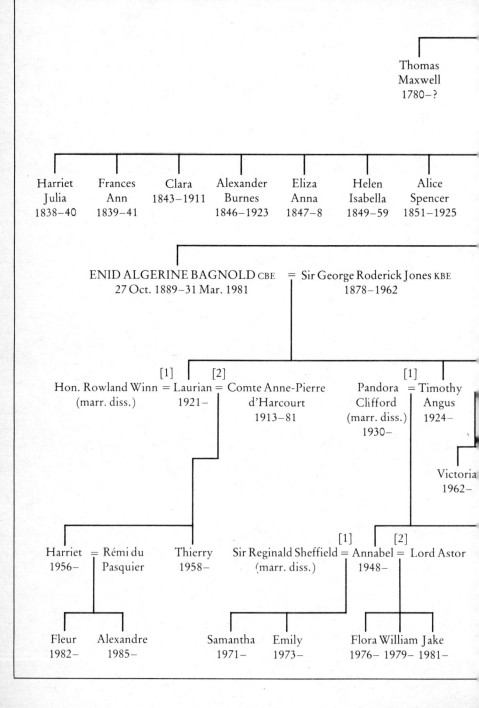

Bagnold Family Tree

Thomas
Maxwell
1780–?

| Harriet Julia 1838–40 | Frances Ann 1839–41 | Clara 1843–1911 | Alexander Burnes 1846–1923 | Eliza Anna 1847–8 | Helen Isabella 1849–59 | Alice Spencer 1851–1925 |

ENID ALGERINE BAGNOLD CBE   =   Sir George Roderick Jones KBE
27 Oct. 1889–31 Mar. 1981   1878–1962

[1]   [2]   [1]
Hon. Rowland Winn = Laurian = Comte Anne-Pierre   Pandora = Timothy
(marr. diss.)   1921–   d'Harcourt   Clifford   Angus
                  1913–81   (marr. diss.)   1924–
                                  1930–

Victoria
1962–

                                        [1]   [2]
Harriet = Rémi du   Thierry   Sir Reginald Sheffield = Annabel = Lord Astor
1956–   Pasquier   1958–   (marr. diss.)   1948–

Fleur   Alexandre   Samantha   Emily   Flora William Jake
1982–   1985–   1971–   1973–   1976– 1979– 1981–

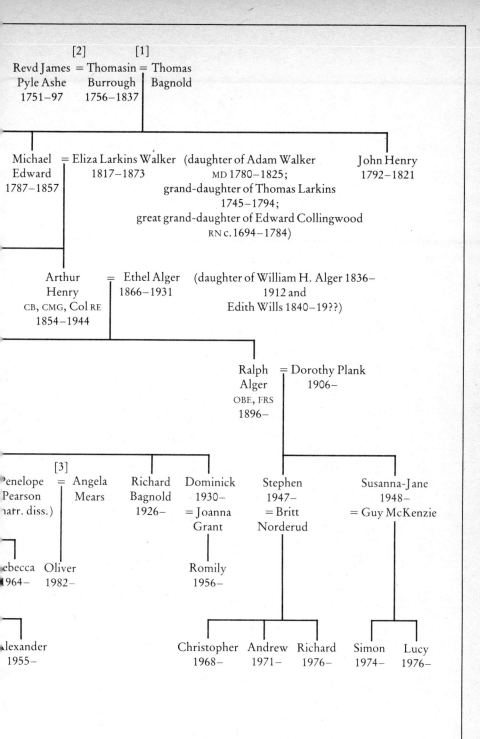

[2]   [1]
Revd James = Thomasin = Thomas
Pyle Ashe   Burrough   Bagnold
1751–97   1756–1837

Michael   = Eliza Larkins Walker   (daughter of Adam Walker
Edward   1817–1873   MD 1780–1825;
1787–1857   grand-daughter of Thomas Larkins
                                                   1745–1794;
                              great grand-daughter of Edward Collingwood
                                          RN c. 1694–1784)

John Henry
1792–1821

Arthur   = Ethel Alger   (daughter of William H. Alger 1836–
Henry   1866–1931   1912 and
CB, CMG, Col RE   Edith Wills 1840–19??)
1854–1944

Ralph   = Dorothy Plank
Alger   1906–
OBE, FRS
1896–

[3]
Penelope = Angela   Richard   Dominick   Stephen   Susanna-Jane
Pearson   Mears   Bagnold   1930–   1947–   1948–
marr. diss.)   1926–   = Joanna   = Britt   = Guy McKenzie
                                            Grant   Norderud

Rebecca Oliver   Romily
1964–   1982–   1956–

Alexander   Christopher Andrew Richard   Simon   Lucy
1955–   1968–   1971–   1976–   1974–   1976–

ONE

Born a Writer

ONE cold autumn day in 1975, two elderly ladies paid a visit to a well-established jewellery shop in Philadelphia. Both women bore an aristocratic mien that was not out of place in the formal atmosphere of Bailey, Banks & Biddle. As the salesman brought out gold bracelets for them to look at, he noticed something unusual about the elder of the two. She had wispy, brownish hair framing a face that had evidently been handsome. Time had etched only a few lines around her still bright eyes, but had sucked away the fullness of her cheeks, making her aquiline nose appear more prominent. She retained a generous mouth and a determined square jaw. She was tall, although a little bent, with a heavy bosom tapering down to slim legs and fine ankles. Her feet were bare.

Wandering around Philadelphia in the fall without shoes excites comment. People stared. Who was this woman? Was she mad? Observing that her companion was Katharine Hepburn, their curiosity doubled. Had they seen the hoardings of Philadelphia's Forest Theater, they might have guessed. Katharine Hepburn was starring in *A Matter of Gravity* by the English playwright Enid Bagnold.

The journey to Philadelphia for Enid Bagnold had not in any sense been straightforward. She left Heathrow airport on 26 October 1975, the day before her eighty-sixth birthday, in a wheel chair. She was escorted by a fully trained nurse who had to bring a supply of five drugs, without which her charge could not live, as well as complicated documentation to satisfy the officials of the US Drugs Enforcement Agency at Philadelphia airport. 'I don't suppose we shall ever see her again,' commented one of the nurses as she left.

Bringing the play to Philadelphia had been almost as difficult as bringing the playwright. Enid Bagnold never found writing easy. She was, by her own admission, 'not a born writer but born a writer'. Her difficulties increased with age. She wrestled with words, discarding the weakest and retaining only the fittest. This play had almost beaten her. Another version had been a disastrous failure in 1968; but, since then, she had rewritten most of it several times. She was making revisions to the end, even after it had been performed in Philadelphia. But she was a courageous writer, not intimidated by criticism, and the spur of ambition, as she neared ninety, was still digging her sharply in the ribs.

A graphologist once described Enid's handwriting as that of a 'natural communicator'. True, she was a profound observer of the human condition with a deep desire to communicate what she saw; but she wrote unhampered by political or social considerations and did not subject her observations to intellectual analysis. Arguably, had she done so, her writing might have lost some of its freshness and appeal. She worked intuitively; honest enough never to avoid her own reactions, but individual enough always to avoid clichés. This made for an originality of expression bought, occasionally, at the expense of clarity. Many a critic found her later plays confusing and muddled with a hint of madness; but she had always written about herself, fascinated by her own impulsions and impressions of places, events and people. Now the victim of a stroke and heavily dependent on morphia following an operation, her own world was confused. Although her ability to get in touch with life never faltered, increasingly, it was not the life audiences wished to learn about nor, she believed, that actors and directors understood.

Going barefoot in the city in October was not simply the action of a crazy woman. She had always found shoes restricting and painful, but only in her seventies had she gained the confidence to shun them. 'Remember this when you are seventy-seven,' she wrote to a friend, '(it's as a gift to you that I say it) that nothing has lessened the ecstasy of walking with bare feet over the dew, between the shades of apple trees, down a slope to write . . . they say people can't feel as much when they are old. They can.'

That Enid Bagnold was chiefly interested in her own sensitivities she never denied. Once asked, 'Are you talking of you? Or me?' she replied: 'When one feels strongly it is always of *me*.' But Enid's introspection did not end there. She had been concerned from an early age to define what the 'me' was going to be. Many people, especially writers, construct a past for themselves. The difference with Enid was that she was living her own fantasy. She became what she wrote and she wrote what she became. Thus a biographer, tracing the points where life and art impinge, finds in the case of Enid Bagnold that they are rarely separate. It is simplistic to look at Enid's writing purely as a *roman-à-clef*, as no key can take account of composites, inventions and inversions. Equally, however, she was unable to people a purely imaginary world. The fictional worlds that she created were so close to the real world as she knew it that they became as one. There were elements of Enid in every woman she wrote of, but, more than that, imperceptibly Enid had become a character from an Enid Bagnold work.

Enid's children, too, were to become inextricably entangled in the myth. Her husband, Sir Roderick Jones, however, was deliberately excluded, for 'Lady Jones' was a quite separate character. Sometimes she was useful and on occasions both she and Enid Bagnold pulled together.* But the 'me' always referred to Enid Bagnold. As she wrote to her father, '"With love and many happy returns on the birthday of Enid Bagnold" is the nicest thing because however much you are married you remain proud and conscious of yourself as yourself ... it always warms me to see my own name.'

The Bagnold name meant a great deal to Enid. She was conscious of her Bagnold inheritance as a shaping force far stronger than any attributes her mother's family, the Algers, had handed down. She felt, as she grew older, that she was locked into the ancestral line where she belonged: 'I grew out of the dead and I can't forget it.' Nor did she forget that it was a line of brave, hard-working ancestors who believed in excellence and success. Her father saw to that.

Enid's father, a colonel in the Royal Engineers, devoted his retirement to tracing branches and even twigs of the family tree. 'Sometimes I believe in a little ancestor worship,' he told his daughter, after he and Enid's mother had trekked round England searching church records and gravestones for biographical data. Mrs Bagnold also visited the British Museum and the India Office, carefully copying out any interesting references. Finally, in meticulous calligraphy and stretching over several pages, Colonel Bagnold set down for posterity his children's lineage.

Enid had planned, before old age set in, to examine all the family documents and papers which her father had carefully preserved; but, although the boxes had been in her writing-room since 1945, it was only when a burst tank threatened their existence some ten years later that she began to take an interest in them. She had none the less already developed a great feeling for the family from which she had sprung – how 'sperm has been ejected through two hundred years to arrive at me'.

Enid's great-grandfather, Thomas Bagnold, a brewer, was born in 1751. In 1779 he married a west-country girl, Thomasin Burrough, seventh daughter of James Burrough, bell-founder. Thomasin's claim to royal descent may be seen as an indication of her social aspirations, and marriage with the brewer Bagnold, for whatever reason undertaken, was unlikely to satisfy these ambitions. Her frustrations revealed themselves in a fiery temper, which Enid believed both she and her father had inherited. This hot temper may

---

* She wrote to *The Times* on 29 November 1973, asking the Editor to publish it as from Lady Jones but to sign it 'Enid Bagnold': 'In order that by using both names I may reach a larger audience.'

have been the cause of the couple's later separation; when Thomas's brewery business foundered, Thomasin's ire was roused. Thomas went to Eccleshall, where he died in 1797. Four years later Thomasin married again, a gentleman of some fortune, the Reverend James Pyle Ashe. This marriage, at St Clement Dane's church in the Strand, was recorded in *Gentleman's Magazine* under 'Marriages of Remarkable Persons'. Mrs Bagnold of Arundel Street was moving up in the world: her new husband, the magazine recorded, was nephew of the late Chancellor Hoadly, of the diocese of Winchester, a poet and dramatist appointed chaplain to the Prince of Wales's household in 1736.

At all events, Thomasin cannot have been an easy mother, as her three sons – Thomas Maxwell, Michael Edward and John – all left home at a tender age to seek their fortunes abroad. Enid's great-uncle Thomas joined the Portsmouth division of the Royal Marines in 1797, aged seventeen, not to see his family again for forty-one years. He was captain of many ships and recorded his adventures in a remarkable diary, much more than a log of events. Duels, skirmishes and drunken brawls among the men are vividly reported as well as a frightening voyage when yellow fever struck and about two-thirds of the crew died. Fellow officer Edward Dix, writing later about 'that dreadful visitation from heaven', praised the young Bagnold for his most humane assistance 'in administering every comfort to the living . . . and ready to perform the last pious duties over the bodies of the dead.'

Captain Bagnold's bravery notwithstanding, on 8 January 1810, he appeared before a court martial at Woolwich. He was cashiered on evidence – cooked, according to Enid's father – that he and a fellow captain had extorted sixteen guineas from a recruit to give him his discharge. However, after protestations of innocence to Lord Cochrane (afterwards Lord Cochrane of Chile), under whom he at one time served, Bagnold was, after twenty-one years, reinstated. 'Thus ended a history of injustice,' commented Enid's father.

While Thomas had been away at sea, Michael, Enid's grandfather, also felt similarly constrained by his mother and left home at fourteen. He sailed from Gravesend on 11 April 1802 in the *Sir Edward Hughes* as a volunteer in the Bombay Marines. He arrived in India four months later and saw action immediately 'against the piratical states of Malwan'.

Barely fifteen, he was then part of Sir John Hayes's forces employed in the Bay of Bengal against the French cruisers and he fought at the storming and capture of the forts of Muckey and Soosoo on the coast of Sumatra. Two years later he was among a party of rough young men who landed on one of the Andaman Islands and went ashore for a drink at a shack kept by a native proprietor. This hapless individual had just died, probably from cholera, and was lying in his coffin. Michael, eschewing the customary quantities of liquor, incurred his companions' wrath. 'All screwed', as Michael described the gang, they determined to rectify this state of affairs. Tipping out the innkeeper, they replaced him with Michael, whom they rendered unconscious. They then laid him at the water's edge. When the waves, tilting his coffin, finally woke him, he found himself floating out to sea. Thus chastened, he left the Marines, and, upon arrival in India, managed to improve his prospects by becoming an ensign in the Third Bombay Infantry.

Most of what is known about Michael, who ended his days as a major-general in the Hon. East India Company, is contained in a series of letters he wrote from the time of his marriage in 1838 onwards. Enid's mother, in a typically selfless act foreshadowing her treatment of her own daughter's letters, later typed out Michael Bagnold's letters stretching over several volumes. They tell the personal life story of a general, as he moved among the rajahs and their mistresses, and of the social life of India at that period – 'A little jaunty, a little trivial, and not really to be compared with the mind and way of writing of his elder brother,' Enid commented.

Thomas and Michael met again in 1838 at Blackfriars Steps in London, when Thomas took his younger brother to 7 High Row, Knightsbridge, to see their mother. According to family lore, Thomas said, 'Mother, here's Michael.' Thomasin Pyle Ashe looked at her son and said : 'What, that ugly man, my son ? Never !' Ugly or not, Thomasin did not flinch some years later from asking Michael to return to nurse her and his stepfather. The General wrote back from India: 'In that case shall you leave me your fortune?' History relates that the answers from both parties were in the negative.

As neither mother nor career could provide him with the capital he needed to cushion the last years of his life, Michael looked instead to a wife. During a rare trip home on leave, he had met and decided to marry Eliza Larkins Walker, a young girl then living at Reading. Eliza came from a long-established seafaring and ship-owning family. By 1777, Eliza's great-grandfather had set up a bank in connection with his burgeoning ship-owning interests. Eliza's grandfather, Thomas Larkins, was a captain in the Hon. East India Company and her father, Adam Walker MD, a surgeon of East Indiamen on many ships. He died in Burma, when he was head surgeon of the flotilla under the command of Sir John Hayes.

Michael was fifty-one when he proposed to Eliza, thirty years his junior, but his leave expired before she had made up her mind. He then wrote to Eliza, sending her the money for her trousseau and passage, explaining that this was not at all because he took her coming for granted, but because the passage was so lengthy and he was no longer young. He waited on the quayside and she was there. They were married at Christ Church, Byculla, Bombay on 1 January 1838. They had eight children, four of whom died in India or were buried at sea. The surviving offspring were Clara, Alexander, Alice and Arthur. Enid's father, Arthur, was born in 1854, just three years before his father's death at the age of seventy-one. Enid was always struck by the huge span in ages between her grandfather, born two years before the fall of the Bastille, one year before the trial of Warren Hastings and a year after the death of Frederick the Great; and herself joining the world on the edge of the 'gay nineties'. Equally striking was the way in which marriage to Eliza had at last brought the Bagnolds a measure of financial security through alliance with trade.

Arthur Henry Bagnold was born on 18 March at 6 Cunningham Place, the London home of some cousins. The General was having a splendid new house built for his retirement at nearby 14 Hamilton Terrace, but this was not ready in time for the birth of their youngest child. The villas and terraces of St John's Wood, a leafy Victorian suburb of north London, were at this time attracting residents of the utmost respectability. For the most part they were 'professional men, city merchants and West End tradesmen, retired officers from India and the Colonies and merchants from Australia'. These gentlemen were taking advantage of the double delights of seclusion and social homogeneity afforded by the vicinity. Because of the excellent and genteel omnibus service, most of the new houses were built without stables or mews, which had the desirable effect of excluding the working class more completely than had yet been possible.

Arthur and his three siblings were at first all taught by Miss Smart, a governess who later developed senile dementia and tried to murder another old woman. Miss Smart was the illegitimate daughter of a man called Knight and in her senility she would not sign anything other than with the name Knight – a characteristic which Enid, forever fascinated by a murderer's mind, found intriguing.

At nine, Arthur went to a school in Brighton and three years later followed his elder brother to Cheltenham. There he rose quickly to the top class, where he remained for two years. At school, he designed and made an early wooden bicycle, a feat which required a scientist's inventive brain as well as a craftsman's manual skills. This rare combination of talents would mark him out from the common soldier.

At sixteen, the young Arthur entered the Royal Military Academy at Woolwich, a fellow cadet with the future Lord Kitchener. He passed out in 1872 and was commissioned a lieutenant in the Royal Engineers. After

Woolwich, Bagnold was sent to Aldershot, where he distinguished himself principally for making the first telephone in England. Mr (later Sir) William Preece, Chief Electrician Post Office Telegraphs, had just returned from America with a prized possession : the first pair of telephones ever seen in this country. When Mr Preece came to lecture about the telephone to the officers at Aldershot, Enid's father listened carefully and took notes. He managed to construct a new pair of telephones entirely from his notes.

The Royal Engineers were at that time in charge of the incipient telephone system. Arthur Bagnold arranged the first set between the officers' and the men's quarters at Aldershot. Telling his servant Shrapnell to listen in, he went back to his own position to use the revolutionary instrument. The young Bagnold spoke into his telephone : 'Shrapnell, Shrapnell, can you hear me ?' Silence. 'Damn, it doesn't work.' Then Shrapnell wandered out of the trees, white as a ghost, trailing the cable behind him. 'Sir, sir, I heard yer voice.' In her autobiography Enid commented how, on his eightieth birthday, she telephoned her father from South Africa. He was as awestruck as had been the faithful Shrapnell.

Bagnold was next ordered to Cyprus, under occupation by British troops, where one evening he dined with Kitchener in his tent. He returned home in 1880, but the following year he was in South Africa, leading a section of field telegraphs to join the force under Sir Evelyn Wood, and laid one hundred miles of telegraph line from Newcastle, in Natal, to Pretoria, but saw no fighting. After another year's respite in England, by August 1884 he was on active service again, this time in Egypt. As a member of one of the two expeditions sent to relieve General Gordon, he was trying to work his way up the Nile cataracts, but the expedition learned of Gordon's death while at Dongola. For his services in Egypt, Bagnold, who had been promoted captain in September 1884, received a mention in dispatches and the brevet of major. He stayed on in Egypt until 1887, during which time he organized the recovery of a colossal statue of Rameses II weighing a hundred tons, which had been submerged in a lake. On his return home in 1887, he spent thirteen months on engineer services at Plymouth and Cardiff. While in the west country, Major Bagnold met and fell in love with a beautiful twenty-two-year-old, Ethel Alger. She had golden hair, violet eyes, an eighteen-inch waist and some talent for sketching.

Ethel's family, the Algers, were long-standing and prosperous Plymouth residents. Her mother, Enid's maternal grandmother, was a daughter of Alderman Wills of Plymouth. Ethel's father, William Henry Alger, had inherited a large chemical and fertilizer manufactory at Cattedown, of which his father was one of the founders. William Alger was brought up in a family of devout Plymouth Brethren, more than one member of whom became a missionary. William, not without some difficulty, increasingly discarded a faith in God, turning his religious zeal instead to philanthropy.

William Alger was for many years a conspicuous figure in the public life of his native town. That he was a man of considerable wealth is indicated by his ownership of Widey Court, a magnificent mansion, where he lived for several years with his five children and eight servants. Widey is mentioned in the Domesday Book and, during the siege of Plymouth (1644–5), Prince Maurice, who was in command of the Royalist troops, had his headquarters at Widey. King Charles I, while at Buckland Abbey, held court at Widey, after which it was always known as Widey Court. Evidently the Algers left this house by the late 1880s as W. H. Alger, JP, is next listed in the Plymouth directories at Manor House, Stoke Damerel, also a substantial house of fine style and proportions, where Enid was to stay many times during her childhood.

The four surviving Alger children made a strikingly good-looking family group with their fair hair, dark eyes and shining complexions. In 1885 Ethel, the elder daughter, was sent, like most girls of her class, to be groomed at a finishing school abroad. Nellie Ravenhill, who was to become her closest friend, remembered her arrival with her father and mother at the Dusseldorf establishment. 'She was dressed in a lovely seal skin, trimmed with beaver, and hat to match. She came down to the evening meal in a beautiful crimson plush tight fitting bodice with a merino skirt and a mass of little frills . . . she made a very pretty picture with her lovely hair. Everyone made much of her – we had never seen such luxury.'

Ethel was rather shy and not very good at lessons, but she excelled at singing, especially ballads. Nellie often accompanied her on the piano and said that nothing ever gave her greater joy than hearing her friend's lilting tones. Ethel Alger spent much of her time in Dusseldorf improving her voice, studying for a time with Lotte Lehman; but the object of such an establishment was ultimately to turn girls into wives and on her return to Plymouth, the business of finding a husband began in earnest.

Ethel did not lack for suitors, though few of them were suitable. She and Nellie would often go to the afternoon ship dances, of which there were many every summer in Plymouth. More than one young sailor was struck by Ethel's beauty and charm. A curate who caught a glimpse of her at a garden party came to call a few days later. Ethel agreed to see him. Presently she came out crying, 'Oh, Mummy, you must go in and see Mr. R; he has asked me to marry him and I said "yes" but I mean "no".' Soon after this she was sent away to recover from an infatuation with a most impecunious subaltern. Although she 'caught' men easily, she was terrified by the result.

Ethel was singing at a musical evening on 9 April 1888, when Major Bagnoll (as she wrote in her diary) introduced himself to her. She told her diary that he was a 'well-made, broad man, good height, brown hair tinged with red, a kind of auburn. Long fierce moustache, blue eyes.' By September, Ethel was refusing invitations, 'as Arthur did not wish me to go without him'. The couple wrote to each other regularly during this period. Ethel's fifty-eight letters, which Arthur Bagnold cherished throughout their married life, were all, he said later, 'of the most affectionate and loving character and they exhibit much serious thought on the part of the writer'.

At the time of Ethel's meeting with Arthur, William Alger had just completed his second term as Mayor of Plymouth. During his mayoralty (1885–87) Alger and his wife had received the King of Portugal and had celebrated Queen Victoria's Jubilee with appropriate pomp and circumstance. 'Many useful works for the benefit of the town were inaugurated. . . . Mr Alger ungrudgingly placed his time, energy and money at the service of the town to uphold its high traditions.'

This life-style suited Mrs Alger, a devout church-goer and resolute snob. Mayor Alger, when confronted with his wife's ambitious social arrangements, usually caved in. 'My dear, you do just as you like', was his frequent rejoinder. But it was more that she was relentlessly complacent about her own position in provincial society than that she was trying to climb higher. When Ethel began to receive the determined attentions of the thirty-four-year-old Major Bagnold, Mrs Alger was not displeased at the prospect of the liaison culminating in marriage. She hoped, no doubt, that his forceful personality would be a controlling influence on her lovely but immature daughter.

It was a propitious match, combining as it did brains with beauty, and female accomplishments with military decisiveness. Bagnold dignity and distinction was now coupled with capital and social position. Ethel and Arthur were married on Wednesday, 19 December 1888, from the Manor House. Nellie Ravenhill was chief bridesmaid and the couple spent their honeymoon in Nice and Monte Carlo.

When they returned, Arthur took up a post as an instructor at the School of Military Engineering, Chatham, and they moved to Borstal Cottage, a pretty, Georgian house in Rochester, Kent, with a magnificent view up the Medway Valley to the Cuxton Hills. It was there, ten months later, on 27 October 1889, that their first child was born: a healthy girl christened Enid Algerine Bagnold.

TWO

I Don't Regret the Little One being a Girl

COLONEL Arthur Bagnold appeared to Ethel's friends as being 'terribly severe . . . and selfish but the best possible partner for Ethel's temperament and upbringing.' That he was a man of some experience, who had not forfeited the pleasures of mistresses while on foreign service, was never talked about, but doubtless evident. He cared nothing for music and singing, and Ethel rarely went to the piano after they were married. He was also quite uninterested in female fashions and adornments, and hated married women 'decking themselves'. Ethel always dressed well, but was no longer preoccupied with appearances and was far more anxious to make her husband happy. She was an utterly devoted young bride and overjoyed to discover that she was soon to be a mother.

The pregnancy was uneventful and Ethel continued to ride almost until the birth. Although there was a small obstruction at one stage during labour, all went well. 'When you do see your grand-daughter, I think you will be pleased with her,' Arthur wrote to his father-in-law a few days later. 'How Ethel could have produced such a gigantic infant is a marvel.'

He added significantly, 'I don't regret the fact of the little one being a girl a bit.' Nor did he. Within certain obvious restrictions of the age, Arthur Bagnold displayed liberal views on a daughter's upbringing and Enid was given the same advantages, admonishments and practical instructions as a son. Within days, Ethel was completely captivated by the infant, although she found lying in bed for the customary three weeks rather a tiresome business. 'However I've got my baby by my side. It is not a bad little thing . . . it has very long arms, long fingers, long legs and toes, it is nice and soft to touch. It squeals a lot and sleeps a lot – I think I get fonder of the little thing every day.'

Enid's own earliest childhood memories are of the pride her mother took in her young daughter's quick brain. She learnt to read by the age of four and remembered with glee shouting out the advertising slogans as the train steamed past. Also at a young age, Enid felt instinctive scorn for her grandmother Alger. This was mostly because her grandmother did not view the child with the same adoring delight as did her own mother. Enid was disdainful, too, of the way Mrs Alger dragged her obliging husband every winter to what she called (much to Enid's amusement) the 'Reveera'. In her early years Enid spent much time in the company of her grandmother. Ethel had been a very young bride and not completely out of the family orbit when she had married and in any case, Arthur was working hard at his career and was often away. As Edith Alger frequently came to stay at the Bagnolds' cottage or as, more usually, Ethel took Enid to Stoke Damerel, there were plenty of occasions for Edith to chastise her daughter for not being strict enough with the child who was, she feared, growing up both spoilt and a rough tomboy. Although Arthur disliked his mother-in-law, he tolerated her influence for his wife's sake.* During the visits to Stoke, Enid could appreciate the luxuriance of her rich surroundings – the yellow brocade of the drawing-room and the lush plants of the tropical conservatory – but she deeply resented having to share her mother's love with the woman who seemed to come between them.

However, it was for her grandmother's attitude towards religion that Enid felt the greatest contempt. Her grandfather was by now an agnostic and, much to his wife's humiliation, refused to accompany her to church. 'Grannie was always name-dropping about God. You'd have thought He was an earl,' Enid wrote. When Grannie Alger climbed into her carriage to attend church without her husband, 'she wore a dainty look of sorrow as though she was leaving him in Hell', Enid remembered.

It was through Edith Alger that Enid learned about the fine gradations of class. '"People", she indicated with little h'ms and smiles, "were born on shelves and very nice if you were near the top one."' There were always many relations in church but although spoken to afterwards, the young Enid was astute enough to observe that they were never invited back to luncheon. There followed, after church, a round of social calls to elderly relatives – Great-aunt Mary Grace, who gave her shortbread; Great-aunt Lizzie, whose neck was broken; and Great-aunt Bertha, who gave her substantial fortune to missions. These were visits which left Enid with pocket-money and a sad impression of the inhumanity of old age. The afternoon, when staying with Grannie, was punctuated by further 'calls' to people of high standing in the neighbourhood.

For six years it appeared as if Enid was to be Ethel and Arthur's only child. She secured for herself during that time an unassailable position in her parents', especially her mother's, affections, and was perfectly accepted, when her grandmother was not there, 'as a rough little girl. If a boy is what mothers want then the first child is all but born a boy.' Later Enid became

---

* The Bagnolds housed a marble bust of Edith Alger, but, after Ethel Bagnold's death, Arthur threw it into a pond.

dimly aware that there had been other pregnancies, but these had ended in miscarriage.

When Enid was six, she made a workmanlike sampler map of Africa. However, by far the most tumultuous event in her life that year was the arrival of her only brother, Ralph Alger Bagnold, born on 3 April 1896, at the grandparental home. As a treat for Enid before the baby arrived, her mother agreed to her having a pair of mice to look after and suggested a letter for her to copy to her father thanking him for allowing her the animals. Enid rejected the proposed letter. 'I don't want to send elder words like that. In my letter I shall send my young ones.'

She was evidently an articulate child, often making precocious, if un-original, observations. Ten days after Ralph's birth Ethel reported proudly:

'Enid said this afternoon: Mummie, what are these two things I have got?

'Breasts, my dear.

'Can I suck my own breasts and if I did should I have milk like you?

'No.

'Then why have you and why haven't I?'

However hard the child tried to shock her mother, the reaction was in-dulgent laughter. But if Ethel Bagnold spoilt her beloved first-born, Enid's father stood for no nonsense. Obedience, not love, was his creed. Enid did love him all the same and respected his sense of justice, although she did not feel close to him. She absorbed and never forgot his maxims and little practical tips. But as a child, it was his strictness that concerned her most. Enid was whipped at least three times before she was twelve. The first occasion, Enid graphically recalled, was at Brompton Barracks when she was five. She dared her friend, Molly Main, to run under the belly of a horse as it stood harnessed after a church parade and while the groom was away having tea. At first, Molly was too scared, but Enid, longing to outdo, herself ran twice beneath. Eventually little Molly complied and Enid repaid her with every flower she could find in the garden. Even at that tender age, Enid was impelled by a desire to harden her will against fear and for a mastery of herself. The subse-quent whipping was for endangering her friend's life.

Although he mellowed with age, Arthur Bagnold began married life with a fierce temper. Nellie Ravenhill, while staying, was shocked to see him throw a potato at the maid, telling her to give it to the cook as he couldn't eat it. But he was rarely cross with his wife, and the world into which Enid was intro-duced was one of domestic security and harmony. Her mother's all-embracing love gave her a confidence which stayed with her almost all her life and her father's strict set of rules inspired in her a sometimes strange respect for discipline.

In the years after her brother Ralph's birth, Enid went very occasionally to school; a Mrs Thomas's was one she attended in Plymouth, but she was mostly educated at home by a governess called Miss Lewis. Visits to her grandmother were still plentiful and Miss Lewis often accompanied her now. Her letters home indicate that she was never bored. She filled her days with visits to the pier, the aquarium, the beach or, less happily, the dentist, who filled many of her teeth. Enid at eight and nine seems constantly to have been at the dentist, her well-developed love of sweets and chocolates resulting in both front and back teeth needing attention. She was made to write lines on the subject one day when she forgot to clean her teeth after lunch: 'As this proceeding has been especially laid down for me to carry out daily by my mother in view of the fact that my teeth have been in a bad state and have caused me such pain, and my parents much anxiety, trouble and expense, verily I am a naughty child and thereby promise to undertake to try and be more obedient in future.'

Enid's father, meanwhile, was making steady advances in his career, but progress in the army meant regular moves. Enid reckoned that, before she was nine, they had been quartered all over the South of England. Arthur Bagnold with his highly original brain and generous fund of practical common sense was no ordinary soldier. The War Office recognized this when they sent him in August 1893 to a conference at Niagara to discuss the future of the generation and transmission of electric power by alternating or direct current. From around 1896 onwards, Major Bagnold contrived to be based in Plymouth, from where he was sent to Malta, Gibraltar and other outposts of the Empire to work on coastal defences. Much of his work at this time concerned the Brennan torpedo.

In 1896 Major Bagnold was nominated for election as Vice-President of the Institute of Electrical Engineers and would probably have become president in due course. He declined the honour on the grounds that, although he had been associated with the military application of electricity for nearly twenty years, there was no further military appointment open to him in that direction. In 1899 Bagnold was promoted lieutenant-colonel and, just before Enid's tenth birthday, went out to Jamaica as Commanding Officer, Royal Engineers. His wife, two children and Miss Evans, the governess, followed behind in an old banana carrier called the *Don*. Their eighteen-day voyage was so stormy that it gave Enid a lifelong distaste for travelling by sea:

I was in an upper berth above an old lady, and my mother and Ralph were next door. Water came in from a broken pipe and the trunks got loose and swam about the floor. The old lady cried out again and again that she was dying. I was too sick to care. The stewardess came in with two men carrying a stretcher. 'She's making so much noise, dear, we're putting her in another cabin.' She was making no noise then. She was dead.

When they finally reached land, it was as if Enid's creative powers suddenly took hold. Images of beauty now arose in her mind which were never to be completely discarded. She remembered her Jamaican childhood with greater affection in old, rather than middle, age and in her eighties would often recall with great clarity her impressions on arrival there. As the ship rounded the first spit of land, she smelled the mango trees and glimpsed the oysters hanging on the dangling red tree roots. 'This was the first page of my life as someone who can "see". It was like a man idly staring at a field suddenly finding he had Picasso's eyes.'

She had a clear image, too, of her first morning at Up Park Camp in Kingston. 'Having a tropical breakfast on a tropical verandah with the transparent theatre green of bananas growing all round,' Enid wrote. Later that day the entourage was driven up the mountain in a buggy and pair by a coachman called Zinc to Halfway Tree, a patch of sandy ground with a wooden inn where the party transferred to horses. The trunks were loaded on to mules and, led by another mule, they set off for the final ascent, avoiding the frequent landslips, to a disused coffee mill called Coldspring House.

Coldspring House, which was to be the Bagnold home for the next three years, made plain its history by its great wheel dividing the house through the middle. The bottom of the wheel rested in a huge pit of water, home to a colony of frogs who croaked throughout the night. The flowering coffee bushes which still smothered the plantation and the cement barbecues on which the berries were dried were yet further echoes of the estate's former life. It was a large and battered house, which no one else in the camp had thought habitable. The bedrooms were infested with bats and the so-called kitchen was a hut upstream, where the appallingly primitive methods of the native cooks possibly went unnoticed by all but the inquisitive young Enid. Nonetheless, Colonel Bagnold thought it would do admirably and was able to pay a mere £24 rent per year for it.

William Hickey spent a night there in 1776. He wrote that it was:

One of the most romantic and beautiful spots I ever beheld, where stood an admirable mansion consisting of fifteen spacious apartments, from every one of which the magnificent city of Kingston, with the shipping, Port Royal and intervening rich and fertile country met the eye; a spectacle so sublime and magnificent I certainly never did see. The temperature of the air was delicious, forming a wonderful contrast to the extreme and burning heat we had been in only one hour before. At the back of the house rose the majestic and awfully grand mountain towering above the clouds in which its summit was completely enveloped.

The house was quickly made comfortable for Mrs Bagnold, the children and servants; Colonel Bagnold lived in Kingston during the week and came up only for weekends. They considered themselves a fairly frugal military household, but, as a menu for a dinner party given on 2 February 1900 indicates, they lived well. That night, they offered their guests Caughway oysters, turtle soup, king fish, sweetbread soufflé, filet de boeuf, saddle of mutton, turkey and smoked tongue, plum pudding, apricot jelly, sardines, ice cream and dessert.

Unquestionably Jamaica at the turn of the century was an island of exquisite beauty, with its fern-covered blue mountain slopes and trickles of water dripping from hill streams. The rich air hung heavy with the highly scented fruits and flowers; the trees more often than not dripping with thunderous rain-water. But the extreme poverty of the islanders ensured that it was also a life lived within the narrow confines of the 'garrison set', where tennis, polo and army dances were the highlights of the social round. Enid breathed in details of army life and, although she rebelled against the trappings of military existence in her adolescence, by her later years she felt warmly nostalgic about it all. Her father's silver hat with the white cock's feathers on the Sunday parade ground, the reveille bugle announcing dawn through the still cool air and, most exciting for her, the soldiers' 'gaffs' (concerts). Being allowed to stay up for these was a privilege that made her feel almost grown up. She spent hours collecting ferns, drying some for pasting into a scrapbook; others she smacked on to her father's black sleeve and the print of the fern, in gold or silver powder, remained on the cloth. 'Does it still exist? Does anything exist of the past? Or does it live much more strongly and more alive in the memory?'

Books, other than cookery books, had little place in this world and Enid read nothing that she remembered. 'It is so difficult to get suitable books for her,' Ethel wrote to her mother. In fact she seems to have had very little at all in the way of formal education at this time, since Miss Evans had been promptly despatched home. A new French governess, Mademoiselle Gattey, was appointed, but seems to have had hardly more success. Ralph, although six years younger, attended some lessons, but detested having to learn French and, as Enid managed to terrify Mademoiselle, the children enjoyed 'perfect freedom'. A third child, Mary Adams, the daughter of the army doctor, shared the lessons, but little else, with Enid.

Like the tropical undergrowth, however, her imagination flourished. Perhaps it is not surprising that it was nature, rather than the arid schoolroom, which provided the young Enid with her first spur to creativity. She saw grasshoppers leap ten feet into the air, butterflies as big as bats and lush foliage which made her grandmother's conservatory appear a pale imitation. Every morning she rose early to milk her own goats – at one time she had seven kids – and to tend her own small fowlyard, where she kept three hens. Most exhilarating, however, was her discovery of horses. For her twelfth birthday her father had given her a hunting crop as she was, by then, allowed to exercise her favourite horse, La Poupée, every morning. 'I love that, and I am going to teach Mlle to groom, saddle and look after the horse and donkey. Of course, I can do all that myself,' she boasted in a letter to her aunt.

Horses so captivated Enid's spirit that when she was in bed at night she would attach long tapes to her toes and pretend she was driving the chestnut and buggy or a pair of greys. In the afternoons she occasionally went for long rides with General Raper and his daughter Hilda and adored the experience even when it rained. But much of her time was spent cutting out horses from sporting magazines (made of thicker paper than today's variety), carefully choosing only those facing in the right direction and of a uniform size. She would gloss the coats by gentle rubbing and then, with twigs to whip their sides, make them race each other. These paper horses were her most private world, shut up in a box when not in use and shared by no one except, thirty-five years later, her fictional creation Velvet Brown.

Enid had learnt to ride upon arrival on the island on a gentle white mule called Queenie, bought from the governor's wife, Lady Hemming. She took to it immediately, sitting far back on the rump as the natives did, until two young soldiers made it their business to teach her properly and took her out for short rides on a pony. Of course, she developed a hopeless crush on one of the soldiers, Lieutenant Usher, an officer in the Leinsters, but he in turn was in love with Enid's mother. One day, when he was there, Ethel, perhaps looking for an excuse to send her daughter outside, picked up her hand saying, 'Darling, your nails are filthy.' The child ran away sobbing.

'After that I couldn't live without loves,' Enid wrote of the occasion in her autobiography for, after the 'golden lieutenant', she invented other loves. 'She told nobody, but had chosen among her parents' friends, heroes on whom to hang her adoration – stimulating her heartbeats – a little drug-taker.' Perhaps Enid did not recognize at the time how deeply she craved affection – a vulnerability which cloaked an otherwise stark independence. The episode provided her with another spring-board into a private world of premature emotions and imagination.

High-spirited as she was, it is hardly surprising that Enid was often in trouble. Queenie once came into the house and, much to Enid's delight, stole a loaf of bread, while the cat and her kittens sat on the table licking the butter. Enid's father was furious when he discovered them and the animals and child were all given a sound beating. On another occasion Enid sat with her friend Mary chewing oranges on a bank above the bridle road. They drank the juice and spat out the pith and pips. 'A platoon of soldiers marched below us towards Newcastle, a sergeant at their head. I spat pulp on to a cap. I was pleased with the aim, but frightened.' And with good reason. Arthur Bagnold apologized to the sergeant, paid for a new cap and beat his daughter. 'It never crossed my mind that it [the beating] would do me any spiritual harm. Nor it did,' said Enid.

Enid's discovery that she enjoyed writing poems was another cause of friction with her father, partly because she indulged herself at night with only the bats and the pale moon for company. He was worried she was not getting enough sleep and that she might end up an insomniac. Justly, he made her give her word of honour that she would limit to three nights a week. She promised she would.

If Mrs Alger had been worried that Enid was becoming a tomboy, how much more so would she have been to see her grand-daughter during her Jamaica days. A big girl already at twelve, Enid weighed 7 st. 3 lb. and was 5 ft. 2¼ ins. 'I'm afraid I shall be six foot before I've done,' she bewailed in a letter home. Enid was allowed out alone riding from tea-time to bedtime and chatted to any groups of natives she met; she played for hours among the coffee bushes and streams with her imaginary friends. These childhood years were full of dreams and longings – dreams of impossibilities and, above all, a longing that was almost a frenzy to be different, to be great, to stand out.

Her grandfather sent her, for her twelfth birthday, £5 enclosed in a note full of Victorian admonitions about the importance of using the next few years well. 'They are of paramount importance to you. In them your character will be permanently fixed . . . train for a life of usefulness and intellectuality and goodness instead of frivolity and selfishness,' he advised her. There is no indication that her parents were worrying about preparing her for more ladylike pursuits, but they must have been aware that lack of suitable companions was causing her to draw in upon herself.

By March 1902 Arthur Bagnold's command in Jamaica was over and the family returned to England. During the voyage home Enid, still living vicariously, played cupid to an attractive young lady who was enjoying a mild flirtation with the handsome ship's doctor. The twelve-year-old gloried in every nuance of this shipboard romance and overstepped the bounds of her own duties by adding 'don't despair' or 'she loves you' on the bottom of one or two notes.

The ship sailed into Plymouth Sound on 12 April, and lodgings were found for the family at Ryde on the Isle of Wight. To relieve the tedium, Enid decided to relive the shipboard affair herself. When Colonel Bagnold discovered, hidden among the crocheted lace mats of the sideboard, four pages of affected, sentimental outpourings on love, teeming with corroborating incident and data, he was convinced his rapidly maturing daughter had a lover. 'I want his name!' Colonel Bagnold yelled. 'There isn't anybody!' Enid screamed back, as she ran out of the room sobbing. Eventually her parents believed her, but they kept an ever more wary eye on their daughter's curious habit of writing. Poems and imaginary love letters were not all she was composing. In 1902 she wrote a little fairy play, which does not seem to have been preserved among her papers, perhaps because it caused a good deal of unrest in the family. Her grandfather told her that he had read the play with considerable interest, 'but none the less, my dear grandchild, don't do it again. If the imagination is allowed to run too far ahead before the judgement and intellect are trained to accompany it, danger comes.' Mr Alger continued in this vein for over three pages.

However, Enid did not stop writing. She penned a sombre verse 'On the death of a newly-born infant' to her Aunt Clara, in which she compared the short life to a stunted bud. Rhyming and imagery came easily, but she was no intellectual. The outdoor life was still important to her and she desperately wanted her own pony, promising, among other things, never to quarrel with Ralph if her parents would give her one.

After a few months at Ryde, Arthur Bagnold was appointed Chief Superintendent of Building Works at Woolwich Arsenal, south London. The Bagnold family moved to Warren Wood, a large, mid-Victorian gothic house near the top of Shooters Hill, which became Enid's first settled childhood home. Shooters Hill, so-called because it had been a favourite shoot of Henry VIII, retained a strongly rural aspect with its dense bluebell woods. Yet it was only eight miles from London Bridge. Soon after the move, Enid appeared to develop a patch on one lung. Colonel Bagnold decided that the best all-round method of treatment for his daughter was to send her to a boarding-school on sandy soil.

Thus, as if by 'divine, frail accident', Enid came to Prior's Field, near Godalming in Surrey. The school was in its infancy with only about twelve girl boarding pupils, but growing quickly. Mrs Huxley, the headmistress, was the grand-daughter of Arnold of Rugby and the niece of Matthew Arnold. She was married to Leonard, son of Thomas Huxley, and Mrs Humphry Ward, the popular novelist, was her sister.

It was an unconventional school, with the girls allowed unusual latitude in choosing their activities. These were heavily biased towards art, literature and the theatre with little emphasis on arithmetic. Mrs Huxley's influence on the girls was immense : 'We all loved Mrs Huxley and thought her word was law,' one pupil remembered. Until Mrs Huxley came into Enid's life, the only women Enid knew were dependents. Whatever their other qualities, 'they were only wives, stuffed into married quarters'. Mrs Huxley was small, slender, kind and reflective : 'I had never thought of thinking before I spoke,' Enid confessed.

Enid went with her mother for an interview at the school and Mrs Huxley turned to the girl and asked what she liked doing. 'Writing poetry,' she might have responded, but instead she announced boldly, 'I like games,' as she watched through the window some girls hurdling. She had never played 'games' in her life.

In her search for popularity, Enid was guided by the girls' school stories of her day. To be a heroine clearly demanded feats of outrageous courage and daring and thus, for the next five years, Enid determined that 'cutting ice' with her schoolmates was to be her main goal. Being fat, clowning came naturally to her, although sometimes she misjudged the effect in terms of lost self-esteem. The other girls were intelligent and included Professor Gilbert Murray's daughter Rosalind, Maurice Hewlett's daughter Pia, Sir Arthur Conan Doyle's daughter Mary, and Lady Jekyll's daughters Pamela and Barbara.

'Odd that at such a school as this the gym, the games field and possible popularity should be my heaven,' Enid Bagnold wrote for the school magazine nearly seventy years later. How odd was it? Never, by her own admission, an intellectual, yet Enid was acutely aware of the impression she was making on others. The 'gamesy' image was fostered partly as an anti-intellectual pose in front of the brilliant Huxley boys, Julian, Trev and Aldous. One day this fat, clownish girl might surprise them.

By day she kept grass-snakes in her desk and hatched silkworms in her bedroom. After a science lesson on antiseptics, she cut ENID into the flesh of her wrist and then rubbed the cuts with sawdust from the gym floor. Just as she had dared her friend Molly Main to run under a horse, she now persuaded her classmate Margie Wetzlar-Coit to jump from one of the cottage roofs, as she had already done. When Margie tried, she broke both her legs in the process. By night Enid used to crawl out of her window on to the sloping eaves and wander from one roof to another admiring the moonlit scenery. This continued until she was spotted by the drunken cook. Another time Enid climbed down the lavatory pipes and was found by Mrs Humphry Ward, asleep in the bluebell wood. Not surprisingly, she often found herself sent to Mrs Huxley for punishment, but was barely even rebuked. Enid watched the headmistress blush a little before explaining why such escapades could not be allowed in a school. Then she told Enid it was time she began to think beyond herself and about living in the world.

A small beginning was made in that direction by Enid's confirmation in March 1905. Although resisting always anything that smacked of sentiment in religion, her confirmation classes were more subtle. 'The whole affair was offered under a beguiling aspect of intellect, of freed thought, of a dazzling enlightenment,' she wrote in a memoir of her youth. The man who confirmed her also inspired her and was, more importantly, endorsed by Mrs Huxley. He presented the course as though ethics and history were the subjects to be focused upon; and Enid felt her emotions expand in the process.

She was blissfully happy during her days at Prior's Field, as her letters home indicate. Although mostly concerned with clothes, lacrosse matches and the teachers, she evidently already had a talent for telling a good story. For her sixteenth birthday her parents offered her a Kodak camera, but she begged instead for a book of Yeats poems, for, in spite of her daring exploits at school, she was still writing poetry. None of it was very good and it included some eulogies to the games mistress. Occasionally she exchanged verses with Mrs Huxley's son Julian, who was away at Eton. But the poems were mostly a very private affair, written in bed at night, of which the other girls knew nothing.

Mrs Huxley had attended a congress of teachers in York and it was there suggested that, once in every schoolgirl's life, an essay in verse should be set. And so the girls at Prior's Field were told to try their hands at the story of the quest for the golden apples of the Hesperides. As the rest of the school groaned, Enid grasped at this opportunity to outshine her peers, to be noticed. 'I listened to girls who went about so unversed in verse that they could not see that "dove" made a natural marriage with "love". I wrote my Hesperides on a grand scale. It had inset choruses and rhymes (copied from Swinburne) in the middle of lines as well as at the end. I did think it might be hard to beat me. That DID occur to me.'

When the day came to announce the winner, several well-known parents sat on the dais. Enid was at the back of the room in her grey uniform tunic with a red braid sash, a dress that made her look busty. The Jaeger stays, which all the girls wore, did little to reduce the impression of a fat girl. Her hair was pulled back in a short plait and her face was 'as scarlet as my sash with hope'. Mrs Huxley announced that the result of the experiment was satisfactory and very interesting. She congratulated all the authors. ' "But there is one poem . . ." she said. I lost the end of the sentence but I heard "Stand up Enid Bagnold." The gasp of amazement and disbelief as heads turned around from the forms in front of me has never been forgotten. It was utter fame, naked and eaten young. It could never come again.'

Enid's father, with great pride, had the seven-page poem printed and her grandfather presented her with £100 for her achievement, but no accompanying congratulatory note for fear this might encourage her too much. Mrs Huxley sent the poem to W. B. Yeats and then took Enid to an evening party at his flat in Tavistock Square, at which Enid wore a pink woollen dress with a boned lace collar and black boots. Yeats told her, 'If you want to write poetry never touch politics,' advice which Enid might have done well to heed.

The next term Mrs Huxley suddenly fell ill. At the same time, as a reward for her prowess at poetry, Enid was segregated from the rest of her class and taught Greek in the rose garden. Without Mrs Huxley at the helm, the magic of the school disappeared for Enid. She left before reaching the sixth form and Mrs Huxley's death soon after caused Enid her first terrible grief.

Notwithstanding, Enid at seventeen was obstinately unfinished. The battles over church, far from subsiding, were growing more intense. As her father considered church-going 'Satan-chasing', Enid begged to be allowed to stay at home like him. On Sundays her stomach began to churn at the thought of a beautiful morning being wasted among congregants she did not know, but detested none the less. She barely followed the service, thinking only of how she hated the self-satisfaction and sad mediocrity she thought she perceived in these people. She felt herself burning to be different from them, to make a mark in the world. Automaton-like, she knelt for silent prayer, but, carried away with her own secret vision, sank her teeth into the pew in front. Week after week, she screamed inwardly : 'O God, give me fame.'

In an attempt to smooth out some of Enid's rougher edges, Colonel and Mrs Bagnold decided in 1906 to send her to Lausanne. Here the first assault on language and literature, poise and polish, drawing and darning was to be made. Madame Bollinger's establishment was, at the beginning, 'bearable though insipid'. Rapidly it became so loathsome that 'I hate the very name of Switzerland,' Enid wrote in a letter, begging to be allowed home. She enjoyed the drawing classes or, rather, enjoyed being complimented on her sketches. She was thrilled to meet Paderewski and to watch Sarah Bernhardt. 'I have seen Sarah Bernhardt. I have breathed the utterest depths of tragedy and I have seen a dramatic woman in her real and only life,' she confided in her diary. But the multitude of petty rules, the cost of extras which left her permanently short of money and, above all, the dreariness and meanness of life at Villa Thioleyre made her very miserable indeed. When she discovered a pawnshop she thought that, by leaving her watch there, she might just make it home to England.

Her parents counselled caution in her dealings with Madame Bollinger, her father well understanding how easily his daughter lost her temper. When

Madame Bollinger accused Enid of possessing evil spirits and not being a lady (as she did not sit up straight), her parents were finally convinced and summoned her home immediately. In her autobiography Enid claims nearly to have murdered Madame Bollinger during their final row, but, if so, she gave a rather different account to her parents at the time. More likely this was the first of many stories she retold in which the original grain of truth acquired several accretions over the years, until it made such a good tale that fact conceded to fiction.

Paris, by contrast, was a year of great happiness for Enid. Determined that their daughter should acquire some refinements, her parents secured her a place in great haste at Madame Yeatman's Protestant Institute for Young Ladies (Villa Leona), a much more stylish and expensive school. Here at last Enid began to worry about traditionally feminine pursuits. She was taught the art of *maquillage* as well as how to make the most of her rather thin hair. She started wearing it up with a huge coloured bow behind 'like the Americans – awfully chic'. She discovered how delightful extravagant Parisian clothes could be, but worried that cod-liver oil, given her whenever she had headaches, was making her fat. When she tightened her stays, they cut into her flesh. 'I make a gallant attempt to be Parisienne', she wrote to her mother, 'but my failures are frequent.'

Clothes did not occupy her mind entirely. While in Paris, Napoleon and votes for women also entered her thoughts. One moment she was writing a novel about Napoleon from the viewpoint of a soldier who fell at his feet and worshipped him, the next she was writing a novel about a nun who yearned to be a devil. Fantasy having considerably more appeal to her than reality, she was envious to learn that her schoolfriend Winifred Bright had nearly gone to prison as a suffragette. 'I am fearfully keen on the vote', she wrote to Winifred, 'but I am rather vague on it.'

Although she enjoyed dozens of dances and balls while in Paris, she seems to have been uninterested in male partners. Her closest relationships were with girlfriends and her passions reserved for stage idols such as Sarah Bernhardt. The sophistications of Paris had ill-equipped her for the rigours of 'coming out' in an English garrison town. The problem of how to lead an intelligent and striking life while living at her parents' suburban home was to occupy her for the next twelve years.

THREE

An Artistic and Bohemian Milieu

WHEN Enid arrived home at the end of 1907, she had some ideas about what life ought to hold for her, but few clues as to how to realize them. She knew little about the upheavals of the contemporary European art scene, but was aware of the scores of private art schools offering hundreds of young women desperate for independence and stimulation a socially acceptable means of escape. Enid, nosing out adventure, toyed with the idea of attending the Slade. She also considered a course of further education in foreign literature at King's College, London. Eventually, a compromise was reached. Several afternoons a week she attended the nearby Blackheath Art School, where classes were taught by the talented but volatile Hugh Bellingham-Smith. The rest of the time, she was the daughter of the household attending to social calls, with all the unfilled leisure time that was the bane of every intelligent Edwardian girl's life.

The parameters of the permissible were, however, expandable. When she explained to her parents the necessity of her being allowed to paint nude models, they eventually agreed. She also secured her parents' permission to attend Thursday matinées at the afternoon theatre in London. She argued that the audience was 'most respectable. . . . The Afternoon Theatre is the intellect theatre (Yeats and people) and the rabble don't go.'

In spite of these minor privileges, Enid still felt as if she was waiting for the moment, marking time until the great unspecified adventure walked into her life. Colonel and Mrs Bagnold also viewed the art classes as a spare-time activity for their daughter; in their eyes it was a safe enough variation on the inexorable theme of military balls and coming-out dances.

The ritual of 'coming out' did not involve Enid in being presented at Court nor, apparently, even in her having her own grand party. Coming out was intended simply to introduce her to a sufficiently wide circle of men for a husband to present himself. Her mother, generally accompanying her daughter to these dances as chaperone, could not hide her anxieties over Enid's awkwardness, but seemed unable to advise her how to do better. New clothes were chosen and made, not always very successfully when Enid insisted on having a hand in the design, by a local dressmaker; and Enid tried to perfect the intricacies of frizzing, steaming and pinning her hair. Julian Huxley escorted Enid to one or two dances, but any romance that might have blossomed was quickly blighted when he wrote to her describing the intimate interior arrangements of a frog.

Colonel Bagnold's position ensured that most invitations which flooded in to tea and garden parties, dances and balls were of a military flavour. Each occasion filled Enid with an eerie dread, since the men – or rather boys – who with clammy hands put their initials on her dance cards fell far short of the image she had formed of the man who was to carry her off to adventure. Her enforced waltzing partners were merely cadets, frequently spotty and red faced, with buttons missing or dirty gloves. She vowed never, never to marry a soldier.

One young girl with pouting, carmined lips caught Enid's eye. As she puffed raffishly at her cigarette-holder, she assumed an easy manner in talking to men at these functions. 'Sex appeal' clearly made this girl interesting. But what was sex appeal, and how did you get it?

Happily for Enid it was not long before she met this dynamic creature. Dolly Tylden was the daughter of General Tylden, recently arrived in the neighbourhood as commander of the garrison. Dolly, who was much smarter and more refined than her name might suggest, had an unusual little snub nose, a fine pointed chin and an attitude that managed to combine impertinence with self-assurance. An opportunity to meet came one Sunday when, after a subdued row, Enid had submitted to church. Walking home together afterwards, Enid discovered that, although her new friend did not much care for church either, she managed to laugh at the preacher and confess her boredom with a rueful air. As the two reached the Tyldens' imposing Georgian mansion, Bloomfield House, they paused only briefly before Enid was invited for lunch and the friendship quickly forged.

Thus Enid, captivated by her new friend's chic, observed all. As well as red on her lips, there was powder on her nose and several highly original rings on her elegant fingers. When the two went upstairs to Dolly's bedroom, Enid could not help remarking on the large bookshelf which ran along the complete length of one wall. 'Are these your father's books?' she asked – a strange question in view of the very few books that her own parents possessed. When Dolly asked indignantly why they should not be hers, Enid replied rather feebly that she did not look like the owner of such an impressive collection. Dolly's bedroom bookcase was a revelation. It held more books than Enid had ever read in her life and of a quite different kind. At school and abroad she had read classics and poetry. But here were books newly published, written by her own generation. The girls then talked of what they had done with their short lives and what they planned to do.

'Something's bound to happen,' Enid observed casually.

'Nothing will happen unless you make it,' stated Dolly. Enid, finding her new friend an enlightened guide on the subject of men and how to manage them, bravely admitted that she had never been kissed. Dolly did not consider this of grave importance. Perceiving that Enid was trying too hard with unsympathetic material, Dolly explained that she should not take so much trouble trying to make men like her. 'It's only vanity that makes you want to explain yourself to everyone. Don't fuss about being understood. They haven't the least desire to understand you. Take them as they are.' Enid considered all this sound advice for Dolly, although only one year older, spoke as if she had the key to life.

Under Dolly's tutelage, Enid began to register some small successes with men. When an embarrassingly shy young man, Lieutenant Hill, asked her to marry him, she considered the request as frightening as a rape. That he had already taken the precaution of securing Colonel Bagnold's permission shocked her still further and she ran out of the conservatory screaming.

Although still large, Enid was losing some of her eleven stones. Full cheeks heightened the effect of beautiful slanted eyes, through which shone her intense vitality. Clearly she was attractive to men. There were other proposals also rejected, before she received her first kiss.

During a visit to the garrison theatre, Enid had been admired by a certain major in the group. When he invited Enid to tea at his London flat she accepted. She was going to town to the dentist with her mother and hoped by various subterfuges to contrive one illicit hour with him. She had not pre-pared herself for the speed of his attack. Like the heroine of her novel *Serena Blandish*, 'she had no idea that the treatment of her was monstrous. How could she? She had no standards.' He kissed her as soon as he had poured out the tea. 'I caught sight of my face in the glass as my hat went sideways. How far would he have gone, how ridiculous his watchchain and in fact how like a father,' Enid remembered some sixty years later.

In her haste to escape, Enid fell and grazed her knee, which she had some difficulty explaining to her mother. Nevertheless she recounted the adventure in minute detail to Dolly, who listened approvingly. To seek advice from her mother, who had had no difficulties in attracting men, would have been useless. Ethel Bagnold ladled out a generous helping of clichés, including the inevitable: 'Don't worry, darling. Mr Right will soon come along.' Charac-teristically, Enid wanted Mr Wrong.

Six years younger, her schoolboy brother Ralph could not understand her state of mind either. In 1909 she wrote to him at his boarding-school, Malvern College, that she was spending most of her time in London attending suffrage

lectures and meeting friends for lunch, an exaggeration designed to excite his
envy. She confided her adolescent aspirations to him : 'Some day we'll have an
attic in town and I'll keep house for you and cook the meals on a gas stove and
there'll be a parrot and a Persian kitten and you'll tell me all your adventures
and I'll put them in a famous play that I shall be writing. It'll be fun and we'll
belong to some advanced club and be in an artistic and Bohemian milieu. . . .'

Enid's Uncle Lexy was of greater comfort. Urbane and good looking,
Arthur Bagnold's elder brother won a classics scholarship to Balliol and was
then called to the Bar. Although he spent his later years in insurance, he was a
literary man at heart and, after his death, a number of his highly romantic
poems were discovered. He gave his niece great practical encouragement with
her poetry, suggesting once, for example, that she study Keats for his
imagery. When she was regularly visiting London, he always made her welcome at his home in Warrington Crescent, which he shared with his elder
sister, Clara. On her death-bed, old Mrs Bagnold had begged Lexy to look
after the ugly Clara, born with a lip so hideously deformed that no man would
marry her. Uncle Lexy complied, but maintained a second establishment for
his mistress and two daughters. Since Uncle Lexy often came to Warren
Wood for advice on some aspect of their upbringing, Enid was aware of her
two illegitimate cousins. However, they were not a suitable subject for family
conversation. Their existence was a closely guarded secret from Arthur's
other sister, Alice, who had married a Canon Clay and now lived with her
twelve children in Windermere. Enid and Ralph occasionally spent weekends
with their Clay cousins, but felt oppressed by the religious atmosphere,
particularly the Sunday silences while sermons were being composed.

In 1907, Enid saw her first poem published in a highbrow magazine called
English Illustrated, soon followed by another in *New Age*. She had for years
been sending contributions to various publications. They were mostly rejected, but with handwritten letters encouraging her to persevere. *New Age*
was a weekly magazine, widely read and highly praised. Its circulation in 1908
had reached around 20,000 and if there were a particularly lively or controver-
sial edition, it might sell out within a day. Many of the best contemporary
names wrote for *New Age*, including Arnold Bennett, whose 'Books and
Persons' column (signed Jacob Tonson) was considered the best literary
column in London.

Uncle Lexy was pleased at his niece's success and may even have interceded
on her behalf with his younger brother because Colonel Bagnold despised the
free-thinking politics of the *New Age*. Enid bought it surreptitiously, against
her father's advice. None the less, when his daughter's poem appeared in its
pages, he rewarded her with her own workroom. This was the first of Enid's

'tower rooms'. Cold and inaccessible, it was approached by a narrow stair-case and nestled inside a gothic turret perched on the left side of the house. The Colonel saw to it that the study boasted a solid carpenter's bench with two vices, a gas fire and a gas-ring for melting glue bought in thick slabs for book-binding.

In this room Enid began to acquire the discipline of work, which sharpened, like her wit, over the years. Now, if she had nothing to do, she no longer resorted to taking her bicycle to pieces, nor to waiting outside the house of Hubert Bland, the well-known philanderer husband of E. Nesbit, in the vague hope that he might appear and seduce her.

If her parents hoped that this concession towards independence would stem her restlessness, they were mistaken. Early in 1910, she was despatched once more to foreign parts. Curiously, in her autobiography, Enid remem-bered her three months' stay with a family in Marburg in Germany as pre-ceding Paris and Lausanne, an indication that she always viewed this episode as a retrograde step, for, apart from cream-filled pastries at tea, Enid found life in Germany dull, but she endured it with noticeably more maturity than she had displayed three years earlier in Switzerland.

When she returned home this time, she knew precisely what she wanted: an affair. It took her a few months longer to identify a possible lover. From the very first, Dolly and Enid had shared a ceaseless quest beyond the bounds of the social life around them. London had always been the Mecca, whether for hats, lunches or theatres. Exhibiting several of her etchings at the Blackheath Art Club was fleetingly gratifying, but did not slake Enid's thirst for life; nor did her brief flirtation with politics. In 1910, H. H. Asquith's Liberal government blocked the 'conciliation' bill on women's suffrage which it had promised to the Women's Social and Political Union. As a result, the suffragettes again took to the streets in increasingly furious protest. Enid, for her part, stood outside a polling booth on election day in 1910 collecting signatures in favour of votes for women, shouting all the while, 'We are non-military, non-party' – insufficient activity for an arrest, which Enid would have welcomed.

A close friend of Enid's at the time was the brilliant young artist Claud Lovat Fraser. Lovat was a year younger than Enid, but his extraordinary talent was already glaringly apparent. He came from a prosperous, middle-class family living in Kensington and, after leaving school, spent two years in his father's legal practice before his devoted parents actively encouraged him to pursue an artistic career.

Although in his tight sleeves, high velvet collar, pantaloons and silk hat, Lovat looked every inch a dandy, he was also kind, charming, sensitive and gentlemanly. Colonel and Mrs Bagnold must have been beguiled by his charm or fooled by his youthfulness, as they did not raise the customary objection to the time their daughter was spending alone in his company. Enid and Lovat explored London together. She found him a stimulating friend with a ready laugh and an ever-watchful imagination. When Enid suggested they go to visit the tarts in Leicester Square, Lovat jumped at the idea. Wherever he went, a pencil, brush or pen was scarcely out of his industrious fingers. According to his friend Haldane Macfall, a retired army officer turned art critic, Lovat enjoyed 'the vision of the true artist . . . that all-valuable quality of the born artist, the compelling urgency to utter the objects seen as *he* has seen them.'

Despite their enjoyment of each other's company, Enid and Lovat did not become lovers. And, if Enid had any regrets in her old age, it was that she had never experienced love with a young partner. 'I feel I've been done out of it . . . I never got that beautiful groping side of the other's love. I was led. I was too gauche and ferocious in my shyness, that only experienced, older men knew I could be "taken".'

In 1911 she had only her schoolgirl's instinct for adventure without any womanly intuition of how to get it. She had taken to buying *New Age* and had noticed in it the work of W. R. Sickert. When, looking casually at an advertisement at the back of the magazine, she saw that he ran a school, her juvenile imagination alighted on him as a possible candidate for her affection. Sickert was experienced, middle aged and extremely attractive. He had a lock of red hair falling across his forehead and his sardonic humour exerted a strong fascination for the opposite sex. Divorced from his first wife, Ellen Cobden, he had indulged in many affairs since then but, in July 1911, concluded an arduous search for an understanding and undemanding wife by marrying a former pupil, Christine Angus. Although the idea of lessons from Sickert did not excite Lovat, good-naturedly he agreed to accompany Enid and Dolly and effect an introduction to Sickert. Dolly was at first worried by the idea, complaining that she could not draw a line. 'All the better,' Enid told her. 'What teacher would not give his right eye for a pupil with a mind like yours, a clean slate. You've got to draw, it's my only way out.'

Dolly required little persuasion; the Bagnold parents more. However, Bellingham-Smith, after a serious illness, had been given the sack from Blackheath and Enid eventually managed to convince her parents that if she and Dolly travelled to London together, there would be few differences from her life at Blackheath.

At twenty-two, Enid was not lacking in feminine allure, which even the huge new painting overall bought at Dolly's behest could not completely hide. On the first morning at Sickert's classes, she sat in the farthermost corner of the room, hugging her portfolio of Blackheath charcoal nudes. Her heart pounding, she looked around at the work of the other students, considering it faint and indecisive by comparison with her own bold outlines. As she drew, she became convinced of the excellence of her own sketch. Soon the master would come round and inspect. He could not fail to be impressed.

When Sickert finally entered the room and sat down by the easel of the nearest student Enid was enchanted. 'He was all that rumour had pictured, even more. He smiled at some remark of the man by whose easel he was busy and I thought it a charming smile.' Soon he stopped at Enid's work and paused. 'What school have you learnt at?' he asked.

'Oh, I've hardly been anywhere, a month or two at Blackheath. But I work at home.'

'This appals me,' he finally let out as he sat down. 'It is like a poster. Whoever made you draw like that?' he added before walking on. 'You might have drawn it with an umbrella.'

Enid sat silently, crushed into an abyss of despair, hoping only that Dolly had not heard. Her crimson cheeks must have betrayed her anguish, as Sickert returned to her shortly and, more gently now, explained his theories of drawing: pencil not charcoal, lose the harsh outlines. . . . He took her on and no student could have been keener to learn. Lovat he refused, however; according to Enid he considered his talent already too well formed.

'In those days', Enid wrote, 'the journey three times a week to London was such happiness that I resented even the companionship of Dolly. I never bought a morning paper or read a book but sat stiff and upright in my corner of the railway carriage watching the five papers spread in front of me on the opposite seat, my eyes noting every trifling physical detail of the occupants with the same thirsty excitement as if I had discovered some unique physic [*sic*] phenomena.'

She joined an illustrious group painting with Sickert at Rowlandson House in Camden Town. There was Silvia Gosse, daughter of Sir Edmund Gosse, who was in love with The Master; Harold Gilman, who brilliantly captured Silvia's self-effacing qualities in his 1913 portrait and Ambrose McEvoy, later to command high fees for his flattering portraits of society women. Sickert was a born teacher who relished being able to convey his feelings. His pupils, a 'devoted and dull' band of women in Enid's opinion, listened and watched in rapt attention.

Enid took stock of the scene before her. Dust (particularly on mirrors) was especially cultivated by Sickert for his masterpieces from everyday life in a drab bedroom or kitchen. 'He loved the abated light that got muffled in the glass.' Sickert called this 'blonde ... It was a love-word. The folds of a dirty sheet in shadow, the model's naked body on the bed, her flesh, green-shadowed, melting into the surrounding wood, rep, leather, reverberating softly in a splendour of unpolished light.'

Enid continued to work with Sickert, on and off, for several years. She was one of the privileged few, allowed to 'help' by smoking his waxed-over copper plates with a candle. She also had what he called 'fun with acids', but her fingers were 'shaking with dread'. Captivated by the way he made squares on the drawing paper with an exquisite little object in a leather case 'I stole [it] from him and kept [it] for twenty years and then it went.' In the early mornings at his studio in Red Lion Square, his small côterie would sip bowls of coffee, prepare by Thérése Lessore, later to be his third wife, while Sickert, in a towelling robe after an early morning swim at the public baths, talked as he worked. Frequently Sickert took Enid out to lunch at Shoolbreds, an emporium in Tottenham Court Road, and there he would expound to her his views on life, marriage and women. 'If you write, you can carry all that along with love : you can pour love into it. But drawing, painting – it's for nuns.' A note, addressing her as 'Dear delightful & amazing', went on to ask her if she ever slept in London. 'If so would you BREAKFAST here at 9 sharp. Any day including Sunday. I should then get you ALONE for which I thirst – and have always thirsted – and shall continue to thirst. . . .' A sentiment Enid later dismissed as 'airy love'.

Sickert gave her many of the first pulls of his etchings. He also gave her a drawing, spontaneously undertaken one day when she arrived wearing a new dress. The drawing emphasizes Enid's commanding presence at twenty-four and, to her delight, was published in *New Age*. For all the banter and Enid's high hopes in advance, she did not become Sickert's mistress. Painting, for Enid, had offered a route for escape, not a means of expressing any deeply felt meaning of life. Under Sickert she had consolidated her talent, but it remained derivative. Lovat disapproved of the Sickert-product she was becoming and told her so in a drawing portraying himself as the 'truer, sterner, kinder friend'.

Meanwhile Dolly, who now wanted to be known as Violet, had decided the time had come for them to live in London. She found a flat in Chelsea, the rent for which would be twelve shillings a week, and asked Enid to join her. Colonel Bagnold, who in myriad ways had pandered to his daughter's mas-culine yearnings, now had to be approached for this biggest favour of all. Enid worked out a plan of campaign but chose the wrong moment, breakfast, to launch her first assault. There was no real discussion ; her father, in furious mood, simply walked out of the room. But by the evening he was prepared to discuss the matter. First she told her father that General Tylden's daughter would be living with her, which did not weigh at all with him. Then she told him that she needed experience 'like a man', and he half understood. He said he could not possibly increase her allowance of £75 per year, but if she could live on that. . . . The battle was won.

Ralph Bagnold thinks his parents were not particularly shocked by Enid's request; that they had long since recognized her strong will and decided that the wisest counsel was to give her her head. Ethel Bagnold, however, and the conservative Alger family were worried about Enid's future. 'If you scold me in this way by every post, I shan't look forward much to getting your letters,' Enid wrote to her mother. She bitterly resented Ethel criticizing her new circle of male friends. 'The men I meet in London are, believe me, one and all without any solitary exception, *pleasant friends* . . . when you oppose my knowing these men with freedom, I think I am driven into a defence of them which suggests that they are more to me.'

By late 1912 Enid had taken up residence at 18 Rectory Chambers, Church Street, a quiet Chelsea backwater. Chelsea, then, was a thickly populated, urban district which still considered itself a village. Long the haunt of writers and artists, the smarter reaches now attracted prosperous top-hatted profes- sional men and their families, but ragged children were still to be seen running barefoot in the side alleys. Banner-waving suffragettes sometimes marched down King's Road and the smell of paint was in the air.

The flat boasted three bedrooms, a sitting-room, kitchen and bathroom. By day, Dolly and Enid spent much time painting each other and a third friend from Woolwich, Kitty Foord Kelsey. Kitty, who worshipped Enid, occasionally served to play the piano while the other two Double Bostonned. By night, to save money on heating, the girlfriends would sit with their feet in a zinc bath full of hot water. Rolls might be stolen from a restaurant. It was, Enid knew, 'mock poverty'.

'It is rather fun,' she wrote to her mother. 'The char is a very good one and does everything and cooks a splendid breakfast and calls me and gets the hot water ready just as though we had a house full of servants.' Perhaps she embroidered on the truth in order to quell her mother's fears, but in any event it was scarcely a true Bohemian existence.

By the time Enid arrived in Chelsea, Dolly could already count on a collection of writers, artists and art-lovers as her friends. A determined young lady with no creative pretensions herself, she was developing a fledg- ling artistic salon with At Homes every Wednesday. It was at one of these that Enid met the brilliant and gaunt young French artist Henri Gaudier. 'A dreary little thing, supposed to be a budding marvel,' she described him to her mother. Lovat Fraser was the life and soul of these parties, but Enid could hold her own. On one occasion, she poked fun at his flowing dark hair with a withering, 'Lovat, do get some hair-pins and be reasonable.' Haldane Macfall considered Enid Bagnold not only a 'a very beautiful girl' but was also impressed with her witty and impromptu caricatures of Lovat and Gaudier. No one had expected talent from a colonel's daughter.

Sophie Brzeska, the deeply neurotic Pole who shared Gaudier's tortured life and entertained illusions of authorship herself, was furious when she heard Enid's art praised. 'Not at all; her drawings are still and photographic, their only merit is that they strike a likeness. Miss Bagnold is a writer not an artist,' she shouted, before being dragged away.

Enid never liked the puny Frenchman with the wispy strands of beard pencilling his jaw-line; she thought him too cold and prickly for friendship. Nor did she like the older woman, passed off disingenuously as his sister. Gaudier, at twenty-one, was two years younger than Enid and an inexperienced sculptor. But Enid could not ignore the electrifying effect of his artistic brilliance. 'Gaudier shot into our group . . . like a mechanical wasp, a slight, powerful, steely creature all strings and ceaseless quiet noise,' Enid recalled in her eighties. 'Within his head the wheels were never at peace and the hum lay on his lips from which poured talk, invention, criticism, intolerance, gibes, enthusiasm, everything that makes up a mind that can use itself.' Gaudier was most clearly etched in Enid's memory wearing a loose, blue linen smock, only half tucked in with a belt, with his long front hair hanging in a string across his brow, standing on a deserted, windy and icy cold underground station. The last train has gone. But Gaudier, impervious to heat, cold or hunger, tries to keep the group waiting as if a train might yet come. His long arms are waving wildly and impatiently, trying to draw the others closer around him. 'Not at all out of affectation but because he wanted us to hear, hear, hear, what he'd got to say – something which, at that time of night, I don't know that I was up to; extraordinary things about problems with angles and economies of clay. I don't know that I understood it. He would get up a fierceness and it nearly always ended by our pushing off and leaving him behind.' Even Lovat, the first of the group to be excited about Gaudier, eventually quarrelled with him. Gaudier could be furiously abusive to those who, as in the case of Lovat, had helped him most.

In 1912, Gaudier sculpted a head of Enid. As he worked for only three years as a full-time artist before being killed at the Western Front in June 1915, and he smashed some of his works in frustration, those that remain are highly prized. Struck by her beauty and strong features, Gaudier wrote to Enid Bagnold in March that year 'to know whether you could sit now for the portrait head I promised to give you'. He thanked her for her wholeheartedness. It is not known exactly when Gaudier began the bust. In Enid's memory the sessions with Gaudier took place in winter, with daylight rapidly fading. But although she may have visited Gaudier during the winter months it appears that he did not start work on her head until May. Gaudier complained that, although he expected Enid to come every day, she kept him waiting, diverted by her writing. In this he was probably justified; by 1912, Enid was increasingly involved in journalism.

Enid wrote to her mother at the end of May : 'Gaudier has done a *wonderful* head. Very big, rather over life size in clay, with hair and combs and neck and a bit of collar. It's simply extraordinary, exactly like.' Why did Gaudier make the neck so long and thick ? He claimed that he preferred his models to stand or walk about. Yet Enid recalled that she was sitting, on a dais perhaps. Gaudier might have felt particularly aware of his own small stature in her overpowering presence. Never concerned with trying to please, it is more likely that he was interpreting what he perceived as the arrogance of the middle-class student confronted with the grim struggle for existence that Sophie and Gaudier were forced to endure. Enid was aggrieved that the pair considered her, with but £75 per year, a society ne'er-do-well. Had she known that in one year, Gaudier's total earnings were £47.10s.0d., she might have shown greater sensitivity to their plight. Instead she annoyed Gaudier by her 'everlastingly "Oh, that's nice"'. She was, she admitted later, too, 'urbanely fat'. Even later, when he was famous, Enid did not show an appreciation of him as an artist first. Interested, as ever, by her own intuitive reactions, she continued to describe how he appeared to her as 'a hard, disagreeable little creature, with a curious rattling voice like a machine-gun and a complete unawareness of when he was being a bore.'

She hoped Gaudier would give her the bust for nothing, as, evidently, she originally sat to him at his request. But, as she told her mother, she was reluctant to suggest this as the clay must have cost a certain amount. Gaudier knew well that Enid liked it enough to want it cast, but believed she was ashamed to ask because she had left it so long. However, he reported to Sophie in November : 'Yesterday evening I met Enid Bagnold in King's Road ; she asked me to do a plaster cast of her head.' Gaudier did not like 'that plaster business [which] puts my rooms into such a state of filth that it is simply disgusting to look at.' Yet Enid must have decided that to have it cast in bronze was too expensive. Macfall's friend, Major Smythies, whose portrait bust Gaudier also completed that year, paid £12 for his bronze head. She agreed to pay Gaudier £3 for her plaster head.

Sixteen years later, after Sophie's death in destitution, H.S. Ede of the National Gallery wrote *Savage Messiah*.* This was an account of Gaudier and Sophie based on their diaries and letters which, for the first time, laid bare the drama of their impoverished lives. Ede often visited Enid Bagnold during the preparation of *Savage Messiah* and asked her to write an account of her memories of them for use in the book. 'When it came, it was long and elaborate, and not in any way suitable to go with the rest of *Savage Messiah*. ... Her first conversation with me was so true and exciting and then her "story" so drawn out.' Ede tried to edit Enid's piece and an unsatisfactory correspondence ensued, which failed to satisfy either party. Ede was then summoned to meet Enid's husband at his club. Here negotiations began in earnest as to exactly how Miss Bagnold's 'Bohemian' youth should be presented.

Jim Ede believes that, in 1930, Enid's concern was prompted not through any shame she felt for her pre-marital life-style, but because 'her set-up was very society ... and she knew that her husband would not like it'.

She began her tale for *Savage Messiah* with the words 'It's a horrid story', a phrase which later she wished excised on stylistic grounds. Eventually she allowed it to remain, because she thought the removal of other phrases in Gaudier's letters more important. Enid's version of how she sat to Gaudier in his bare little Chelsea attic with the squalid, unmade double bed is one of the most memorable scenes in the book.

While I sat still, idle and uncomfortable on a wood chair, Gaudier's thin body faced me, standing in his overall behind the lump of clay, at which he worked with feverish haste. We talked a little, and then fell silent; from time to time, but not very often, his black eyes shot over my face and neck, while his hands flew round the clay. After a time his nose began to bleed, but he made no attempt to stop it; he appeared insensible to it, and the blood fell onto his overall. At last, unable to stand it any longer, I said: 'Your nose is bleeding.' He replied: 'I know. You'll find something to stop it in that bag on the wall.'

Looking in the bag, Enid found a pile of dirty clothes and selected what she presumed to be long-legged drawers. She tied them around his neck, obstructing his vision and after a time the cloth became soaked through with blood.

Gaudier wrote in his diary that Enid 'lives with Dollie', but in the published version this had to be changed to 'staying with'. He wrote: 'The Bagnold still has the same peculiarity. In the middle of a conversation she

* The book later formed the basis of a play called *The Laughing Woman* by Gordon Daviot and a film, *Savage Messiah*, by Ken Russell.

rushed away to the Embankment without saying a word.' The next phrase: 'and we learned from the other two that she would not be back until midnight, it was then 10.30', Enid emphatically wanted removed from the Ede book. Gaudier concluded: 'Affected of course, but in spite of that she is the most interesting of girls – she at least tries to understand and get in touch with things.' That Enid was quite happy to be called affected, especially when contrasted with interesting, but minded that people should know she was out alone at night, tells as much about the conventions of her subsequent married life as it does about her carefree days before World War I.

At all events, in December, the cast of the head with its overlong neck was ready. Gaudier took it to Enid's by wheelbarrow, and left it as she was out. Dolly and Lovat, poking fun at Gaudier or Enid or both, rouged its cheeks and lips, put blue on its eyes and hung a dress under its chin. Enid was hurt; she wept bitterly. But the make-up rubbed off and the head remained in her possession until one year before her death.

Within months of Ede approaching her for her memories, Enid herself approached Jacob Epstein, the New York born sculptor of Russo-Polish descent, who, she found, was her new neighbour in London, and asked him to make a bronze copy. Suddenly it dawned on her that the student study for which she had resented paying £3 was a rare work of genius. She grew nervous when she thought how easily it might be smashed. Epstein, who had known Gaudier in London, made the copy for Lady Jones, as Enid then was, in April 1930. She paid him £17 and was delighted with it. 'In a curious way, it looks much better than the original,' she told Epstein. 'Now that I have the bronze I somehow feel that the plaster has arrived in a kind of harbour.'*

---

* Both the bronze and the plaster are now owned by Enid's grand-daughter, the Viscountess Astor.

FOUR

Sliding into Madness

THE major cause of Enid's distraction at the end of 1912 was Frank Harris. She had already started working for him while Gaudier was trying to finish her head. At the same time she was returning for weekends to Warren Wood. Always more interested in life than in books as the true educator, she grabbed, during the week, at everything she thought comprised Artistic Life.

Lunches at Eustace Miles, the vegetarian restaurant in Soho, now became frequent. Eustace Miles might have been known as 'the place where people who look like garden pests eat like garden pests', but Enid was not interested in denying herself the pleasures of meat. She was attracted by the other diners rather than the food. The poets Ralph Hodgson, W. H. Davies and Edward Thomas were all regulars. Hodgson, then editor of *C. B. Fry's Magazine*, had a permanent table. There he sat with his lethal bull terrier tied by a thick chain to a chair beside him, holding forth about purity in art while polluting the place with his 'Captain Beard' tobacco. Bellingham-Smith, her erstwhile teacher, married to Hodgson's sister-in-law, sat sadly pontificating in another corner.

Sometimes Enid went to Dan Rider's bookshop in St Martin's Lane, the acknowledged centre for Harris-worshippers to congregate. Lovat Fraser introduced both Enid and Hugh Lunn (who later wrote as Hugh Kingsmill) into this wide-eyed circle, waiting, in the smoky atmosphere behind the heavy curtain dividing them from mere customers, until 'Frankie got a paper'. Lovat also induced his father to put up most of the money to buy Harris's new paper, *Hearth and Home*, a 'blameless' ladies' weekly journal to be staffed by acolytes from Rider's bookshop.

Harris, at fifty-six, was past his prime. The large nose, protruding ears and waxed moustache were not exactly assets. But by his talk alone he could enthral. Lunn, Middleton Murry and Dan Rider had all, at one time, come under his spell. His books on Shakespeare, Wilde and Christ had established his literary reputation; and if, in his own mind, he sometimes confused himself with those he wrote about, it was a confusion he encouraged others to share.

To Enid his very ugliness was an attraction. Meeting him was 'like being run over by the ocean'. But she also saw him as a direct link not only to Shaw and Wilde but to the most fashionable of modern writers and journalists.

When she was sixty-nine she was persuaded to write a review of a biography of Frank Harris by Vincent Brome. She hated reviewing, but of Harris she wrote:

He made sin seem glorious. He was surrounded by rascals. It was better than meeting good men. The wicked have such glamour for the young.

If a doubt sneaked in he made the doubt glorious. Caught out in a lie he laughed his great laugh, and that had its dash. But all the time he was a ship nose-down for disaster. He could pull the stars out of the sky but he flushed them down the drain. Yet what a talker! What an alchemist in drama – What a story teller! It's as impossible to reconstruct the thrall as to call back the voice and power of Garrick.

By September the evident excitement of her new position on *Hearth and Home* shone through every letter to her mother. 'Your child, as well as being so brainy and so "very young" is also very wise – and paddles her canoe with the utmost aplomb – and the stage villain and arch deceiver Harris turns out to be an excellent [and 'fatherly' deleted] ruffian – protecting your child from well-meant officiousness on the part of gentlemen with diamond rings and grey nails.' Her parents, alive to the dangers, warned her 'not to take any new step'. But Enid asked whom they could possibly have in mind! 'Lovat? The Ads Manager? All the rest are unfortunately provided with wives. Your child is a wise child and thoroughly efficient. . . . Of course there's Lunn but he's rather spotty.'

Harris recognized slave labour when he saw it and worked his new protégée hard. She alone of the staff got in at 6.30 every morning and typed, sometimes producing four articles in two days. Harris soon asked her to put in an extra hour's administrative work, flattering her by saying Lunn had tried this and failed. 'I don't mind doing it – it will teach me more of the business of the office than anything else; I mean in case I had a paper of my own.' Before long, the paper's drama critic Kenneth Hare left and Enid stepped into this breach too.

Among the articles she produced for this short-lived paper were interviews with two great ballroom dancers of the day Oscar and Suzette, the writer E. Nesbit and the painter John Lavery. When she travelled to Esher to meet Mrs Annie Besant, then looking after two Indian boys, one of whom was believed to be the Theosophist Messiah, the cub reporter discovered the need to be well informed before an interview. Mrs Besant treated her kindly, wrote much of the article herself, and left Enid to fill in the gaps. Being unprepared for an interview was a sin which Enid, once established, never forgave. Harris thought Enid's piece 'the best talk with a woman I've ever seen'.

She also invented recipes and pronounced upon furnishing, which made Rider guffaw. 'Now what do you know about the arrangement of the home, Miss Bagnold, ha ha ha. If it were the arrangement of the universe. . . ." Her most stimulating assignment was an interview with Katherine Mansfield for a series on young women writers. Enid never understood her. '*Never* till I read *Bliss* fifty years later and found the girl whom I missed when I met her – imprisoned for ever in the crystal of her own words.' Mansfield and Murry, although originally part of the Harris set, were fast becoming disillusioned with their previous idol.

Throughout that autumn, Enid was ecstatic about her elevation to the literary world; above all, seeing her name in print. She began to resent covering routine events because 'I only feel reporterish and not at all important'. She nursed a vague suspicion that Harris ought to have been paying her more than the thirty shillings for which she had to ask each week. But then he beguiled her with praise and she no longer minded how hard she worked for him. He also took her out to lunch, usually to the Savoy or the Café Royal, and sometimes he introduced her to his famous older friends. Enid luxuriated in Harris's fame and glamour as she reflected on how far she had travelled.

After five months, *Hearth and Home* collapsed. Enid barely noticed that most of her friends, unable to stomach Harris, had drifted away too. Ralph Hodgson, whom she considered her mentor, was disgusted by her involvement with Harris, refused to speak to her for a year and wrote a poem about her called 'Eve':

> Picture that orchard sprite,
> Eve, with her body white,
> Supple and smooth to her
> Slim finger tips,
> Wondering, listening,
> Listening, wondering,
> Eve with a berry
> Half-way to her lips.
>
> Oh had our simple Eve
> Seen through the make-believe!
> Had she but known the
> Pretender he was!
> Out of the boughs he came,
> Whispering still her name,
> Tumbling in twenty rings
> Into the grass.

She paid scant attention, but moved on with her chief to the next venture, 'a tainted little property' entitled *Modern Society*, which Harris acquired in

1913. By now Hugh Lunn and Enid Bagnold were virtually the only staff left. So absorbed was Harris in Enid – the conquest vital to him in restoring his shattered self-confidence – and so consumed with financial worries that his literary contributions were negligible. And Lunn, 'a glorious friend but lazy', was expending all his energies in observing the office romance. He was constantly badgering her to tell him the details, and she, being proud of the affair, talked. Enid alone was the star writer on *Modern Society*. For its pages she modified Maupassant, rewrote recipes and copied cartoons, putting her own name to them all. She was quite shameless and would, by this time, have done anything for Harris. 'I was sliding into madness.'

Harris had emotionally seduced Enid on the very first occasion they met. She knew it. The actual event was simply a question of timing. Believing himself to be the great initiator, his preference was for virgins. He liked first to win the girl's trust, affection and preferably her adoration; then to discover everything possible about her by ruthless questioning. The intellectual fore-play concluded, he would proceed as swiftly as possible to the task in hand.

Picture then, how, on the day selected by Harris, he propelled Enid to-wards her inexorable fate. Steering her firmly by the arm, he led her away from the hurly-burly of Regent Street, with its noisy street vendors, into the rich sensuality of the Café Royal. Together, they walked beneath the laurel-crowned initials over the entrance barely glancing at the smoky haze of artistic conversation beyond. They avoided the red plush banquettes and marble-topped tables of the public dining-room with its ornate mouldings, gilded goddesses and cupids, but slipped instead up the side staircase, finally reaching the privacy of an upstairs room.

After lunch, Harris told his young assistant that sex was the gateway to life. 'So I went through the gateway in an upper room in the Café Royal.'

That one sentence, which caused Enid so much heart-searching to produce fifty-seven years later in her autobiography, is all she ever told of the event. By that time her husband was dead; she asked her children if they would be offended by the revelation and they laughed. But, when the author of a new biography of Frank Harris asked her for further details, she declined. Phillippa Pullar wrote:

Unfortunately once she had published her account nothing could be added. She had nothing more to say. Nobody, she felt, could have disposed of a first seduc-tion so elegantly and briefly as she did in her autobiography.... It was stated without emphasis – like a vaccination – and then left. She admired it herself so that anything further (as contributed by her) would be an inelegance.

That afternoon, 'at the end of the session', Enid went to Warrington Crescent for dinner with Uncle Lexy and Aunt Clara. She could concentrate on nothing but her lost virginity, considering herself 'like a corporal made sergeant'. Nowhere is there any intimation that she had found the experience enjoyable or fulfilling, an expression of mutual love. For the gospel according to Frank Harris was passion: the greatest thing in the world was not love but passion.

Hugh Kingsmill, although without naming Enid, recalled a conversation with a woman who had once loved Harris:

As if only with his help would one pass into the kingdom of experience. What nonsense all that was – about Passion and Freedom! And how it impressed one!... Yet there *was* something there – a tangled, troubled light.... I still see the horizon of his eyes and talk flaming like a sunset and yet it's gone – how it's gone! I suppose because it was all so unreal. I thought it was real enough then but there was too much 'Love' and too little natural affection.

Kingsmill's observations of the minutiae of the Bagnold-Harris affair formed the basis of a novel entitled *The Will To Love*, written while he was a prisoner-of-war at Karlsruhe and published in 1919. Enid is thinly disguised as Barbara Guest, a 'modern English girl, clever, but no bluestocking, tall, active, and healthy.... Love interested Barbara more than anything else, but she had little gift or inclination for ball-room trifling, and would generally intimidate her partners by the abruptness with which she swept away their small talk in her anxiety to discover if there were anything individual and original in their dispositions.'

Barbara meets the well-known, but eclipsed, writer Ralph Parker (Frank Harris) on a train and soon finds herself indulging in an illicit affair with him. The story ends with a tawdry but successful attempt by Parker to blackmail Barbara's parents. Even though Harris was well known for his deceit, there is no evidence to suppose that the dénouement was based on reality. Kingsmill's heroine is attracted to Parker partly out of youthful rebelliousness but also because she feels sorry for him. By recounting stories of the neglect and persecution he claimed to be suffering, Harris was for ever arousing pity among his listeners.

Enid's version of her affair with Frank Harris, told with evasive simplicity, scarcely gives an impression of the passion generated or indeed of its duration for well over a year. Kingsmill's Barbara, however, 'longed with all the force of her nature to be with him again . . . "it must be love", she concluded. She had given him her youth, her innocence, and so she loved him. And yet – it wasn't quite what she had dreamed love to be.'

Enid did not speak of this book. Proud though she was to have been sculpted and painted, her literary portrait met with less favour. The novel found no place either in her autobiography or on her bookshelves. When Kingsmill showed Enid the manuscript, she was horrified to discover not only that the heroine was to be called Enid but that she lived in Woolwich. 'I think you are very much fettered by circumstances,' Kingsmill upbraided her when she pleaded for changes. 'Writers who wish to write sincerely ought to be on ticket-of-leave, cut by all their relations and without any reputation to bother about. This applies most of all to gentlewomen, poor things.' In spite of his high-handed tone, however, Kingsmill obliged his erstwhile colleague.

Still relying heavily on her mother's love and approbation, Enid had no intention of 'cutting all her relations', even if matters were not always harmonious. Whatever their private anguish, Enid's parents had until now always supported their daughter. Enid's liaison with Harris, even if they were unaware of its full implications, unleashed their deepest concerns. In a typewritten letter Arthur Bagnold reminded his daughter of her position in society. 'You come of gentle stock and your parents and relations are gentlefolk whose social position must be maintained and respected.' Yet, he continued, she was now employed as an Art Editress of a penny weekly paper of low repute. 'This paper is one which never had anything but a poor reputation and is carried on by a man who, though clever, appears to have little or no business capacity – a man who holds and expresses views in the paper of a nature with which none of your relatives, not excepting your young brother, care to be associated.' Finally, Colonel Bagnold suggested to his twenty-five-year-old daughter that she was spoiling her chance of marriage to a gentleman. 'Surely he would think if you can interest yourself in being associated with such a paper ... you must not be above touching dirt in other ways.'

Enid's reply to her father's rebuke is lost. But there is some evidence that the 'double life' with Harris was taking its toll on her nerves. When her grandmother Alger took her to Nice for a holiday in February 1913, a bumpy red rash spread across her face and her hair began to fall out. A local doctor diagnosed depression and warned her that she would always suffer from this. It would scarcely be surprising if she were worried about being pregnant. She wrote to her mother urgently asking when her 'visitor' was due. Years later she recalled for her daughter-in-law the agonies of jumping up and down and 'swilling the gin down each month'.

Her loyalty to Harris was sternly and publicly tested early in 1914. Drama at *Modern Society* was a daily occurrence. The bailiffs had arrived more than once but, on each occasion, Harris's possessions were let out of the window on a rope in the nick of time. Overburdened by financial difficulties, facing several writs and suffering from gastritis, Harris became more reckless in his attacks as his sense of personal insecurity deepened. These culminated in a libel case brought by Lord Fitzwilliam against the paper. Full reports of the trial were carried in every newspaper. In court, Harris had thundered at the judge in a voice usually reserved for errant waiters. The tipstaff tapped him gently on the shoulder and led him away to Brixton gaol for contempt of court.

Meanwhile Enid, failing in her naïveté to grasp the gravity of the charge, had spent the morning shopping. Harris had told her that he was hosting a luncheon at the Savoy for Sarah Bernhardt (he was, in fact, merely a guest) and Enid decided to buy for the occasion a magnificent white silk hat with a large white feather which she had been eyeing for some weeks in Mme Henry's, the Bond Street milliners. Unable to afford its three guinea price, Enid was allowed to take it only after she had undressed and found a Cash's name tape on her old school vest, a gesture that proved her identity, as well as her youth. Thus behatted, Enid returned to the office and waited in trepidation for the one o'clock appointment. At half past two, the telephone rang and she was told about the prison sentence.

At first distraught and then furious, she was still fierce in her devotion to Harris and easily assumed responsibility for publishing the paper, dimly aware that otherwise it would lose its stationer's licence. 'Fired by my editor, I determined to be great too, to rally his friends around the martyred leader.' She wrote to Bernard Shaw, James Pryde, Max Beerbohm, Haldane Macfall and Joseph Simpson, asking them, instead of the usual contributors, to fill the paper. Leaving the other pages blank would, she thought, add to the effect.

Shaw, on a handwritten postcard, refused: 'You can't put an elephant to hatch hen's eggs,' he told her. He explained to Beerbohm why he was not helping. Harris, he believed, had to pull himself together. 'Miss Bagnold is not able to dry-nurse him out of his difficulties.' Joseph Simpson sent a sketch and, best of all, Beerbohm provided her with a drawing of himself and Frank Harris at a restaurant table with the caption: 'The best talker in London with his best listener.' Beerbohm's only proviso was that this should be used neither as a cover nor as a poster, because 'as you so well understood, I did not want to be portraitist to "modern society".'

With the Beerbohm trophy in hand, Enid eagerly went by bus to Brixton to discuss the next issue with Harris, having first received her father's permission. Colonel Bagnold had reluctantly agreed, because to desert a friend in need would have offended his standards. Enid wrote:

Frank Harris was brought out at a smart pace across the prison yard by a warder, and entering a glass room . . . spoke to me across a wide wooden table, sitting at the farther side. He promised me that Max's stipulation should be faithfully kept, but he did not seem pleased with either Max or me, only gratified on his own account. On leaving the prison I was fascinated by the way in which the inner prison gates were shut before the outer were opened and you were left in a tunnel watching the pale faces of other visitors.

A day or two later a man delivered a heavy roll of posters with Beerbohm's drawing thereon. The realization that, even from prison, Harris was quite able to continue lying and cheating sent Enid, in a white fury, racing to Beerbohm's house. She explained what had happened. Beerbohm took her back to the office immediately to fetch the posters and then on to the printers to collect the block. Finally they descended the Savoy steps to the river, where they threw the whole lot in. As a reward, Beerbohm gave Enid the original drawing.

The Frank Harris who emerged from goal unshaven and shaky at 5 a.m. one day was in many ways a broken man. Enid was there to meet him and the pair got into a taxi bound for the Café Royal where, according to Enid, Harris hoped he would be able to spruce himself up. 'What will people say to me?' he murmured to her, his courage ebbing away for the moment. Enid felt as if he were sapping hers.

For those she loved, Enid would always do anything. But Harris's behaviour over the poster had disillusioned her. And, even before that, the previous few months had worn her down. 'Not with him, but with that remorseless, downhill, losing fight, money going, chances going, concili-ation thrown again and again to the winds, health going, energy poured out upon nothing, fury spent against something that not only doesn't heed but doesn't hear.'

Harris went almost immediately to live in the South of France and then to America. He had often told her he would go to America, get a divorce and marry her. 'But it's a good thing he didn't really. Not that he could have, I expect.' Enid was again swept off by her grandmother for a holiday in France and then, no longer employed as a journalist, went back to live at Shooters Hill, never again to leave it entirely until she married.

FIVE

What a Soldier of Fortune is Every Unmarried Girl

ENID'S brief taste of freedom made it difficult for her to settle down to the conventions of suburban life expected of a girl of her class. Frank Harris had shown her that following the urges of one's nature was not necessarily disastrous; she still had the courage, but no longer the opportunity to experiment.

'I seem to have to trundle off in pursuit of spurious amusement that always turns out to be dust,' she wrote to her mother after a particularly desultory few days at Inkerman Barracks in Woking. Or again, from Royston: 'Remind me next time that it is pretty boring and don't let me forget and come.' The monotony, she moaned, even made her tire of strawberries. One weekend was particularly insufferable as her fellow guests 'call themselves Bohemian and that just shows what they are. Anyone who calls himself or herself a Bohemian is sure to be an art student with a touch of Kitty in them. I hate them and they hate me.'

The tennis and weekend parties were also, she complained, preventing her from getting to grips with writing a novel. She had long promised Harris that she would write a character sketch about him; other subjects that she toyed with were 'the sex question, the woman question, the great free life that a woman ought to live', none of which adequately caught her imagination. When she was not writing she was book-binding; an occupation which 'did quite well instead of Frank Harris'. However, writing a full-scale novel, which she had yearned to do since her schooldays, still eluded her.

Enid's return to the parental home when Harris left the country was greatly eased, however, by the arrival of some glamorous, flamboyant and worldly neighbours. The Baroness Catherine d'Erlanger was a French woman of noble birth and very decided taste. Anything that glistered she wanted in her court. Full of imagination and ideas herself, she had a great natural instinct for talent in others. Those she thought worth protecting and helping she would collect as part of her entourage; but her spontaneity ensured that, just as easily, they could be forgotten. 'Where you are loved for no reason you are dropped for no reason,' said Martin, the butler, in *Serena Blandish*.

One such protégée was Paula Gellibrand, a beautiful girl whom Catherine befriended, according to some simply because she liked exquisite things around her. Catherine's enemies pointed out, however, that the delicate blue-eyed blonde with a perfect figure but little to say acted as a perfect foil for Catherine's own daughter, the dark-haired Baba d'Erlanger. The two became almost inseparable and Baba's quick-thinking intelligence was shown off against Paula to its best advantage. Freddie Guest* fell madly in love with Miss Gellibrand and commissioned Augustus John to paint her.

Catherine bought houses in the same way that she acquired people. Her London residence, 139 Piccadilly, was a magnificent building, a former home of Lord Byron and perfect for entertaining on a grand scale. But for weekends the Baroness considered it wildly amusing for guests to drive eastwards down the Old Kent Road to Shooters Hill where she had discovered a fine Palladian mansion. Falconwood, set amid forty wooded acres, had been built over a period of three years and was finished in 1867. The wife of the first owner, Lord Truro, died within two years and was buried by him at night in the grounds. The site of the grave was never known and an attempt to dig up the remains revealed only dogs' bones. When the d'Erlangers bought Falconwood, it boasted an impressive tiered garden leading down to a grass tennis-court and the bluebell woods beyond. Above all, it was next door to Warren Wood.

Enid, turning her 'ardent snobbish eyes, mad with interest' on the *beau monde*, soon wandered through a hole in the hedge. Announcing her credentials boldly, she told the Baroness she was a journalist poised to write books. She knew that her inadequate clothes and schoolgirl fresh face were not enough. 'Whatever I have looked like, and what my face has not carried, I have always had a sort of vitality that did instead.' She managed to put herself over. But the d'Erlangers were installing a hard tennis-court and Enid's immediate entry ticket was her facility with a tennis racket. She quickly became a daughter of the household.

The Baron Emil d'Erlanger was a banker of Hamburg–Jewish extraction; a kind and patient man, indulgent of his wife's whims. She, a tall, striking woman with vivid red hair and flared nostrils, bowed to few conventions. Her lover was Hugh Rumbold, a transvestite. 'I never fathomed the sexual life of either of them, whether towards each other or alone,' Enid wrote. Perhaps not. But she watched, intoxicated, as the Baroness dressed in the morning, drinking in the sophistication that she hoped could remain within her.

The Baroness could be both a warm friend and a dangerous troublemaker. Enid, inevitably fascinated and influenced by her, longed to be part of the

---

* Capt. the Hon. Frederick Guest CBE, DSO.

brilliant, uninhibited, cosmopolitan, and above all rich society that had suddenly arrived on her doorstep. Aware that she was tolerated at first simply as the girl-next-door, she determined to make her mark on this new world. 'I was swimming on approval in a new electric sea.'

With hindsight she rationalized the change in her life. 'I turned round from my artistic friends to society friends. As a writer I wanted to have the naked stuff of people who were not writers who knew each other on totally different lines but, as it were, tuned each other up. If you're always living with painters you're always dealing in the second hand. It interested me much more to be with people who were doing things rather than watching others doing things.'

By her twenty-fifth year, Enid had forged some independence for herself at home by virtue of having lived in London for nine months. But, she insisted later, she had 'rebecome a virgin'. Although the d'Erlangers' world was a far cry from the military respectability of her father, the only objection her parents raised to her spending as much time as she did in their set was when the Baron established a hen yard beneath her father's bedroom window. The cockerels woke him every morning at four. Enid eventually managed to persuade the Baron to relocate the chickens and her father was placated.

Enid often stayed at 'one three nine Pic'. Here, first a liveried footman and then a butler escorted guests up seemingly endless steps eventually to be announced in the drawing-room. Enid told her brother that she was falling over butlers throughout the house and the bathroom, with a silver bath let into a marble floor, was a wonder to behold. Enid had her own room there with blue walls covered in tiny gold stars.

Sometimes, parties went on all day and then at night Catherine might take one or two close friends out to the theatre for the last act of a play. Or else, upon a whim, they might descend in large numbers on a favourite restaurant in the early hours of the morning. It was an impulsive life, always with something amusing being dreamed up. Enid well knew that, as her patron did not suffer bores, she had to be amusing too. But the role of court jester had been marked out for her since school and she did not feel uncomfortable in the part.

Serious artists and intellectuals were not at home in such gatherings. But among those who watched her performance on the d'Erlanger stage were Eric Caledon, the charming, slightly shy, Irish bachelor; Edward Knoblock, the New York-born playwright; the beautiful Ruby Peto; the wild and gay Nancy Cunard and the promising actress Julia James. Basil Blackwood, who later wrote to Enid from the trenches, was amongst this circle, as was George Grossmith, the comedian, and Duff Cooper, then working in the Foreign

Office. The Princesses Marie and Violette Murat, the diplomat Matila Ghyka and Paul Morand, not yet the novelist he was to become, were also regular visitors. Among other hostesses, Enid met Lady Ottoline Morrell and Lady Cunard – 'sublimely idiotic and yet wonderful' – and the Marchesa Casati, renowned for once having two chained lions prowling at one of her balls. Lady Diana Manners, the most beautiful woman of her generation, made more than a fleeting impression. Although electrified by the 'blind blue stare' Enid was not yet brave enough to strike out for friendship with her. Enid wrote to her mother at the time: 'she's awfully nice but makes a lot of noise' and waited thirty years to know her.

In August 1914 events in the world took hold of her life. The Bagnolds were holidaying on Dartmoor when war with Germany was declared. Enid immediately joined the Red Cross. She had recently begun to keep a journal and the war became, of course, a constant background theme. Before she was even qualified, one of her first duties was to attend at the railway stations as the wounded returned from the front. 'The great trains with the Red Cross gleaming in front of them edged slowly, softly, carefully in against the plat-form. There was awed silence as the doors opened, nobody alighted, and the stretchers were carried to the train. . . . The wounded came just as they were, their bandages soaked in blood.' They were rushed to the nearby Royal Herbert Hospital at the foot of Shooters Hill, a 700-bed mid-Victorian insti-tution. The Herbert had been built in the wake of Florence Nightingale's experiences in the Crimea and named after her staunch friend and supporter, Lord Herbert of Lea.

In November, Enid gained her Red Cross certificate of proficiency. She wrote in her diary:

I am sick, sick of the war, sick of the unending misery in these hospitals here, sick of the jargon, the real belief in mistaken ideals, sick altogether of the excuse of ideals at all to marshall and protect the worst passions and abuses, the poorer side of personal and national spirit. . . . To live in a period of war is to be frightfully unlucky, to have delicacies, arts, intricacies of thought, any personal spontaneity of living purposely sterilized in everyone, everything, every journal, book, amusement, about one.

I am unable to turn pain and loss to an account. . . . I am not inspired to any turn of thought. I find nothing provocative, nothing suggestive.

Painting, however, seemed to offer a way back into writing. Her scorn for art students notwithstanding, Enid had taken up etching with Sickert again early in 1914. And this time she often worked alone with him. 'It occupies all my days and makes me happy. . . . I ought to be writing, straining miserably and wearily to write. I've heaps to say and I can't say it. . . . I think of beautiful things which people would take pleasure in reading if only I could take trouble to learn to use the medium.'

One day as she was folding her Red Cross dress to put it away in the chest of drawers, Sickert leant over to kiss her:

I was very thrilled; I felt a whirl of sensation as I sat deep in the end of the bus. . . . But the drawing is better than the kisses. It's wonderful to be happy all day long. And now, curiously enough I am more sure than ever of my real deep attachment to Frank Harris. I have been very *intimate* with him, personal touching intimacy of heart and mind and outlook. He holds so much of me, made so much of me himself and cares for what he made like a gardener. Sickert's given me a real gift; my love of drawing, my perceptions, my talents and through the drawing I hope again to write poetry. It would be a fine thing to be the finest painter in the world. But *I* would sooner be a little poet.

Frank Harris, 'the wonderful first to me', had too great a hold on her for their affair to die. It lived on in a series of coldly passionate love letters which Enid herself realized were far more eloquent and expressive than the novel about him she was struggling to write. Buried away in her tower room she typed out copies* of her own letters and pasted them into the journal she wanted no one to see until she died. She called it her Death Journal. Interspersed among the letters are musings, poems and some letters she received, although there is only one original from Harris and an extract typed out by Enid.

The correspondence was, for Enid, a literary exercise conducted with a master craftsman: 'Ah Frank, Frank, make me a writer, me too! I am one . . . that's the gruesome part of it. Yet there may never be a word of mine on a printed page. Oh Frank, Frank, finest lover in the world! Come back and let's have our life and love together.'

Many of her letters were concerned with the purity or jealousy of their love. 'No frailty touches us in our relation to each other,' Enid wrote to Harris. 'No vagaries, whims, tempers, misunderstanding, jealousies blur our understanding of the other's written word'; sentiments more easily committed to a typewriter than spoken aloud. At other times she talked of their mutual talent for love-making; 'Oh I want you, I want you so. Let me listen again to your laughing assurances that it's "alright . . . quite safe" and . . . like

---

* As these were not carbon copies, it is impossible to know whether they are 'as sent'. However, she described them as such when discussing their republication with John Randle of the Whittington Press in 1980.

the beginning of the world. Then the final gentleness, your divine intimacy and tenderness.'

Perturbed but flattered by Harris's request to send him some nude pictures of herself, Enid searched among her friends for an obliging photographer. Dolly would have nothing to do with Harris and Kitty would have been too shocked. But when Harris thanked her for the prints before she had even posed, she realized that the request had not been made of her alone.

Enid was aware that Harris 'whom I know to be alive with all the riches of sex dowered shall I say with purses of the gold coin' was bound to be enjoying the attentions of other women. Nonetheless the sure knowledge of this shocked her. She told him:

I don't love you the less, Frank, for having asked someone else. . . . I almost love you more, shall I say, more lovingly, more tenderly; there is a side of me which feels for you as if you were the most wonderful child in the world . . . and who would cavil at such a child for swearing, stealing the jam . . . what you will. For in physical betrayal there is nothing; I see that and insist on it firmly.

It was a brave pose that Enid tried all her life to maintain. But beneath the proud words there was certainly pain. Pain when a letter from Frank Harris 'accidentally' included one from a girl who had worked in the office with them in the *Hearth and Home* days. Realizing that Frank and this girl had been occasional lovers throughout her own affair with him was the final betrayal that spurred her to tell Dolly one day in 1916, 'Oh I shan't hear from Frank any more. It's all over.' In fact, Enid's letters continued until October 1918, four years after she last saw him.

T he shock of discovering that she had been sharing Harris, not only with his wife, was all the greater for Enid, because she had spared him few details of the new man in her life.

'The taste for me is apt to corrupt the palate and unfit it for common fare,' Harris had once warned Enid. But there was nothing common about Prince Antoine Bibesco. Enid was introduced to the Roumanian diplomat at Catherine d'Erlanger's London dinner table. Antoine was tall and severely handsome. His dark hair, swept straight back, revealed the receding temples of his thirty-seven years. A man for whom female conquest was shockingly facile, his thin, hard lips and impenetrable gaze betrayed, to those who cared to look, a teasingly cruel nature. A direct descendant of the Kings of Moldavia, he cut a dashing figure in society and his friendships, once given, were not fickle.

As much Parisian as Roumanian, Antoine grew up among the cream of artistic talent. Saint-Saëns and Fauré, Liszt and Wagner among musicians; Anatole France, Pierre Bonnard and Edouard Vuillard among writers and painters, all frequented the Rue de Courcelles salon of his mother, Princesse Helene Bibesco. It was here too that the young Antoine, then studying in Paris for the Roumanian diplomatic service, first met Marcel Proust. A close friendship soon developed between Proust and the Bibesco brothers: all three inhabited a childish world of secret names and twisted words. Thus the Bibescos became Oscebibs and Marcel, Lecram. For Antoine, in love with the telephone often more than the person to whom he was speaking, the special name 'Telephas' was invented.

Enid told Harris of her meeting with the handsome Prince. 'A.B. defended you the other day. Someone said you wrote of England as a traitor and A.B. exclaimed: "No no! Rather he writes of her weeping as a man speaks of a mistress with sorrow and tenderness."... I think you'd like him. It's a pity I can't' – later annotated by Enid, 'and then of course I did!'

It is not difficult to see why Enid caught Antoine's eye. Physically, she was striking. Once qualified as a VAD she was often to be seen in the neighbour-hood in her starched white apron and dress on her brother's Douglas motorcycle; he, since August 1915, had been serving with the 20th Division in France.

Constantly 'fretting to be more extrovert' she was, in October 1915, one of the first women accepted to work in a munitions factory at Woolwich Arsenal. The war was going badly and complaints about shortages of shells were reported back home. 'Art indeed! Here to my hand, were more astounding possibilities.... It was up to us to correct all the deep-rooted convictions of women's illogic, of women's unfitness for mechanics, from the mind of man. We were the pioneers,' Enid wrote at the time. She worked from eight in the morning until eight at night with one and a half hours off for lunch. Payment was from thirty shillings (£1.50) a week with promotion to supervisor expected to follow swiftly.

'I expect it will be ghastly hard work, but awfully "*la chose*",' Dolly wrote enviously when she heard about it. 'I can see you sticking your chest out and saying "Now, my man ..." and settling strikes and making speeches and always with a large black smut on your nose, but it won't spoil the effect, only make them feel you're a fellow worker and all that kind of thing.' In the event, Enid hated the job. Being 'head of a gang' appealed to her but the three-hour lectures on muzzle velocity, fuse construction and the composition of explosives she found less than stimulating and the primitive sanitary conditions appalled her. She complained to the Home Office that her male workers treated the factory shed as a public convenience and the fouled air had caused several of the women to suffer septic throats. On 10 November she handed in her notice.

To Antoine, she appeared overflowing with more than a measure of originality. Her conversation effervesced – but her written talent had to be disciplined, nurtured, even bullied. He was highly amused by the unbowdlerized account she supplied of her affair with Harris. This small worldliness made her a more interesting companion but never a potential wife.

When asked later how long he had remained in love with her, he replied 'three days'. For her part the attraction was fatal. She never loved anyone as much again. Everything she subsequently attempted was to prove to Antoine how she had triumphed in life. For one year, before sleeping at night, she would pray to a God she barely believed in: 'Please, make Antoine marry me.'

There was another reason why Antoine encouraged a friendship with Miss Bagnold. He was devoted to his elder brother Emmanuel who had been disfigured by a stroke which had weakened his facial muscles. Constantly taunting Antoine with threats of suicide – he had already made two attempts – Emmanuel wrapped a blue scarf around his face and required friends who had not known him before. Enid did not displease him. She amused him. On the first occasion they met he put only an arm around the door, grabbed some dried flowers from a vase and thrust them at her as a present. In one of the many pencilled notes he sent her, he wrote, 'The sky is grey and so are my thoughts. But when I look at your eyes I remember the sky has been blue and may be so again.' Thus Antoine was using Enid to keep his beloved brother alive.

Enid was now living very intensely. Although the regular Zeppelin raids filled the London sky with billowing white smoke, the war did not appear to curtail her social life. Of course, there had been deaths among her friends. The most harrowing for her was in the autumn of 1915 when a flying hero, Captain Roger Mapplebeck DSO, was killed while she watched him on a trial flight. 'He was charming and young, shy, gentle, proud but one of many like him, dead.' However, under Antoine's inspiration, she was at last writing again; poems at first, then small sketches and stories. The Bibesco brothers 'brought me up I was their child. They were my Oxford and Cambridge and the Sorbonne.'

In an unpublished satire Enid wrote at this time, 'A Tragedy in Trafalgar Square – A New Study of Hamlet, Prince of Denmark', she captured Antoine's combination of melancholy and *joie de vivre*. When Ophelia asks how he is or where he is, he refuses to reply, the questions being too personal. 'Something witty please,' he asks.

Proust's biographer, George Painter, considers there is in Enid Bagnold's work 'a strand of lucid French imagination which appears also in the work of the Bibescos' friends, Giraudoux, Cocteau and Morand and even in Proust himself and is connected in its origins with the unwritten art of [the Bibescos].' Foremost among the duties of friendship for this arcane society of French aristocrats and intellectuals was the 'constant exchange of deadly and inviolable confidences.... One of the most interesting pastimes of friendship was to introduce one friend to another and see whether they took together or disliked one another intensely: this was called "operating a conjunction". An indispensable element of conversation between friends was gossip,' Painter wrote.

Chief delight of the group was to visit old churches. To Enid was extended the great honour of being invited to accompany the Bibescos – this 'cruel and miraculous' pair – on their visits to England's Gothic churches. Before the first of these outings Enid was 'sick with nervousness and hardly slept'. At 8.30 the following morning the Bibesco Daimler drew up outside Warren Wood:

Antoine sprang out first with a grim nervousness. I almost closed my eyes as another figure stepped out and stood also on the pavement. I got in, sat down in the far corner and Emmanuel handed me snowdrops. We moved forward, Emmanuel sitting between us well forward resolutely that I might not see his face. We sat like this all day, till 4 o'clock and I was nervous and unhappy.

Once at the church, Emmanuel would often enter first and then rush out with a staged gesture: 'We'll go back now, it's much too beautiful for you to see.' Enid wrote a poem to Emmanuel after a particularly wonderful day with the brothers in January 1916, keenly expressing her awareness of her inferiority towards them.

> How will it fare with me . . .
> When by some valley some old Park rolls near,
> And o'er the streaming lawns the deer
> Scatter and flee,
> When at the very portals of the Abbey door
> I pause, and pause, . . . and dare no more?
> And when beside your intimate delight,
> To me the beauty is aloof and hidden out of sight?

For her talent in verse, the Bibescos rechristened her Virgilia, a name she wore proudly along with the diamond and onyx brooch which Antoine gave her. 'Virgilia' had not been chosen lightly by the Bibescos. Antoine perceived that this talented and attractive young girl was using a natural gift for

self-dramatization to create a character for herself. Aeneas, too, the invention
of Virgil, was a legendary hero creating a myth around himself. Since Enid
wrote poetry and Virgil's epic poem, if pronounced without diphthongs,
becomes 'The Enid', the name was perfect. The analogy might even have gone
further: if Enid were cast as a Roman epic female type perhaps Antoine took
to himself the role of Aeneas, the hero who left the East to found a great
dynasty and empire in the West.*

Enid's photograph albums of this period show the threesome at Lavenham
in Suffolk, Kirton in Lincolnshire, Peterborough Cathedral, Crowland
Abbey, Stewkely, St Botolph's Church at Boston and Walsoken, Norfolk.
Enid is invariably relaxed and smiling, slimmer than at any time previously,
wearing elegant black suits (black to please Antoine) with a large velvet
beret.†

She confessed to her diary: 'I am aware of an immense adaptability in
myself. Only tell me what will please you and I will become it. . . . I do begin
to feel something in a church. Maybe it's only like learning Russian . . . for
someone like Ivy Low.'‡

Intellectually aware that a refusal could draw him closer while blind
adoring love merely distressed him, Antoine was, she knew, 'playing the
woman to my man . . . Antoine's strength is in his detached elusiveness – mine
is in my . . . I meant that I woo – he retires, beckoning.' In the spring of 1916,
Enid was helplessly in love. 'You do, you do make me happy." Enid wrote to
Antoine. 'I have not been happy like this, happy on the right lines . . . happy
without a hinterland of black thoughts and regrets . . . for years.'

When Antoine said he would telephone, Enid was unable to concentrate on

---

* George Painter thinks that, according to this analogy, Enid may have 'represented all three of the Virgilian heroines, Dido Queen of Carthage (so madly in love
with him that she could only react to his leaving her by burning herself to death),
Lavinia princess of Latium (his destined bride for the ultimate production of Julius
and all the Caesars) and Camilla (the Amazon maid who runs about shooting his men
in the war against nearby tribes of anti-Trojans, till slain herself to his sorrow, a
parallel to the hockey-captain side of Enid). Later, the daughter of the Prime Minister
of England seemed a still better equivalent of Lavinia.'

† Perhaps the brothers took the opportunity to explain to Virgilia the legend of
Crowland. 'The abbey owes its founding to Guthlac, son of a Mercian nobleman, who
gave up his military career, turned monk and decided in 699 to live as a hermit in the
Lincolnshire Fens. He was brought by boat to a chosen spot on an island where a sow
with a white litter lay under a willow tree – details which are reminiscent of the passage
in Book VIII of Virgil's *Aeneid*, in which Father Tiber advised Aeneas on the site
where Alba was to be founded. The Crowland site, Anchor Church Field, is about a
mile from the ruins.'

‡ Ivy Low (b. 1889): radical journalist and writer who, on 22 February 1916,
married the Russian revolutionary Maxim Litvinov.

anything until he had done so. He, of course, more practised and less stricken, never rang when he said he would. 'Oh, had you meant to ring up ? I had forgotten you were going to,' she occasionally managed. If he asked her to lunch at their house at 114 Grosvenor Road, she tried, but was unable to refuse. 'As regards Antoine, I am sure of nothing.'

The brothers' constant use of the telephone, especially timed, so it appeared, to interrupt Bagnold family meals, was not the only point at issue between Enid and her parents. As the visits to churches usually required at least one night away the inevitable lies made the strain at times intolerable. But then a chaperone was found, the Bibescos' beautiful young cousin Marguerite Lahovary. Emmanuel wrote, with excessive politeness, to Ethel Bagnold asking whether, as Marguerite would be with them, they could use his house on the Thames at Marlow as a staging post. Occasionally a telegram had to be sent stating that they would have to stay as it was now too late to return, but carefully adding that his cousin was in the party. Mrs Bagnold, replying with unintended veracity, invariably acquiesced: 'She is getting such an education through you.'

Books, especially chosen for Virgilia's tutelage, often arrived by special messenger. 'They educated me, as it were, in the basement below Proust. Proust was alive then and I wasn't thought eligible for the ground floor.' Voltaire's *Candide* was among the volumes sent and its effect on Enid was immediate. She had already developed a detached, wrily sardonic tone in her letters to the Bibescos ; her frequent references to herself in the third person were almost a carapace, shielding her from the inevitable wounds to come. But reading *Candide* sharpened and crystallized her approach and she was to use this to brilliant effect in *Serena Blandish*.

The books, hats and especially the brooch worried Enid's father. Victorian morality dictated that such gifts, if not followed by a proposal of marriage, compromised a girl. He told her so. She, maintaining to him that it was quite different now, none the less begged Frank Harris : 'Tell me how to marry him. Tell me . . .'

Christabel McLaren*, who saw Antoine and Enid together at this time, thought they would marry : 'For you both looked radiant when you were together – like a classical God and Goddess . . . your height, your carriage, blazing eyes and your radiance gave you the ambience of a Goddess.'

The abstract charms of marriage tempted her not at all. She was sickened by those who kept telling her she 'must marry. . . . Not for mating, not for the joy of sensuality, not because my hands are out against your hands and

---

* Later Lady Aberconway.

nothing under heaven gives me strength to hold my body back but because . . . because. For reasons, my dear.'

When Dolly, now Mrs Eric Crundall, and Lovat Fraser, happily married to the American singer Grace Crawford, exhorted Enid to marry, she was unmoved. She had recently received three written proposals from a doctor, a civil servant and a soldier which she had no difficulty in turning down. They were useful only to brandish in front of Antoine. Enid's attitude appears to put her squarely among the freely emancipated females of her day – the Ann Veronicas – who eschewed domestic woman and the social system that glorified marriage. After all, a sexual adventure outside marriage had been an aim for some years.

But Enid's attitude was born not out of any conviction that all females should have greater freedom; it arose from a personal longing for adventure within herself. This confused vision led to an entry in her diary in 1913: 'Dominate me, imprison me that I may have the pleasure of rebellion, the freeborn pleasure. Set me free as air and I'm a slave of a woman waiting to be taken.' Her views changed little in the succeeding years.

Catherine also encouraged her to marry – but not to Antoine. Mischievous as ever, she was unhappy with the results of her own handiwork: 'She likes conquests kept *inside* her house,' Antoine told Enid, relaying also that Catherine had warned him how Enid would try and set a trap for him.

In the autumn of 1916, Emmanuel rang up one day to invite Enid to go with them to America for three weeks. She knew this would never be permitted, but worried too, if she were to go, how she would react to Harris. For Harris was still acting as her father confessor. 'One thing you wanted to know about. Did Antoine give me more physical pleasure than you? My dear, he hardly gave me any.' On 18 October she wrote:

Well now, that is all ashes; or not at all bitter like ashes but past like a little wind, like blown leaves, leaving me with certain pictures in my mind, certain experience – all to the good but past, in the sense that I know his value, see that he has no other temperament beyond the *jouissance célébrale* [sic] of a sort of sex-curiosity, know that he's kind, gentle . . . capable of *tendresse*, hyper-sensitive to faults of style and literature . . . that he is my friend, that we no longer sleep together . . . and you have the picture.

In spite of the brief yet magical happiness she had enjoyed with Antoine, she wrote, 'Oh dear me, Frank, what a wonderful life I might have had if you weren't in America.'

SIX

The Letters I Might Have Written You

WHEN her relationship with Antoine faltered, Enid turned to a woman friend. Irene Cooper Willis was six years Enid's senior, she had a striking, Hispanic aura and was brilliant. One of the first women students at Girton, she became a convinced socialist and barrister. 'She looked always as though about to answer Shylock with beautiful indignant gravity, shy but rigid for the right,' Enid wrote of her.

Friendship with Irene offered Enid intellectual stimulation and brought her to the periphery of Bloomsbury, but was not enough to win her acceptance there. Irene came from a large family living close by on Shooters Hill Road. Enid often walked there and back for dinner and was tolerated because 'my chatter was a change, I think, from their own conversation, and they flattered and "admired" me.'

At first, Enid was malleable enough to be influenced by Irene's strong personality and independent mind. Fascinated, too, by the manner of her dress and the way she pulled her shiny black hair behind her ears, fixing it with two dark green combs, Enid copied her for a while by wearing a white collar with cascading linen frill. Sometimes she even borrowed Irene's clothes when she went to stay with her.

Towards the end of 1914, Irene Cooper Willis had been introduced to Bertrand Russell, as a research assistant. Very quickly he too fell under her spell but she, finding little attraction in any man, spurned him. It was not long before she intensified her feelings towards Enid. Enid, although realizing that Irene had 'a fantastic propensity to get hurt', was often irritated by Irene's political views, especially her support for the Union of Democratic Control (UDC). This, to Enid, represented a 'shapeless, formless, colourless fossildom'; she preferred something new and alive.

In November 1915, she forbade Irene to speak to her again until she, Enid, had written something – a threat against which her friend railed. 'I felt quite sure before the day was over I should hear your voice on the telephone arranging a meeting. . . . Considering that when we are together we generally spend the time in miseries and in reproaching ourselves for being Unlit

Lamps*, it seems from the practical point of view a waste that we should throw away these salutary opportunities and imagine that we should burn briskly without them.' She signed herself 'your spurned, though loving, Irene'.

Vita Sackville-West was also a friend of Irene's and through Irene met Enid. Writing to Enid some thirty years later, she described Irene's loneliness after the death of her companion, the writer Vernon Lee†:

The one thing I can give her is affectionate friendship. I can't stir her emotions as you evidently can because she never had that sort of feeling for me at any moment. I always suspected that she had for you and also suspected that through you she had been hurt in some way – rather embittered. Though she has never hinted it, let alone said so explicitly. Perhaps you found it necessary to be – what shall I say? – stand-offish; I don't know. Oddly enough, I have no idea even if you are what people call 'like that' (probably 50-50, like most people of rich natures) and consequently can't tell if you would have been likely to respond at all.

Vita doubtless perceived the situation accurately, but the friction between Enid and Irene may have been caused by little more than Irene's dislike of the d'Erlanger social scene, which still held Enid in its thrall. Irritated as Irene was by Enid's lack of political sophistication, she nonetheless continued to act as her confidante for many years.

Enid was soon absorbed in her hospital work. She believed 'nursing puts one more in touch with the spirit of men who fight than any other woman's job now.' If she had been worried before about being able to turn pain and loss to account, writing to Antoine about life at the hospital suddenly gave her a voice. Her descriptions of the impermanency of hospital life – 'an everlasting dislocating of friendships and combinations'; of the red-caped sisters' cold dedication to rules – 'a relation is the last straw'; and of the helpless pain and suffering of the men, in the days when lack of drugs meant 'he must stick it out', were both poignant and poetic. It was Antoine Bibesco's galvanizing genius not only to recognize the talent and insights of this very junior nurse but to compel her to make something more permanent of the haunting images she was creating for his benefit. When she wrote him endless letters about the misery she was witnessing, he questioned coldly, 'Why not keep something for yourself?' Recognizing her poor memory, he advised her to write down every day's events at the hospital.

* A phrase taken from Robert Browning's poem 'The Statue & The Bust':
  And the sin I impute to each frustrate ghost
  Is the unlit lamp and the ungirt loin.
  The Unlit Lamp was the title of a novel by Radclyffe Hall, published 1924.
† Her real name was Violet Paget.

She kept herself apart from the other staff, fearing that to enter their cosy world of gossip would blunt her artistic perceptions. In this way she was able to contemplate the laying of hospital trays: '65 trays ... it takes me an hour to do. ... I make little absurd reflections and arrangements taking a dislike to the knives because they will not lie still on the polished metal of the tray but pivot on their shafts and swing out at unbeautiful angles when my fingers have left them.'

Sometimes Enid believed that a literary success might win Antoine back. 'I am the Potter, why should the Potter love his Pot?' he asked. For he had always made his own feelings clear. 'Don't care for me too much; it's no use. Besides does it not stop you from getting married?' But Enid did not love him the less simply because he had warned her of his limited interest in their affair. My love will change that, she convinced herself. Antoine saw his role in Enid's life as instigator not lover: 'I'm going to make something of you one day.' He enjoyed her letters, not as the recipient of so much love – he was embarrassed by it – but in admiration of the elegant turns of phrase and witty little water-coloured drawings that invariably accompanied them. 'Your letters are brilliant,' he told her. 'But really, don't scatter yourself. Believe me, either passion or work. ... There is only one way – steady continuous work.'

For Antoine Enid worked. 'These are the letters I might have written you,' she inscribed the first page of her *Reflections of a V.A.D.*, which she illustrated and bound especially for him. There was no moralizing in the reflections and the tone was unemotional, but the pain was sharply observed, as in the episode when the father of a dead officer seeks some last words about his son from a surviving soldier:

In a very few minutes the citizen went past my bunk door, his hat in his hand, his black coat buttoned; taking back to his home and his family the last facts that he might ever learn.
At the end of the passage he almost collided with that stretcher which bears a flag. Of the two the stretcher moved me least.

Antoine, urging her to send the manuscript to William Heinemann for publication, returned his copy.

By the summer of 1917, Enid found herself involved in a messy entanglement. Irene had a younger sister, Gwynaeth, who was twenty-two, very attractive, slight and dark with wild short hair and looking sixteen. She too had a good brain, but was unable to resist the entreaties of any man. For her, the pleasure was in being able to give, to say 'yes', not in consummating the relationship. Gwynaeth Cooper Willis made no secret of having slept with innumerable men, who, to Enid's horror, were almost all boring and mean-minded.

Enid recounted to Frank Harris what happened next. 'Anyway, I resolved at once that Antoine had better cure her. At least he could give her a higher standard. . . . So one day I planned a lunch and failed to turn up myself, having first of all secretly given her (not him) carte blanche as to her behaviour. I swore I wouldn't be jealous and of course haven't any reason to be.' Enid's introduction seems extraordinary, although she was presumably not aware that Gwynaeth and Emmanuel were already lovers. Emmanuel's discovery that his brother and Gwynaeth were indulging in an affair unleashed a torrent of abuse. 'Poor Gwynaeth, she is so fickle that she can't even be fickle continuously,' he taunted her. Enid tried to defend her friend. Emmanuel would have none of it. 'Of course, one brother may suspect you of duplicity when brother number two is your partner.' To Gwynaeth he wrote vindictively : 'See Antoine as often as you can. You won't see him long. Soon he will curse you, yea even the memory of you.'

The ugly recriminations that ended Emmanuel's affair with Gwynaeth greatly depressed him. His threats of suicide were now repeated daily. On 22 August, Emmanuel rang up from his country home to make sure that Enid would be available that day to go to Antoine in London. Shortly afterwards she received a telephone message to go immediately to Grosvenor Road. She knew this time that Emmanuel had taken his life. Antoine, chiding himself, remembered his brother's warning : 'Look out for my gay days. Look out for when I'm top of my form.' It had been a gay summer. For hours that night Enid and Antoine walked along the embankment together, sometimes silent, sometimes discussing death, Antoine occasionally threatening his own.

Then, but only after receiving her father's permission, Enid stayed the whole night, comforting Antoine, fortified by hot chocolate and, at dawn, croissants. Nothing could have saved Emmanuel but Antoine had worshipped him. He told Enid that he had only ever loved two people, his mother and his brother. Enid, by that remark knowing how little she must have meant to him, nevertheless believed she was a help to him that night.

When they finally motored to Emmanuel's house, they learned he had taken poison and hanged himself on the back of his bedroom door. In his will, which was found lying next to his body, he bequeathed to Enid £120 'less £20 because I am angry with Virgilia', no doubt a reference to the Cooper Willis débâcle. There was also a note for her. Suddenly, as the last person to have spoken to Emmanuel, Enid was once more intricately caught up in the web of Antoine's life. She sat in the car with him at the funeral, listened as he poured out his innermost thoughts. And then he suddenly withdrew from Virgilia. He shunned society and reverted to his natural passion for secrecy. He wrote to her : 'Please don't mention to me ever either this letter or its contents – or don't mention to me your silence about it'; haunting words that signalled the end of a phase in her life.

Enid's manuscript had been passed on to the writer and critic, Desmond MacCarthy, then a reader at Heinemann. He lost it on a bus one day. There was one other copy, made from carbons, which Enid had given Ralph Hodgson, away at the war, and this was now urgently sent for. At all events, Heinemann decided to publish what was from then on called *A Diary Without Dates*.

Enid was no stranger to Desmond MacCarthy. They had first met at Irene Cooper Willis's family home in 1913, when Irene was trying to end her unhappy relationship with him; he, deeply in love, was baffled by Irene's coldness. Desmond MacCarthy proved a far less demanding friend for Enid. By 1917 Enid was enjoying some success with her poems appearing fairly regularly in the *New Statesman* and the *Nation*. She sent one to Desmond MacCarthy for his comments and the friendship between them blossomed. 'I dropped a seed and you send me back a flower,' he told her. As well as poetry they discussed Irene Cooper Willis and how Desmond might win her over. A man of exceptional charm and intelligence, he easily won Enid over. But she loved his talk more than the man. Desmond, in turn, luxuriated in the company of women. Enid he found not only attractive but amusing and witty; above all he praised her for her courage and energy – qualities which never wavered in Enid any less than Desmond's admiration of them. Desmond valued a conversation for its depth and detail and he urged her never to be afraid to bore. In his view, those who jumped from one inconsequential topic to another were life's real bores. Although close to the 'Bloomsburies', he was too eclectic in his friendships to be tied to any one group. He was equally at ease among aristocratic or political gatherings as he was at literary and intellectual parties. And so, he performed a valuable service to Enid, introducing her and her book around.* 'You are going to make me into something. You are going to do some more "potting",' Enid wrote to Desmond in gratitude.

When he took her to Garsington, the wartime home of Lady Ottoline Morrell, she begged him not to leave her alone among so many unfamiliar writers and artists. Afterwards he told her that Ottoline had remarked, 'Why did that vamping girl hang on to you?' In fact, she recognized (but only just) Hugo Rumbold, returned from the war wounded and dressed as a lady's maid.

---

* In her autobiography Enid refers to Desmond's Oxford education (p. 197). He studied at Cambridge; an inaccuracy her husband would have found unforgivable.

Thus attired, he set to removing the ladies' wet stockings after a walk. He surely knew that, as an officer in the Guards, dressing as a woman could bring him to a court martial.

Enid was justified in fearing her reception among such lions, but, all her life, she never gave up trying to enter the den. On 29 January 1918, Virginia Woolf wrote to her sister Vanessa Bell after seeing Desmond MacCarthy:

I have scented a minute romance for you – I am afraid only a figment, but still better than nothing. Did you ever meet a woman called Enid Bagnold – would be clever, and also smart? Who went to Ottoline's parties and now lives at Woolwich and nurses soldiers? 'That disagreeable chit?' Yes that is my opinion too. But she has evidently enmeshed poor old Desmond. She has written a book, called, as you can imagine, 'A Diary without Dates', all to prove that she's the most attractive, and popular and exquisite of creatures – all her patients fall in love with her – her feet are the smallest in Middlesex – one night she missed her bus and a soldier was rude to her in the dark – that sort of thing. Desmond insists that I shall review it in the Times. First he writes a letter; then he comes and dines; then he gives me the book; then he invites me to lunch with a Prince Bibesco who is apparently one of Bagnold's lovers; then he writes again – and every visit and letter ends with the same command – 'For God's sake review this book!'

Virginia at first refused, but thought she might agree in time: 'Bagnold has said to him "Now I won't kiss you" (or whatever it is they do) "until you've got my book reviewed in the Times."' Bagnold has him in her toils. 'The question is, am I a match for Bagnold? You would be, of course, but then I'm so susceptible. Bagnold paints too.'

Virginia Woolf did not review the book and, as Enid walked with Desmond on Hampstead Heath, she mourned with some bitterness the fact that Desmond himself would not review it – he gave her friendship 'instead', he said. She rejoiced, however, at his new name for her – Lionetta – because she was not quite a lion. Came the day of publication and Enid found herself almost a celebrity. 'The world is before me,' she wrote to Frank Harris in March. She had already sent him the book, hoping that as editor of *Pearson's* magazine he would review it. 'I have looks (better than I ever had); this isn't conceit it's simply that I do look better. I am without nerves, no one frightens me, people even know who I am when I dine out. This sounds incredible on one little book but it has the good luck to be so as my reviews have been copious and very long and because people have talked about it a good deal.'

She was not overestimating her success. Her descriptions of unfeeling hospital routine were picked up by the *Daily Mail*, which was exposing a scandal in a similar hospital in Rouen. Within half an hour of publication, she was sacked by the matron of the Royal Herbert Hospital for breach of military discipline.

William Heinemann published 15,000 copies of the slim volume, for which she was paid threepence per copy. 'So I shan't be opulent on it.' But it opened many doors for her. Through Antoine she met Lady Desborough, the renowned hostess. 'I have given the pleasure of your book to so many and I cannot tell you with what enthusiasm it has been received,' she wrote to Enid. John Galsworthy invited her to contribute to *Reveille*, a new government quarterly he was editing. In the first flush of success, Antoine took her to Chelsea to meet the American painters and hostesses Ethel Sands and Nan Hudson, where the new writer was received with cordiality. Cynthia Asquith, daughter-in-law of the former Prime Minister, found the Diary 'wonderfully gripping, pitiless and true, and so vividly written. [Robert] Nichols says it's the only good English thing of the war – bar Siegfried Sassoon.' Antoine also arranged an introduction with Cynthia, who considered Enid 'quite pretty in a fairly ordinary yellow-haired, fresh-complexioned way, '*not* remarkable looking but quite a good talker and an appreciative, stimulating listener.' Sibyl Colefax, the greatest lion-hunter among all the hostesses, also took an interest in Miss Bagnold now. She found her not quite 'up to the standard but not so far below it : so she held my hand, passed me round to her back, still holding the hand, while she talked to someone else.'

Sir Philip Sassoon, MP, then Private Secretary to Field Marshal Sir Douglas Haig in France, wrote to her from the Front : 'I suppose there is not a VAD in France who has not now begun to keep a diary in emulation of you – and paper is so scarce.' Meetings with the poet Robert Nichols and H. G. Wells soon followed. She had been seated next to Wells some years previously when the Mayor of Woolwich, sensing literary talent in young Miss Bagnold, had effected an introduction over a lunch. But in 1918, thrilled by her first literary success, she renewed her acquaintance with him. This time, she stipulated the Cottage Tea Rooms in the Strand as a rendez-vous. It was a shabby little restaurant, with extremely poor food, which had been a favourite haunt of former days. 'My reason was that I really can't stand even being seen lunching with him. The last label on earth that I want … is that.' She was unmoved, she claimed later, by Wells telling her over lunch she was his type and suggesting they might enjoy a mild flirtation. This was simply 'another feather in my silly cap'. She extricated herself from the attempted seduction and Wells sent her an amusing drawing recording the occasion.

In her autobiography, discussing the apparent conquest, Enid telescopes the pre- and end of war meetings, perhaps accidentally. But it is clear from her journal that the Cottage Tea Rooms lunch took place in the spring of 1918 and she writes there as if meeting Wells for the first time:

To speak honestly . . . I didn't much like him. When I think of the best of his books he certainly wasn't that. He told me 'the story of his life' in four words and it sounded and looked like a little black dot on paper . . . . It isn't fair to one's life . . . to toss a few laughing words of contempt out into the air and pretend that one has told the tale. After all, one knows even from his books, that he has, after his own fashion, been very fond of a few people. Then why talk of it to a stranger, and make it seem thin and papery and old, when once it must have had a life and a flower.

Her eagerness, fifty years later, to claim publicly an attempted seduction by Wells would, she knew, meet with disapproval in certain quarters. Did she think by fudging the dates to lessen this scorn? 'I hope Rebecca [West] will forgive this story,' Enid wrote in her autobiography. 'I ought not, ought I, to have told that story here and there. But I did. I couldn't help it: it was heaven. I owed him no love-responsibility.'

In any case, Rebecca West, who in August 1914 had given birth to Wells's son, Anthony, took a rather different view of Wells's attraction to Enid Bagnold. 'I do not say that H. G. would not have had a love affair with her if the circumstances had been more favourable, but the facts were quite different,' Dame Rebecca told Wells's biographers, Jeanne and Norman MacKenzie, in 1973. 'I think he would not have had a love affair with her very happily because she had had an affair with Frank Harris, which to both of us was rather the all-time low.' The illustrated post-cards from Wells to Enid, some of which Enid reproduced in her autobiography, 'were sent off under my eyes and meant nothing', Rebecca West continued in her account of the friendship.

Impressed by sales of her first book, Heinemann agreed to publish a volume of her poetry. *The Sailing Ships* contained mostly work that had already appeared in newspapers and magazines but Enid designed the 'wrapper and decorations'. Not yet thirty, she wrote in the foreword: 'Writing prose is very difficult, writing poetry is rare, living is very amusing, and growing old is the easiest of all.' H. H. Asquith, the former Prime Minister, had been so impressed by her first book that he wrote: 'I must get hold of Enid Bagnold's poems: she is a clever creature.'

Painting had helped her create the visual images that were always to be a strong aspect of her work. The image of herself with a ship on the sea, was one she had nurtured for many years. In her 1916 attempt at autobiography she wrote that, as a child, 'I did not envisage the possibility of shipwreck. Now I know it is possible and that keeps the zest and the skill to steer, bright and eager.'

SEVEN

My Dear Virgilia, You Have Wrinkles Under Your Eyes

AS the war drew to a close, Enid had plenty of male friends and admirers, but none with whom she was intimate. The literary affair with Frank Harris had been revealed for what it was: the pursuit of an unattainable ideal, and the passion excised from her relationship with Antoine. She wanted love, not lovers, and, as she grew harder to please, began to wonder if the two were incompatible. Her professional life, however, appeared to be on a surer footing, although her main difficulty was still an inability to conjure purely imaginary situations and characters. Once again, she was in search of fresh creative springs.

Antoine Bibesco sensed this and told her she should volunteer as an ambulance driver in France. 'It will be awfully chique [sic] to go.' Although the war ended on 11 November 1918, women drivers were badly needed to ferry the sick and wounded and even the dead, until men had returned to civilian life. A senior VAD who remembered Miss Bagnold at this time described 'the really startling psychological effect' she had on the older female recruiting officers. 'It was not what she said that shook us . . . it was rather the way she looked and the vital, challenging "feel" of her. She had better looks, a wider vocabulary, a quicker wit than the rest of us. She carried herself proudly and, moreover, she knew how to wear her clothes.'

She was accepted, sent on an elementary course of automobile maintenance, and left for France on 22 November. Mrs Bagnold, with tear-streaked face, had pressed some gold sovereigns into her daughter's hand. Three days later, Enid arrived in Bar Le Duc, northern France. The winter of 1918 was bitterly cold and Enid spent her first night in an unheated room in a peasant's shack without blankets, covered by wet sheets and a dirty eiderdown. The work was long and hard, often starting at 5 a.m. and ending at 11 p.m. Night driving with few lights unnerved her. The girls were expected to do all the maintenance on their cars, cleaning, oiling, greasing and changing tyres. They were not allowed to retire until their vehicles were in perfect order for the road. If a breakdown occurred, the FANY had to sleep in a nearby ditch until help arrived. The roads were often mud tracks with huge craters. 'No one cares, everyone drives like hell, there isn't any light and if you were to lose a "*blessé*" I don't suppose anyone would know.'

After a few weeks she wondered if she would be able to last the six months. Her greed for adventure, fuelled by her search for literary inspiration, had despatched her to France. But there was neither the time nor the privacy for writing. In one room, fourteen feet square, lived seven women and several rats. 'It's a ghastly lonely life, but wonderful experience, I suppose.... I am secretly delighted I wasn't here during the War, quite hard enough as it is without being kept awake by bombs all night.' As her first Christmas away from home loomed, she told her parents she was 'happy-ish'. To console her, she asked for Antoine's blue crêpe de chine handkerchief with his initials on to be sent out.

In the New Year, however, when she was sent to Verdun things began to look up. She lived in this underground tunnelled city for four days, the first woman most of the men had seen for months. 'All the cooks and orderlies and men in the mess – the whole garrison are so interested at my staying there and clean my shoes and bring me water in turns.' The day she left Verdun, Marshal Pétain gave a ball. 'Isn't it dreadful. I've no time at all to write, and dance till two every morning nearly.... It's all divine and I am having the most startling success – I feel sixteen and I can make jokes in French just like I can in English and people give me flowers.' A week later there was a fancy-dress ball for which she managed to buy twelve yards of white cotton gauze and a local dressmaker turned it into a fabulous crinoline, 1830s style, within a day. Enid painted blue and green flowers all over it and at the ball 'the commandant and his officers toasted my dress as the prettiest'.

This ball scene was beautifully recreated in her first novel, *The Happy Foreigner*. For although Enid complained there was no time for writing, at home her dutiful mother was typing out all her letters, which formed the basis of the story. As she began enjoying herself more, the idea for the novel suggested itself. Quite obviously, it was to be a simple romance set against the background of a devastated post-war France.

At the end of January she moved to Metz and could now tell her parents she was very happy. 'I have a most delightful (what American women call a Beau – only it's a foul word) here, who never leaves me for a minute at parties.' Captain André Gustin was tall, fair-haired and thirty-five. He knew Antoine slightly, spoke no English and Enid found him utterly captivating.

She did not tell her parents he was married. Most of her drives now were with him too and she spent all her free time in his company. None the less, when Antoine sent her a telegram inviting her to Paris on St Valentine's Day, she did not hesitate. In her stained khaki uniform, she drove her Panhard limousine from Précy-sur-Oise to Paris, parking outside Antoine's magnificent house on the Ile St Louis. She, wanting a bath as much as anything, expected at least that they would lunch together. He, having other ideas, told her he had to go out unexpectedly. 'I have ordered your lunch here and I shall be back in an hour and a half. I have to meet my future father-in-law, dear Virgilia.' Quite possibly, she thought Antoine would never get married. But Emmanuel, in his will, had told Antoine to buy a diamond bracelet as his wedding gift to Elizabeth Asquith, daughter of the former prime minister. It was, in Emmanuel's eyes, a dynastic match. As Enid sank back into the bath, alone in Antoine's flat, she convinced herself that, in any case, she no longer loved him. She wrote to her parents disingenuously: 'Antoine and Elizabeth are awfully suited.'

'I got over the shock ... and now I seem always to have known it,' she told Desmond from Charleville. In any case 'I have been so, so in love'. Only the romance with André kept melancholy at bay. 'You know, I told you, that it was a sort of tiresome vice with me that quite young men always bored me. And suddenly to discover one that didn't was quite new and wonderful.'

March came and Enid was still negotiating heavy snowfalls and suffering appalling cold. To get into bed she had to crack open the frozen sheets. Then André was demobilized. He still saw Enid every other week when he returned to inspect the war damage sustained by the factories he owned. But she was quickly disappointed in him. 'What a pity when people take their uniform off; civilian clothes are so ugly.' Not only that. He had grown fat now he no longer had to live off army rations. In *The Happy Foreigner* she vividly describes one of these reunions when Julien takes Fanny up the mountainside intent on telling her his plans for rebuilding his ruined factories. She listens uneasily, no longer in love nor in tune with his aspirations:

Pointing into the night, he continued to unfold his plans, to build in the unmeaning darkness, which, to his eyes, was mountain valleys where new factories arose, mountain slopes whose sides were to be quarried for their stony ribs, rivers to move power-stations, railways to Paris and to Brussels. As she followed his finger her eyes lit upon the stars instead, and now he said, 'There, there!' pointing to Orion, and now 'Here, here!' lighting upon Aldebrande.

Her own adventures were not entirely over; she spent several weeks sharing an empty house with an unattractive billeting lieutenant. 'It's probably improper, but it's the only choice,' she comforted her parents. As the wartime romance with André faded, she began to focus on her life back in

England. She contemplated inviting Logan Pearsall Smith to Woolwich for some tennis as she thought her overarm serve would be greatly strengthened after cranking up so many army vehicles. More importantly, there was her novel to be written while the scenes and images were still fresh in her mind. She returned to England in April 1919.

As Frank Harris had predicted, her age and experience were making her more, not less, attractive. But Enid had never been short of proposals of marriage. Her journals are peppered with names of men such as Jack Franklyn, William Rawle and the 'awful [John] Aldford', long since forgotten by her, who, she claimed, wished to marry her. To Frank Harris she wrote in 1918, 'Offers of marriage have been my fortune lately. The book [*A Diary Without Dates*] seems to encourage them. Young men long to be "understood", and when they read my book they think they have found a wife who will spend her life in understanding them. So they propose. I have had four since it came out in January.' In her autobiography, she wrote: 'At twenty-eight, in spite of my "mistress" attitude, I began to get engaged to people.'

The first was 'a racing man' who annoyed her by complaining in a loud voice at Woolwich station that workers smelled. The engagement was rapidly called off. The second was a red-haired 'gentleman-farmer-squire'. This wedding might have gone ahead had it not been for perished rubber. When all four tyres punctured one night through lack of use during the war, Enid, the expert on car maintenance, suggested stuffing hay into the tyres in order to get them to the nearest garage. But the man had no jack and an argument developed which terminated the romance.

Ivor Guest, Viscount Wimborne, a hugely rich and renowned Edwardian womanizer, had also been paying Enid some attention lately. Enid had known Ivor and his brother, Freddie Guest, since Falconwood days. Wimborne had arranged a magnificent hamper of sweetmeats to be sent to her in the Ardennes, and occasionally suggested they meet for dinner in Paris while Enid was in France. Then he invited her to the family estate in Rugby, Ashby St Ledgers, where his long-suffering wife, Alice, Lady Wimborne, did her best to put Enid at ease. The grand life-style of powdered, bewigged footmen and a Rolls Royce to meet her from the station appealed to Enid. She especially liked being allowed to drive the Rolls herself. But cubbing, the weekend's main activity, made her sick with apprehension, and she disliked her host's arrogance. She told her father that in a revolution 'I should think Ivor's [head] would go in a second.'

In some unpublished notes about the Guests – 'the very word excites me' – Enid recorded how 'I found that I attracted each Guest as though it was the same Guest. There were a number of them, each with identical impulses as from an ancestor. The approach was the same, the inevitability; I shook with silent laughter. It was zoological.' None of these men offered her passionate love, nor, more importantly for her, the firmness and decisiveness which she craved.

Another of her suitors at this time was Sir Tudor Walters, a Government Front Bench spokesman, who occasionally invited her to listen to him speak in the House of Commons. Through his good offices, Enid was invited to work in Vienna with a Friends' Relief Mission, helping distribute food and milk to undernourished families. Antoine, married for nearly a year, was still writing her 'daily bullying letters' advising her both to get married and to work at her writing. A visit to Vienna might provide inspiration for the latter, she reasoned, although it was unlikely to help with the former.

Among the older women introducing Enid to eligible men was Lady Sackville, mother of her old friend Vita Sackville-West. Vita, now married to the impecunious diplomat Harold Nicolson, had never lost touch with Enid. In 1919, they resumed their acquaintance. Enid was fascinated by Vita and made herself a black velvet beret exactly like one Vita wore. Vita sent Enid a little Chinese amber elephant as a token of their friendship.

Lady Sackville thought that Sir Roderick Jones, at forty-two widely considered to be a settled bachelor, might be the ideal husband for her new young friend. He was a small, dapper, self-made man who had spent his formative years in South Africa and had rapidly risen to become proprietor of Reuters, the international news agency. Although titled, he was no aristocrat. He lived in South Street, Berkeley Square, with his doting aunt, Mrs Susan Faulkner, a hundred yards or so from Lady Sackville in Hill Street. She suggested that Sir Roderick might tell Enid from first-hand experience what conditions were like in Vienna – what food, clothes and medicaments she might need to take. When Sir Roderick obligingly said he would get his secretary to see to it immediately, Lady Sackville admitted this was not quite what she had had in mind.

Roderick shied away from meeting potential marriage partners for a number of reasons. The circumstances of his birth and early upbringing were shrouded in mystery, partly because he never referred to them himself. In later years, more in exasperation at how little she knew than because she believed it to be true, Enid sometimes told friends she thought he was illegitimate, but there is no corroboration of this. According to his birth certificate he was born on 21 October 1877 at Dunkinfield in Chester. His father was Roderick Jones, a hat salesman, and his mother Christiana Jones, née Gibb. The boy was called George Roderick, but soon dropped George. In his autobiography *A Life in Reuters*, he dismisses his early years in one sentence : 'Born in England, where my education was supervised and given a strong literary and biblical direction by my Scottish grandfather William Gibb (a cousin of Queen Victoria's favouriate Archbishop of Canterbury, Archibold Campbell Tait, and along with him prepared for the church), I joined his married daughter then living in Pretoria after my father's death.' There is some evidence for supposing that Christiana Gibb had married beneath her. The year after George Roderick's birth, such money as his family had was wiped out in the City of Glasgow Bank crash. This momentous event left Roderick no capital with which to launch a career. More importantly, it also branded him with a deep sense of the squalor of poverty. From then on he retained a horror and loathing of genteel poverty, of debts unpaid, of tradesmen dunning.

At sixteen, Roderick was sent out to his aunt in South Africa where he found work as a sub-editor on a small Pretoria daily, the *Press*. Promotion came quickly once it was noticed that he had become not only an eager reporter but also fluent in Dutch. Leo Weinthal, Reuters' chief correspondent in the Transvaal, picked him as his personal assistant. Through Weinthal, Jones met President Kruger and became friendly with Generals Smuts and Botha, and with Dr Leander Starr Jameson. With his friend Leo Amery he scooped the opposition by interviewing the Boer commandoes. At the end of the Boer War Roderick returned to London to direct the South African services of Reuters and within four years, and still only twenty-seven, was sent back by Baron de Reuter to take charge of the South African operations. There he stayed for ten years, rising in society to become Master of the Cape Hounds.

Roderick Jones clearly understood from an early age the value of cultivating good friends in high places. Lord Gladstone, the first Governor General of the Union of South Africa, would obviously be a useful ally. 'He was never out of Government House,' Lord Gladstone's niece, Pamela Lady Glenconner, recalled. He had long since focused on headship of the entire Reuter organization as an appropriate outlet for his vigour and vision. When the Baron, faced with insurmountable losses, shot himself in April 1915, Roderick pressed to have himself posted back to Head Office. Now he staked out his claim to take over Reuters. He could not have done so without the support of important contacts.

Reuter shares, which before the war stood at £12, were down to below £4 as rumours abounded of mismanagement of the company and depletion of its reserves. Roderick, who had managed to build up a certain stake in the company, realized that, given the wide shareholding and a board in disarray, foreign interests might succeed in acquiring Reuters. The principal shareholder at the time was Mark Napier, to whom Lord Gladstone had both introduced and endorsed Roderick. Jones and Napier offered £11 a share for the whole company. In the transaction which followed, and which in current terminology would be known as a management buy-out, the Union Bank of Scotland advanced the required £550,000 (being one hundred per cent of the purchase price) on 'the security of Reuters as a going concern'. The bank required three guarantors, one of whom was Lord Glenconner, unconscious perhaps of a conflict of interest, as he was also Chairman of the Union Bank of Scotland.

Having borrowed the money personally to buy Reuters' shares, Jones reviewed the options for the repayment of the loan. Reuters owned a bank, the disposal of which Jones considered to be a major item in his planning. Thus in 1917 the bank was sold for a sum which Jones, too modest to name, none the less described as 'entirely satisfactory to Napier and me'. Without explaining precisely how this exercise in corporate asset-stripping assisted him, personally, he explained that 'the proceeds . . . enabled me, inside a year, to repay long in advance of the stipulated time, the loan made . . . by the Union Bank of Scotland.'

In August 1919, Mark Napier died leaving Jones, now knighted for his war work with the Department of Information, as sole shareholder. Jones had incurred some criticism for not relinquishing his ties with Reuters while working on British Government propaganda. As Jones explained in 1918 to the author John Buchan, who was at this time head of the Information Department and was the South African 'contact' which Jones 'was to use the most relentlessly' : 'Today my word is law and I can get done swiftly many things which would take longer and be more difficult if I had to work through somebody else at Reuters.'

All of this work had, of course, taken up most of his energies as well as his time, but the delights of female society were not entirely forsaken. Such relaxation as he allowed himself was taken in the company of the Hon. Mrs Algernon (Guen) Bourke. Mrs Bourke, seven years older than Roderick, had been married at eighteen but separated from her husband, the son of the Earl of Mayo, for many years. Guen Bourke was a ravishing beauty, tall and majestic, who had a daughter nearly Enid's age. There was never any question of Roderick marrying her, although one of his most treasured possessions was a lock of her golden hair in a leather case with their initials on either side. She remained a lifelong friend, outliving Roderick, but Mrs Bourke was cast more in the role of protectress than temptress.

'I was no misogynist or misogamist,' Roderick explained in his autobiography, 'but I remembered Francis Bacon's warning about marriage and giving hostages to fortune. I had longstanding and inescapable family monetary commitments. I was not eager to add to them. Moreover, I had always been fearful of being permanently tied up to another human being whom I might find incompatible and want to escape from.' In this frame of mind Roderick declined Lady Sackville's lunch invitation. However, the following week there was a party at Mrs Valentine Fleming's house in Hampstead and he agreed to drive some of the guests there, meeting first at Lady Sackville's.

It was a brilliantly sunny March day with a piercing blue sky and biting east wind. Enid had just bought herself a three-quarter-length fur coat from Revillon in Hanover Square – or rather, she had not bought it, but Mr Revillon himself allowed her to have it 'on a down payment of five pounds' if she promised to buy her trousseau from him. When she remonstrated that she was not even engaged, he replied: 'With that coat, you'll be engaged in a month.' That day both she and Roderick arrived early at Lady Sackville's, as had one other guest, Lord Berners. The three were milling around the lapis lazuli hall table and Roderick offered to take her coat. 'No one takes my coat. It's all I have,' she replied. Decisive as ever, Roderick fell for her instantly, or so he always maintained. At all events, a wife who could act as hostess for a man of his position was no bad thing. He told Lady Sackville over lunch: 'I mean to marry her.'

During the next three weeks Roderick took time off work to motor down to Shooters Hill several times. Often this was on the pretext of giving Enid some advice or information about Vienna. Enid's departure with a friend, Moira Tillie, was now imminent. Roderick, although 'not exactly Daddy's type' – Colonel Bagnold hated all journalists – also had many qualities of which Enid's parents warmly approved. They found him 'honest, open and frank'. As they pointed out to her, 'His experience of men and matters must be considerable and he must be unusually able, or he could not have climbed up the ladder as he has done in the space of some twenty years or so.' They were by now more than ready to see their daughter forgo her bachelor life.

Then he proposed. Far too clever to suggest that Enid should not go to Vienna, Roderick gave the impression that he was allowing her every liberty. He organized a Reuter press pass for her, advanced her £50 expenses, and arranged a chauffeur-driven car to meet the two girls at the station in Paris. He took her writing seriously and had proofs of *The Happy Foreigner* delivered by hand to Heinemann's for her. On the Thursday morning of departure, a small party gathered at Victoria Station to see her off. Antoine, taking her aside, informed her icily: 'My dear Virgilia, you have wrinkles under your eyes,' a fact she denied. He advised her to marry Roderick without delay.

A few days later Roderick himself was in Paris. He had managed to get the girls transferred from a military train leaving for Vienna on Monday to one leaving almost a week later so that he and Enid might enjoy a few days in Paris together. He filled Antoine's flat, where Enid was staying, with magnificent roses and iris; he bought her lace handkerchiefs from Worth and a large bottle of scent. They dined at the most expensive restaurants post-war Paris could offer. And when they said goodbye on the steps of the wagon-lits it was Enid who called Roderick back for 'one last burning kiss'. 'It's all very corrupting and I suppose I shall have to get married,' Enid admitted to her parents.

After a week of high living and frivolity in Paris she was hardly in a frame of mind to accept the squalor and privations which now confronted her in Vienna. She loathed her stay there and constantly contemplated coming home. The young men appalled her; either they had been dismissed as Communists from the British Army or else were American farm boys from the mid-west who prayed a good deal. No one ever had a bath and much of the food was inedible, especially scrambled egg made of bad Eggo. Instead of getting out and meeting the poor she found herself saddled with terribly boring office work. She saw rioting in the streets, including one anti-Jewish demonstration when the crowd beat a Jewish woman and tore her clothes. Although she heard stories about malnourished babies, 'I haven't seen much really to distinguish it from other slums.'

Roderick, all the while, was sending her daily love-letters in the Foreign Office bag. He flattered her for her fine ankles and beautiful countenance, and made a business-like proposition as to what their future life together could offer her. 'With me you will have a better opportunity of self-development than with many men – we shall travel together, see interesting people and interesting places and you shall have your tower room, sacred to yourself and time for your writing.' At the end of April, she moaned to her parents : 'This is the dullest adventure I ever went on.' But she had already made up her mind what to do about it. The next day she sent Roderick a telegram asking him to send her a 'wire which will afford good reason for my returning immediately'.

In later years, because, like any writer, Enid always knew how to embellish a good story, the account of how Roderick persuaded Enid to marry him underwent a subtle transformation to which Roderick acquiesced. He promised, as a gentleman would, at the time to say 'NOTHING about your telegram asking to be summoned back'. According to Enid's later version, 'I married him because he made me.' When Reuters' Vienna correspondent brought her tickets to Paris 'because Sir Roderick thinks it advisable that you should return next week as he says there will be a great deal to do before the wedding', she claimed to have thought, 'The nerve. The almighty Nerve. . . . The tickets, the audacity, got me on to the train. I meant to have it out in Paris.'

She meant to do no such thing. She had asked Roderick to send a strongly worded telegram enabling her to leave Vienna because she was hating it. She knew perfectly well she was going to marry the man and then accompany him in July to the Imperial Press Conference in Canada; and she wanted to. She also knew that, by the time she had told the Quakers of her change in plans, Roderick had lunched individually with her mother and father, submitting to intensive questioning from each, and the whole matter had virtually been settled. Quite possibly she was not in love with him. 'It bores me dreadfully to leave home, dreadfully. I'm heavenly happy at home. But I rather want to marry Roderick too. It's rather one up to me. . . .' Only her new name displeased her amid all the arrangements. 'Isn't Lady Jones a nightmare name? He must get a peerage,' she was already planning. Roderick came out to Paris to bring her back. He bought her a magnificent engagement ring costing £400 from Boucheron and they went on to the Ritz for lunch. On the way home Enid lost her passport. Roderick, who travelled on a diplomatic passport, just laughed. But Enid observed wrily that once married, such forgetfulness would have been cause for a major row.

And so, in her thirty-first year, Enid decided to marry Sir Roderick Jones KBE, eleven years her senior. By fostering the impression of being an unwilling bride, forced to the altar, Enid was, to some extent, the victim of her own narrative powers. If love were absent, many assumed that money must have been an overriding motive. But although the taste was easily acquired, Enid was probably truthful in insisting that she did not marry him for money. Roderick had told Colonel Bagnold at his club that many people assumed he was richer than he really was. He estimated his income at between £5,000 and £6,000 per annum with the bulk of his capital tied up in Reuters shares. Although, quite naturally, Enid enjoyed the material luxuries he lavished on her, in the early days of their marriage they had to curtail their proclivities for extravagant living. They liked people thinking they were rich, but it was not until 1926, by which time he was able to realize some of his capital, that this was actually true.

Several of her friends considered them an ill-matched pair. They found Roderick's precision dull compared with Enid's exuberance and sparkling wit and pointed out the couple's physical disparity. She, at 5 ft 10 in, was almost a head taller than he and much more sturdily built. When they danced, which both enjoyed, his head nestled in her ample bosom. At a dinner-party a guest once asked, 'Can you lift your wife?' Before Roderick had time to reply, Enid had swept him off his feet saying, 'No but look! I can.' Enid was a modern, independent girl but her future husband was conventional, had a reputation as a martinet and was a man who liked things done his own way. Dame Ethel

Smyth had, only a month before Enid's departure for Vienna, warned her against marriage as an interruption to her career. 'I am certain that if you make anything but writing your first objective or try to blend it with something else you'll be making an awful mistake. One can't serve two masters.' Vita Sackville-West, in the midst of her own marital turbulence, wrote what her husband called a 'foolish, hard little letter' opposing Enid's marriage to Roderick Jones. But Enid 'flamed indignation' at Vita's objections and was unshaken in her resolve. Sickert, flatteringly, wrote to her from France: 'Human nature being what it is, the notion of your marrying is disagreeable to me while a hundred lovers would only leave me thrilled with sympathy and vicarious pleasure.'

These friends did not, however, know Enid as well as she knew herself. 'I like discipline. I like to be part of an institution,' were the opening words of her first book. 'It gives one more liberty than is possible among three or four observant friends.' She recognized her own characteristics unusually clearly. She had grown up in the security of a highly disciplined military household and felt her greatest freedom in bending rules as far as possible. But rules there had to be. As each day passed Enid found herself becoming increasingly dependent on Roderick, a weakness she had been contemptuous of in other women and guarded against in herself. She wrote to Roderick on the eve of their marriage about her past views on love: 'Yes, love, I know, but it shan't ever wreck me. I won't be wrecked by a human creature like myself. But now you could, Roderick. I'm leaning every day, leaning more. Why not? I'm marrying you; you love me. It endures. Yet at the same time I know what a departure this is, how new. Not perilous with you.'

Perhaps her father's words weighed with her too. 'I do counsel you to marry when the Right Man comes along ... up to the present I have been inclined to think that you have sought happiness by yearning for praise, for notoriety and for being made much of. But if [a woman] gains the love of and gets the praise and appreciation of a husband she will be happy and contented and the happiness will last.' Her mother was thrilled by the engagement. 'You will find your life so much richer and more complete in every way. If you and he are as happy as Daddy and I have been for the past thirty-one years you will do very well.' But above all, whom else could she marry? She had been engaged at least twice, lived abroad alone twice and been seen around with Antoine Bibesco too long for tongues not to wag.

Ever conscious of the dramatic possibilities of an entrance, Enid insisted that their engagement be announced before she returned to London. Once home the process of 'getting to know each other' was shelved in the excitement of planning the wedding. Extremely proud of his fiancée, Roderick

hosted an intimate lunch for twenty-four at Claridges on 20 May which gave
Enid a foretaste of their future social life. Viscount Gladstone, Lord
Atholstan, Sir Ian Hamilton, Viscount Burnham, Sir Campbell Stuart and the
Earl of Lytton were among the guests to whom he introduced her. Wedding
presents began pouring in; Enid was particularly struck with a silver-fox fur
jacket from Antoine Bibesco, but did not know that this had been his wife
Elizabeth's idea. Roderick gave his bride a leather-bound copy of the
Apocrypha – 'I don't know what it was specially that he wanted to convey',
Enid wrote in it later. 'I wish I knew.' He also gave her a tortoiseshell and
silver-gilt dressing-case. 'I don't know how to thank you. How can I make
you realize too that I wouldn't hurt a hair of your head, . . . that I think of you
with a tenderness that is quite near tears, that if anything I said made you look
astonished, bewildered and then hurt I couldn't bear it, I'd never mean it, I'd
do anything first,' she wrote to him.

On the afternoon of 8 July 1920, Chelsea Old Church was filled with bay
trees and red roses. To the strains of John Milton's paraphrase of the 136th
Psalm, the bride entered, smiling confidently and enjoying every minute, as
she admitted later. She wore a magnificent gown of palest gold silk net with
classically simple lines. It was held in at the waist by a band of gold leaves and
gold tissue apples were appliquéd all over the dress. A wreath of gold leaves
and apples around her fashionably bobbed hair held the veil and long train in
place. She had complained at the price of all this finery: £75.1s.6d., but the
dressmaker told her that nothing was skimped to make it less beautiful –
everything was of the softest and most expensive.

Her two young pageboys, Basil and Nigel Napier, wore outfits designed
by Enid in brown and yellow silk. The four winsome bridesmaids, Lady
Hermione Lytton, Lady Cynthia Lytton, Miss Celia Bigham and Miss Rosen
Daniel, Enid's cousin, wore shortened versions of her own dress. The Archbishop of Cape Town officiated, assisted by Enid's uncle, Canon Clay. The
reception was held at Number 6, Cheyne Row, the house of the Hon. Mrs
Trevor Bigham, lent for the occasion. 'What a splash *The Times* made with
Asquith and [Lord] Northcliffe signing the register. In fact it looks most
splashy in *The Times* altogether,' Enid wrote to her mother the following
day. The guests as named in *The Times* seemed more like an extract from the
social register than from Enid's address book; the process of exchanging
friends, which began when Enid gave up her Chelsea flat, now led her into a
completely new milieu. Harold Alger told his sister Ethel: 'I felt it was a
family success and a big step in the family rise to have a London Society
function like yours.' Afterwards Roderick and Enid were driven away to
Puttenden Manor, the Napiers' fifteenth-century manor house in Lingfield,

Surrey, which had been put at their disposal for a quiet few days before they sailed to Canada.

The weather that week was glorious and Enid spent the few days at Puttenden in a childlike state of excitement. She was extremely happy that Desmond MacCarthy, now literary editor of the *New Statesman*, had published a short story of hers, 'Vivien the Spinster', a cynical tale of love and coming of age; she was enjoying practising with the new typewriter given her by Ralph; she adored being called 'my lady' by the bevy of Napier servants and she was indulging her naturally sybaritic inclinations. Roderick wrote to his mother-in-law, only half-jokingly: 'She's steadily overeating herself; what can we do about it?'

A few weeks before the wedding, *The Happy Foreigner* had been published. In the event, it was a highly impressionistic piece of reportage, poetic journalism more than a novel. Enid's powers of observation and her ear for the triviality of most dialogue were ideally suited to such treatment and the book was well received. While at Puttenden, two reviews appeared which cheered her immensely. Rebecca West devoted two columns in the *New Statesman* to the book. 'Now here at last in Miss Enid Bagnold's *The Happy Foreigner* we have a good book that is written from the point of view of the Lady.... Her eye for landscape, not made glassy by any moral preoccupation, any sense of the necessity to feel a holy horror against the aggressors, has enabled her to give a uniquely vivid and impressive picture of the desolation of the war-ravaged areas.' Six days later, in the *Athenaeum*, Katherine Mansfield described Fanny as 'almost without fear, nothing can overwhelm her or cast her down, because it is her nature, and unchangeable, to find in all things a grain of living beauty ... a pioneer who sees, feels, thinks, hears, and yet is herself full of the sap of life.' It was an accurate description of Enid herself, determined as she was to wring happiness out of her existence. She basked in praise such as this from Mansfield and West.

On 19 July, Enid and Roderick embarked on the ss *Victorian*, a luxurious Canadian Pacific liner, and the beginning of married life. Enid considered the other passengers 'a host of horrors ... I am easily the nicest.'

EIGHT

We'll Be Such a Success at a Marriage

THEY were not such a success at a honeymoon.

Enid's trousseau from Revillon, five cabin trunks full, were, she considered, well received by the older matrons on board. 'But', she wrote to her mother, 'no one has asked me officially who made them.' Coming to terms with being of secondary importance to another person, as she was to Roderick on this trip, was an unanticipated constraint. Only the reviews of *The Happy Foreigner*, sent on by her parents, cheered her. 'Here, where I'm only a bride, it's a joy to remember there's a country where I am occasionally something else.'

The weather was cold and squally. Enid, a poor sailor at the best of times, felt seasick during the entire voyage. She was also in pain with cystitis, rheumatism and sore lips. To avoid the mealtime scrutiny of the older women, she often ate alone in her cabin, where she gorged herself. She then suffered appalling flatulence. Lady Burnham, the doyenne of press wives, told Enid it was her duty to come up on deck and be with her husband. 'Enid really is a dear', Roderick wrote to his new in-laws, 'but she will overeat. I am trying to keep her down to salads and grapenuts but it is like riding a pulling horse.'

The miserable crossing was followed by twenty-six cramped days and nights on a train travelling across North America. All the press delegates lived entirely on the train in compartments which Enid, doubtless exaggerating, reported as about five feet square. 'We don't bath, but just dab cold water over ourselves. . . . The great anxiety of each day is the hunt for the aperient. For that reason we leap out of the train at little stopping places and take hurried, busy exercise.' Such excessive scatological concerns were hardly conducive to romance. Nevertheless, Roderick was tender and considerate towards his bored and sick bride.

She complimented Mrs Faulkner (whom she now called Tanta) on how well she had brought up Roderick. 'He knows how to make a lady's bed when she has untucked it because it is hot, and how to put a lady's dressing-gown on when she is eating breakfast in bed and catching cold, and how to take her stockings off if she is feeling giddy from the train rocking, and how to rub ammonia on her bites . . . really he might have been married all his life the way he seems to be used to it.' The pampering and ministrations came easily. But so did the rows. For Enid, it seemed, could not be controlled like other people who worked for him. Tempted to laugh in private at the pompous magnates holding forth in every city, Roderick worried that she might let him down in public. But the importance of 'keeping up a front', that loyalty was the thing, Enid knew instinctively. She also learned, more slowly, as she watched him work until the small hours, what a passion he had for his 'other wife' – Reuters.

That two such obstinately strong characters, marrying relatively late in life, should find the constant proximity of another body oppressive is perhaps not surprising. They had discovered at Puttenden that single beds were essential if either was to sleep properly. Even when thus separated they were occasionally too close for comfort. One night in a hotel in Calgary, Roderick was dreaming heavily and kept throwing his arms out and hitting Enid until she lost her temper and woke him up. He sprang out of bed, burned his hand on the radiator and stubbed his toe on an earthenware spittoon. In a fury, he picked up the offending object and flung it out of the window, six floors up, narrowly missing a passer-by. Within minutes a policeman knocked on their door seeking an explanation and Roderick, with all the imperiousness his slender frame could muster, told the officer that, if he wanted his name, he could find it downstairs.

Ethel Bagnold sympathized with her daughter and told her that, if she had the luck to have single beds, she should pull them further apart in future. 'I am going to put your bed in the spare room so that you can have a separate bed each whenever you are down here.' This distaste for sharing each other's bed (or at least Roderick's distaste, which Enid was too proud to counter) does not necessarily mean that the sexual dimension of their marriage was not important; increasingly, however, that became the case. They were by no means alone among their generation in preferring the privacy of sleeping apart, but it entailed a diminution of shared intimacy which, for Enid, who craved 'to be known', was arguably a disaster. On the threshold of her first relationship which promised to provide emotional stability as well as physical pleasures, the combination, she found, eluded her.

As they journeyed on, confined in their compartment, Enid complained that she was never allowed to see the 'real' Canada of forests and wild animals. 'They hoick us from banquet to banquet and take us over steel plants and round the towns.' She found each town the same, some bigger, some smaller, with indifferent shops. By the time they reached Washington she decided she preferred to stay in her hotel bedroom reading about more interesting towns elsewhere in the world. Ibanez's *Four Horsemen of the Apocalypse* amused her more than the delegates' tour guide. Even New York barely aroused her. She was upset because she had been looking forward to a meeting with an American publishing house, The Century Company. But they had just rejected a short story of hers, 'The Benefactors', stating: 'To publish it anywhere in this form would certainly add nothing to your literary reputation'. While in New York she decided to fire her London agent James (J.B.) Pinker; in future, Roderick was to deal with the business side of her contracts.

She was, in short, more than ready to return home by the autumn of 1920. Tanta, having prepared the South Street flat and moved out herself, warned the new incumbent that, among other things, Roderick needed eight fine and two bath towels per week. Enid was to have her own room in the flat for writing, of which accommodation her father most heartily disapproved. 'Reasons are, I think, obvious.' Enid settled smoothly into her new routine. Getting married, she told Antoine in December 1920 'is the most satisfactory arrangement made in all my life. I never knew what balance was before. I never knew what it was to be quite contented and mentally fat and not look abroad for amusement any more. How domestic I am.' Roderick was at the office all day and Enid spent the morning shopping, the afternoon writing (she told Antoine she was hard at work on an idea for a new novel) and the evening going out with her husband. They took to riding together in Rotten Row – until Roderick fell and suffered concussion. She had not yet come to terms with her name. 'I went to a party the other night and I was twice introduced as Lady Smith,' she moaned to Antoine. 'The second time I corrected them and said it was Brown and they got confused and remembered it was Jones and blushed.'

She noticed, too, a changed attitude amongst her erstwhile friends:

All the old ones are jealous because they think Roderick has £40,000 a year which is a cruel myth . . . started by Sibyl Colefax. . . . And the same with lots of women I knew when I was the recipient of all they had to give. They can't bear my change of position, they can't bear to ask me to dine and not need anything from them. If I tell them I go on buses just the same and have only bought one coat and skirt since I had my trousseau they say: 'Oh well darling, I suppose you don't want it now, now you can buy up half Revillon.'

When, in December, her old friend Vita Sackville-West came to lunch with her lover Violet Trefusis, Enid felt awkward with them:

They are both on the look out to find some change for the worse in me because I have married. They come wrapped in Persian lamb and astrakhan and watch me and use quiet voices and I, flushed, raising my head from social accounts in an old jumper, forget myself and say in the voice befitting Woolwich parties, 'Won't you sit down?' and then they giggle.

Enid felt more at ease when she and Roderick were invited to stay with the Gladstones at Dane End, or even with the Wimbornes at Rugby, where she noticed that she was given a much more impressive suite than in her single days. Roderick took her for a long weekend to Paris, the first of many such trips in their marriage, and bought her new hats.

In the spring of 1921 Enid was disconcerted to find herself pregnant. She was very sick, did not enjoy the sensation at all and thought she must be carrying an ape, a suggestion which brought about a sharp rebuke from Ethel Bagnold. Mrs Bagnold's letters to her daughter during her first years of married life are vivid reminders that, far from fleeing the restrictions of the parental home, Enid had swapped one master for two. And yet, the teenager who had rebelled against her parents' conventions now accepted their admonitions with scarcely a murmur. Her parents were shocked at Roderick for allowing his pregnant wife to drive. Mrs Bagnold feared that if he did not insist on Enid living a quiet, restful life, knitting little cardigans for the baby, he might end up with an invalid wife and a fretful, nervous child. Even holding a heavy book was to be forbidden.

Enid was better able to heed her mother's advice when they moved to the country a few months before her confinement. Bidborough Hall in Kent was a large, mock-Tudor mansion which gave Enid the chance to sack Roderick's manservant, whom she had discovered reading her private letters. Once at Bidborough, reluctantly and unsure of herself, she began real housekeeping and established a proper staff of butler and several maids. At the head of the hierarchy from now on was Frederick Cutmore, hired by Roderick from a previous situation where he had ruled over five footmen. Although principally intended as Roderick's valet, Cutmore was given a wide range of household duties, from attending bells to ironing Roderick's shoelaces, putting out clothes and seeing to fires. 'He knew things we shall never know again. He knew how the fingerbowl got on to the gilt fruit plate and how it got off again . . . he knew what hired waiters expect for their dinner, who carried the silver tea tray and who set a match to the spirit lamp, how hunting boots were cleaned with blood and a bone. . . .' Although himself married with a family, he never spoke of his wife and generally accompanied Roderick when he travelled. He was tall, good looking and dignified and, much to everyone's embarrassment, was frequently mistaken for the Head of Reuters during those trips.

Mrs Faulkner did not stint on advice for the young bride and suggested that the new nursery be situated as far from Roderick's room as possible. Roderick's fatherly love would depend on how seldom he heard the new baby

1 The Bagnold family home on Shooter's Hill, London

2 Ethel Alger, Enid's mother

3 Colonel Arthur Bagnold, Enid's father, aged eighty

4 Enid circa 1896
5 At Burnham on holiday: Enid standing
next to her father (*back right*), and her mother (*seated centre left*)

6 As a young lady of seventeen
8 The young journalist

7 Lovat Fraser in fancy dress
9 Frank Harris

10 A woman of the world   11 Prince Antoine Bibesco   12 As a VAD in 1918
13 On 8 July 1920, Enid Bagnold married Sir Roderick Jones

14 Enid and Roderick on their honeymoon
15 Laurian's christening in January 1922:
(*left to right*) Rudyard Kipling, Lady Sackville, Viscountess Gladstone, Roderick,
Col. Bagnold, Viscount Gladstone, Enid and Laurian with her nurse

16 Timothy and Laurian in the night nursery
in the garden of North End House, October 1926

17 Enid with Richard, Timothy and
Laurian, Rottingdean, 1928

18 Cynthia Noble, Enid, Timothy, Laurian (*at back*), and Dorothy and Arnold Bennett, 1928

19 Randall Neale at Reuters
20 Albrecht Bernstorff, Enid and Diana Strathcona, 1933

21 Enid with Donald Strathcona, Colonsay, 1934
22 Roderick and Enid playing chess

cry. On 9 October 1921, Enid's first child, a daughter, was born. She had returned to Warren Wood for the birth, which, in spite of the midwife getting drunk and failing to appear, was straightforward. The elderly doctor arrived at twelve noon and gave her a morphia injection and chloroform at 2 p.m. He tied Enid's legs to the bedpost and asked Roderick to assist in place of the midwife. One hour later the baby was born. The pains, Enid told her brother, were 'as though an outside power were forcing you through a sausage machine ... but the waking up is marvellous. You float to life on a soft morphiac wave of popularity and acclaim.'

It took but two days (her own assessment) for the scarcely dormant maternal feelings which Frank Harris had seen so clearly, to appear. At birth, the child had a tiny bloodspot in her eye which Enid could not bear to look at. Once this was overcome Enid's sense of motherhood, her ideal of founding a family, took hold and became one of the focal points of her life. And with it, the great wish to be 'someone' was gradually transmuted into the great wish to be remembered, especially by her children.

Ethel Bagnold revelled in her new grandmotherly duties and fussed busily about her daughter during the customary resting period. Enid stayed at Warren Wood for six weeks. The new parents dithered over a suitable name and for some days the infant was Charmian. But then Lady Sackville, who was to be a godparent, suggested Lorraine, after the region in France, and they decided on a modification of this – Lauri-Anne, or Laurian. The other godparents were Viscount Gladstone and Rudyard Kipling, whom Roderick knew from South African days. His appearance at the christening three months later at Bidborough village church ensured maximum publicity for the event. Enid chose a large black hat and wore a plain black dress, which could not hide the fact that she was, once again, overweight.

On the Sunday after Laurian was born, Enid decided to tell her husband everything about her past life. Still in a highly charged emotional state, she broke down and sobbed out half the story while Roderick listened calmly, interjecting periodically, 'I will not fail you.' There were no recriminations. The next day Roderick went away – a long-standing arrangement to visit an old friend – but letters flew between the pair reenacting the midnight scene. Enid had owned to 'four bold loves – but Roderick, there is something I hope to God you believe; there has never been a baby.'

'What must last night not have meant to you? The effort, the recalling of memories, the recital. It fills me more and more with wonder.' Roderick told her he admired her for her courage in not holding anything back and that he was now rejoicing that it was all over, 'that your craft, frail and yet so wondrously preserved, has sailed safely out of its ten year tempest into serene waters, which I pray will last you into eternity.' The next day Enid thanked him for his understanding. 'Roderick, I do worship you – you are my central pivot. . . . I beg your pardon for spending so much of myself before I knew you and all I can say is that it's like the milk, the more is taken from me the more comes in'; a typically earthy simile of bodily functions.* But now, her confidence restored, 'We shall forget about it and I'll make you proud of me somehow. What a foundation we have – Oh we'll be such a success at a marriage.'

It is hardly surprising that these confessions did not come earlier in their relationship. They were married quickly and the honeymoon left them little time alone. Perhaps full disclosure might have lost her Roderick. Yet the birth of a child focused Enid on the need for a clean slate through honesty, which was always one of her strongest attributes. She may, however, have felt some lingering guilt at not revealing everything sooner as, in her autobiography, she talks of sitting in a cornfield at Dane End during her engagement and telling Roderick about her past loves. Roderick apparently replied: 'What a mug I've been. All these pretty girls I've known – would they have slept with me?' – a note of false naïveté from a forty-two-year-old man of the world. The episode as recounted by Enid was, more likely, another of her 'amusing' stories that she came to believe in herself. The precise nature of Roderick's 'understanding' is illuminated by the knowledge that he spent the three days immediately after Enid's repentance at Paultons in Hampshire, the home of Mrs Guen Bourke.

Life buried in the country with a baby was particularly lonely for Enid, as Roderick spent Monday to Friday in London staying at his club. They wrote to each other almost daily, but it was a dramatic contrast to her previous life. Enid was fortified by the steadfastness of Roderick's love and pride in her, but he was not an easy man to live with. He left her lists of things he wanted done and telephoned half-way through the morning to make sure she had carried them out. One day, shortly after their honeymoon, he left his spectacles at home. Enid blamed herself entirely: 'You have got a fool wife. I'm so ashamed.' She searched frantically for them and then went to the station to put them on the train for him.

In his office he was a complete autocrat and the staff were terrified of him. Every messenger was instructed in the strict ritual of the arrival and departure ceremonies. In the morning, this required a senior messenger, known as 'the MD's boy' (Managing Director's), to be waiting at the front entrance ready to

---

* She once told Cynthia Asquith her work was like 'beautiful vomit', but added: 'I mean nothing derogatory by this filthy simile'.

dash out into the street to open the door of Sir Roderick's Rolls Royce as it stopped precisely opposite the front steps to the building. Meanwhile the hall-porter ensured that the only lift was waiting to whisk Sir Roderick up to his office. The procedure in the evening was similar except that a police constable was always at the corner of Carmelite Street to halt the Embankment traffic, thus saving Sir Roderick any delay. When, later, traffic lights were installed at this junction another messenger was despatched to jump on the rubber pad which controlled the lights, ensuring they changed to green at the right moment.

James Lees-Milne, at one time Sir Roderick's junior secretary, was appalled by

an office routine from which no deviation was permissible in any circumstance. He demanded from his underlings the strictest observance of infinitesimal minutiae. For instance, every object on his desk had to be arranged each morning with meticulous exactitude. The edges of the in-tray must be flush with those of the out-tray. The silver calendar, turned for the day, two inches to the left of the clock. Pencils newly sharpened, and clean nibs in pen-holders. The penwiper at right angles to the blotter, freshly filled. Telephones and intercommunicator slightly staggered at an angle of, say $22\frac{1}{2}°$ from the chair. . . . If the softest of the three india rubbers was not found on the left-hand side of the row on the allotted tray and adjacent to the red (not blue) sealing-wax, Sir Roderick's displeasure could be terrible.

Yet his letters to Enid reveal a tenderness, ardour and pride in his wife which few who knew the public face of Sir Roderick Jones would guess. He told her: 'You see things in me which nobody else has ever seen and has ever expressed. Loving you . . . transcends everything and is become the sheet anchor of my existence.' Enid hated being parted during the week but they could not yet afford to buy a London house. Roderick, by his passionate letters, tried to alleviate both her loneliness and her vexation over the 'servant problem', which dragged on until the end of her days. The heavily servanted household of pre-war days had disintegrated and, although there were still plenty of maids around, Enid was not good at selecting the right ones, nor at regulating them and remembering not to interfere herself. Laurian initially caused her much distress when she appeared overjoyed to go with her nannie and upset to be with her own mother. In August 1922, in need of a change of scene and more stimulating company than the maids could offer, Enid drove herself to Menabilly in Cornwall for a week's holiday alone. She stayed with her friend, Mrs Reginald McKenna.* Perhaps this brought home to Roderick

---

* Pamela McKenna (née Jekyll) was at Prior's Field with Enid.

the need to find a London home and by the winter, they were established at 13 Hyde Park Gardens, Antoine's house, now vacant.

A happy consequence of the move back to London was the new doctor. In the spring of 1923, Enid had a sudden and acute case of suspected whooping-cough and in July, it was decided she needed a tonsillectomy. Harold Waller was forty-two at the time he became Enid's doctor. The son of a missionary in Central Africa, he was a man of high principles who devoted most of his life to working among the underprivileged mothers and babies in east London. He would work unstintingly until the early hours if either patient or nurse needed his help or guidance. The nursing staff revered him as a saint. At the same time Dr Waller ran a fashionable, private general practice in Chelsea; Gladys Young and Peggy Ashcroft were two of his patients there. He was a tall, slim and debonair man with wavy grey hair, deep-set blue eyes and long, sensitive hands. He was always immaculately dressed; he wore a Homburg hat, carried a rolled umbrella and a tin box with his sandwiches. A man of considerable courtesy, charm and humour, he was widely read and could talk in great depth on a wealth of subjects.

Enid was utterly captivated by Harold Waller. His enthusiasm was infectious. She imbibed every word of his advice. Friends remember how, from this time on, her entire conversation was peppered with what Dr Waller believes, Dr Waller says or Dr Waller thinks. Harold Waller influenced Enid's ways and views of life more completely than anyone she had met since Antoine. Ignoring the conventions of patient/doctor relationships, Enid bounded straight into friendship with the man. She sent him copies of her books and he wrote her a long letter of appreciation and praise, urging her to 'turn the famous Ford towards Chelsea' and come and see him one day. Immensely warmed, Enid replied: 'My busy doctor troubles to write to me by hand and the lazy patient answers by typewriter.' It was a chatty letter discussing her habits of working and the house where she was living – but when she went for her next appointment Dr Waller's German wife greeted her icily. Dr Waller himself, rather embarrassed, said, 'Oh, by the way, there's one thing I must tell you. When I write you an appreciative letter you mustn't write me anything appreciative back again.' This incident had the not alto-gether surprising effect of fanning Enid's interest in Harold Waller still further.

To convalesce after her throat operation, Enid went to stay in August with some new friends at their house in Sussex. Sir George Lewis, a prominent lawyer, and his beautiful wife Marie, lived at The Grange on Rottingdean village green, just a short walk from the blustery sea front. It was thought that the air would do her good and this time Laurian came too. Enid was determined to make a quick recovery because Roderick had a major world tour planned to start at the end of 1923. It was to last ten months and take in America, India, China, Hong Kong, Japan and Ceylon. Enid, hating her lonely weeks in the country, was bent on accompanying him and Roderick raised no objection. They arrived in New York at the end of August, spent ten days in Canada and a long weekend in Maine as guests of Mr and Mrs Frank Noyes, President of Associated Press. Then they went on to stay with the Bibescos in Washington where Antoine was now Roumanian Ambassador. But here Enid discovered that she was once again pregnant. Frantic telegrams crossed the Atlantic and on Waller's advice, she was despatched back to England. A temporary home on Shooters Hill was found for her and Laurian. This house, called The Rookery, was a stone's throw away from her parents' home, where she was to wait for the birth.

Throughout her pregnancy Enid obeyed Waller's every dictate: vigorously walking for two miles every day, strictly regulating her diet and extravagantly changing all the baby layette she had chosen so carefully for Laurian. Waller babies had to wear only wool for the first six months. Vita came to stay one night with her new friend, Geoffrey Scott. 'I believe she is going to show me as her poor artistic friend who lives in the suburbs . . . make a sort of chic of my squalor.' Another day she had tea with Ethel Sands 'where I had a minute success – Virginia Woolf was there, your dear Pearsall Smith, Arnold Bennett . . . and finally Antoine arrived out of the blue.' Enid drove Antoine home, about which she then wrote and apologized to Roderick:

Don't mind about it, darling, I just tell you because it happened. I mean I just register that I did drive him there, but it hasn't the slightest significance. I only dwell on it because at the word Antoine, I know you will, a little, and I want by dwelling on it completely myself to clear it like a bad fog away – I couldn't *trompe* you with the Archangel Michael . . . not even immaculately.

Nonetheless, when Enid wanted to see Desmond MacCarthy, recuperating after an illness, she asked permission first. 'I could have brought him down for the night and taken him back the next day – but I thought you might not like it.' Roderick grudgingly scrawled. 'Have Desmond down.' He had, after all, just sent a parcel of Chinese silks to Mrs Bourke. Roderick wrote at length and regularly. He told her she could look for a country cottage as a weekend retreat but that, until he knew with more certainty how things would work out at Reuters, they simply could not afford a permanent London establishment as well. He was always sensitive, about any remarks from Head Office that he might be enjoying himself on these trips and he instructed his wife to paint a gloomy picture to the Napiers and other office people of what a difficult time he was having and how straitened were their circumstances. But to the Sibyls and Vitas of the world, she was to betray no concern whatever. Not that there were, as he reminded her, any real grounds for anxiety, at any rate with regard to income. The lavish presents that he sent back to Enid from every port of call included several cashmere shawls, necklaces, bedspreads, fans, handbags, amber, pearls and tortoise-shell. 'It's like counting eastern merchandise in the Bible,' she told him.

Roderick was universally treated as a special envoy from Britain, treatment which was, however, no less than he expected. Magnificent receptions and banquets were given in his honour, sometimes in the presence of royalty, and 'Government House' was always put at his disposal. Enid recognized how important the pomp and circumstance was to Roderick. 'I love you for your simple sincerity and lack of make-up about yourself . . . can you imagine, shall I say, Osbert Sitwell or Pearsall Smith, loving it too, but considering it more effective to snigger and sneer and say "what operatic tinsel".' The months without Roderick dragged. But, for the first time in her married life, she was able to settle down to a regular pattern of writing. She was delighted by H. G. Wells's flattering mention of her *Diary Without Dates* in *The Dream* and copied out the relevant section for Roderick. Wells had written: 'Nowadays, of course, nobody reads the books of the generals and admirals and politicians of that time, and all the official war histories sleep the eternal sleep in the vaults of the great libraries, but probably you have all read one or two such human books as Enid Bagnold's *Diary Without Dates* – or Barbusse's *Le Feu*.' Goading her on was a fierce determination that she would have a book as well as a baby to show Roderick on his return. Something to make him proud of her again. 'It's so marvellous to me to realize that you believe in my writing. It's almost too much to believe of married life.' In the event he was home before either made their appearance. But the discipline of having to bring forth something by a certain date without the distraction of a social life suited her, and the resulting novel was one of her best works.

The seeds for the satire *Serena Blandish* or *The Difficulty of Getting Married* had been sown in the days when Enid was living in and out of the d'Erlanger household. The novella was almost ten years in germinating, but distance only sharpened her perspective. She had tossed around several ideas over the last few years for turning her own prolonged adventure into fiction. But once she had focused on Voltaire's method in *Candide* of telling the most impossible series of events at breakneck speed as her vehicle, she found the narrative flowed effortlessly. At the very moment when the most preposterous events are taking place, the characters utter highly moral explanations. The Voltairean method, well suited to such a simplistic parody, she handled as if it were her own.

The story centred, as the sub-title suggests, on a penniless but beautiful young girl's desperate search for a suitable husband. A Brazilian countess takes her in hand and eventually a nobleman is found as her bridegroom. Only during the marriage celebrations does Serena realize that, although 'she had not known where she was going, nor where the countess was hurrying her, to what false brilliance of marriage, to what fabulous and déclassé world ... she was marrying the son of a negress.' Martin tells her that it is better to be married in Ethiopia than single in London. The authoress begs the question.

Not surprisingly, Antoine claimed *Serena* as his 'spiritual child'. 'He took an interest in his friends to the point of pursuing their squeaking souls ... he buffeted me, punched me, pinched me. At last the stream began to flow,' Enid wrote. Antoine, whose butler was called Martin, became distilled into the book's butler of that name, freely dispensing advice to the naïve heroine. His particular brand of cynicism, combined with a capacity for devotion, is stamped across the book. But there was also an element of Cutmore in Martin. Cutmore's inborn contempt for women and effortless efficiency in ruling the household so distressed Enid because she felt she could never live up to his high expectations. 'He is never impressed by anything. . . . In fact he is rather like Antoine.' Enid mused that, since Cutmore might easily recognize himself in Martin, 'Cutmore will think I am in love with him – what a fresh dilemma.'

'Nobody on earth knows what were the reflections of Martin. It may be that he did not really care for women. It may be that he had real pity in his heart, or it may be that he liked to have his finger in every pie.' Thus was Martin described in *Serena Blandish*. He was 'the dark God who drove the chariot of [Serena's] fortunes', just as Antoine had driven Enid's. 'Please do not handle my character,' Martin demands.

Catherine d'Erlanger was barely disguised as the Countess Flor di Folio, who saw herself as a businesslike theatrical agent arranging the contracts of stars.

She has the mind of a child, the energy of a wild animal, and the health of an immortal [Enid wrote in *Serena Blandish*]. She was no snob, and though still beautiful and very rich, she had a delightful flair for bad society. There had been a time when the most exclusive persons had accepted her invitations, but having everything in the world that she wanted, she had tired of them, and her growing fondness for the disreputable, the curious and shady, for all quacks and purveyors of sham goods, sham art, bogus literature, her passion for imitation fur, imitation tortoise-shell, imitated antiquity, had led her at last to the pitch of appreciating an imitation aristocracy, and with the cunning of a child, which thinks it takes in all the world, it had delighted her to palm off bogus dukes upon genuine duchesses.

Lord Ivor Cream was a caricature of the dashing Lord Northampton, who had made such a strong impression on Enid when she stayed with him at his home, Castle Ashby, in 1918. Five years previously he had been involved in an extremely unpleasant breach of promise case in which the plaintiff, Miss Daisy Markham, had been awarded the substantial sum of £50,000.

It was widely assumed that Paula Gellibrand, Catherine's 'adopted' daughter, was the role model for the heroine. Paula fitted much of the description of Serena, her ethereal looks adding to the foundling quality she possessed; sharp-tongue society watchers commented that Paula's marriage to the Duke of Casa Maury mirrored the ultimate fate of Serena, who married the Count Montague D'Costa. Hardly surprising for, as Enid had written to Antoine, 'Fancy Paula Gellibrand getting married. And to a little decadent Marquis too. That was a find for me. That settled the end of [the book].'

Enid never admitted that Paula Gellibrand was the inspiration for Serena. When Arthur Calder-Marshall wrote an appreciation of Enid Bagnold's work in 1954, she asked him to cut any reference to Paula. But, if the heroine were not Miss Gellibrand, many might jump to the conclusion that she must be based on Enid herself – a conclusion which she was able to refute the more vehemently by maintaining that another girl, who was not part of 'The Set', namely Gwynaeth Cooper Willis, had been the original for Serena. As well as Paula, aspects of both Gwynaeth and Enid undoubtedly went into the composite character – the last line of the book was, after all, a reference dangerously close to Enid. Describing the relief on Martin's face when he sees Serena safely married, she wrote: 'There had been moments when he had been half afraid he might have to marry her himself.'

For Colonel and Mrs Bagnold the idea that their own daughter might have been such an adventuress was beyond contemplation. The mere fact that she knew about and had written of such lurid events shocked them profoundly when she sent them a manuscript. 'It is a loathsome production,' Colonel Bagnold wrote to his son-in-law. 'It is a work of which I am ashamed as being the production of my own daughter . . . of which you ought to be ashamed as her husband.' If the book were published it would put a barrier between him and Enid. He foretold of consequences too terrible to think of if publication went ahead. But if she were intent on this, he would, at all events, spare nothing to have the name of Bagnold removed. Her mother, too, wrote four pages of notes accompanied by a letter in gentler vein. The book was very clever, she conceded, but 'what an odious bit of society life'. She begged Enid not to be angry with her, her comments were those of an ordinary, unintellectual woman, but she could not escape from concluding, 'I hate the book and fear your reputation will drop most awfully and Roderick's too.'

Their batch of letters to Enid and Roderick arrived on Saturday 17 May, just a few days before Enid's second baby was due. Mrs Bagnold was well aware that 'such a shock might have a serious effect on your condition'. She decided nevertheless that the effect on Enid's children of publishing such a book would be far worse. Enid accepted their rebukes uncomplainingly, but never contemplated dropping the book. She decided to publish anonymously and negotiations with Heinemann continued throughout the summer.

After consulting with John Buchan, Roderick proposed a sliding scale of royalties, rising to 25 per cent after 5,000 copies sold. Charles Evans, the new managing director, professed to be horrified but eventually agreed to an advance of £50 and a royalty of 25 per cent after 7,000 copies had been sold. The first edition was, in any case, to be approximately 3,000 copies. Evans greatly admired Enid's writing and considered the book 'an extraordinarily brilliant piece of work . . . rather than let it go unpublished we would be quite willing to issue it anonymously or under a pseudonym.' Had Enid chosen the latter course it is quite likely that the writer's identity would have been overlooked. By citing 'A Lady of Quality' as the authoress, she ensured that an air of mystery surrounded the book when it was finally published in December 1924. A society guessing game began in earnest.

Mrs Bagnold's criticisms can, to an extent, be justified. Sixty years after it was written, *Serena Blandish* appears offensive. To contemporaries it was no more than a bitter comedy of manners, blithely capturing the wicked and gay spirit of post-war London society which had, like the story's heroine, lost its self-respect. Published four years into the decade that has come to epitomize fast and standardless living, the book was a child of its time. It attracted considerable publicity and curiosity and within three months had sold out. The *Evening Standard* reviewer considered it 'vastly entertaining' and the *Times Literary Supplement* called it 'a brilliant tract for the times'. Rebecca West wrote Enid a warming letter of praise about *Serena*:

I think it exquisitely written, and, like everything you do, good poetry. There's a passage about marriage and love ('which dies at a request') that made me feel like tears just by its cadence. It is so amazingly true, too. . . . It's queer you should have written *Serena* just when I'm labouring on the same subject in a semi-tragic novel. Mortifying too, for I shall never invent anything so marvellous as Martin.

Enid was scrupulous, publicly at any rate, in denying her authorship but several people surmised. One newspaper claimed it was undoubtedly the work of Elizabeth Bibesco, and Antoine, feigning fury, threatened to sue. Enid secretly believed that Antoine, the true friend, had fanned the whole affair to draw further attention to the book. When Catherine d'Erlanger read

Serena, she was greatly insulted by her own portrait and threatened libel action, but after Sir George Lewis, acting for Enid, asked Catherine if she recognized herself, she decided to drop the case. She did not forgive Enid and they never saw each other again. Almost immediately *Serena Blandish* aroused interest in New York and several successful playwrights were proposed as possible dramatizers.

Enid was well satisfied with both productions of 1924. On 29 May, Dr Waller had delivered her of a healthy 8 lb 5 oz boy, whom they had already decided to call Timothy. 'Timothy Angus and Serena Blandish were twins carried during the same nine months,' Enid wrote. But if it appeared to her as if the wicked fairy had attended Serena's christening, she ensured that Timothy's godparents were no less illustrious than his sister's. They included Leo Amery, then Colonial Secretary, General Smuts and Vita Sackville-West. With Dr Waller's constant advice and the help of an excellent nurse, Ethel Raynham-Smith, Enid thoroughly enjoyed this baby. He was, Enid told friends proudly, put out at 6.30 a.m. and kept out in all weathers until 9.30 p.m. The hood was put up on the pram only in pouring rain. Apart from arguments with maids – one nurse whom Enid discovered wiping the lavatory seat with her handkerchief caused her particular consternation – the lady of quality was again happily sinking into domesticity and motherhood.

With two young children and Dr Waller's emphasis on fresh air, the need for a country cottage had become pressing. In the summer of 1924, the Lewises again invited Enid and Roderick for a weekend. They particularly wanted to show the Joneses a pretty house that was for sale opposite their own on Rottingdean village green. The house, or rather two houses joined, had once belonged to Sir Edward Burne-Jones and later to the painter William Nicolson who designed the beautiful entrance hall with orange and black squared linoleum. There was, and still is, a painting by Burne-Jones in the corner of a bedroom to amuse children made to stand there.

While Enid waited outside in the Delage sobbing, Roderick agreed to buy North End House for £3,000. It had character, but was rather more of a country cottage than the Queen Anne mansion, arrived at after a long drive through a deer-studded park, which Enid had envisaged for her family. But it was close enough to town for Saturday to Monday guests and, although rather small, they built a new wing 'so we can have Desmond and Lady Buckingham together'. They had, in any case, taken a lease on yet another London house, 24 Berkeley Square, where they were to live during the week and in the winter.

NINE

The Beauty of a Young Man

EVER since their marriage, Roderick had been preoccupied with a
reorganization of Reuters which would enable him to realize some
capital. Only then could they live in the style to which all their friends
believed they were accustomed. On 3 December 1925, after long and arduous
negotiations, Roderick was able to announce that, through the creation of a
Reuters Trust, the Press Association had acquired a majority interest in
Reuters. Jones argued that his sole purpose in selling to the Trust was 'to place
Reuters above the variations in ownership and control that would result from
its continued dependence upon the life of one individual'. However, this
partial sale resulted in Jones receiving £63,000 and, under the terms of the
Trust, Jones was able to retain an interest of nearly 25% in Reuters which was
now valued at over £300,000. 'How frightfully happy I am', his wife told him,
'that tangible, shining (metaphorically) money is there, and what a giant you
are to have scooped it out of this cold English soil.'

After the sale, Roderick remained as Chairman and Managing Director,
little changed in the autocratic manner in which he ran the company. The
provincial newspapers, he insisted revealingly, encouraged him to continue
to manage the Agency exactly 'as if it were still my private business.... The
advantage of one-man ultimate control was that no time was wasted in
superfluous consultation and argument.'

Similarly, as his household expanded, so did his manner of exercising
authority in that sphere too. 'You are in audience and a damned tyrant; what
a perfect combination and one that any woman would give anything to have
as a husband,' Enid wrote in a submissive moment. At other times her
apparent inability to attain the high standards he set for organizing the household devastated her. This perceived failure had an arresting effect on her
writing which almost dried up under these parched conditions. Many of the
rows at this time between Enid and Roderick were over planned alterations
and additions to the new house. Enid's idiosyncratic style in interior decoration initially irritated Roderick, with his more conventional view of
appropriate decor. Eventually, he became proud of it.

Every summer, until the Second World War, Enid would hunt around

Brighton's ubiquitous antique shops for second-hand (or 'almost antique') Regency furniture. Many of the items on which her eyes alighted were not expensive – like an alabaster plinth head, covered with grapes and leaves, that cost just five shillings – but were bought for their effect in a particular spot. She knew, with her artistic vision, how to transform ordinary objects; she painted green ribbons and gold edges on the sides of the shelves of an ordinary bookcase – trying to copy a pattern she had noticed on some Wimborne chairs.

One day, she idled away her creative talents inventing a special table for the children. 'When you let down the hinged panelled sides you have a low, enormous play table in the middle of the drawing-room', she explained to Desmond. Once opened, the table was to incorporate a theatre, a workbench, a basin, forts, drawbridges, tunnels, deserts, etcetera. She knew it would take years to make and Roderick would surely object to its presence in the drawing-room, but, she made Desmond promise, 'Don't tell Lady Cynthia about it, or Wells, or any of the people who deal in good ideas for children.'

In an unpublished sketch written shortly after their move to North End House, Enid encapsulated a typical argument. The couple in the piece, Sir John and Lady Danesworth, were 'rich, cultivated, occupied in the world'. Sir John was complaining about a new pelmet board.

'It's monstrous and scandalous ... that that pelmet board under that valance shouldn't have been painted. Or made of mahogany. It's common, unpainted deal.'

Lady Danesforth, burning with indignation, told him no pelmet board was ever painted.

'I could have had this one painted perfectly well. I simply didn't because it's not usual. You're not supposed to look underneath.'

The row continues with Sir John, fretting that the unpainted board makes them appear to be cost cutting, finally walking out of the house. Lady Danesforth, finding that 'time had dimmed her courage', slipped down through the hall and followed him, miserable that on the first day of the weekend after a heavy week of work, she had driven him out of the house.

'She had told him she hated the job she had put her hand to, she loathed running the house he had bought. Of what use was money if the woman you were prepared to adore threw up her hands and rebelled at the work which no one else in his family life but she could do?' Lady Danesforth posed the question. Lady Jones could not answer it.

In spite of the extra cash, the Joneses could not easily find a suitable London house to buy. The following two winters were spent at 113 Eaton Square and 96 Cheyne Walk respectively. In the summers, Enid went down to Rottingdean with the children and Roderick stayed at his club from Monday to Friday. Each week, in vain, Enid begged him to try and come down for longer. 'I know I must but it doesn't seem as though I could live only on weekends. Oh my darling – after all we haven't fifty years together in front of us.' Roderick's main joy of his weekend visit was a ride with Enid – and every Monday he wrote to her, thanking her for giving him a calm or exciting two nights, almost as if she were the owner of a guest house, or his mistress.

During the days alone, she spent three hours every morning in a room allotted her for writing.* Often she produced little more than a letter, a poem or a page of notes or ideas for her journal. In the afternoons she usually swam. She adored bathing in the sea and, much to the locals' amusement, walked down Rottingdean High Street in her costume, sometimes twice a day, even though she was, by 1926, pregnant with her third child. She was a strong swimmer but the exercise was taken largely at the behest of Harold Waller. At his suggestion also, Laurian and Timothy had their beds taken outside in the summer and they slept in the open beneath a pergola all night. Several society magazines found this so extraordinary that reporters were sent down to Rottingdean to write articles about Lady Jones, an expert on child welfare, and her outdoor night nursery.

Occasionally Waller would spend a day in Rottingdean with Enid and her children; Enid was intrigued by what she termed his 'yearly spurt of friendliness when Mrs Waller is away in Dorset'. They walked together over the Downs, he holding forth on his pet subject, the unhappiness of married life and she, starved of male company, flirting mildly. He was not immune to Enid's immense charm and vitality. 'It is so long – so very long – since anyone took the trouble even to pretend to value me that I am all flustered at reading your note.' But when she pressed him to stay he resisted. 'Better, I think, to picture you from here as you describe yourself (with my own embellishments added) . . . your husband I leave out wilfully.' Three days later, he explained further : 'I need no car nor wings to waft me to Sussex, Delilah. It is not priest-hood. There is a tiresome woman great with child. . . . I await her summons.'

On 10 May 1926, in the middle of the General Strike, Dr Waller delivered her third child, called Yorick for the first few weeks of his life, but then Richard Bagnold Jones. This child was born at 113 Eaton Square and Nurse Raynham Smith again returned for an extended period. Roderick, due to

---

* Within months of acquiring North End House Roderick also bought the seaside boarding house called Gothic House which abutted it. The room at the top of the spiral staircase in this new building was earmarked as Enid's new Tower Room, as Roderick had promised her before their marriage.

leave on another long trip around the time of the birth, was delayed by the Strike and did not get away until 27 May. Coming to terms with his possible absence, Enid acknowledged that the husband was a dispensable element in the birth process. She was by now writing extensive notes on her experiences in childbirth.

As soon as she was fit, Enid moved down to Rottingdean with the babies, nurses and maids, and tried to organize herself into a sane routine of writing. The last time that Roderick had gone away, his absence had resulted in *Serena Blandish*. But this time, she wrote to him in Honolulu to confess defeat.

I had meant (with all the resolution and strength that is in me) to have at least part of a book ready for you on your return. But I can't do it. I have sat for weeks, morning after morning, all the morning up in the spare room, or in my bedroom, or down here in the garden room, trying, trying till I was sick.

She blamed the breastfeeding for making her feel mentally heavy and stupid.

I am so afraid you will be thinking I have done it, and it is bitter enough not to have done it without meeting your disapprobation as well. So I warn you in time. I really have tried till I was nearly blind with trying, sitting facing the typewriter, wrapped in rugs and staring at nothing and *thinking* of nothing. I have no spring of fancy and no outlook or anything and no nice words lying about in my head, and worse than that, no central idea at all.

Even her letters to Roderick at this time were in some ways a disappointment. He begged her for some of the witty little drawings she had always sent to Antoine but she told him that if she tried to think of them, they were not funny. 'A drawing is a sort of involuntary cackle or chuckle, jerked out of me like a hiccough – I should love to do them for you for I know they make you laugh but I can't. I expect feeding Richard isn't good for that sort of spirited flip of the mind.'

Unquestionably it was not. Under the Waller routine, Richard was weighed after each feed and when he did not gain, Enid was subjected to 'fierce breast massage which makes me have to hold my wounded chest in my hands'. She also had to go for extra long walks to increase the milk. The massage, the feeds and the walks took up almost all of the day. She had, however, spent 'months of sweating' that summer over a short ghost story for an anthology being edited by her friend, Lady Cynthia Asquith. Flattered to be asked, and afraid of being thought a fool if she refused, she agreed. But it caused her enormous difficulty. 'It is very bad,' said Enid in a covering note. 'I couldn't have believed that writing, which can sometimes be a faint pleasure to me, could have been so dislikeable, and such a task.' In spite of Cynthia's warm approval, Enid wondered only whether Cynthia's judgement was good.

In November 1926, both Roderick and Enid were dangerously ill with influenza which, in Roderick's case, turned to pleurisy. Both had temperatures of 104°F and both had spots on their lungs so that 'we nearly died'. When Laurian, Richard and three of the servants succumbed as well, Waller advised a holiday, somewhere warm and dry. And so a trip to Egypt was organized early in the New Year. Enid's brother Ralph, then stationed in Cairo, acted as their guide. She did not care for Egypt with its mummies, dead Pharaohs and tombs. 'Who wants to have it hammered into them that it's almost useless to lift a finger between birth and death, that everything has been said and done already and that women die like dust and leave their wretched jewellery behind?' she wrote to Moira, her friend of Vienna days. But she enjoyed the camel and donkey rides so much that they decided to bring a large white donkey, complete with all its native trappings, back with them. They came home via Paris, where Enid was joined by her mother, and the two women stayed on an extra week, shopping. Enid had always adored Paris. For her, this was the best week of the entire holiday. 'We stayed at a cheap hotel and did everything at tiny restaurants and drank vodka and got back the flavour of pre-marriage cheapness and heavenliness.'

A few months later, Roderick had to return to Paris and Geneva, for a major conference of international press magnates. Following her illness Enid had shed much of her extra weight gained through pregnancy and she jumped at the opportunity of going with him. She bought several new outfits for the trip. The manager of the Reuters Paris office, Randall Neale, met Sir Roderick and Lady Jones off the train at Paris and the three of them had dinner together at L'Escargot. Randall Neale was then, like Enid, thirty-eight, extremely good looking with sparkling green eyes. A decisive, autocratic man about whom colleagues in Reuters had complained because of his high-handedness and tyrannical manner towards subordinates, he was easily angered. He had, none the less, great intelligence and charm.

Separated from his wife, he had lived in Paris for several years and knew every restaurant, café and night-club. Enid romanticized; surely this was the sort of man she could fall in love with. 'Neale – your name has mentioned volumes. Must I unlearn all those tricks? When you were spoken of my heart leapt. I invented excuses to prolong the talk. I ran you down. I did you injustices. In my spirit I gambolled and adored your name. All lovers are willing to incur ridicule. All that your name evokes is still within me,' she wrote in her journal.

Although they saw very little of each other during that trip, Enid moved on to Geneva in a state of high excitement. To Antoine she admitted, 'I have been asleep for seven years, having children, and now, thank God, I am thinner and men like me again, and I realize that there is one kind of life when you are fat and another when you are thin.' Meeting Neale had awakened her to the possibilities which life could still offer her. In Geneva she made two more new friends who stimulated her in other ways. Baron Oliver de Reuter, a nephew of Roderick's baron, was thirty-three, dissolute, deaf, half bald, brilliant (in Enid's view) and eccentric, with marvellous poise, figure and manners. His charm was 'indescribable at present but I hope to get him in a play'. His constant companion but not, Enid surmised, his mistress, was the Princess Duleep Singh, half Hindu and half Scottish, the child of a seventy-year-old Rajah and a sixteen-year-old Scottish dancer.

In the company of this mesmerizing pair, Enid played chess all day and night. By 3 a.m. the Baron gets 'obstinately drunker and drunker but his manners are always just as good'. Enid too, her head swimming with cocktails and ideas, drank champagne ceaselessly. 'Roderick is divine and lets me do what I like, because he knows I am obsessed with his character and I want to write about him.' In October, when Richard was christened, Baron Oliver de Reuter was invited to be one of the godparents.

That autumn and winter Enid and the children spent entirely at Rottingdean. She wrote numerous sketches and vignettes about Paris and Geneva, the Baron, and being in love. But she could not write a book. 'Shall I ever ?' she wondered. 'Work I do all day long but manual work. Tearing about doing this and that, trying to run a house that grows larger over my head, like a showman holding up his own round of wooden horses, but work of the mind, none.' The builders had now begun incorporating Mrs Elliott's boarding house into North End House and the deafening noise from knocking walls down did not help. It was a particularly lonely time for Enid because of a tragedy at her friends the Lewises' house. Sir George Lewis, overworked and depressed, had fallen under a train, an accident widely believed to be suicide. Lady Lewis rang Enid the night of his death and she stayed with her until four in the morning when she went home shaking. Soon after, Lady Lewis and her children left Rottingdean and let their house; Enid greatly missed their warm friendship and neighbourliness.

Before the year was out, Enid and Roderick found a London home at last. 29 Hyde Park Gate was an impressive house built in 1800, with a large garden standing in the shadow of the Albert Hall. They had fewer rows over this house, partly because they sought professional help for the changes required. It was gutted and Sir Edwin Lutyens redesigned the interior. For the dining-room he converted the two smallish reception rooms into one long olive-coloured chamber of 'great and simple beauty'. But his masterpiece was the square drawing-room at garden level. To enter, guests had first to come down a magnificent wide oak staircase with a rope handrail. At the top of the stairs, one looked over and down at the other guests below before disappearing behind the wall of the staircase to reappear at the bottom – a dramatic entrance which Enid loved. Through four long french windows, the drawing-room gave on to the garden, in the design of which Lutyens also took a hand. He bordered the whole area with fig trees growing on a trellis, and filled the corners with large pots of madonna lilies. At the foot of some large stone steps, he arranged a striking terrace of black and white paving stones.

Lutyens took great pains over Enid's writing-room, which, again, had to be approached by steps – two one way and two at a right angle. For the bottom of these he designed, as a typically humorous touch, a copper newel knob which swivelled. His idea was that if she awoke, inspired, in the middle of the night, she could run down the stairs and pivot, with the ball under her palm, directly into her writing chair. Most of the second floor was turned into a rather cold and draughty nursery, rumoured to be the largest in London, with a parquet floor on which the children could bicycle, and strategically placed pillars, good for hide-and-seek.

They commissioned Allan Walton, a fashionable artist who decorated Marcel Boulestin's first restaurant in Leicester Square, to paint a fanciful representation of Regency Brighton's Old Steine on a glass panel flanked by mirror glass pilasters. As a joke, Walton added a paddle-steamer in the background and the piece hung in the hall. He also marbled for them the tops of two dining tables (which were big enough to seat twenty-eight) in olive and charcoal with a brass rim and inset with a narrow brass filet. The workmen stayed almost a year until the winter of 1928, transforming the house into a palatial residence for splendid entertaining. Roderick thought it Enid's fault that it was not ready sooner.

Ruling over two households was an immense undertaking for Enid. The establishment had now swollen to nine indoor servants, two nurses, nursery maid, a chauffeur, two gardeners, a groom, a strapper and Cutmore. Cutmore was theoretically in charge of supervising all the other servants, but he could not prevent them from regularly handing in their notices at the most critical of moments. If the notice were accepted, it was Cutmore's duty to prevent contamination of the new nursery maid by the old. But his prime role, once they were ensconced in Hyde Park Gate, was overseeing the weekly move to the country. But, although this was undertaken with the precision of a military operation, it generally overran someone's 'half day' at each end, provoking further upheaval. The cook was given the money for rail fares for some of the servants and a taxi was ordered to meet them at the other end. Cutmore's silver canteen had to be loaded into one car (from 1930 until the outbreak of war this was a Rolls Royce Sendenca de Ville); Enid herself liked to drive the second. Roderick preferred to be chauffeur-driven in the Rolls and had a speedometer installed in the back because he felt it was his, rather than the chauffeur's, duty to control the car. The milk and papers had to be stopped in one house and started in the other and, for longer absences, caretakers were established in the empty house with a list of instructions.

Regular visitors to Rottingdean all had particular requirements with which Cutmore was expected to be familiar. Some liked the bath run for them, others preferred to run their own. Colonel Bagnold liked a small white bath towel, as well as a bath sheet, and the hot-water bottle placed right down to his feet, not in the middle of the bed. Each of the visitors' rooms, which Roderick expected Enid to make sure came up to the high standards he was used to in Government houses abroad, was to have biscuits, a bottle of water, glass, matches, books, writing paper, envelopes, post-cards, fresh pen nibs, sharpened pencil and full ink-pot. Not surprisingly, when she ascended the steps to her tower room, even if she had nothing particular to write about, she was aware of salivating as her hand touched the door handle at the thought of leaving domesticity behind.

Occasionally she saw a glimmer of humour in the domestic round. One morning, cook disturbed her at work, 'a thing no one has done before', telling her to go immediately to the chemist. There she extorted a packet of snapshots belonging to one of her maids. The pictures showed five of them, dressed in their employer's bathing dresses ('of which I have a whole cup-boardful, being a specialist in bathing'), sitting, some of them on expensive new garden furniture and others astride Mahmoud, the Egyptian donkey, and 'the hall boy of fourteen grinning adolescently among them . . . I gave the first row and saw the first tears at 10 o'clock yesterday morning and the last row and the last tears at a quarter to eight as I was dressing for dinner.'

Mrs Basil in *Call Me Jacky* says that, during the seventh year of her mar-riage, she might have been tempted to murder her husband. The traditionally difficult seventh year was not a good one for the Jones partnership either. During the course of a meeting between Roderick and Sir Edwin Lutyens at Hyde Park Gate, Lutyens talked about his nineteen-year-old daughter Mary and his worries over her involvement with the Theosophist Movement and its leader, Krishnamurti. Roderick impulsively suggested that Lutyens should ring his daughter there and then, and ask her to join them for lunch at Claridges. It was, according to Mary Lutyens, 'the beginning of a friendship that was to change my life radically. . . . For all the peculiarity father must have found this friendship preferable to my association with Krishna.' The effect on Roderick and Enid was equally dramatic and subtly changed the nature of their marriage.

Thereafter Roderick, fifty that year, met Mary almost every day when he was in London, and most weekends Mary was invited to stay at Rottingdean. Roderick also wrote to Mary every day, letters which were hand-delivered by a Reuter messenger boy, and he gave her a tin box with a key and her initials on in which to keep them.* Yet Mary herself never realized that she could have been a danger to Enid : 'It always seemed to me that you and Roderick had complete understanding . . . your marriage was unique.'

Enid coolly observed Mary at first, realizing she was on the verge of discovering life. 'Mary is nineteen and ready to sacrifice anything. She wishes to make life an experiment; she believes that in her day something may happen. And she is right to believe it.' Soon Enid, too, was captivated by Mary's dark shyness and naïve sincerity. She was also worldly enough to realize that the most effective way to neutralize such a young and impressionable rival was to turn her into a friend. It was not difficult, as Mary was almost as bowled over by Enid's charm as by Roderick's chivalry and dependability. For a young girl hoping to be a writer, becoming enmeshed in Enid's web was a heady experience. Enid encouraged Mary in her writing and taking a leaf out of Antoine's book, instilled in her the importance of discipline; three hours a day at your desk even if you have nothing to say. At weekends Mary found herself joining in conversations with literati such as Desmond MacCarthy, H. G. Wells, Arnold Bennett and Logan Pearsall Smith, but felt embarrassed by her immaturity, by her certainty that no conversation of hers could contribute to the success of a party. 'Once, to my utter shame, I did amuse the company in your house,' Mary reminded Enid years later. One Saturday lunch, amidst such a gathering, Mary was asked which horse she had been allotted for her ride with Roderick the next day. She replied : 'Roderick is going to mount me.'

Enid was, according to Mary, 'sweetness itself. . . . You were to me rather like what the Baroness d'Erlanger was to you – except that I worshipped you, was quite a bit in love with you.' Even when Roderick showed Mary an inkpot on his desk made from an elephant's foot and she, turning it upside down to admire it, spilled all the ink on to the carpet, there was not a word of reproach from Enid. Sometimes he would drive Mary out to Richmond in the morning and they would breakfast at the Roebuck Inn, on the edge of the park. Most Thursday nights Roderick took her dancing at The Embassy

* When the time came for Roderick to ask for his letters back, Mary was aghast to discover as they exchanged letters that her grammar and spelling had been corrected in the red pencil so hated by his children and staff.

where he had his own table. To all this, Enid never raised a murmur. Physically they were far better suited for dancing together than were Enid and Roderick, and Enid sometimes resorted to a professional dance partner, Gordon Dowd. For Mary's twentieth birthday Roderick bought her a diamond watch bracelet from Boucheron. At the same time he gave Enid a similar but less stunning smaller one. Mary believed, with some justification, that as long as Enid could entertain the literary friends who bored Roderick, she preferred to know that her husband was happily occupied with a young girl.

In any case, Roderick had told Mary that he and Enid had a pact. Either partner could have any number of flirtations as long as they did not actually sleep with anyone else. This pact was causing Enid some difficulties. In June, she and Roderick had again visited Paris and renewed their acquaintance with Randall Neale. Then in July, an opportunity arose for Enid to spend three days in Paris alone, escorted everywhere by Neale. Both considered it a magical time in spite of the physical limitations which Enid imposed on the relationship. She told Neale it was to be nothing more than a 'romantic attachment', something *'hors catégorie'*. Ever since Frank Harris she had looked upon the consummation of an affair as a disappointing detail for a woman, sometimes less exciting than holding hands. Neale told her he accepted her restrictions. Nevertheless, after dining at a restaurant in Montmartre on the last day, Neale paid the bill, tipped the waiter and then said: 'And now we have time to have our coffee comfortably in my house.'

Enid, slowly picking her thoughts and her words, told him: 'If I refuse I am in the immodest position of being the first to suggest what has not been suggested. There is no reason which I can think of why I should not go. Therefore I must fall back on that frail barrier of convention which is meant for such situations.' Neale, realizing her reluctance, replied instantly by ordering two coffees from the waiter. The moment passed and Enid pondered on the opportunity lost. 'The beauty of a young man, which I missed in early youth, began to torture me. . . . We are never at the right moment for love.'

Enid returned to England and, once more, found herself infatuated with a romantic ideal. She rushed to the post every day longing for Neale's letters, and as she took her daily bathe, thought only of the France which was just beyond her gaze. Transporting herself back to the Place du Tertre, his arm around her shoulder, she felt 'so warmly in Paris that the water gave me scarcely any shock. . . . Walking slowly up the village street in my wet dress I am alive with certainty. I only think "what a long way through the night".'

Neale did write: 'Now I naturally think that I did not make half enough of those three days. There was so much more to be said . . . *et ce fut merveilleux'* – a letter across which Enid scrawled in pencil: 'This is that worn and fingered morsel of paper, the first love-letter from a new lover, wherein by constant reading I try to read more than is written.' She looked for more florid declarations of his love and his innermost feelings, because, for her, that was all part of an affair. His letters were a disappointment. Her own reply to his first letter she copied out, stuck into her journal, and then digressed into analysing her own feelings of love. 'To be quite honest (and I know the horrid labels that sentence might earn), writing to me is more than being in love. But marriage is more important than writing. . . . To be then, in love, steals nothing from my husband. On the contrary, it lights me. It turns thought and beauty and desire on like a stream. Feeds him as well as me, and all around me.'

Enid's absorption in Randall Neale enabled her to view with greater equanimity Roderick's flirtation with Mary Lutyens. But Neale was, from the start, in an impossible position. For the three days in July Roderick had advanced Neale any sum up to a total of Frs. 24,000, to be accounted for later 'in connection with Lady Jones's visit', although Enid recognized that 'Neale is going to be miserable at being paid for'. In July, Roderick sent Enid a copy of the office memorandum which made clear that Neale had been instructed to go to Geneva at the end of August when Roderick and Enid were also due to be there. He wrote on Enid's copy : 'Madam, I venture to send the enclosed in the belief that, conceivably, it may interest you. I am madam, your most humble obedient servant, Roderick Jones.' Annotated by Enid, 'RJ's blessing on my Neale adventures.' Neale, though pleased at the fresh opportunity to see Enid, wondered if it was 'a machiavellian design to have me in Geneva near you but a prisoner in the dungeons of the League ? . . . I suppose I shall be kept with my nose to the grindstone and hardly see you at all,' he wrote dejectedly. Only too aware of the delicacy of the situation, Neale advised that her envelopes, which bore a blatant Rottingdean postmark, should at least be typewritten.

Naturally enough, Enid raised no objection when Mary was invited to this trip. After Paris and Geneva, the party spent a few days at the Auberge du Père Bise at Talloires, just south of Geneva. It was a beautifully quiet spot with the restaurant on the edge of the Lake Annecy where they dined every evening. Long creepers encircled the restaurant garden and only the occasional steamer disturbed the mirror calm of the water. One day it rained incessantly but was dry enough by the evening for the foursome to take their customary dinner, at separate tables, outside. Noticing the chairs were still wet, Roderick rushed back inside to fetch a cushion for Mary. Such thoughtfulness apparently did not occur to Neale and he left Enid, who was watching Roderick and Mary, to manage as best she could. Considering herself humiliated, she was furious with him and burst into uncontrollable sobs. She dismissed Neale and ran to Roderick who put his arm around her comfortingly. Mary, although temporarily abandoned could not fail to be impressed. 'You were unhappy and Roderick was instantaneously with you – his love, his protectiveness, his chivalry, his loyalty all yours like St George in "Where the Rainbow Ends". That was what he must always have been to you and you to him. . . . You were never within a million miles of losing him to me – he worshipped you,' Mary wrote to Enid many years later.

A doomed relationship from the start, the affair with Neale had been dealt a death blow. Although she continued to see him on an occasional basis for the next ten years, she was lured to Paris more by Chanel and Reboux (the milliners) than by Randall Neale. Hoping Talloires was a place where she might get ideas and calm for writing, Enid remained there, sitting all day in an open boat in her bathing things, with her typewriter propped between her knees, while Roderick went on to Geneva. She put together some incon-sequential thoughts on Aristide Briand, the French Foreign Minister, and his evasion of journalists at the League of Nations. The piece was published on her return in September in the *Observer*. Roderick considered it a 'gem' but Antoine chided her for wasting time by 'writing little articles without any interest (I haven't read it yet) simply because suddenly you feel that you want to see Enid Bagnold in print. Look at the watch and the calendar; every minute time is moving on and you waste it! You can achieve but you must work . . . one must limit oneself. Our imagination is the friend of our laziness. Start on one subject and stick to it.'

She also brooded over the bizarre events of the past few days. Had she been right to fling Neale away? 'I ought to have kept a scrap of him, just to dance with.' She told Roderick that whatever affairs they had, they must never jeopardize their own relationship. 'Though I have had qualms from time to time in weak moments that we might be risking something in the light of . . . shall I call it the "string of continuity". Yet it was just that string that we couldn't break and so we have both dared to thread other things on it.' Mary, Roderick and Enid came home via Holland as Mary had wanted to take her friends to meet Krishna at Castle Eerde. Enid then went to Paris again while Roderick and Mary returned home via Amsterdam.

The events of the summer of 1928 had a salutary effect on her. Watching Roderick becoming increasingly engrossed in Mary had worried her in-tensely and perhaps it was only the independent friendship that had grown up between the two women which saved the Joneses' marriage. By the autumn her new green Tower Room was finished. Roderick never went in it, but many were the notes she composed there for him: 'I do love you so much,' she told him in November. 'You are all I have really, you and the children. I have a wretched passion, which I must control, to be the only person in the world to you. I know that's absurd, but it's a sort of bad instinct.' Being a 'devoted mother' came easily because Enid firmly believed in her own children's superiority. Many were the letters to Roderick in which she boasted about Laurian and Timothy, showing up neighbouring children to be behind both mentally and physically. Vita noticed this and called her, to her face, 'a prig about being a mother'. She said Enid was 'constantly declaring that one baby did not weigh as much as her own, or had eczema or was not fed properly'. Her husband, Harold Nicolson, felt uncomfortable visiting North End House because of a feeling that the children were being thrust at visitors. She was ambitious for her children. Sensing great artistic talent in Laurian, Enid determined that she should have no formal education at all, at least until she was seven, but preferred instead to take her to admire famous paintings. She was always drawing pencilled outlines for her children to colour and sent them to painting lessons when they were in London.

At five o'clock every evening the children were brought down to their mother to be entertained. For one hour she was theirs entirely and could always devise a different imaginative activity for them. Sometimes it was playing with flour and water, sometimes making intricate model villages, sometimes reading, or, best of all, telling them her own made-up stories, but never anything to do with music, which she hated. She had a natural flair for getting on with her children. A tremendous power to affect them she had too, but was equally good at listening when required and never patronizing. 'She could not merely bridge, but altogether ignore, the gap of years,' recalled Timothy. 'She could chat without being parental. She could be amused. The child felt not merely that it was loved ... but that its company could be a pleasure to her.' Her views on the children's upbringing were decided and although some, such as breastfeeding and inclusion in adult conversation were quite advanced, others were curiously old fashioned. She took them swimming in an often freezing sea, believing it was good for them ; she had a nurse, as opposed to a nanny, in full starched uniform, to look after them in what struck many visitors as a clinically hygienic, almost spartan nursery. And she fostered 'yearning toys' for the children 'so as to give them unsatisfied desires'. Certain toys were put on a high shelf in the nursery 'so that they can look at them during meals and long and long like dogs round the table, when the meat smells lovely and sometimes ... when you're good, then you get them but never for long enough.'

For someone who was acquiring a reputation as an expert on child welfare, children in general left her unmoved except as a yardstick to show up her own favourably. Devotion to Harold Waller, however, brought her the closest she ever came to charitable work. Inspired by him she worked tirelessly for the organization which he and Nurse Raynham Smith set up, the Babies Club in Danvers Street, Chelsea. This was the first private welfare clinic for children in London. It was, according to the newspaper reports on the day it opened, 'a West End club to teach rich mothers East End wisdom'.

'A West End mother, when she has her first baby, has probably never handled one before. She surrounds her baby with too much attention and attention of the wrong sort,' Lady Jones told reporters attending the club's launch. 'Very often the baby does not get enough fresh air ... whereas the East End baby is out-of-doors all day long, and very often she gives the baby the wrong clothes – long heirloom dresses weighed down by the embroidery – which do not allow the child to kick its legs about.'

Enid had learnt Waller's lessons well. But she was not chairman of the committee and Waller was angry with her. She dashed off a hurt rejoinder : 'I do not like publicity seeking any more than you,' she told him. 'If I did I could get all I want outside the Babies Club. It is not particularly chic or amusing to figure as a domestic philanthropist.' Waller naturally forgave her. He was fond of her, and she was useful to the club. She persuaded several rich and important people to join, and almost the first large reception the Joneses held at their new London house was in aid of the Babies Club. The nursery at Hyde Park Gate was regularly used as a lecture hall for club speakers. Enid designed the cover of a special Babies Club Recipe Book – the hoods of the prams were up 'because they are easier to draw' – and worked hard to promote it in spite of the previous jibe from Waller. And she was involved on their behalf in a large amount of correspondence and administration for bazaars as well as touting for new members.

Why did she do it, with so much else already interfering with her writing ? Because she knew that if she had to 'stand up before God's fierce blue penetrating eyes I should say "I cared for the Babies Club because Waller ... inspired me."' By 1929 however, the club was in serious financial difficulties. Enid proposed that Dr Waller should write a book on child care. For every section he wrote, she promised to donate £100, up to a total of £600. She could not offer any more because the sum represented the full amount of her part-share in the film rights to a play 'and that is all the spare money that I have at the moment of my own'.

The play in question was *Serena Blandish*. The American writer, S. N. Behrman, had been captivated by *Serena* from the moment he first read it. With no idea who the author was, he asked his agent, Harold Freedman, to secure him the rights. Even before he secured them, he set to work on the dramatization, so impressed was he by the book's 'tough awareness of the metallic facts of life'. Jed Harris, one of the most successful producers in New

York at the time, wanted *Serena Blandish* too. When Enid was sent Behrman's first draft she complained about a name given to a new character. Apparently it 'conveyed rugged strength which did not altogether conceal the hard fact that he was a poor weakling.' Unwittingly, Behrman had chosen the name Roderick. Soon after this Behrman himself was in London for the opening of his play *The Second Man*. Enid seized the opportunity to invite him for tea at Hyde Park Gate and offered to give a lunch party for him later in the week at Sovranis, a fashionable new restaurant in Jermyn Street. Whom would he like to meet? Behrman, with dry New York humour, reeled off some of the best-known figures in contemporary English literature. They chatted some more about *Serena Blandish* and he left. Came the day of the lunch and waiting for Behrman in the restaurant foyer were Arnold Bennett, H. G. Wells, Desmond MacCarthy and the rest of Enid's literary set. He was bowled over.

Behrman's version of *Serena* did the rounds of New York managements throughout 1928 but was constantly rejected on the grounds of expense. One set was to be on top of a bus, another in the Countess's limousine and, with all the beautiful clothes required, it was thought to be very special and sophisticated. Jed Harris, however, was extremely wealthy and did not mind the cost. He had a contract with the actress Ruth Gordon, and saw this as the perfect starring vehicle for her. One of the major difficulties in staging the play was its ending with its implied sense of failure for Serena as she realizes her husband is a half-caste. As Ruth Gordon commented: 'They would have torn down the Morosco Theater if we did that.'

In Behrman's adaptation Serena refuses riches to run away with the Countess's secretary to Monte Carlo – a more tactful ending which somewhat obscured the point of the original.

The rehearsal period for *Serena Blandish* was, according to Behrman, 'a never-ending vortex of misunderstandings which engendered lifelong enmities.' Henry Daniell was brought over from London to play the disillusioned Lord Ivor Cream and another English actor, A. E. Matthews, played Martin. Matthews seemed unable to learn his words. He had one line: 'The orchestra will play Gershwin and Brahms' for which he always said 'Gershwin and Brahm'. Finally Harris could stand it no longer and shouted 'Brahms, Matty, Brahms'. Matthews looked very astonished, took off his glasses and asked, 'Why plural, dear boy?' Harris accused Constance Collier, then at the very peak of her profession, of trying to play the part as an English lady instead of a Brazilian Countess. And there were two very costly orchestras, one at the back of the curtain, the other in the front pit, to be coordinated.

By the time the play moved to New York on 23 January 1929, the atmosphere among the cast was poisonous. The *New York Times* had reprinted an out-of-town review which panned the show ; nonetheless, several reviewers gave it high praise. Harpo Marx was at the opening night and telephoned Ruth Gordon immediately to tell her it was 'just great'. Enid never went to New York to see it nor, out of deference to her father, did she associate herself with the play at all. But it ran for some ninety performances which, for a high-brow play in 1928, was not unsuccessful. Bette Davis said of *Serena* : 'I just saved up my money and I went to see it and then I saved up my money again and I went to see it again.' *Serena Blandish* was Enid's first play. Harold Freedman, not yet her agent, wrote to her : 'I hope that now this is on you will write a play of your own and send it to me as soon as you have finished it.' She told Freedman that she had already written a quarter of one 'but it has no cut about it'. There is no evidence that she had started to write a play but the lure of his flattery began to eat into her.

1929 ended badly. Enid broke her forearm and wrist cranking her car, and was in great pain in St George's Hospital, unable to write at all for several weeks. The break was so severe that it never healed completely. But she was longing for another baby. A new baby made Enid feel romantic – it was, she often told her husband, 'like having a tiny lover out in the pram'. And by the end of the year, aged forty, she was delighted to discover she was pregnant for the fourth time. Mary Lutyens, in her innocence, was shocked to learn of this but Roderick consoled her. 'My dear little girl,' a phrase which he used rather incongruously for both Enid and Mary, 'you'll understand some day.'

In February 1930, Mary Lutyens married Anthony Sewell. Roderick, finding the wedding too painful to attend, went away to Paris. Laurian and Timothy were invited to be bridesmaid and page ; Enid noticed that Mary was wearing the gold bracelet that Roderick had given her.

TEN

I Feel a Dictatorship Longing Coming Over Me

ALTHOUGH Enid believed that her marriage might easily have crumbled within the first seven years, she felt that from then on it grew steadily more robust. Giving advice to a young friend undergoing marital difficulties many years later, she advised her to return to the nest, even if it were made of thorns, and not to seek both love and comfort together. 'If you want the romance of love, and of course you do, you can have it as well in time. Somebody will light you up. You can't expect a husband to do it. He only does it once.'

Roderick and Enid played chess together almost every evening when they were together at home. 'But I don't think we ever get any better; we are so up to each other's openings and stratagems,' he once commented. As in chess so in life. From now on their partnership was marked by loyalty, not fidelity, respect but not passion, liberty but not licence. The bonds of matrimony did not break because they were tied so loosely.

The Joneses' fourth and last child, a son Dominick, was born on 18 August 1930, delivered and nursed once again by the Waller–Raynham Smith team. On the same day Enid's first children's book made its appearance. *Alice and Thomas and Jane* was a series of adventures which had originated as stories made up and told aloud to her own children. Like her other books, it was rooted in experience. Thomas (eight), Jane (seven) and Alice (five) live in a village called Rottingdean 'in a strange shaped house because it kept on being more and more houses'. There were cooks, governesses and nurses; the children wore 'Fortnum jersies' and the father turned lunch-times into lessons on the Boer War.

But, as she explained in a foreword, while the children in the story 'ran about the house and rushed about the village and did all the things my children would like to have done . . . my children sat still.' Thomas (drawn more from Laurian than Timothy), the most daring of the threesome, is made into the eldest. His escape to Dieppe is the centre-piece of the book, although such an adventure was very far from anything that Timothy or Laurian might have been allowed. He certainly would not, as in the book, have gone unpunished. Earlier in the year, Enid had tried to buy a whip for the children at Harrods. When told by a shocked assistant that they were no longer stocked, she bought what she wanted in a pet shop. It hung in the hallway of North End House, alongside the riding crops for use on the horses. Emphatic that being whipped by her father had done her no harm, Enid perhaps wanted to show that her children were chips off the old block. Family discipline was always Enid's preserve. Only years later, when the problem of schoolboy homosexuality arose, was Roderick called in to pronounce – the subject was considered too serious for Enid. But then, in the middle of the lecture, Roderick shied off.

Alice and Thomas and Jane appealed on many levels. Everything was described very simply so that none of the thrills, for example of being wound up a cliff in a bucket, making a getaway through a smugglers' cave or eating snails, alone, in a French restaurant, were blurred over. What child could resist such adventures? Her sharp-edged sense of observation and good ear for dialogue, lent to a highly improbable chain of events an air of humorous reality. When a policeman questions the children drawing on the pavement, Alice looks up at him and says:

'My sister might be deaf and dumb.'
'Is she?' asked the policeman.
'I can't tell a lie,' said Alice, 'but she easily might be.'

Thomas, full of worldly wisdom, is good at explaining things to his sisters.

'Why are there always nuns on the cliffs?' asked Alice.
'Because the Downs are Roman,' said Thomas.

And the imagery, always her strong point, is made particularly accessible for children. 'Look at the sunset,' says Jane. 'The sun was being murdered in his bed and was sending up streams of blood like a squashed octopus all over the sky.' *Alice and Thomas and Jane* was a sort of glorification of 'the nest', which had now become the leitmotif of Enid's life. Several of the illustrations, all in an appealingly naïve style, were by nine-year-old Laurian, which made Enid particularly proud of this book.

It was a charming but rather boastful piece of work, the tone of which, in 1930, was not unacceptable. Enid Bagnold was not the only children's author of the time who believed instinctively in the idea that what was suitable for one's own children was valid for a range of others. A large body of early twentieth-century children's fiction (*Winnie the Pooh* is perhaps the best known) made use of the technique of the author's voice intruding or featured the author's own children as central characters. *Alice and Thomas and Jane* was universally well received. Naomi Mitchison, reviewing in *Time and Tide*, asked what was Enid Bagnold's peculiarly entrancing quality? It seems to be that she takes the ordinary child's values seriously and understands them and puts them in touch with some absolute. . . . [The stories] are the kind of stuff which childhood's intensest feeling is made from . . . the irony which hardens the book up and keeps it together is not from without, from a more refined and elaborate consciousness, but from within, so that there is no laughing at, only laughing with. To be able to get down to one's subject like this is an extremely rare quality.

Even Desmond MacCarthy wrote about *Alice and Thomas and Jane*, although still not a full review. Introducing an extract from the book in *Life and Letters* he said : 'Children like stories of possible adventures in a world of facts as much as impossible ones in a world of marvels. Perhaps most children even enjoy them more, the matter-of-fact world being still sufficiently marvellous to them. You can take the pleasure out of any game of make-believe by saying "That is not the way things happen. . . ."'

Enid's apparently cosy existence was, however, shattered by the death of her mother on 12 July 1931. Ethel Bagnold, at sixty-four, suffered a sudden heart attack while staying at North End House for the christening of Dominick. Enid had been in the room with her, gossiping just a few minutes before she was 'simply blown away like the wind'. Enid's long-standing and profound fear of death was greatly intensified by her mother's early demise; more importantly she realized she was herself no longer a child. Within a short space of time Enid became quite ill with a heart problem. 'The worst thing is, she thought me wonderful – that one never gets again,' Enid wrote to Vita. Enid tortured herself that perhaps her mother had not known how much she loved her, 'because I often went for her. . . . I feel as though my public has gone – she was that. I bullied her, teased her, collected everything for her, rang her up every night for ten years, even from France, made her laugh, dazzled her, thrilled her, abused her about her clothes, couldn't keep away from her . . . does it become again worthwhile to do anything ?'

Enid, wearing a fawn coat of her mother's, went away immediately with Roderick to France while Ralph stayed with Colonel Bagnold. They went on to Talloires again but everywhere seemed gloomy to her. Being abroad did not help her come to terms with her loss, and when her health declined further in the autumn, Waller prescribed sodium luminal morning and night to soothe her. But in the autumn, a heart specialist advised that the only cure was for her to go away at once and alone. 'Actually I ought to be alone', she wrote to Marthe Bibesco (Antoine's cousin by marriage) who had invited her to go and stay with her in Roumania. 'I have only got one month out of ten years. . . . Roderick would have let me go away before but I shouldn't have had the brave wings to go unless a doctor ordered me.' She was planning, so she told Marthe, to go to the South of France, Marseilles probably, not because she wanted warmth or sun – that would distract and tempt her away from writing – but because it was an area she knew and in Marseilles 'there is at least a danger of rape . . . it is terrible to live so long without a danger of rape.'

On 1 November 1931, in old clothes and with a knapsack on her back, Enid set off for Provence, but not alone. Her country friend, Ruth, Lady Monk Bretton*, recuperating too from an illness, decided to accompany Enid, at any rate for part of the trip. After a night in Paris, the two women took a train south but after stepping off the train and walking a mile up the street to the hotel, realized that they were not going to be able to spend a whole holiday hiking with knapsacks. Enid had a typewriter in hers. They saw a man with a donkey and yellow cart outside a restaurant and asked the price for the pair. A bargain was struck at three hundred francs, but the animal was a beast to control. 'Its behaviour is brave, plucky, tireless but mostly governed by sex.' Stopping as it did every few yards to smell manure pats, the women made slow progress and caused frequent traffic jams. It was hard work looking after the creature. They oiled its harness, cleaned and repainted the cart and made sure at the end of each day that he had enough to eat and drink and a comfortable place to sleep. Enid considered it a perfect way of seeing the country and, as they mostly walked alongside the cart, of taking mild exercise.

She wrote very lengthy, detailed letters to Roderick, her father and the children. Years later, Timothy went to Provence and told his mother it was the only place he had ever been which was 'exactly as I imagined. You must have described it well.' Ruth went home after two weeks. Although Enid missed her company, she hoped she would now settle down 'to try and allay that haunting itch that drives me to want to write'.

But Oh my darling [she wrote to Roderick], I am so homesick for you. Don't you think you could come out and spend a week walking? With two people it's all the greatest fun. With one alone, it's a bit dismal especially when one has these heartbreaking failures over not being able to write. I have no gifts. They're all illusion. Perhaps I shall never write the book I want to. What I put down on paper seems so trivial, so far from what I want to say, I want to make a full rich picture, and it's all tinny. Your-at-the-moment-very-despondent (but possibly easily cheered up you never know) Enid.

A mere hint from Roderick that he might come was enough to set her working. Falling back on past successes, the obvious approach was an account of her travels with a donkey, 'a sort of day to day Diary Without Dates'. If she put down all the details now, it could be polished once she was home. Sometimes she believed she would be much happier if only she could cure her urge to write. 'It is like a Calvinistic conscience. I would so much rather be grooming the donkey, mending his harness, nailing little luxury attachments on to the cart. But here I

* The former Ruth Brand married Lord Monk Bretton in 1911.

am instead, grinding out words like a mania and not really liking it at all, yet only soothed and "good" when I do.'

At the end of November, Roderick came out for a few days to bring her home. She had been away for only four of the requisite six weeks, but had had enough and was awaiting his arrival like an eager child for Santa Claus. Once together, however, they argued. Enid, eating frugally for weeks to economize, was furious about the amounts Roderick now handed out in tips.

Back at Rottingdean, she eagerly set about finishing her travel notes. Her tried and tested style was little changed from the reportage treatment of her first two books, *The Happy Foreigner* and *Diary Without Dates*. But this time she had nothing remotely as gripping for her subject matter and the piece was punctuated with more random thoughts and observations, including the admission that literature did not stir her. She had taken Sterne's *Tristram Shandy* with her but found it unreadable. 'A terrible little classic . . . that one ought to have read when one was seventeen.' She continued: 'Sometimes I think, ashamed, that while I am cracking the sugar off the cake, and calling myself a writer, and behaving towards myself as though all fodder could come from within, there are those people . . . who really care for literature . . . who read and read, who call themselves nothing but who really know.'

She sent the story, *Kiki – Donkey in France*, to H. G. Wells for his opinion. But he told her frankly of its shortcomings; it was too personal and without general appeal. Wisely, she accepted his advice and never sent it to a publisher. But the episode did little to boost her confidence and a further three years elapsed before she conceived of another idea worthy of a book. Increasingly, she was unable to view her inability to produce a major work calmly and this was threatening to cause her real grief.

'I am, of course, no real reader,' she had written in *Kiki*. Only one or two books had made her 'whole life take a leap forward' and among these she numbered *Orlando*. Her mind now turned particularly to Virginia Woolf's classic about Vita Sackville-West, as Vita, who had been contemplating going to France with Enid, had just sent a poem dedicated to her instead. In it she describes Enid as

> An eagle, happy in a cage,
> (If such a thing might be,) that had forgotten
> The crags and storms and ocean's splendid rage,
> A free and lonely spirit once begotten;
> Now tamed to peck the groundsel through the bars
> And to esteem a kindly self protection
> Above the danger of the windy stars.

'I can't tell you what I felt when I read it – I'm so proud,' Enid told her. Vita – the only friend, in addition to the Bibescos, to call Enid Virgilia – understood the importance of the security offered by the bars, especially because the eagle knew how to open the cage by herself and how far away she could fly.

Several years before, at a dinner-party given by the Lewises, Enid had met Count Albrecht Bernstorff, a large jovial German, Counsellor of the German Embassy since 1922, who reminded her of a character in a Dürer painting. One year younger than Enid, she described him as: 'nearly a giant, perhaps six foot six, certainly at one time weighing twenty stone, somehow younger than in young middle age, blond as a baby, bald, but with the remains of curling tendrils above his ear.'

Bernstorff's ancestry was Swiss on his mother's side, with a preponderance of oriental scholars and sages. His paternal ancestors were Danes, at least two of whom had held high political office. With such a background, it was hardly surprising that his span of knowledge and outlook on international affairs were reminiscent of an all-embracing Renaissance figure, a knight who in the mediaeval sense had the ability to look at the world as a whole. Interestingly, Enid considered that in knowing Bernstorff she accepted his 'pennon' – the knight's protective flag on his lance. During his ten years in England Albrecht Bernstorff became a well-known figure in London society. He dressed elegantly, drove a convertible Armstrong Siddeley and frequented the best restaurants and clubs. He did little to hide his homosexual tendencies.

Albrecht Bernstorff had first come to England in 1909 as a Rhodes Scholar at Trinity College, Oxford, and since that time had been captivated by the British. He responded to the spontaneity, tolerance and informality which he encountered among the upper-class English with whom he mixed. 'Once we Germans learn to laugh as they do, we shall inherit the earth,' he wrote in a handbook for students. In 1918, following his country's defeat, Bernstorff had been sent as a representative of the German Foreign Office to the Allied Commission of the Rhineland. From then on, he was convinced that only a democratic and pacific Germany could return to a position of economic affluence in Europe.

Albrecht delighted in enriching his friends' lives by introducing one to another. From about 1929 onwards, he was a constant weekend visitor at Rottingdean. Among the friends he brought were Gabriel Beer Hoffman, a portly Austrian would-be writer who talked a lot, Donald (Lord) Strathcona, a Dornford Yates character who sported all the latest fashions including a hairstyle which encompassed his ears like mudguards, Geoffrey Eastwood, a bachelor clerk to the House of Lords and Klop von Ustinov, then Press Attaché at the German Embassy. Albrecht and Klop were known as 'Big Pig' and 'Little Pig' respectively. Albrecht was a regular guest, too, at the Hyde Park Gate dinner-parties which Roderick believed were such an essential prerequisite of his position at Reuters and which Enid leavened with her own literary and social friends. One of her more original ideas in the late twenties was to give 'Boxing Parties'. Dinner was served as usual in the dining-room. Afterwards, Lutyens's drawing-room was converted into a boxing ring, with the twenty or so guests seated at small tables on a balcony all around. Enid, temporarily fascinated by the sport, gave at least three of these parties and friends remember, by the bloody noses of the participants, that they were by no means stage fights.

However, when convention required, Enid could be relied upon. Roderick relished the opportunities afforded by his sumptuous new house to indulge in the rituals of wine, port, cigars and coffee, to see his silver displayed all gleaming, and his servants hard at work preparing and serving. Enid, only half-jokingly, once referred to spending a whole day overseeing the preparation of food and rooms, but then, not having time to take a bath, throwing an extravagant gown over her dirty body. Not that she took no pride in the dinner parties ; the display of luxury gratified her too. Sometimes she spent hours planning and designing drawings on the menus. Guests sometimes saw her scribbling an instant note of complaint if she considered anything had gone wrong with the food, and sending it down to the kitchen with the dirty dishes. In January 1931, while the Round Table Conference on India was sitting, the Joneses gave a dinner-party for the principal Indian delegates, including Jinnah, the Moslem leader, and the Maharaja of Alwar. The latter caused a considerable flurry by enquiring in advance whether there would be meat or meat-based sauces, leather-seated chairs, heavy curtains which might conceal an assassin, or cats to which he was allergic.

Visiting dignitaries from a variety of countries were regularly offered hospitality in London or Sussex. When Herr Raumer, as emissary of the Third Reich, came to Britain for a short visit, he was promptly invited down to Rottingdean for lunch. Also invited were the Ustinovs and their adolescent son, Peter. During the lunch, the Nazi official extolled the efficiency of the New Germany : 'I only have to press my bottom', he boasted (meaning button), 'and four policemen come running.' Peter, captivated by the imagery, dissolved into giggles. Sir Roderick, stony-faced, signalled that the youth be removed from the room.*

* The Jones/Ustinov friendship cooled after Klop von Ustinov applied for British nationality. According to Peter Ustinov, Sir Robert Vansittart, the Permanent Under-Secretary of State for Foreign Affairs, suggested Jones as a possible sponsor, but Jones declined 'on the grounds that such an initiative might have offended the German Government'.

From the first, Enid's imagination was fired by Hitler's rise to power in Germany. She viewed the German dictator's actions in a romantic light; they brought colour and excitement to ordinary German people and could bring peace to Europe. It was up to Britain to keep 'steady' and grow accustomed to 'this volcanic resettlement of Europe ... there will be troubles to come', she conceded, 'jew-baitings, imprisonments, purges but we must swallow them and in the end that united kingdom will bring peace.' Some of this attitude was in the air that any upper-class English woman breathed in 1933, but Enid was not simply mouthing the views of others. She was intuitively hooked by the excitement of the changes in Germany in spite of being, by this time, on intimate terms with Bernstorff, who hated the Nazis. Hitler was the antithesis of everything that he and his family had for generations believed in and hoped for. He tried hard to explain to Enid the historical truth of events in Germany. They were attuned to each other in almost all things but this. Albrecht considered himself 'completely at your feet ... behind all our words are forces quite beyond the control of us little human beings ... as eternity and passion take us beyond ourselves in those rare moments of ecstasy, beyond the reach of our willpower.' Enid recognized: 'You have always had an enormous influence on me.' Yet in spite of such enlightenment, proffered by one she trusted in so much else, Enid's views from this time until the outbreak of war, became increasingly sympathetic towards Hitler. Albrecht, for all the love she bore him, scarcely made a dent in them.

In the spring of 1933, Enid decided she should see for herself what was happening in Germany. 'I speak German badly but I sop a lot of knowledge through the pores of the skin and I expect I shall be filled with impressions,' she had written to Colonel Lawson of the *Daily Telegraph* before she left. Roderick, 'which is divine of him', agreed. She was to stay most of the time at Albrecht's family estate, Stintenburg on the Schall See in northern Germany, where there would naturally be other guests acting as chaperones. Stintenburg was a flat, marshy area with wonderful sunsets and excellent hunting and fishing. The richness of life at Stintenburg, with its many servants and sumptuous food, reflected the Danish influence; noticeable too was an underlying German austerity.

Immediately she arrived, however, Enid was in trouble with Roderick for not telegraphing. Roderick telephoned in furious mood and threatened never to let her make such a trip again. But the real cause of the trouble was, once more, 'the pact'. Enid had told Roderick about 'one or two indiscreet suggestions B. had made', adding: 'Be happy, darling, be comforted. Nobody has hurt me or you and only very slightly (and flatteringly) wished to do. Bless you, my dear dear.' Roderick expected her to telegraph every day; 'but what am I to say – still unraped Saturday evening.' Bernstorff considered Roderick's domination over Enid terrifying and told her he would send Roderick a telegram: 'German Government undertakes interest itself in your wife.' This missive Enid managed to forestall.

While in Germany, she brooded much about Hitler, his speech to the Reichstag on 17 May ringing constantly in her ears. She had brought some work to do – a translation from French into English of *Alexandre asiatique* by Marthe Bibesco. Antoine had been nagging Enid for years to do this. It was a typically Bibesco fable, with its emphasis on youthful success which Antoine had taught Enid to prize more than love. Although she completed most of it during the trip, her mind was on the Nazi phenomenon.

I wondered what had caught me so really in the movement in spite of its persecutions and book burnings [she wrote to Roderick]. It was the same thing that caught me over Russia, the revolution, the construction of the Soviet. It's a vital movement onwards to something. At least it's the negation of liberalism in both cases. . . . I am so sick of the dreary socialist-communists, growling, carping and doing nothing. The tone of the *New Statesman* and the tone of the Hitler movement is the difference between life and death. Sicker still of Liberals, like Violet [Bonham Carter].

Seeing Albrecht in his family surroundings likened the Bernstorffs in her eyes to the Asquiths in England; she scorned what she deemed the ineffectual liberalism of both.

Enid planned to go to Kiel, where Hitler was addressing a rally, then Hamburg and Bremen. She explained her itinerary in great detail to Roderick in advance, making special play of the fact that nowhere would she and Albrecht be staying in the same hotel. None the less she could not resist: 'I would rather like to do this motoring trip with Bernstorff, like you did with Mary,' a jibe that made Roderick 'sore all day'.

Immediately she returned Enid sent her article on 'The New Revivalism' to *The Times*. 'Ten days is not much and I cannot pretend to arrive at any conclusions,' she began her article. It was a long piece, spread over three full-length columns. Written with an underlying tone of great sympathy towards the Nazis, it mostly recounted why individual Germans she had met supported the new regime.

Even the anti-Nazis admit that Hitler is a sincere man. To the Nazis he is almost divine. . . . Without doubt, it is treated as a new spiritual awakening. And we know well enough from the past what excesses, what cruelties, what intolerances can be done in the name of the Lord. If Germany is, as France says, 'the mad dog of Europe', it may be because it is mad to act from the heart and not from the head. . . . I am sure that nothing of this is directed at all against the outer world.

Scores of letters poured in, almost all complimentary to Enid, which served only to reinforce her views. Albrecht also returned to London but at the end of the summer, having made no secret of his opinions, was recalled to Germany. Enid was the first person he rang with the news and they met that evening for dinner at the Eiffel Tower restaurant in Soho. He was, by then, 'head over heels in love' with Enid.

Enid wrote to Geoffrey Dawson, Editor of *The Times*, asking him to publish a leading article lamenting Albrecht's recall. And, just before his departure, she hosted a large garden-party in his honour. For eight days, until Albrecht left the country, they were constantly in each other's thoughts or company. On the day of departure Enid drove him to Folkestone. There they were able to spend a few last moments together embracing. Albrecht later wrote to her that those 'last minutes . . . made me feel that we do belong to one another a bit and the parting kiss !' Philosophical as ever, he was already planning how soon he could return and, more importantly, when she could come over and stay with him again. 'What a friend you have been, and *will* be,' he told her.

The months after Bernstorff's departure were among the lowest in Enid's life. At home Richard was causing her deep anxieties. He seemed very different from her three other children, and yet she was convinced he was 'queerly clever'. Doctors diagnosed a problem of incoordination and suggested a variety of old-fashioned treatments which the elderly Nurse Hull fell in with to little avail. In this matter Roderick was of no comfort whatsoever to his wife or to his son. An enthusiastic young nanny, who had originally come as a temporary in 1930, but had stayed until 1933, brought far more fun into the children's nursery. But now she was leaving to be married. 'She has become . . . the backbone of my country home and a bulwark to me. How we shall carry on without her I can't think.' However, Nurse Brighty badly wanted to keep Richard for as long as it proved possible in her own new home, and Enid, realizing that this was where he seemed happiest, agreed. 'She has been, and is eager still to be Richard's salvation.' The admission of failure with one of her children implied in letting him go, made this a most difficult decision. It was especially painful because only a few months before she had despatched her first son Timothy to boarding-school in Oxford. She never forgot the look on his face as they parted on the station and felt a little bit of him was lost to her for ever after.

The absence of two children, as well as Albrecht, preyed on her mind. She had not published anything for years, and toyed with the idea of writing a play about Bernstorff. In a rough sketch she pencilled the following :

'"Is it the *German* you want in me?"

'(Kindly, lyingly) "No – No – the man. (But it *was* the German.)"'

She aimed in these scenes at contrasting the creative mind (herself) with the non-creative (Bernstorff) 'filled with images of lust – wine – content – desire –

snobbery – kindness'. From these notes, it might appear that the self-restraint with Bernstorff was not merely physical. She felt herself as an 'artist' his superior and therefore believed her vision of world events to be broad, creative, imaginative; his – narrow, liberal, intellectual. Thus she refused to be swayed by him. She enjoyed his company, was flattered by his attentions but also, according to these notes, was apparently aware of the ambivalent nature of his sexuality.

Enid felt desperately alone and a failure in 1933. Donald Strathcona, 'my Scottish Laird', was paying her some attention. They often went riding across the Downs together and he gave her lavish presents, including a very special Leica camera, then unknown in England, to replace her old box Brownie. She recognized unequivocally that Roderick gave her considerable independence. 'Has any other husband ever welcomed his wife home with such a letter when he knows she comes straight from the arms of the noble Lord? It is true I come straight from his arms . . . but, Oh Roderick, they mean nothing to me . . . even when I kiss him I am just play-acting to gain time to feel and I don't feel. Perhaps it will come.'

If Strathcona, sometimes accompanied by his wife Diana, was her only diversion, Roderick was scarcely without young female company. The children, now old enough to notice the weekend arrangements, began calling the girls who were invited to stay, 'Daddy's little bits'. These girls were the recipients of Roderick's flowers or affections at various times. Among their number was the beguilingly pretty Jeanne Stourton, who in 1938 married Lord Camoys.

Cecile Dechaume, the music student daughter of the French portrait painter, Charles Geoffroy-Dechaume, was both talented and beautiful, but not yet twenty. Enid encouraged the friendship and bought her a magnificent silver dress to wear out for dinner with them in Paris. But Cecile, as Enid knew, was too spirited to experience real affection for a fifty-five-year-old. When Enid returned from a pleasant evening with the Austrian Ambassador, Baron Franckenstein, she sat at her typewriter and wrote Roderick a note: 'Twenty to two a.m. Married life has a lot of charm. Don't forget that, when you feel depressed about Cecile. . . . I can only tell you that I am devastated at finding you asleep. I feel lonely beyond words.'

Many were the bedtime notes, pushed under his door or left on his breakfast tray, that she wrote him in this vein. On 31 July 1933, at seven minutes to one, she pencilled: 'Oh you're asleep, it's desolating. It is the most chilly, unsociable thing in the world to run upstairs and find you asleep. I feel I can hardly go to bed.' But if Roderick had no one to cherish him he was irritable and depressed and life was difficult for Enid. So much so that in one note she wrote: 'How I wish you could have a *Mary* over again.'

Also by 1933 she was no longer able to see Harold Waller regularly. He had accepted a new job in London's East End which meant that he had less and less time for his private work, including the Babies Club. 'I hope you will get a far better doctor, but I hope you won't ever like him very much.' His departure tempted Enid to leave the 'damned old Babies Club' and she agonized over this during much of 1933. It was no use, she explained, telling her she ought to care for the Babies Club because it does good to humanity, as she was not made like that. 'You can use me for its objectives by inspiring me through individuals but that's the most you can do to me.' But Dr Waller persuaded her to stay. He was not, after all, deserting the club completely himself. 'Oh what a dear you are, and what a lovely thing to have you there in life to pull me straight – bless you!' Enid wrote.

By the late summer her distress manifested itself in an acute rash on her face. The red patches, swollen and itchy by turn, spread down her neck and, too embarrassed to see anyone, she told her friends she had a bad case of nettle-rash. Now as she went to bed – 'a dismal sight just doctored for the night with ichthyol' – she felt she had little physical appeal in any case for Roderick. On 9 October 1933, she went into a nursing home for a complete rest. Although she told Roderick he was making 'that beastly face *so* much easier for me by your sweetness about it and by your concern', at the same time, in a long letter from the hospital, she told him that she could not live without his good opinion, 'and I seem to have lost it. What you feel is ... she's a bad housewife because she pretends to be a writer and as a writer she produces nothing. So she *is* nothing. Charlotte Brontë had at least written *Jane Eyre* and *Shirley* before she married Mr Nichols and went and did the dirty on him by dying in childbirth. But I've died in housebirth and done the dirty on you and have only three inferior books to show for it. . . . I suppose I ought never to have married. But I did so want to be loved and have children.'

The rest cure had little effect nor did the remedy suggested by another specialist. Believing the rash to be the effect of light on her skin, he advised her to wear scarlet – she bought a scarlet skirt, a lined scarlet hat, a scarlet sunshade and wore them (in conjunction with taking arsenic as prescribed) for six weeks. Her troubles were too deep. But she promised Roderick she would try harder with the housework in future. 'As it seems I can't write I may as well not make a muddle of both.' She also ordered some new outfits with matching veils and 'I am preparing to launch myself veiled on society.'

The autumn of 1933 she went out but little, preferring to lie at home and ruminate over world politics. She read Vernon Bartlett's book *Nazi Germany Explained* and was enthralled. 'It has arrived by reason at the things I have only arrived at by jumps and by the back of my mind.' She wrote congratulating Mr Bartlett and explaining that, since her own article, her views on Germany had developed further. 'I am aware of the "dictatorship longing" coming over me. (I don't of course, want it for myself, but for everybody else!) I'm not at all sure it isn't a kind of hunting for God.' So impressed was she with Bartlett's thesis that she sent it, as well as another book which she admitted showed the 'half-mad side of Germany', to Ralph, then serving in Hong Kong, as his Christmas present that year. A few months later she contemplated joining the Blackshirts in England. 'Those who joined the Nazis early got preferment later! Now's the moment. It's just going to be the thing . . .' she wrote to Roderick, asking what he thought. One of the reasons she gave him for wanting to join was that 'it would be so riling for Wells'. Not sufficient reason, she realized on reflection, for such a dramatic step.

She tried to harden herself to the effect of her veiled appearance on other people but frankly considered she had a face 'painted like a drunken clown at the circus'. Arriving at Timothy's boarding-school to take him out was such an ordeal that she hid in the car and sent Roderick to fetch him. In November, H. G. Wells gave a dinner-party, apparently intending to announce his engagement to Moura Budberg, an event which, to the surprise of few, did not materialize. Harold Nicolson wrote in his diary: 'And there was Enid Jones, who had an outbreak on her face and arrived veiled like the Begum of Bhopal.' Not surprisingly, she preferred to stay at home.

Albrecht was deeply worried about her. Convinced there was nothing physically wrong, he believed that hers was a case not for dermatology but for psychoanalysis; 'that some internal mental conflict (to put it crudely) is reacting on your skin and it is typical of such cases that it should affect the skin of your face.' He urged her to visit a recommended psychoanalyst in London. However, priding herself always on her openness and lack of neuroses she took no more notice of his medical advice than she did of his political intuition. Their relationship, mostly conducted by letter, but interspersed with trips to England, grew strained. 'Darling, have you given me up because I can't be enthusiastic about Hitler? If you wish to keep me with all my faults I am only too glad to remain your – friend. Though one day I should like to be that in a fuller sense.' Enid had no intention of acceding to Albrecht's desires. She had seen Neale 'shivering and longing' before a dinner date, expecting more than she was prepared to give. Albrecht, with his homosexual reputation, might have appeared a safer companion, yet now he too wanted more than friendship. Enid resisted only partly because of Roderick's insistence. A much stronger impulse was her own disinclination towards sex. Holding hands and kissing was fine, but she saw little prospect of pleasure for her in anything more. 'Only negresses have orgasms,' she once instructed her son, when the subject of sex arose. Enid indulged in affairs to satisfy her romantic, not her carnal, desires.

Early in 1934, her rash cleared up, temporarily, of its own accord. In February, Roderick and Enid went to New York for a few days, a trip which, although short, prompted her to make a will. She had many unfinished literary fragments, some of which she thought might be publishable and asked that these be shown to Desmond MacCarthy, Vita and Harold Nicolson and Virginia Woolf. 'Perhaps as Desmond has known me for twenty years, he can paint some kind of portrait of me so that I can feel that in some way I am caught together and tied up in a not inelegant parcel.' A few weeks later, the whole family, minus Richard who was still with Brighty, went on their annual skiing holiday to St Anton.

She now felt able to resume her social life and in March attended a boasting party, a small Chelsea gathering hosted by Logan Pearsall Smith. According to the minutes, Lady Jones made several boasts. One referred to a remarkable poem she had written aged sixteen, another declared she had been twice picked up by the late Duke of Rutland, a third that Howard Spring once described a book of hers as having been written by a 'licentious and libidinous old man'. Above all she could swank that 'she was so rich she put 3d. instead of 1½d. on her letters'.

For at least a year, Donald Strathcona had been pressing her to spend a holiday with him at his home on the Island of Colonsay, near Oban in the Scottish highlands. He painted her a tempting picture of life aboard his yacht there, promising her peace and quiet to do some writing. 'How easy it is to be happy up here. . . . Take care of your splendid and angelic self and don't curse the day when you first met this dull old dog.' In May 1934 she accepted, Roderick's attentions being happily engrossed elsewhere.

Later that summer, Albrecht came over. Although their views were as far apart as ever, she loved his wit that ensured 'every meal was a party' as his huge frame sank into a chair, his worldly-wise observation and, above all, his steady devotion to her. He understood her motives and her complexities and he was patient with her. It was the affection, the being fond of, that she needed more than sex, and which he offered her. She wrote, albeit with her husband in mind, 'When I look back on the paint of sex, the love like a wild fox so ready to bite, the antagonism that sits like a twin beside love, and contrast it with affection, so deeply unrepeatable, of two people who have lived a life together and of whom one must die, it's the affection I find richer. It's that I would have again. Not all those doubtful rainbow colours.'

ELEVEN

The Absolute First-Hand Vision of Things

THE family scrap-books, or 'baby books', assiduously maintained by Enid since marriage, detailed all the major and minor Jones' achievements. Sometimes she relied on newspaper cuttings but often she wrote a short account of the occurrence herself. Acute fear of death increased her belief in the importance of posterity and so Enid, the original 'Recording Angel', preserved first letters, first drawings, first sayings, first locks of hair along with school reports, height and weight charts and every other aspect of her children's progress. From 1930 onwards, the baby books are suddenly full of horse affairs – pictures of the children riding, accounts of gymkhanas or newspaper tables of prizewinners.

Laurian, by the age of nine, was an accomplished rider. 'Her ambition is to own a livery stable and to walk about in riding breeches with her hands in pockets,' Enid told Tanta, a few months before buying Laurian her first pony, Jim. That summer, Laurian won a cup at the Rottingdean Gymkhana, where trophies were presented by 'Lady Roderick Jones'. The following year the Joneses acquired five more horses: Tom Brown for Timothy, Sir John for Roderick, and The Pie for Enid as well as Jennifer and Dartmoor, a two-year-old unbroken filly bought for forty shillings at the Princetown Pony Fair, which Laurian broke in herself. They were kept in some of the fourteen dilapidated loose boxes next to the field at the back of North End House. More than a century old, the stables had stood idle since the Joneses had bought the house.

That the Jones children entered the Sussex gymkhana scene in the early 1930s with such a burst of determination and drive owed much to the efforts of a strong-minded personality, one Bernard McHardy. McHardy, with his slight build, curly red hair and leathered face, looked every inch the former steeplechase jockey he was. But he had given up professional riding by the time he came to Rottingdean unemployed and hoping to find work among the still plentiful racing stables and livery owners of the village. He stayed longer than he might have done because he fell in love with a pretty local girl, Isabelle Sandever. At seventeen, she was ten years his junior. McHardy was a devout Catholic and usually went home every summer to the remote Caldy Island, off the coast of Wales, where his family ran a farm for a group of Benedictine monks. But one summer, to be near Isabelle, he stayed in Sussex and found a job teaching the Asquith children to ride. General Arthur and Mrs Betty Asquith and their four daughters, Mary, Jean, Susan and Christine, had, since 1928, taken a house on Rottingdean Green for the summer months : Kipling's former residence, The Elms, which now belonged to the Joneses. The Asquiths introduced the Joneses to riding as Jean, Sue and Laurian became immediate, close friends.

McHardy's unusual blend of romance, religion and toughness captivated Enid and worked on her imagination. She wanted him both as a teacher for her children and as a character in a story, for there was an air of mystery about McHardy. Enid knew about the yellowing newspaper cutting showing a horse falling under its rider which McHardy carried around with him. She, believing he had lost his nerve after a dramatic fall in an important race in Belgium, invented a glorious past for him. But Isabelle maintains his racing career had been a much more humdrum affair with no dramatic falls or loss of nerve. McHardy slept for a time in a small workshop at the back of the Asquiths' garage; according to Enid, 'he was for a time a tramp. . . . I found he was sleeping in a cupboard off the garage on a cement floor'. At all events, she offered him a small sum to be their groom, which he accepted, and from then on he slept in one of the loose boxes at the end of their garden which had been used to house the straw. With few modifications, this remained his home for the next ten years. Laurian worshipped McHardy. Soon she and Timothy were regularly winning cups and rosettes in gymkhanas from Devonshire to Richmond. The 'establishment' was increased to thirteen horses as McHardy 'invented us as a horsebox family and through delirious summers we trailed after success'. Neither Richard nor Dominick ('Tucker') cared much for riding. But 'the management' (Laurian and McHardy) forced five-year-old Tucker 'like a child actor on to our stage'.

McHardy taught the children not only how to ride but also how to win : a competitor about to overtake was to be given a quick jab in the horse's ribs. He gleefully shared his horse knowledge with Enid and she devoured it. A story she often told against herself well illustrates her recognition of the debt she owed him. Enid was convinced that one of her mares was in foal but McHardy insisted she was not. Both agreed to ask Mrs Asquith 'because she's a real lady. McHardy knows I'm an upstart where horses are concerned.' She knew, too, that McHardy was 'more important than the governess, more important than a mother', a generously painful admission for Enid. She had developed a particularly tight bond with Laurian and was, to an extent, living vicariously through her. 'Oh what a strange thing it is to have a second life and second girlhood for me,' she once wrote to Marthe Bibesco. On summer evenings Laurian would be summoned, while happily playing in The Elms' garden with the Asquiths, to chat to her mother in her bath.

Enid hoped very much to be able to influence her only daughter. Although she experimented with a variety of educational establishments for Laurian, her willingness to abandon formal education was evident. It stemmed partly from a vague belief that a narrow system of exams and tests might impede the flowering of any artistic talents. Even reading, Enid believed, might stunt the girl's natural imagination, a view to which one governess took the strongest exception. Enid often discussed 'the vexed question of education' with Betty Asquith as her girls and Laurian sometimes shared lessons during the summer. During the winter months, when they went up to London, the schooling problem was exacerbated. In November 1930, she decided to take both Laurian and Timothy away from their school 'because it is so stuffy. That William the Conqueror was 1066 (I hope this is right) . . . we can't expect to teach them more than this in these wretched little schools that are opened in converted concrete houses in London. . . . I don't really know what to do . . . what I have is outlined in my mind so flimsily that the children will probably not be educated at all and then I shall be sorry.'

But Laurian's increased attachment to McHardy aroused Enid's occasional jealousy. When Laurian hit her head on a rock while swimming, she went to him first for help. Another time, the children decided to have a midnight picnic in The Elms' garden and invited McHardy. But the next day Laurian's conscience pricked and she told her mother, who was furious. 'Like an old-time nanny he was beginning to edge me out. He stopped consulting me. I was to have the trouble without the interest.'

However, Enid regained the interest and the gymkhana life made her happier than she had been for ages. She even cancelled a cocktail party for which the invitations had already been sent as it interfered with riding arrangements. It was a big troupe that set off for gymkhanas: Enid, Betty, McHardy, sometimes Isabelle and all the young. Watching her children perform and win was, for Enid, almost a spiritual excitement that brought her closer than anything else to religious fervour.

These horses . . . these children, this toil and fun of it all [she wrote to Betty]. The chat about 'straight shoulders' and the gossip about 'square quarters', the small profit and extreme loss account at the gymkhanas, the grappling with the horses, divorced from the ritual of grooms – which is our luck and joy. All this is yours and mine and most people don't taste it in the same way. . . . How right I am to write a book about 'girls and horses'. Only you and I really know them as a collaboration.

By the summer and autumn of 1934, Enid was, at last, utterly engrossed in this new subject. It would probably have remained an elegantly written, if rather dry discussion of the female–equine relationship, had not a chance remark from Geoffrey Eastwood set her thinking on a different track. He asked at lunch one day if she still had 'that terrible piebald that jumps everything'. When Enid said yes, he told her she should 'stick it in the new book and jolly well make it win the Grand National'. It was almost as if the words, so quickly spoken, had a magical effect of lifting the book into literature. Enid knew that her intense preoccupation with stable life was vivid to her. But until this remark she was writing without a purpose; now the images at the back of her mind moved to the front. They began to speak as one scene after another super-imposed itself on her mind, all rushing towards the race itself as the dramatic climax. 'I was fascinated by the idea of extreme notoriety applied to a very pure person, a child in fact, who neither sought it, barely recognized it, and certainly made no capital out of it.' Thus the documentary for adults was transformed into fiction for adolescents although Enid always clung to her belief that the short-lived drama of the book was less important than the sustained relationships of the girl with her horse and family. She would often inscribe copies of the book with: 'This is a book for grown-ups not children', an endorsement easier to maintain in the 1930s atmosphere of sheltered adult fiction, than now.

The story of *National Velvet* has today passed into folklore. How Velvet Brown, the youngest daughter of a country butcher, wins a horse in a raffle for a shilling, which turns out to be a natural jumper. How the horse, called The Pie, is entered for the race by paying a hundred gold sovereigns that Mrs Brown had won in her youth for swimming the Channel. How Mi Taylor, her father's assistant, trains her for the race and takes her to Aintree disguised as a foreign jockey, James Tasky. How Velvet and The Pie win – because it is their to-getherness that matters – only to be disqualified as she falls with exhaustion after the race and the organizers discover that she is a girl. In spite of all the excitement the book ends on a moralistic downbeat – life must carry on. 'But the achievement remained; Velvet had shone a wonder, a glory, a miracle child – but she was now able to get on quietly to her next adventures.'

National Velvet offered a hymn of praise to the enduring qualities of middle-class family life. The quintessentially English, Brown family, rooted in the Sussex countryside, consisted of four girls and a boy: Edwina, seventeen, Malvolia, sixteen, Meredith, fifteen, 'all exactly alike like golden greyhounds', and Velvet, the youngest, at fourteen. 'Velvet had short, pale hair, large protruding teeth, a sweet smile and a mouthful of metal.' The youngest child, four-year-old Donald, who accumulated spit in a bottle, was Enid's own son,

Dominick. As any youngest child, he was allowed privileges unthinkable in his older siblings. Mr Brown was a quiet, unassuming man who worked hard at his business and disliked the idea of his children having horses because of the cost. Matriarch of the family was Mrs Brown, an enormous woman whom Velvet loved and admired and whose approbation Velvet would always seek. She was

solid and silent. She did not talk much, but managed the till down at the shop in the street. She knew all about courage and endurance to the last ounce of strength from the first swallow of overcome timidity. She valued and appraised each daughter, she knew what each daughter could do. She was glad too that her daughters were not boys because she could not understand the courage of men, but only the courage of women. Mr Brown was with dignity the head of the family, but Mrs Brown was the standard of the family.

Although the book was dedicated to and inspired by Laurian, she was not the model for the heroine. Enid's own girlhood – her keenness for riding forced to find its outlet in racing paper horses and pulling on makeshift reins while in bed – was still vivid to her. And as she grew up, the passionate will to succeed had not abated. This was the essence of Velvet. In addition, Jean Asquith lent other shades to the portrait of Velvet and her three sisters provided inspiration for the Brown sisters.

But, as was clear to anyone who lived in the neighbourhood, in creating the Browns Enid had borrowed freely from the local butcher's family, the Hilders. The Hilders, of old Sussex stock, and their four daughters fascinated Enid. She had written of them years earlier in her diary as the 'belles of the village' and originally called the story 'The Slaughterer's Daughter'. It was not simply the physical attributes of the girls but the very Englishness of the whole family which gripped Enid's imagination and enabled her to breathe life into every detail of the humble cottage existence she created for them. Although Mrs Hilder may have assumed that Mrs Brown was an altogether unflattering caricature of herself, she should not have overlooked the fact that Enid was also trying to portray something of her own nature. It was not an entirely successful attempt – Enid in 1934 still had more feminine allure than she allowed for. But the way she saw herself in relation to the rest of the family is revealingly accurate. Roderick was at this time little more than a remote figure-head to the children and, strict though she was, her children always considered her the source of family fun.

Thus inspired, Enid could write at great speed. She was determined that everything in this dream story be absolutely accurate, and, in addition to checking regularly with McHardy, made a careful study of the Jockey Club Rules and went to the Liverpool Autumn Meeting at Aintree. That day she did exactly as Mi did in the book; she started from Becher's Brook at a jog trot, saw them come over, started back again, running slowly and got back just after the win when the horses were galloping past the post.

Christmas 1934, the Joneses spent quietly at home. Cecile Dechaume and Geoffrey Eastwood were staying, but Enid worked when she could. By the first week of January, she was able to send to Heinemann all the proofs of *Alexander of Asia*, her translation which she had finally completed after sixteen years, as well as her manuscript of *National Velvet*. Laurian, then thirteen, had again illustrated this and Enid was particularly proud of her simple line drawings which, much to the anguish of some future publishers, she always considered an intrinsic part of the work. Anything more would, in Enid's opinion, have turned it into the children's book which, she insisted, it was not.

Enid was pleased with the finished work, not in a conceited way because she admired her own style, but because she knew she had captured the atmosphere of stable and garden that meant so much to her and the Jones children in the summers of the early 1930s.

It was that special atmosphere which trembled and blew its way into *National Velvet* even though the places and persons had become in some unsought manner altered and superimposed. When the book was finished I knew I had caught something back out of the passage of time at least for our family. . . . And if the book is liked I dare say it is because it was done so intensely for ourselves.

By the time she sailed for South Africa with Roderick, Laurian and Timothy on 18 January 1935, she considered 'everything has been sorted out – cover, adverts, contracts with Heinemann'. She had new photographs taken for the publicity which show her unsmilingly poised, almost hard, wearing a black hat and coat. There were even some tentative approaches from film companies but Enid did not entertain any real hopes of reaching agreement as she was insisting on retaining a hand in the writing of the scenario and the final direction. 'Awful terms and no film company is likely to agree without a struggle.' At all events she had decided to hand the matter over to Harold Freedman, 'the ablest agent I know', with whom she had corresponded over *Serena Blandish* but had not yet met. He could, she thought, do well for her in England even though he was based in New York. Her principal concern on her departure was, however, once again her teeth; one of her lower molars had broken the week before and was to cause her 'fiendish pain' throughout the holiday.

By the time she returned in April, *National Velvet*, her first novel in ten years, had been published in England to immediate acclaim. In the United States, Thayer Hobson, Chairman of William Morrow, had taken it rather reluctantly. He told Enid, when he visited her in hospital where she was recovering from appendicitis, that he did not foresee the story selling well in

America. 'It is charmingly written in its way and one of the pleasures we publishers sometimes afford ourselves is to be able to publish an unfinancial bit of writing' – words which did not endear him to Enid. But Charles Evans believed in the book, considered the descriptions brilliant and persuaded Hobson to back a hunch. It was selected as Book of the Month in England that April and in America that May. Several film companies were now showing keen interest in *National Velvet*. Pandro S. Berman, then a producer at RKO studios, thought the role of Velvet would be perfect for Katharine Hepburn. Universal were enthusiastic too but Paramount made Enid the best offer and a contract was signed in June 1935 with an outright payment of $40,000.

In spite of their urgency to sign the contract, Paramount then hung fire. Whenever Enid wrote asking them what was happening they told her preparations were coming along. The major difficulty was in casting Velvet. The role had to be played by a child who was genuinely fond of horses, expert at riding, spoke with an English accent and had, what the studios termed, 'star quality'. In the first few months Paramount's favourite was Lesley Ruth Howard, the thirteen-year-old daughter of Leslie Howard – but in the next eleven years before the dream was finally turned into celluloid, thousands of young girls were considered for the part that began to gain a reputation as the 'role in a million'.

The reviewers praised *National Velvet* unstintingly. Raymond Mortimer thought it 'one of the jolliest, raciest books I have read in years – a novel calculated to sell by the ton and, at the same time, likely to be gobbled up by the most fastidious'. Hugh Walpole wrote : 'I haven't the least idea what genius is and it is a word one is chary of using, but Miss Bagnold has something that belongs to genius – the absolute first-hand vision of things.'

In Rottingdean itself, however, the reception was rather different. The Jones family had never become fully integrated into the life of the seaside village and Enid was always wary of the 'half-acid half-affectionate nature of the village gossip'. Locals considered the Joneses rich, new arrivals from London and could not fail to notice the fleet of large cars (they had a Buick, a Rolls Royce and a Dodge) that regularly brought down important guests, for there were parties most weekends during these years. Several of the maids lower down the hierarchy were local girls who gossiped about the 'goings on' and Enid herself felt some ambivalence towards the weekends full of people. She sometimes ordered thirty-six Sunday newspapers so that her guests would occupy themselves silently for longer in the morning. She hated all the preparations required 'and the moment they are gathered together in the garden-room I slink out if possible, murmuring something under my breath as though I had been called on a message and go and dig in the field.'

Many of the Joneses' habits, although unexceptional by London standards, were considered unnecessarily ostentatious in Rottingdean : Roderick liked to have McHardy stand outside the parish church with a horse saddled and waiting immediately after the Sunday service. The children with their governess and string of ponies were not village children. By making the Browns a butcher's family it was not difficult to identify them with the Hilders. Everyone in the village knew that Mrs Hilder had been an exceptionally good swimmer in her day. She was deeply wounded by Enid's fictional portrayal of her as a bossy, over-large matron. She barely knew Lady Jones who, she felt, had not had the decency to talk to her in advance of her plans for fictionalizing the family ; she did not consider they were, as Raymond Mortimer had commented, lower middle class. Perhaps what rankled most of all was that Enid did not even buy her meat from them.

Admiral Langford-Clarke, the Joneses' nextdoor neighbour, taking the honour of the village upon himself, sprang to the Hilders' defence. Trust had been betrayed. He told Mrs Hilder he would go immediately to Bacon's book shop and demand that the volume be removed from the window display. Whether his will prevailed, history does not relate, but the reverberations rumbled on for years and Enid's estrangement from village life, already noticeable, grew more acute.

As the excitement from the success of *National Velvet* died down Enid once again took up the domestic mantle. And in the summer of 1935, her skin rash returned. Again doctors were at a loss either to diagnose a cause or prescribe a cure. But a holiday alone was assumed to be helpful. Her friend Ruth Monk Bretton, now widowed, was called upon again to accompany her to France to the village of Clos Norman. Heat, sun, wild strawberries and cheap red wine made the rash marginally better but did not cure it. Perhaps Enid did not know herself, or was too proud to confide in Ruth, but her friend guessed that Enid was not happy about her arrangements at home. Enid could not endure Roderick's displeasure. Sometimes she needed to be apart from him because the weight of his want of praise made her, literally, ill. Ruth, in any case, once again had to return early, this time with stomach trouble. Enid cabled home 'face worse, useless staying unable resist catching midday train today'. She had been planning to see Neale in Paris but did not feel up to it and asked Roderick not to tell him she was passing through. The rash came and went during the rest of the summer. In October she went again to France, staying this time at Figeac. 'I go through horrors of depression but just now, after your telegram, feel much calmer. In this hotel I feel protected,' she cabled Roderick. For her birthday later that month she told him not to bother about a present for her 'unless it be a new face'. But this time Enid did meet Randall Neale in Paris, the one enjoyable evening of the trip. Roderick in between dinners at the Ritz and dancing at Quaglinos, told Enid he was glad the Paris evening 'was a success – without violation'. She also did some shopping in Paris – six hats – which provoked Albrecht to comment wrily, that he knew now why he would always remain a bachelor.

In the autumn of 1935, Enid's social life centred on Donald Strathcona. 'Kind old Donald but . . . I feel unkind in saying tedious,' when what she wanted was her husband. 'The worst thing is, I'm not sleeping in your bedroom,' she told Roderick in a note after an evening with Donald. 'Somehow that terrible visit to France made me know more than ever how welcoming and warm and loving you are.' Roderick was not always available to his wife because, following the fashion in highest society, he had become infatuated with an American divorcee. Enid greatly disapproved of Mrs Lois Russell, but knew how 'common' it was to mind. 'Lois is very charming and when I insidiously say she isn't, it's only because I'm jealous.' Placating his wife, Roderick had always insisted that Enid was the only one he really cared for. 'Whatever bye-paths we may tread, on occasion with him, on occasion with her, our main march into the future together is never fundamentally for one moment in question. For myself I cannot envisage life without you.' Gradually she came to terms with her husband's new companion as Roderick's liaison continued throughout 1936. Struggling to put her love for her husband above such vicissitudes, the notes she wrote him when she returned from dinner out were courageous. 'I do hope, hope all will go well with Lois at Quaglinos. I do want you to have all the happiness there is. I love you.' By December she felt able to write 'A Happy New Year my darling. I wish you fidelity with exquisite mitigations.' In a play Laurian was to write, with Enid's guidance, about the weekend parties at North End House,* Mrs Russell becomes Mrs Lois Harmer, 'a pretty little thing who used to work in a teashop'. Even Sir Thomas, the character based on Roderick, comments about her: 'It's one thing taking her to dine at The Savoy but it's quite another having her here in my daily life.'

Albrecht was still in Enid's thoughts, but not in her daily life. As was plain whenever he visited England, usually staying with the Joneses, their views diverged ever more. He wrote: 'I only hope I have not annoyed you by losing my temper over politics. If so, it will only indicate to you the tension in which everyone lives and which is such a contrast to the lovely English landscape.'

Before leaving England he had introduced Enid and Roderick to an up-and-coming German envoy, Joachim von Ribbentrop, then German Disarmament

---

* 'The Long Grass': this never progressed beyond typescript.

Commissioner. But he never hid his scorn for the 'champagne dealer with no qualifications but that he speaks a few languages, which the great Bismarck used to say head-waiters also did.' Enid and Roderick invited Ribbentrop to lunch at Hyde Park Gate and the German made full use of the opportunity to hold forth before influential English people. He stayed until four p.m. When Ribbentrop came again to London, in November 1934, still not with full diplomatic status, they knew that he had been intriguing against Bernstorff in Berlin, causing him personally considerable difficulties. Even though the Joneses found him a bore, he was none the less invited to luncheon for a second time – an invitation which Roderick maintained Ribbentrop himself had asked for to meet the British Foreign Secretary, Austen Chamberlain. The other guests were Margot Asquith (Lady Oxford), Mr and Mrs George Bernard Shaw, the Prince of Hanover, Mrs Richard Guinness, Lady (Helen) Dashwood and Ralph (now Major) Bagnold. Once again the party dragged on until four p.m., with Chamberlain, Shaw and Ribbentrop retiring to a corner of the drawing-room to discourse on world politics.

On 7 March 1936, German soldiers marched into the Rhineland and the ensuing crisis provoked widespread discussion in the press of Germany's internal policies and the sincerity of Hitler's promises. 1936 is often considered a watershed in the thirties: the year when, with hindsight at any rate, the British public became aware of Germany's true intentions. However, on 18 April, Ribbentrop was once again an honoured guest at the Joneses' London home. This occasion caused Roderick some embarrassment even before the dinner as the German Ambassador, Herr von Hoesch, and his wife were also invited. Roderick was well aware that Ribbentrop, if not seated in the place of honour to Enid's right, would cause an unpleasant fuss. But he was below the rank of ambassador. Roderick telephoned the Germany Embassy for guidance and was told by Prince Otto von Bismarck, the Chargé d'Affaires, 'better to ignore diplomatic etiquette rather than upset Herr von Ribbentrop'. Before the end of the meal Ribbentrop began boasting about the Führer's plans and the need to increase Lebensraum. Across the table sat General Freyberg, invited only because his wife Barbara (née Jekyll) was a schoolfriend of Enid's. Freyberg was incensed by the German's speech and began to argue with him. The Germans would never get away with it, he said. A furious slanging match developed with tempers rising on all sides and the party broke up in disorder. Freyberg knew that his hosts were angry with him for his behaviour towards a distinguished foreign guest and Barbara Freyberg was highly embarrassed. Twenty-four hours after the dinner von Hoesch was found dead in sinister circumstances; Ribbentrop then returned to London as his successor.

In June Bernstorff was again able to visit the Joneses and Enid gave a dinner in his honour. For Roderick there was Mrs Anthony Sewell (Mary Lutyens), Miss Jeanne Stourton and Mrs Charles Hoover (Lois Russell); for Enid there was H. G. Wells, Desmond MacCarthy and Lord Strathcona. For politics, Sir Austen and Lady Chamberlain.

By 1936, Enid's performance as a hostess had become critical because Roderick was hoping for a peerage. The submission on Sir Roderick, sent to the relevant authorities, argued

this peerage should not be a decorative appendage to a retiring energy. It should be placed in the active hand of a man who can wield it for Reuters for years to come. . . . The Head of Reuters, in constant negotiation with other countries, sowing debatable ground with the seed of English news *can* say with reason : 'I need this peerage to strengthen my hand and my position.'

There is some evidence to suggest that this line of reasoning was greeted sympathetically in the patronage office and that Sir Roderick was offered a peerage before the year was out. The Asquith family remember that the title Lord Rottingdean was chosen, which gave rise to the quip that he would be 'Lord Rotters of Reuters'. The Jones children and the staff at Reuters were also aware that a peerage had been offered. However, the honour was apparently withdrawn. Quite possibly this was simply because he talked about it before the official announcement was made – a cardinal sin. Or because he was, although slightly, allied to the wrong camp in the abdication crisis of that year. Roderick had met and corresponded with the Prince of Wales (through his private secretary) on more than one occasion in the last few years but was not a friend. However, Jones's deputy and confidant, Bernard Rickatson-Hatt, was closely associated with the 'Bryanston Courterie' of Wallis and Ernest Simpson. By February 1936, Rickatson-Hatt was one of only four people to know that Edward VIII intended to marry Mrs Simpson and that Ernest Simpson would not stand in his way. On 10 December 1936, the King's abdication was announced and Enid, who had spent the evening dining with Randall Neale at the Savoy Grill, then went to see the crowds outside the Palace. It is possible that Rickatson-Hatt's close connection with the Windsor camp soiled the organization he worked for as well as himself in the eyes of the new king. At all events, the hoped-for peerage never materialized.

Early in January the Jones family decamped to Hochsolden in Austria for its annual skiing holiday. Roderick, ill with flu, did not go with them.

TWELVE

Birth with its Horrors and its Beauties

BY 1937 Enid was facing the end of nursery life. Laurian had been sent to the renowned Fraulein Huebler in Vienna. Timothy had won a scholarship to Eton and Richard had gone to a small boarding-school in Kent. Only Dominick was still at home. 'What an empty house this is,' she lamented in a combined letter to her eldest children. Having and nurturing babies had been for Enid a vital confirmation of her femininity. Now almost fifty, she found the acceptance that this part of her life was over cost her some painful soul-searching.

'Am I happy? Oh, quite. But rather lonely without my sense of sex,' she wrote to Marthe Bibesco during a skiing holiday in February. 'I have been so accustomed to letting men be my alcohol. Like Antoine, I treated it a little bit as a spring-board when I wrote. But there. We all have to make quite another picture out of the next thirty years. It's not (I hasten to add, in vanity) that I am *technically* yet at that period but spiritually I am approaching the gates.' Love had always played a more important part in her life than sex and from now on her affairs were with words and ideas. Even so, she began tinting away the grey-haired reminders of her age.

For some years now, at least since the birth of Richard which she had been prepared to face alone, she dreamed of writing a novel that had never before been attempted; a book to glorify a woman's actively creative role as a mother which she felt, after four births, uniquely poised to do. 'You do not know what it is fully to be a woman until you have had at least three children . . . and I am having four,' she told Marthe on the eve of Dominick's birth. She had been making extensive notes of her experiences, thoughts and reactions; now she decided to turn them into her next and, she hoped, her most important work. Gathering and transforming into words a part of her life now over in order to perpetuate the sensations of those years, had already become a hallmark of her writing. The new book was to be unashamedly unacerbic, the collected wisdom of the last fifteen years, a still life of Motherhood. In fact Enid had begun her book about birth several years previously but had put it to one side when *National Velvet* had taken over. Early in 1937 she returned to it. By the spring she was hard at work and cutting back on social life; dinner-parties were 'tiny affairs of only six people . . . and [I] am having no weekends in the way of parties.'

The 'story' begins with the entry of a midwife into a well-to-do country household, teeming with children and servants, about a week before the birth of the fifth child. The husband is absent, on a business trip to India, and from then on the woman in the book is referred to only as 'The Squire'. 'She is rich, strong, fertile and loved woman, with a large domain to rule. The only thing that threatens her happiness is the melancholy of life itself whose vapours she sometimes smells with overpowering strength.' Thus wrote Enid about a character more completely herself than any she had yet created. Her vigour, her determination and pervading sense of healthfulness were conveyed; still it was not the whole Enid, ignoring as it did her feminine charm and wiles. She saw the mother as 'One of those old stable archways with a clock ticking life away in the summit of the arch through which life and her children flow . . . perhaps like an arch over a river, I can get no nearer than that.'

Paradoxically, it was a masculine sort of portrait, and yet men and sex, accepted as necessary for procreation, were purposely eliminated. Everything centres around a small, tightly knit circle of women – the 'English Harem' as she once called it. Men were omitted because Enid had seen clearly during the last fifteen years that 'all the day of a woman's busy family life was made up by herself alone, herself as ruler'. Men are introduced to the book, however, as seen through the eyes of Caroline, the Squire's beautiful friend and neighbour. Caroline is restless and wants to go to her lover in Paris. She arrives one day for lunch to talk about the imbroglio. The Squire listens patiently, 'with her lover in her lap. . . . The complications of love seemed to her indescribably stale, the baby much fresher. Love, love she had heard of love all her life. Every day and every play and every book dealt with it. Every friend went through it. She herself felt like a woman who is old and free.' Caroline was the sort of woman men had in mind in using the term 'woman', but, 'We ought to be called "wumen", some different word. "Wumen" are hard-working, faulty, honest, female males.' There was yet another kind of woman personified in *The Squire* by the midwife. She was gallant and formidable: 'You and those like you have become a third sex.' Enid touched upon, but did not develop in later work, the idea that not all women were motivated by men. 'She' in *The Chinese Prime Minister* is a similarly masculine woman, but not a lesbian. In *The Loved and Envied*, when Cora feels a woman's hand on her thigh, 'she understood a second sex . . . there was room after all for everyone'. Enid often remarked that she would rather see a beautiful woman's face than listen to an intelligent man: 'Isn't that odd and I am not a lesbian.'

Enid was neither old nor free. But, in recognizing that passionate physical affairs were now over for her, she sought the comfort of love elsewhere. 'After forty the sense of beauty grows less acute; one is troubled instead by a vast organ note, a hum of death,' she wrote in *The Squire*. Antoine being the only man she had ever fully loved, the conclusions she drew from the pain of loving him were that, to be in love, it was necessary to suffer. Enid's children, too, having the capacity at least to make her suffer, were recipients of this same great love force. At the same time, writing, which had always been a painful process for her, was, she considered, a little like being in love.

Caroline was undoubtedly suffering in her love affair. The character of Caroline was largely inspired by Enid's friend, Cynthia Asquith. Cynthia, 'with her chestnut Romney loveliness', was not only beautiful but coolly aristocratic. Daughter of the 11th Earl of Wemyss, married to the son of the former prime minister, she had sat to the finest painters of her day including (as a child) Sir Edward Burne-Jones, John Singer Sargent, Ambrose McEvoy and Augustus John. She had slipped into writing by offering advice to mothers in *The Times* and becoming secretary to J.M.Barrie (although she could neither type nor take shorthand). Enid had met her through Antoine, in 1918, but they became friends later. One summer, Cynthia and her two sons, Michael and Simon, had taken a small house in neighbouring Peacehaven. Enid and Cynthia walked together one evening and then sat gossiping in the airy garden-room of North End House. 'You said, sitting on the sofa, "I couldn't do without love." By which you meant "in love". You said that sentence. And from that sentence, which I never forgot, for it rang a bell in me, I evolved the love-woman in *The Squire*.'

Caroline is, however, also the Squire at a younger stage – 'That lovely creature is my youth' – but Enid was now making a positive statement rejecting that part of her life. 'When the baby had gone the light went out of the room. The emptied vase which was the mother turned to her visitor. "We two women", thought the Squire, "are of differing sexes, differing planets. She thinks I am a woman, fit to listen to love, but I am a mother, and I have a contempt and a weariness of such childish things."

What the book lacks in construction it makes up in its poetic vision of motherhood. Plotless, it meanders gently along until the reader is brought up sharply by a highly original turn of thought or the acute characterization of the children. Boniface is erratic, intense, single-minded and a portrait of Richard. He was 'red of face, asking no help, intent upon some inner life which would not swim up into his difficult speech. . . . Inarticulate, eccentric, living like a mole in his world, putting into dangerous execution plans for which no one had the key.' But the most telling portrait was that of the midwife, based on

Ethel Raynham Smith. 'I am virginal and narrow but I am his gardener,' she tells the Squire. Raynham Smith, in reality not given to such lyrical expression, was a small, almost frail-looking woman with reddish hair and blue eyes. Her quiet manner belied the intensity of her belief that motherhood was a perfectable science, for she had 'very high ideals about the the creation of a greater and more healthy race', and that the conditions of birth were critical. Enid's intelligence and willingness to follow through these beliefs had endeared her to Ethel Raynham Smith in a way no man ever could.

I have never ceased to love you and often have had a feeling of some mystical rare link with you that will carry on forever [she wrote to Enid]. I have vivid memories of sudden thoughts of yours about which in odd places we have suddenly talked when I have sensed in you something that carries me into the highest realms of experience, things on which I depend and gain spiritually great help. I have never told you this and sometimes I have felt it so powerfully that I have thought you must have felt it too. Do not think you are ever far away from my most everloving thoughts, you never have been.

Enid did to an extent experience the link too ; *The Squire* is testament. 'In me she set up an excitement, an anticipation of the event, a desire to produce a wonderful child that exceeded anything I had ever been told about my private health and private future. Her serene and bright spirit entered my life and, sword in hand, entered my house.'

The book was completed by December 1937 and, for the first time, was to appear initially in America with serialization in *Ladies' Home Journal* preceding publication there by William Morrow. Payment was not a problem, Hobson assured her. After the success of *National Velvet* he promised her 'just about anything you want that won't bankrupt us', but then baulked when she asked for 20 per cent after the first 7,000 copies. A far more serious cause of concern to everyone was the choice of title. Enid had, in an early version, named the heroine Martha and Hobson liked the title 'Squire Martha'.

But Enid was now obstinately opposed to naming the woman as this would spoil the universality of her theme. *Ladies' Home Journal* wished to call it 'Birth' to which Enid also strongly objected as not giving due emphasis to the varied talents required in a mother. She proposed 'Document of Motherhood' which Hobson thought a crib of Vera Brittain's *Testament of Youth*. By February 1938, the matter was threatening to get out of hand with one title for the American serialization, another for the English serialization (*Good Housekeeping* had taken it), a third for Heinemann and a fourth for Morrow. Suddenly Hobson dreamed up 'The Door of Life', a title Enid always hated for its sentimentality. She had written a book with humour, realism and beauty but, deliberately, not a trace anywhere of sentimentality.

The Squire gave it just the hardness she wanted. An earlier idea of Hobson's, 'Born of Woman', she rejected as a 'MAN-made title which reinforced the Madonna idea, from the conception that man had always had about motherhood. The whole book is indeed an effort to get away from the saintliness of motherhood.'

Enid was not shy about trumpeting her high ideas for this book. 'I really think I may say it is the first attempt in a novel to portray the very first moments of [the maternal] relationship in great detail,' she told Mayer Hobson. She wrote these notes for a foreword to a later edition: 'I thought, if I could get it right, they might read it in China and India. . . . I wanted it to be exactly as objective as if a man had had a baby. I wanted to pin down the quality of the pain and of the love and the surprise and the effect of the birth on the mother, on the other children, on the nurse and on the servants. In many ways I think I did get it right.'

The Squire is a unique book. Inevitably, it has an old-fashioned ring to it today. But, in the days before the ubiquitous ante-natal clinic, when all that women could read to allay their fears about pregnancy was Dr Grantly Dick Read's sober *Natural Childbirth* (1933)*, Enid's open discussion of a taboo subject was courageous. She did not deny that there was pain in childbirth. But she knew that if fear of the unknown led to tension and more pain, by understanding the pain – 'swimming with it' – there could be enjoyment of the birth process. This was an advanced notion. It matters neither that the science of obstetrics has made immense progress since 1938, nor that, it must be said, any woman surrounded by such copious domestic help would relish an opportunity for the philosophical contemplations of birth and its corollary, death. Few women today can reasonably expect that kind of cushion. But, if the paraphernalia of the birth are removed, and the events of the novel seen as in a time capsule, the emotions expressed are universal.

Her mind went down and lived in her body, ran out of her brain and lived in her flesh. She had eyes and nose and ears and senses in her body, in her backbone, living like a spiny woodlouse, doubled in a ball, having no beginning and no end. Now the first twisting spate of pain began. Swim then, swim with it for your life. If you resist, horror, and impediment! If you swim, not pain but sensation! . . . Keep abreast of it, rush together, you and the violence which is also you! Wild movements, hallucinated swimming! Other things exist than pain!

Few mothers would not be moved by such intensity of feeling.

Consumed as she was by her own perception of the importance of this book, she considered the title and jacket critical in conveying the right impression.

---

* Dick Read's most famous book, *Childbirth Without Fear*, was not published until 1944.

From the outset she was terrified lest Morrow might make a 'drawing of a pram in green' for the cover, and the book emphatically was 'nothing to do with babies in the ordinary sense'. It was a book about a mother – a book about herself. It was always the book she felt expressed herself best and the one she gave first to new friends.

By May 1938, Hobson was growing exasperated with her. She was delaying returning the corrected galley proofs, pleading that she was too busy, and she complained about the final jacket when it was too late to change. 'Frankly, I don't like your ideas for the tree of life sort of thing,' he informed her curtly. Everyone knew her by now as the author of *Serena Blandish* but she refused Hobson permission to mention this in the promotional material. As if this were not enough, the dedication she wanted, 'For the Babies Club', was also causing friction. Hobson considered it too clinical, but eventually agreed to the book being inscribed to Harold Waller MD and Ethel Raynham Smith. She explained to Ethel: 'Would I have dedicated what was most important to me . . . what cost me the greatest number of years to create . . . to you and to Harold . . . would I not rather have dedicated it to the husband who begot the children if I had not felt to the bottom of my soul your importance to me and to my road in life.'

In spite of Enid's strictures, *Ladies' Home Journal* in May 1938 called its extracts 'Birth': 'a drama of passionate motherhood . . . a story no woman who reads can ever forget. Some readers will be startled by the daring of Birth.' A few weeks later, the book itself appeared to almost universally good reviews. *Time and Tide* pronounced it

a really important book, a mark in feminist history as well as a fine literary feat. Here at last is a portrait of a woman in her essentially feminine phase of life and yet neither siren nor appendage. The Squire works at her unceasing material task not with the worried air of the silly conscientious modern mother, but rather with the easy splendour of a tigress lashing her tail to put her cubs through their gymnastic paces.

Forrest Reid, in the *Spectator*, considered that 'in its delicacy and precision it is poetry. This is the kind of writing that really is writing, that lifts fiction on to a plane where it need not fear comparison with any other art.'

That it was a book with greater appeal to women than men went almost without saying. Antoine confided to his family that he could barely struggle to the end of it. But he contained his criticism and told Enid only, 'I have to be frank, I don't like the word "nipple" either spoken or written.' H. G. Wells said the book made him feel 'I'd been attacked by a multitude of many-breasted women (like Diana of Ephesus) and thrown into a washing basket full of used nursery napkins.' Vita, too, was 'frankly shocked at some of your outspokennesses. I belong to the old-fashioned school that thinks a baby should not be mentioned until it is in its cradle.' None the less she complimented Enid on her *tour de force*. Other friends were more positive. Harold Waller told her it was 'the strongest baby you've brought forth'. And Logan Pearsall Smith maintained he was so moved, 'It makes me wish . . . that I had been born of your sex to taste the joys which we men never taste.'

None of the reviewers realized, however, an underlying if subconscious symbolism to the book. This does not, of course, mean that she was writing a political tract; far from it. She was by nature apolitical, but, while brooding about the situation in Europe with the images of birth so freshly in her mind, she was struck by certain parallels. Enid had for some years seen the arguments of the various European countries in terms of squabbling children in a nursery. 'We understand France's fear but can you make nursery rules founded on the neurosis of one unlucky child?' In *The Squire*, she took the simile a stage further. 'Birth is always difficult and ugly. I love to see things born,' she wrote in a series of unpublished notes.

We are afraid of Hitlerism. We see in it retrogression. I see in Nazism birth and all the horrors and beauties in birth. . . . A curious inverted situation has arisen. The intellectuals, who should be the first to spot a birth, in this case watch it with horror. Their horror is natural. The birth has become clouded in brutality. It does not even run in blood, like a revolution, but exists with the narrowness, the restriction, the obstinate totalitarianism frowning weight of the ruler of an armed camp. . . . But they have missed a birth!

Early in 1938 she had visited Paris with Laurian, now sixteen. 'How swimming in happiness Paris was,' she wrote to Antoine. 'Then Hitler took over Austria and I *knew* it was good. And nobody else knew. That made me happy. I knew that we were nearer peace. I am prepared for dictatorships. As a mother whose life is utterly bound up with her children I would submit to a disciplined Europe (and its discomfort) if I could be sure that my children wouldn't be torn up in death or the fear of death.'

In October, just a few weeks after the ceding of Czechoslovakia and the Munich Agreement, Enid delivered Laurian to her first real school, Kurt Hahn's* establishment in Germany. Schloss Salem was a twelfth-century Cistercian monastery where the 134 boys and girls 'all work and play hockey and ride together'. Here, she believed, Laurian would imbibe many of the qualities she admired in Germans. She hoped too that the experience would

---

* Kurt Hahn, the founder of Salem County Educational School, was arrested by the Nazis in March 1933 and came to Britain four months later. He founded Gordonstoun School in Scotland along similar lines to Salem.

'do things to you that are good'. The trip also provided Enid with opportunities to take another first-hand look at Germany and its famed autobahns, and to return via Paris for some hats from Reboux and dresses from Yrande, Molyneux and Schiaparelli. She never intended to examine the political realities of Nazi Germany but was, like any writer, always in search of her own sensations. With her innate curiosity and disdain for the petty, the mean or the common, her inability to see anything much more than a mood in the country is all the more surprising.

Enid wrote quickly, while the impressions were sharp in her mind, a long piece about her experiences in Germany. But this time she had some difficulty in getting it published. Even her friend Geoffrey Dawson of *The Times* baulked. However it finally appeared in the *Sunday Times* on 6 November 1938, under the headline 'In Germany Today – Hitler's New Form of Democracy'. She intended in her introduction to make plain that hers was a virgin mind better able to report impressions because it was uninfluenced by Nazi propaganda. 'I received no propaganda into my mind because I had not the means to receive it,' she wrote. But her next sentence was a gift to the anti-Fascists. She admitted, 'I cannot read the newspapers and, though I speak a little German for the common uses of the day, when I am replied to in German, it immediately gets beyond me.' She also informed her readers : 'I met no single person of importance, or even of the upper classes.'

'Immediately you are in Germany you are aware of a blaze and a bustle of activity and gaiety. Children run about, or wobble on their bicycles, shouting to each other. There is vigour and expectancy on the faces, and friendliness. . . . On all sides was the hand of Gulliver in Europe – giant roads, giant traffic, giant buildings and behind them and working in them, a steady, disciplined people, adoring its leader. . . . Are we then to condone their persecution ?' she asked. 'We shall have to accept them as we have had to accept Abyssinia. So violent an evolution is like an operation. . . . Hitler had decided that the Jews were to be no more than the touch of yeast in the bread. The proportion of yeast in the continental loaf is too old and too strange a problem for English minds.'

Enid may have been well pleased with the metaphor but she came, ultimately, to regret the article. 'Of course I was wrong . . . and afterwards I got obstinate through being hit so hard. What does a bull do ? . . . it gets into a corner and goes moveless and dumb.' She was immediately inundated with letters. Edmund Blunden in *The Fortnightly* praised her for her 'brilliant style and . . . the most evident passion for truth', approbation which, in 1938, placed her perilously near the extreme political right. Enid herself was not part of the vociferous fringe of pro-Hitler Britons – Unity Mitford, Oswald

Mosley, William Joyce; her thinking was closest to what may be called the pro-German faction of the establishment which regarded Continental dictatorships as a force for peace in Europe, whereas France's nerves were a threat to it. But by October 1938, this group was rather thin.

There was, as Enid had predicted, a volley of attacks. Among those who found the article most puzzling were Jewish mothers, who could not make the connection between *The Squire* with its hymn of praise to motherhood and the giving of life, and the destruction of life implicit in the Nazi doctrines. Dame Ethel Smyth, who had entertained such high hopes for Enid after her first book, wrote in the following week's *Sunday Times*: 'It surprises me that so brilliant an intelligence should not remember that, except of course in the case of the very young, behind the "keep smiling" habit lurks a dread spectre – the concentration camp.'

By far the most devastating attack appeared in *Time and Tide* by the Labour Member of Parliament for Nuneaton, Commander R. Fletcher: 'If it makes a German happy to beat up a Jew, and if in turn it makes Miss Bagnold happy to see a German happy on his way home after beating the Jew, well, what is a Jew? Not even a "person of importance or even of the upper classes" while Miss Bagnold is both.' Commander Fletcher went on to point out that Enid Bagnold was also Lady Jones, wife of the Chairman of Reuters. 'Reuters, no doubt, owes much to the ability of those Jews whom the firm employs and may even have some Jewish capital. It is a little incongruous perhaps to owe part of the good things one enjoys in life to Jews while at the same time accepting persecutions as part of the natural order of things for them. I hope those who gather news for Reuters are more accurate observers than the wife of the head of the firm.'

Enid was incensed by his swingeing attack. 'I am fair game; I am a writer. I have my own opinions. I wrote my own article. But Commander Fletcher obliques his attack behind me to my husband,' she replied in *Time and Tide*. She did not attempt to vindicate her views on Germany but rather to refute 'the innuendo that of this rich Jewish tree my husband, a Gentile, caught the plums... in Reuters' critical and dangerous hour... Roderick Jones set about rebuilding the shattered and quaking economic fabric of this great Agency,' Enid maintained.

The rebuttal did her little good and the episode cost her dearly in friendships. Philip Guedalla, the historian, sent her a sarcastic telegram. Leonard and Virginia Woolf had always been slightly standoffish to their would-be friend and Sussex neighbour; henceforth, Leonard in particular mistrusted her. Even Maurice Baring, the distinguished writer and wit, who was by this time a close friend in Rottingdean, chided her gently, suggesting she re-read the story of The Emperor's New Clothes. However, by far the most hurtful attack came from her long-standing friend Violet Bonham-Carter. Insisting that it was not a difference in political outlook that shocked her, Violet wrote: 'What surprised me was that you could write with such irresponsible lightness, almost gaiety, of a situation undermined with human tragedy and horror. You are endowed in a rare degree with perception, sometimes attaining divination, you have imagination, you are before all things, a *human*-being.... Did you imagine anything when last week you read about the expulsion of 20,000 Polish Jews.... All boys over twelve were torn from their mothers and shipped off alone.' Violet cited other instances of Nazi atrocities reported in the British press, before concluding: 'This is the background of the "Jones week in a country town" where "children wobbled on their bicycles", you drove so brightly through.... People put different values on freedom, mercy and humanity – I rate them high – but they, and their converse, must at least be treated seriously.'

Enid told Laurian, miserable and homesick in Germany, that she was having a harrowing week. She recounted the attacks, referring to Fletcher as 'Albrecht's jackal', a rather unfair swipe at her friend given that Albrecht had never lacked the moral courage to tell Enid or high-ranking Nazis the pig-headedness of their views. It was, he told Enid, 'difficult enough to hold one's own against the stream and one is miserable if one's friends don't understand one's position'. As Albrecht was struggling to retain the means of his own survival, Enid wrote him a long letter extolling Hitler for evolving 'a better political and efficiency machine to cope with life in 1938 than we have'. But what was much more important, she told him, 'is your fine and loyal letter. Furious with me but not personally angry and still wanting to defend me if you can.'

She might have defended herself better. By saying 'we shall have to accept' the persecutions there is a temptation, with the benefit of hindsight, to imagine Enid was accepting the systematic extermination of several millions of Jews, but in 1938 she did not know that the concentration camps were also extermination camps. The reports beginning to filter through were usually met with shocked, or occasionally defiant, disbelief. She was saying, however, that the persecutions would have to be accepted, because, she believed, Britain could not prevent them. By mentioning the Abyssinian fiasco she was also reminding her readers of what she saw as the futility of opposition. By today's standards her metaphor appears tasteless, her defeatism heartless, but she belonged to a generation a large part of which, having witnessed the slaughter of the 1914–18 War, had lost its heart for a further war; and she was the mother of three sons. Her latest visit to Germany had served only to confirm her view that Hitler seemed good for that country and would be harmless to Britain if he restricted his territorial aspirations to continental Europe. She was to prove a bad prophet.

In the matter of Germany, Roderick offered her some support. Publicly, his stated aim as head of Reuters was to be seen neither offending nor pandering to any government. Privately, he wrote to Laurian telling her that he envied her growing up in this new and unpredictable world. Enid was always careful to show her pronouncements on Germany to Roderick first, in case they might harm him, and only to send them on for publication if he approved. Roderick, who, as head of Europe's biggest non-governmental source of information, was receiving regular bulletins about life in Nazi Germany, considered the article marvellous: 'Such strong meat that nobody I fear will publish it ... because they have not the courage.' In 1938, Roderick was trying to obtain an interview with Hitler and had written to Ribbentrop suggesting that he might 'send to Germany one of my most trusted representatives to interview the Führer or to receive a statement from him and then to render the Reuter organization available for its distribution all over the world'. Ribbentrop refused, the moment not being 'appropriate', he said. In his autobiography, explaining why he turned down opportunities to meet Hitler, Roderick commented, 'Others had been to Berlin or Nuremburg as the guests of Hitler or his entourage; but they were for the most part not under the same necessity as I considered myself to be to keep myself and Reuters no less aloof from possible entanglements whether with Nazism or with any other ism.'

Laurian hated her German experience and begged to be allowed home but, consistent above all else, discipline for Europe and discipline for the Jones family were Enid's maxims for 1938. 'It's a question of learning to be doggedly brave as well as passionately brave ... the difference between bearing sharp pain and death danger, and bearing sickness and tedium.' The pain, Enid reminded her daughter, was just as she had described it in *The Squire*. She had to 'turn to the school and swim in it ... instead of living every second at home. If you live like that, Time won't pass. ... You must show courage over this. What's the good (at least I feel tremendously about this ... in all my relationships with people) of brains, taste, self-analysis, understanding, if you haven't courage. It's almost the most important thing in life.' And then, she asked Laurian, what would everybody think? 'Not only the disgrace from every point of view and from your own of bringing you back, but the anti-climax here.' Eventually Enid relented and Laurian was allowed back a few weeks earlier than planned.

Enid had no new writing projects under way at the end of 1938. Behrman's adaptation of *Serena Blandish* played briefly at the Gate Theatre Studio in September. The then relatively unknown Vivien Leigh was praised for her interpretation of the title role; Stewart Granger took the part of Lord Ivor Cream. But the play was not a huge success – its bright and brittle cynicism seemed out of sympathy with a world veering towards war. It lasted less than three months.

The family went skiing in Klosters in early 1939 and, on her return in February, Enid decided to resign from PEN (The Society of Poets, Essayists and Novelists) 'because after reflection, she no longer feels in sympathy with their aims'. Putting herself thus in the third person she avoided any elaboration. Her real reasons were never divulged. It was not the first time that she had tried to resign but on this occasion no one pressed her to remain.

In June the Joneses gave their last grand dinner-party at Hyde Park Gate. The guests included the Soviet and Chinese Ambassadors and their wives, Antoine Bibesco and H. G. Wells. Even Albrecht, managing one last trip out of Germany, was present. In August 1939, Enid and Roderick went on a bicycling tour of France. Passing through Clermont-Ferrand they heard of the Russo-German pact. They returned home through the night. On 3 September, Britain was at war with Germany.

THIRTEEN

It's a Privilege To Live in These Times

LIKE every urban householder, Enid spent the few days before the announcement of war feverishly scouring Woolworths for essential items that would help protect her family against bombs. Eager to be 'blacked out' by Friday sunset as ordered, Enid set about tacking and hammering, hanging blankets, unearthing crumpled brown paper, painting light bulbs with black paint that dripped when hot and covering car lamps with newspaper: the sort of practical tasks she loved. The preparations complete, she decamped to Rottingdean to give North End House the same treatment. Within a few days that too was ready, with several pairs of zinc buckets, one empty, the other full of sand, long-handled shovels and rakes now cluttering the house.

Once she accepted the reality of war she threw herself into it with gusto, and offered Kipling's house as a hospital. It was to be an annexe for Dr Waller's British Hospital for Mothers and Babies in Woolwich. The whole household was engaged in the preparations with Timothy given floor cleaning and lavatory scrubbing duties. Nurse Raynham Smith was matron in charge. Laurian's main duty was driving some five mothers and their new-born babies in the family's Ford shooting-brake from Woolwich to Rottingdean, where it was hoped they could calmly establish a breastfeeding routine. 'I had only just passed my test: it was winter and icy and once we ended up half-way up a bank. I think the terror of the drive must have stopped their milk,' Laurian recalled.

The London house was soon closed up entirely. Roderick took refuge at the Savoy from Monday to Friday; he could walk from there to his office. Once a week, Enid drove up to join him and also stayed the night, often descending to the 'society' shelter in the early hours of the morning when the alarms went off. When she was in Rottingdeam, she relieved the tedium of her lonely evenings by visiting Maurice Baring, then suffering from paralysis agitans. She was having tea with him one day in January 1940, when she received a frantic telephone message from the producer of a charity panto-mime due to be performed that week at the Theatre Royal, Brighton. Enid knew all about the society production as two members of the cast, the singer

Olga (Oggie) Lynn and her friend, Maud Nelson, had been staying at North End House for a week, and Enid had given a lunch-party for the company. *Heil Cinderella* was a lavish arrangement of the traditional children's story and represented exactly the sort of involvement in the war effort which Enid craved. The ugly sisters were played by the lanky Cecil Beaton and the dumpy Oggie ; the Hon. David Herbert, son of the Earl and Countess of Pembroke, was Buttons ; Prince Charming, the Lady Margaret Drummond-Hay and the Queen, Lady Juliet Duff. Laurian was given a part as a court lady. On 30 January, Lady Juliet Duff was taken ill with influenza. Enid was asked to take over the role that night, albeit reading the part and wearing a costume held together at the back with safety pins. She did not hesitate for a moment and was exhilarated by the opportunity. When her role of deputy seemed likely to continue, Enid made up her mind to do the thing properly and for almost the whole of the night and the next day shut herself up with the script until she was word perfect. But that night, Juliet Duff was better. Enid was asked to step down. Her disappointment was bitter indeed. 'Alas, I wished her dead !'

The revelation to her of how little it would take to commit a murder was an inspiration which, at once, she set about transforming into a play. Already lured by the immediacy of theatrical communication, her brush with the footlights simply proved the fatal seducer. At the outbreak of war, Enid had been working on a play which her brother Ralph, a scientist, had conceived : an inventor, after twenty years' work on animals, has shed new light on the onset of senility. He believes he is able to postpone old age so that the human body suffers no deterioration from about forty to eighty. However, on the day he is to present his findings, he is killed by a motor car. The scene then moves to Heaven, which is full of committees and bureaucracy. The inventor is told he is dead but does not believe it. Finally, he is shown a 'vision' of earth forty years on and the unhappy state to which he has brought the world by extending the life of men in their prime.

To a 1940s audience, *Heaven Only Knows* could have been most stimulating. Enid wrote the dialogue but called on Ralph for answers to scientific problems. They corresponded in a dilatory fashion, trying to knock the idea into a three-act shape. But neither collaborator had a satisfactory way of producing a 'vision' on stage. Although she did not drop this idea completely, she now turned to the murder story, which seized her imagination, and worked on it keenly in the early years of the war.

After the fall of Holland and Belgium in May 1940, the fear of a German invasion of southern England greatly increased. Under the Government's notorious Regulation 18B of the Defence of the Realm Act, several prominent people, including Sir Oswald and Lady Mosley, and, (briefly) the writer,

Henry Williamson, were interned at this time; Enid told close friends of her relief that she was not among them. There is no evidence for supposing that she might have been, nor indeed that she felt either guilt or remorse for her faith in Hitler.* On the contrary, she felt she had been unfairly harassed. 'Really I might easily have been in 18B through sheer obstinacy, through surprised huffiness, no, that's not the word, through outrage at being taken for a supporter when my whole nature is of a person who looks on. If I had known what I was looking on at, it would have been very different. I should have known, but I have frightful gaps in my intelligence.'

Her fear of internment may have been a writer's exaggerated concern, but her fear of an invasion was real enough. The South Downs were vulnerable. Enid campaigned energetically to strengthen beach defences. She wrote to *The Times*. 'The coastal villages can be taken with the morning milk; the question of the Downs ranks with the Maginot Line that was not continued to the coast.' When *The Times*, for security reasons, did not publish, Enid continued her battle by heckling the Town Clerk of Brighton, the Officer in Command, Coastal Defence Works, and Lord Trenchard. She went to the House of Commons to see Sir Edward Grigg and had an interview with General Thorne. Eventually she was assured that everything was being done to prevent an invasion of her village. Having carted all her precious things – baby books, photographs, embryonic writings, up to the cellar in Hyde Park Gate, she now brought them back to Rottingdean.

Before the first year of war was over, as more of her staff were called up, Enid realized that the family could not go on living at North End House, which they could afford neither to heat nor clean properly. She had had a well-stocked reinforced shelter built at The Elms, the Joneses' other house across the green, and, with just two maids and a boy left, wanted to move there as soon as the summer was over. Plankie, Nurse Dorothy Plank, her faithful children's nanny of six years' standing, and the cook had been running a canteen in the grounds of The Elms' garden from 6.30 to 8 p.m. every evening. Almost sixty soldiers came for what was called 'Hot dish hour'. A darts board and newspapers were provided and the small loss was funded by Lady Jones and friends. Inside The Elms, Nurse Raynham Smith was stretched to her limits with the mothers and newborns. Not surprisingly,

---

* Thirty years later, she discussed with her American editor, Edward Weeks, whether she should go into more detail in her autobiography about her pro-German beliefs. 'I am told it is remembered against me and might draw sixty-year-old reviewers to hiss again and distort their dealings with the whole book. I have totally suppressed it and written half a page instead simply saying that I went to Germany, that I was naïve and didn't know what was behind the scenes. I felt it was cowardly so to do but was so strongly advised. I am open to other points of view.'

telling her they would now have to leave was not welcome news. The relationship between Ethel Raynham Smith and Lady Jones had been on shaky ground from the outset of war. The matron objected to Enid's nightly visits to Maurice Baring and told her she should be visiting the mothers instead. Enid considered Ethel was turning into a petty dictator 'who ruined the hospital for all of us from the start', and she complained to Waller.

Waller rebuked Enid and called for a 'tincture of forgiveness. She is a poor frustrated virgin and has tried her poor best to sublimate her sterility by safeguarding the more fortunate. I've never thought of this before but I'm not sure I would love you as I do if you'd been barren and had led a life of cramped virginity.' His words did not sway Enid from her decision to repossess The Elms. Nurse Raynham Smith, disbelieving, wrote bitterly : 'It is not possible, these people's husbands are fighting for you and your children – at present I cannot bear what you are going to do. I dread it for all, especially, I am sure, it will hurt you.' Enid drafted several acerbic replies, but eventually Laurian, 'because neither of us dislikes the other, at the same time we have no special fondness for each other', replied. She told Matron the truth. The Elms was being closed down as a hospital because the family could not afford to run it any more.

With no one left to look after the horses, some had been turned out to grass on the Downs, others given away. But in October, Roderick gave Enid for her fifty-first birthday a fine 1880s phaeton, painted blue with black and yellow decoration. Pin Money, one of the few horses left, pulled Enid around in it and they became a familiar sight locally. With so little petrol available, the carriage was a boon and Enid considered it 'heaven to drive. It satisfies all my horse passion without the trouble and cold of riding.'

In the spring of 1941, she used it to visit Virginia Woolf for lunch. Enid had never managed a relaxed friendship with Virginia. The orgy of disjointed praise she had written after reading *Orlando* failed to win her over. 'How very nice it was of you to write it, and I think to myself with wonder, could she really have liked *Orlando* as much as that,' Virginia replied. But perhaps Enid had overdone it. In any event, Virginia considered her one of Vita's 'second rate women friends', and offered Lady Jones no encouragement to intimacy.

In spite of this, Enid decided to call on the Woolfs, uninvited, one summer's day before the war. She had been asked to Goodwood Races at the last minute by Sir Matthew (Scatters) Wilson and accepted, as it was an opportunity to parade a new Paris dress and matching hat from Reboux, 'a huge, smart-casual panama, never yet worn'. But Wilson was angry to discover she was not a member and that he had to pay for her entrance and her lunch. He was even angrier when the panama blew off in the wind and raced

between the horses' legs. That evening, Enid went impetuously to the
Woolfs, bursting to tell them the story. Leonard believed she felt mortified by
the social disaster and came to them for support and reassurance. She wanted
to be told, he felt, that in a writer's world, hats blowing off were unimportant.
Recounting the episode in her autobiography. Enid maintained that the visit
was simply to share a laugh with the Woolfs. They, however, saw it as further
evidence of Enid's worldliness; try as she might to belong to the artists'
milieu, she could not release her other foot from the 'smart set'.

At the end of 1940, Virginia told Vita Sackville-West that, if she wanted,
she would ask Edith (*sic*) Jones to lunch the same day Vita was coming 'and
I'd slip out into the garden and leave you'. Vita was pleased at the suggestion
as it would 'not only save me a mort of trouble, and would save me from
leaving you earlier than I want, but would flatter Lady Jones no end. You
needn't leave us; we have no secrets. Our friendship is purely platonic and
always has been.'

Later, Enid remembered how strange she thought it that Virginia had asked
her during the lunch if she had any Dexedrine. On 28 March, Virginia Woolf
drowned herself in the River Ouse; a tragedy which Enid saw in terms of a
lost friendship. 'She did like me, I think,' Enid told Cynthia Asquith. 'I think
it was very nearly a friendship and three weeks ago I think it was about to
become one. So I feel a savage anger at myself ... and full of regret.'

As the initial panic gave way to relief that they had not yet been bombed,
Enid was able to turn her mind to matters that always interested her: family
meals. With only Plankie now to help her, Enid was suddenly mistress of her
own kitchen. She remembered graphically, like so many of her class at this
time, the day she discovered where her own utensils lived. Cooking soon
became a work of art, with Enid making use of whatever ingredients were
available and transforming them into some highly original combinations.

But making sure that her children had enough to eat owed as much to a
natural delight in food as to her sharp instinct to hold the family knot intact
under threat of famine. She saw herself as a latter-day Robinson Crusoe. Not
given to self-pity, Enid genuinely believed that, under pressure, her own and
the nation's wits grew stronger. Within a short space of time, the Joneses
became smallholders. Enid had imagined at first that her miscellaneous collection of hens, geese, chickens, ducks, rabbits, a goat and a cow could all feed
happily together off the same three-and-a-half acre patch of grass behind
North End House. But she soon discovered that the cow – a Jersey because of
its high cream quotient – had to be moved twice a day, so she tethered her to

an iron stave hammered into the earth on all the unused tennis courts scattered around the village. This, at any rate, meant fewer cowpats to clear from the lawn. With her growing tendency to lumbago, Enid found the weekly clearing up of cowpats one of her most painful wartime chores.

The cow was not difficult to milk. That skill Enid acquired in an afternoon. She also calculated the breeding habits of rabbits. By husbanding precisely one hundred, she had enough to eat, two a week, all the year round. The does were required to produce four litters a year instead of the normal three. This, she considered, 'shortened their lives but it was their war work'.

Finding enough food for all the animals was a harder task. The rabbits lived mostly on wild grasses and weeds garnered by Enid from the hedgerows, with occasional outer cabbage leaves; the ducks fed on worms and the cow on potato peelings with some mangolds in winter. The geese ate some of the cow's mangolds and the goat ate anything it was given. A pair of Chinese bantams, a present to Laurian, now multiplied to ten, ate 'the remains of the dog's dinner and the dog eats the remains of mine'. The return from all this effort was not inconsiderable. There was a constant supply of fresh eggs and Enid judged her fried rabbit so good that nobody could distinguish it from Chicken Maryland. Sometimes she cooked rabbit in cream for, gourmet that she was, she did not object to the many hours' work involved in setting the shallow pans in the dairy to produce cream – 'more cream than we could eat – hence butter-making'. Plankie took the remaining skimmed milk for the family and, as long as there was enough, Enid would snatch three whole milkings to make a cheese. Boning up on the *Fundamentals of Dairy Science* and engaging in correspondence with rennet manufacturers, Enid eventually taught herself to make butter and cheese. She prided herself on her 'real cheeses with rinds, not one of your so-called cream cheeses hung up in a bit of muslin'. Making a cheese took about five hours but, far from begrudging the time it took from her writing, she welcomed such manual activity as an antidote. She even saw parallels between writing and cheesemaking, the latter being 'a sort of science and a sort of legend, evolved from man's necessities and from the empirical advices and observations of women long dead and gone – a mixture today of higher mathematics and decimals of acidity, mixed with witchcraft and a sort of rough luck. Now and then you throw up a good cheese like a good poem,' Enid expounded in a radio broadcast.

'It was now', wrote Lady Diana Cooper in her autobiography, *Trumpets from the Steep*,

that Enid Bagnold Jones, the torch of Rottingdean, came closely into my life and ardent affection. . . . Most Wednesdays, we two old farmwives would meet at Barnham Market (by train to save our meagre petrol-ration), baskets of produce on our arms, our shoulders hung with nets and sacks, first quivering with living things to be auctioned, then carried back filled with kids and cheeping day-old ducks, often out of control, fluttering free on to the platform – a rough-and-tumble harum-scarum Rowlandson–Caldecott scene of flying feathers, ourselves doubled with laughter at our obstreperous merchandise.

Lady Diana had been the girl Enid most admired. She revered her no less throughout middle and old age. With farming as a common ground, the friendship now flourished. In May 1940, Enid was able to record in the Baby Book: 'Diana and Duff Cooper to lunch.'

In spite of her new interest in farming and cooking, Enid did not give up her old habit of morning writing. Every day throughout the war, she would cross from The Elms to North End House and climb the steps to her Tower Room. The idea which the charity production *Heil Cinderella* had left in its wake was a play to be called *Lottie Dundass*, a name culled from a gravestone in Ovingdean Churchyard.

Lottie Dundass was a powerful, psychological drama about a girl who had a passion for the stage. She was one of seven children from a poor family; the father was in Broadmoor for murder. Lottie has inherited her father's streak of madness but also her grandfather's genius for acting. Because of a heart problem, Lottie is told to give up training for the stage. However, she does not relinquish her ambitions and secretly learns whole parts from plays. The knowledge of her illness serves only to make her 'feel herself lifted out of the common humanity . . . she quivered with the beauty of her own doom – her love of drama was now given death as an ornament.' A play Lottie knows by heart is showing in her town. When the leading lady falls ill and the under-study is delayed, Lottie secures an interview with the distraught manager and is offered the role. But then, at the last moment, the understudy arrives. Lottie takes off her costume, but stands for a moment with a belt in her hands which she was to have worn; suddenly, insanely confident of her own talent, she whips it around the understudy's throat, pushes the body away and climbs into her costume again. Mrs Dundass watches Lottie give a moving perform-ance, only to collapse from a heart attack on stage. But, having already discovered the corpse, she knows her daughter's crime and decides not to revive her.

It was a highly dramatic climax to an exciting, if occasionally unbelievable, play. But the role of Lottie offered tremendous scope for a young actress and considerable interest was quickly expressed in America. On 21 August 1941, at Santa Barbara, California, *Lottie Dundass* was given its world premiére under the direction of David O. Selznick. Dame May Whitty played Mrs Dundass but a new, young actress, Geraldine Fitzgerald, took the starring

role, scoring a great personal hit. The play suffered from one or two deficien-
cies which marked it as the work of an inexperienced playwright and it did
not run for long. The writing was sprawly and some of the characters shallow.
Lottie had six siblings none of whom appear and, more significantly, the plot
required too much explanation with too little action. However, the central
theme of a child ignoring a generation and desperately searching for proof of
her descent from a grandfather she worships is still valid today.

Charles Cochran quickly acquired the English rights, but, much to Enid's
chagrin, took far too long organizing a production. Actresses including
Wendy Hiller and Lilli Palmer were, he told Enid, queueing up to play
Lottie, but he did not want to spoil the play by choosing the wrong one. 'You
have written another "Juliet" – a young girl of twenty with thirty years of
acting experience needed.' By September 1942, he had secured Ann Todd as
Lottie and the play opened, appropriately, at the Theatre Royal, Brighton.
This was the scene of Enid's original inspiration and she had used it as the
setting for *Lottie Dundass*. It lasted only a week at Brighton, but Enid had felt
particularly involved as the Cochrans had stayed all the time at North End
House. On the Saturday night Enid managed a small party with Duff, Diana,
Oggie, Cecil and Sibyl (Colefax), intermingled with new theatrical friends.
When *Lottie Dundass* moved the following year to the Vaudeville Theatre in
London, Dame Sybil Thorndike joined the cast as Lottie's mother, a part
Enid wanted to act herself, 'and I am sure I could have'. Reviewers gave it
wide, and on the whole extremely encouraging notices. Desmond MacCarthy
wrote in the *New Statesman and Nation*: 'It shows marked aptitudes for
writing for the stage.' None the less he did not shrink from pointing out several
'missed opportunities' as he saw them. Ann Todd always listed Lottie as one
of her favourite roles.

Enid's theatrical impulses were further quickened by an unexpected need
for cash. When Enid had shown *Lottie* to Vita Sackville-West, Vita had
confided, almost enviously, to Virginia Woolf: 'It seems to me a play which
would make her fortune, so that Sir Jones' [sic] resignation from Reuters
won't matter in the family fortunes.' Whereas Enid's earnings had always
been regarded as the cream on the cake, extra pocket-money for her to bestow
upon the children at her whim, there was to be for the next fifteen years
at least rather more urgency for her contributions to the family pool. On
3 February 1941, after being head of Reuters for a quarter of a century, Sir
Roderick Jones had been asked to step down.

There are various accounts of the circumstances which led to this event, not
all of which are relevant here. Separated for so much of the war, Enid was not
closely in touch with events in Roderick's world. Nor had she ever been. For

a woman of such innate curiosity her lack of interest in Reuters and her husband's role there may appear strange. She dismissed the great news organization in her autobiography in a few sentences. She viewed Reuters as an institution of ever-present drama, which fitted well with her view of the natural drama of life, but looked no further. But why, of all the people that she knew well, did Roderick never feature in any of her work? Quite simply, because he did not *interest* her. He offered her not fascination but wisdom, not excitement but security and material comfort, not the pain of love but the balm of praise. Characters for books she could find among people she did not have to live with. A few weeks after their twentieth anniversary, Enid was in Fortnum and Mason buying a wedding present for a young friend, when her eyes filled with tears and she had to sit down and write Roderick a note. 'The memory of *our* first breakfast in bed. Oh my beloved companion, what fun we have had. You are such a *man* and such a companion – a bundle of glowing, various *lovable* humanity. . . . I couldn't live without you.' At the same time, Roderick was writing from the Savoy

to the dearest of all women. I write this in these uncertain days lest anything should swiftly befall me and I have no chance of speaking to you. I want you to know and always to remember that from the day we first met ... you have enchanted my life. I am so thankful that you have had the wisdom, the understanding not to be ever in doubt, because, shall we say, of Mary or Lois or now my new little friend. I have been deeply fond of them, it is true ... but *never* to any abatement of my utter and *complete* devotion to you. I write this so you may never harbour a doubt about my complete unfaltering and passionate heart and soul loyalty to you.

Loyalty was certainly the watchword of the moment. In his autobiography, Roderick maintained a lofty silence about his departure from Reuters; this gave the impression that a grave injustice had been perpetrated. That was, in any case, the view he inculcated in his wife. But, in 1930, the Press Association had bought all the rest of the Reuter shares, less one thousand which Sir Roderick continued to hold until his retirement. That Roderick was no longer the owner of Reuters had made little difference to his management of the business. His Press Association colleagues became infuriated by his imperious behaviour and increasingly concerned that Roderick was courting government interference for financial gain which would jeopardize the independence of the news agency. During World War I, Roderick had indulged in, and been criticized for, similar activities. The final straw for the Reuters board was the discovery of a secret, supplementary letter of agreement between the Foreign Office and Reuters, acknowledged by Roderick but which he maintained was only a draft. In return for badly needed financial assistance to the company, the British Government was being allowed to pronounce on the acceptability of Reuters' senior managers. Jones admitted the existence of the letter only under duress when other members of the board confronted him with their certain knowledge. He rushed out of the room and signed his letter of resignation. 'To the last he was, according to his own lights, an honourable man acting in the best interests of his company and his country,' wrote George C. Scott in the official Press Association history, *Reporter Anonymous*.

It appears that Enid was not aware of the details of the board-room coup either then or later, but she knew that her husband was in difficulties and, protectively, sprang to his defence. On the morning before Roderick's fateful board meeting, she paused amid her own writing to compose a letter to him: 'And the thought of you fighting so bravely on the edge of what may be retirement. I long to keep this house intact for you to enjoy ; but more than that I long to find that fate has smiled on your courage and twisted your lot into a new environment among nicer people. Oh, the damnable unfairness and monstrousness of the whole thing.'

The retirement was both an emotional and financial shock for the Joneses. Roderick was offered £4,000 in compensation and a pension of £5,000 per annum. But, to Alexander McLean Ewing, Chairman of the Press Association and a man to whom he would, admittedly, want to paint the blackest picture, he wrote:

My financial situation is causing me grave anxiety. I naturally have been and am retrenching most drastically . . . with four children to maintain and educate . . . and obligations to poor relations which I cannot honourably neglect, plus the necessity of not appearing to make too humiliating a descent (and enough descent there must be without that) from the status and position which I have occupied for a major part of my working life, the task is heartbreaking.

Nobody was to know the circumstances of Roderick's departure, but financial straits dictated that the tax inspector ought to be told 'that you were requested to resign. This is of course the truth. It also makes justification for the payment of compensation which is not liable to tax.'

The war enabled the Joneses to make their retrenchment more quietly than would otherwise have been possible. Dominick, at eleven, was sensitive to the changes as he watched some of the horses sold and the Rolls Royce stored under a giant dust sheet in the North End House garage. He was uncomfortable at the sight of his mother, almost servantless, in the kitchen struggling to make dishes without the right ingredients. The Joneses' gravy had always been made with several pounds of shin of beef – with anything less the world seemed to be crumbling. But these were economies being made by every family in 1941. To Dominick, lack of servants represented 'the denial of all civilisation. . . . What was so awful was that a meal had been a social occasion ever since ever, an occasion at which the servants assisted in the fairytale atmosphere as though they were trying to help orchestrate some special event.'

Enid's support for her husband did not diminish once the immediate crisis had passed. Even when he was out of a job she never refrained from telling him what a strength he was to her. Eight months after the resignation, when the Reuter trust was announced, she fired off a salvo to *The Times*, pleading that 'tomorrow's *Times* should carry the held-back valedictory' which had not appeared on his resignation and made plain how 'he cared so tremendously for the future of Reuters. . . . When he dies something like this will be written but it won't be much good to him and it will be an agony to me for I shall know how sorely he missed it.' It was Enid's idea, to help Roderick fill his day, that he should build rabbit hutches. Roderick applied his customary meticulousness to his new hobby of carpentry and made several for Diana Cooper too, but he was preoccupied with the need to make ends meet and, with constant dark mutterings about the evil (and dangerous) habit of 'living off capital', the children were aware of a distinct feeling of being pinched. When Chips Channon, MP, the diarist, was invited to Rottingdean for dinner, he found Enid 'buxom and vital . . . highly social and full of fire and energy. Sir Roderick seemed ineffective compared to his wife and I should have thought scarcely up to his former important job.' For dinner that evening, Channon recorded that they ate rabbit, washed down with some of Roderick's finest claret.

Two wartime friendships encouraged her further in the direction of the stage. Cecil Beaton, although a renowned photographer, craved a theatrical success as badly as she. They sent each other rough drafts of their plays and back came encouragement, suggestions for improvement and a snatch of gossip. Enid adored all his theatre titbits. In return, she made him cheeses and sent him to look up her brother Ralph in Cairo when Beaton had a War Office commission there. 'Tell him . . . how I am looking like a Roman matron,' she instructed. She also lent Dale Cottage, next door to North End House, to Cecil and his mother for some of 'Dr Rottingdean's ozone cure'. When she read his letters she was filled 'with an immense feeling of loving gratitude'. She told him:

Part of the gorgeousness of having a play done would be to sneak off to eat with you in the intervals and snigger. I know *exactly* how you feel about plays and I feel exactly the same. . . . I have at present such diarrhoea in writing plays, and such constipation in having them produced that, by the time I'm grey, I shall come on to the stage with two sticks, apologizing that I can't also be at my ten other first nights. Ha...!

Cecil was also a close friend of Lady Diana, as devastated by her beauty as anyone, and friendship with him locked Enid further into the charmed circle. The two aspiring playwrights read some of their work out loud to Diana Cooper during the war, but she was less than impressed by either.

The other stimulant for Enid was Edith Evans, by this time perhaps the finest actress in Britain. They had been introduced in the early years of the war by Peggy Ashcroft, when both were appearing in a Clemence Dane play at Brighton. The Evans magic worked immediately and Enid discussed play-wrighting with her for hours. She had hoped to attract Edith Evans to a part in a serious play she was writing, and wrote in some notes for an early draft: 'The mother (Edith Evans) is hard-working, efficient, ex-civilized, ex-beautiful, free of speech, quick temper, loving . . . frantic temper.' Evans was not won over. At the same time, Enid questioned with Cecil whether a play could be made of *The Squire* which might tempt Edith to play the leading lady. He gave her heart but pointed out that 'the children are almost bound to be appalling bores on the stage'. Recognizing Edith's genius and longing to see it work on one of her own plays, remained a prime motive of Enid's play-writing career. As early as 1942, after their first meeting, Enid wrote to Edith:

I suggest that you come down here this coming Sunday in time for lunch (no clothes, just a little attaché case and a toothbrush and the bus); that we don't talk about it at all that day (that's very important, because it's Timothy's leave from his brigade and Laurian will be here and I am three quarters of a mother on Sundays and it bothers me, in front of them, to have them reminded of the writing part and I answer, half-ashamed and preoccupied and feel at my worst about writing and even when Roderick is there I don't like talking about it. It isn't that it isn't important to him and valued by him but I just keep it very much apart until it's finished). . . . Well, to continue after that large bracket – stay the night and that next morning we come over into my writing-room and spend the two hours that I should ordinarily be in front of my typewriter (and staring at white paper) talking very practically, as though we were two hack playwrights intent on screwing out a plot to please the public, good sturdy plot-hunters about the play, its construction, the meat there is to be served up in the first act, the second and the third. We'll talk as though it just had to be done for an exam or for our living.

Edith, then in a stronger position, accepted the invitation to talk but continued to resist being caught in Enid's web.

As the war dragged on, Enid became more involved in her miniature farm, but with fewer helpers. Laurian, since 1942, had been working at Handley Page, the aircraft manufacturers, as a government inspector and lived mostly alone in London. Also in 1943, Timothy had been commissioned into the Grenadier Guards. Enid broke her routine for a few days that winter when, with Diana Cooper, she braved the cold, dark, wartime trains to visit Maurice Baring, who was being cared for by Laura, Lady Lovat at Beaufort Castle in Scotland. It was a sad meeting. Although he did not die until December 1945, Enid never saw him again and actively missed his wit and conversation. In spite of Roderick's presence at home, there was a hint of loneliness in her letters to friends at this time. 'It would simply alter my life', she wrote to Cynthia Asquith, 'to have you, Diana or Vita living in the village.'

In December 1943, Colonel Bagnold died, aged eighty-nine. In an obituary in *The Times*, Enid wrote: 'I cannot say of anyone so full of common sense as my father, so ready to take life as it came, that he was "of the old school".... He was a man of most excellent judgement, and very just; modest, determined and resolutely unsurprised.' Both Maurice Baring and Colonel Bagnold were, in different ways, men she greatly admired. In the closing years of the war her worries intensified about the other men in her life. The letters from Albrecht now dwindled to an occasional trickle. They indicated a tale of exceptional courage and daring, far beyond the expectations of those who had known him in London. Thanks to his 'rabid sister-in-law', he had already spent some months of torture in a concentration camp and had become very thin. Undeterred, he continued making dangerous journeys to Switzerland under the pretext of visiting family, but in fact organizing papers to help would-be escapees.

In the autumn of 1943, Timothy, not yet twenty, was sent to Italy. The following summer, Enid heard he had stepped on a mine in an early dawn advance and been blown sideways with serious leg injuries. Enid rushed down to the village that night hoping to borrow enough money to fly out to him. She managed to raise the cash, but could not get on a plane. At the end of August Enid was staying with the Asquiths at Clovelly when a War Office telegram told her that Lieutenant T. A. Jones had been placed on the 'dangerously ill' list. The communications that followed were sparse. Timothy wrote (or rather dictated) a short note to say he had to have his leg amputated as gross sepsis had set in and his condition was deteriorating. For about a week after receiving this, Enid believed her son must be dead. She asked Vita if there was any chance of Harold arranging to have her sent to Italy with the British Council. But, to her immense joy, Diana Cooper, then in Algiers, flew specially to Naples to visit Timothy in hospital. That Timothy should have such a rare vision of loveliness by his bedside seemed, to Enid, a great comfort. In September Timothy was well enough to be shipped home. Enid spent weeks at a time in the Adelphi Hotel in Liverpool while he recuperated at the nearby Royal Infirmary. Although the rehabilitation period was far from over, Enid was relieved that her only child at the front had, at any rate, emerged from the war alive.

Enid's reputation from *National Velvet* had grown steadily since its publication in 1935. Enid herself was sometimes referred to as 'Lady "National Velvet" Jones'. In spite of wartime paper shortages, it was constantly being reprinted, with school and other cheap editions also available. The story had captured the mood of a determined nation. 'Its huge popularity', wrote Claud Cockburn in *Bestseller* (subtitled *The Books that Everyone Read: 1900–1939*, 1972), 'displayed in those decades of stress and menace showed a facet of English mentality, English requirements. ... The galloping *National Velvet* can certainly not be denied its rating as an authentic spirit of the Time.' In July 1943, eight years after publication, the book was dramatized as a radio serial for Children's Hour with the author as narrator. Enid had also adapted it for the theatre, hoping *National Velvet* might become a children's Christmas classic, a *Peter Pan*. But although there were regular news items naming this or that actress as the latest possibility for the film role of *National Velvet*, Enid had so far derived little joy from the film contract she had so speedily signed in post-publication euphoria.

She had immediately invested in America what remained of her £8,000 ($40,000) for the sale of *National Velvet* film rights. Within a year, the Treasury in Washington wrote that she owed them a further $3,000 in taxes. Advised originally by Irene Cooper Willis, Enid appealed and for three years there was what she called 'unurgent and gentlemanly delay'. She then sought advice from Vita Sackville-West's accountant, Percy Popkin, of Romford, Essex – 'Our Perce'. Never enjoying a sound grasp of financial matters, Enid found his long letters and statements impossible to understand. Vita advised perseverance as, 'I do think he's brilliant. He saves me pounds every year.'

Suddenly Enid received a letter from the US Tax Authorities demanding not only the full tax but a penalty and compound interest, now totalling more than $30,000. At this point, she was advised to pay immediately as the snowball was growing daily and the Americans might distrain on future novels published in the United States. However since the war, her investments had slumped dramatically; to pay the debt she sold what remained of them and had to borrow money from Roderick as well. Popkin's explanation that, 'I am now convinced the [US] Authorities are out to get in all they can, especially from non-residents', was of little comfort. In possession of a sudden fortune of her own making, Enid had bought ponies and typewriters for the children and a gold cigarette case for Roderick. But the ponies died, the typewriters rusted and the cigarette case was eventually stolen. She made no more money from the film of *National Velvet*; it had been an outright sale.

At the end of 1944, the film of *National Velvet* finally appeared. The world première, at Radio City Music Hall in New York, was a resounding success. The critics hailed it as 'a joy... as happy and thrilling a picture as you'll find'. In spite of the biting cold, rain and snow, queues began to form each morning as early as 7 a.m. At times, they extended four blocks. Box office records at the world's largest theatre were broken. In a single day 26,152 people saw the picture and one week attendance reached a total of 176,465 people. Pandro S. Berman had moved to MGM for whom he eventually produced the film in Technicolor, with Clarence Brown directing. But the star was an unknown twelve-year-old English girl living in California, with shiny black hair and large violet eyes who seemed to personify innocence. Until then she had appeared in *Lassie Come Home* (1943) but little else. Elizabeth Taylor had desperately wanted the role of Velvet as soon as she had read the book but she was both too young and too small. 'I loved the part because Velvet was an extension of me. I rode every morning and I knew how to jump.' But she trained hard and ate well and managed to add two inches to her height in three months. During the making of the film, just as Enid had conveyed in her book, Elizabeth developed a great bond with King Charles, the horse used for The Pie. She could jump him six foot bareback and he often followed her around the lot. She was given King Charles as a thirteenth birthday present and kept him until he died twelve years later. Mi Taylor was played by Mickey Rooney, who as a child star was once considered even more of a draw than Shirley Temple.

Wartime communications ruled out the possibility of consultations with Enid. A scriptwriter was sent over to England to watch the Grand National and Aintree was painstakingly recreated, albeit in midsummer, in a Hollywood location. When Enid was invited to a press viewing in London in January 1945, she was

prepared for anything... prepared that Velvet should be 18, in a ball dress dangerously in love with Mi Taylor, the scene laid in Monte Carlo. Thus ready I found I watched the film with delight. ... I had a passing regret for the loss of a few subtleties, I thought once or twice with a brief passion, 'Ah if they had me over there', but when we came to the race I was enthralled. They'd got what of course I could never put in, the heart of it, the excitement, where I'd had to invent and go sideways offering horses, as it were, in a mirror, they could go far better. It's a different medium.

She admitted she was rather tired of it by the fourth viewing. But the fifth time was the official première.

The grey and silver magnificence, the glass vestibules and the chromium corridors of the Empire in Leicester Square – there we hoped to see my name blazed from the hoardings, the queues impassable. We were breathless with the anticipation of a delightful and brassy notoriety as we passed from the empty street into the vestibule. I distinguished my name on the poster as small as the darn on a stocking. . . .

In Britain too, *National Velvet* pulled in the crowds, its excitement appealing to a nation weary of war.

Emerald Cunard, one of many distinguished guests at the première, told Enid she thought it was so good she advised 'sticking to films'. Enid smiled and refrained from reminding her that she had written the book, not the film. But she believed that her future might lie in the film industry when, also that year, the Hungarian-born film magnate Sir Alexander Korda bought the rights of *Lottie Dundass* for the fledgling London MGM. Enid was employed to write the script for this and, at £100 a week, considered herself well paid. Korda supervised what Enid wrote and they discussed the play over lunch every Wednesday at the MGM offices in Belgrave Square. Korda had Vivien Leigh in mind for the title role but she suffered one of her first bouts of tuberculosis before the film was ready. Korda himself then left MGM and Enid was handed over to his deputy Ian Dalrymple. He insisted on an ending which she considered most inartistic, 'stuffing' a play within a play. Much to Enid's chagrin, the film fizzled out and, with the rights tied up, the script languished for years on MGM's shelves.

Basking in her celluloid glory, Enid decided in the spring of 1945 that it was time to give parties again. Some of the guests at this first party since the war were old friends: Desmond MacCarthy, Harold Waller and Helen Dashwood. But there were also new faces, Cyril Connolly, Cecil Beaton, Alexander Korda and Mr and Mrs Hamish Hamilton, indicating the direction of her post-war life.

By February 1945, Enid recognized that Albrecht had probably been murdered. In a final purge, the Nazis had killed nearly all of those who, it was deemed, might have had sufficient authority to be considered possible armistice negotiators. The realization that Albrecht could not be part of her post-war life horrified her:

Albrecht had such immense floatability. I thought I should see him again. He was my very last love before closing time and I liked and respected him as well. Also I wasn't kind to him about Hitler and I feel remorse. I thought in those days that Hitler was a new God and Albrecht a donkey not to see it. And he has paid by being swung on his poor huge neck.

FOURTEEN

The Pessimism of Age

ENID celebrated the end of the war by throwing a party for her two
eldest childen. Since there was no electricity at Hyde Park Gate, she
extemporized with hundreds of white candles stuck into empty beer
bottles and the event was duly reported in the society magazines. To Antoine
she wrote that she had spent the war 'as in a nunnery'. Farming and writing
plays, she told him, had been the twin pillars of her wartime existence.
Sometimes she confused the two: 'With books at least they hatch. But with
plays and films the Hen of Fortune sits and sits and never a peck at the shell
under her.' The goose of theatrical ambition had also laid its egg. *Lottie
Dundass* had given Enid the unparalleled thrill of hearing her own words
spoken on stage. In addition, in the spring of 1946, her play, *National Velvet*,
was finally accepted for production at the Embassy Theatre in Swiss Cottage;
she still believed in the potential of *Heaven Only Knows*; and a fourth play,
about writing, she considered 'rather high-brow but, I hope, dramatic'.

Poor Judas, which she had spent two years writing, was her most serious
work to date. It is the story of an old Czech writer living in Dieppe on the
eve of war. Jules Pasdeloupe Calas is compiling material for an ency-
clopaedic study of treachery. In need of help, he employs a British writer to
lend style to an otherwise dull procession of facts. This man, Edward Mission
Walker, is a poet at heart who prefers to talk about the act of writing
rather than doing it and was based on Desmond MacCarthy. As the Germans
advance, Walker realizes he must flee. He persuades Calas to let him take his
notes and work on them in England. Four years later, he has not touched
Calas's study, but has filled his own notebooks. When Calas arrives unexpectedly and discovers this, Walker talks to him of 'the liberation of the artist to
do what he has to do'.

Enid knew it was a difficult play. She had used it to express some of her
deepest thoughts about the agonies of writing. But, none the less, the initial
rejections by various theatre managements left her 'dumbfounded'. She had
sent it to Laurence Olivier, who turned it down, but 'I don't believe he really
read it.' She also sent it to Hugh (Binkie) Beaumont, head of the powerful
H.M.Tennent theatrical empire. Cecil Beaton had effected this valuable

introduction for her, but Binkie liked it no better than any of the other plays by Enid Bagnold which he had recently rejected. At this point, Enid decided it would be more professional if she found an English agent to hawk her work around. 'She is Joan Ling, which somehow isn't a very confidence-making name.' Joan Ling, however, had great confidence in *Poor Judas*, which she thought a 'wonderful play', although it might 'take some time to sink into the managements' heads'. Miss Ling sent it to Michael Redgrave, who refused it politely on the grounds he was not yet old enough to play Walker, and to Robert Morley who replied, 'I don't quite know what it's about, but it stimulates me – send it to Tyrone Guthrie.'

Enid was growing frustrated by the delays and toyed with the idea of finding a publisher before a theatrical management for the play, but relations with publishers were no smoother. In the autumn of 1945, she had met Hamish Hamilton at a party and was soon discussing terms with him. The only new book she had to offer him was *Poor Judas*, but she was, as she pointed out, like the housemaids, unsettled, and wanted a change from Heinemann. Charles Evans, who had died at the end of 1944, had cosseted and esteemed her, and she always maintained she could only write under praise. The new Heinemann team were strangers to her.

Secret lunches with Hamilton were arranged and a draft contract sent out. Enid required various amendments as well as changing the title of *Poor Judas* at the last minute and then changing it back again. In spite of post-war shortages, she wished to be consulted about the quality of paper, the linen for the cover, the jacket design, and the width of the margins – one of the constant foibles. And she wanted the promise of an eventual collected edition of her works. A contract was signed on 27 December 1945, but on 17 January Enid received a letter from Hamilton telling her: 'After a lot of thought, I have come to the conclusion it would be a mistake for us to publish your books.' He did not elaborate. Her constant demands had obviously caused him second thoughts. Roderick summoned him to Hyde Park Gate to explain himself, but there was a terrific row and Enid told him she never wished to see him again – an interdiction which lasted for ten years.

On the rebound, Enid hoped to catch Macmillan's. But in the summer of 1946, Harold Macmillan had the 'effrontery' to tell her that '*Poor Judas* is not worthy of your powers', and that its publication could bring her neither reputation nor money. Enid took three weeks to reply, not out of pique, she told him, but because 'I received your letter with so much pain I could not write.' She returned to Heinemann, soon to build up a relationship with Dwye, son of Charles Evans, and, although tempted, never left them again.

While waiting for news of interest in *Poor Judas*, Enid went to Paris to stay

at the embassy with Diana Cooper; her husband, Duff, was then the ambassador to France. She had a 'marvellous three weeks'. Diana had turned the
embassy into 'a place where anything might happen, where no party was just
a party and every guest was expected to contribute. If they failed, they would
rarely be offered a second chance.' Enid was invited again several more times.

It was her first time out of England for seven years. She felt badly in need of
a holiday because Plankie, her wartime mainstay, had just married her
brother, by then Brigadier Ralph Bagnold, OBE, FRS. An expert on the
physics of blown sand and desert dunes, Brigadier Bagnold had achieved fame
as the creator and organizer of the 'Long Range Desert Group' during the
war. 'What hell afterwards for me,' Enid wrote in one of the Baby Books following Plankie's wedding at Rottingdean village church. Roderick gave Plankie
away and Timothy was best man.

Before 1946 was out, however, Joan Ling's faith was rewarded. In November, at the Bradford Civic Theatre, although not the London venue to which
Enid aspired, *Poor Judas* had its first public performance. Esme Church, the
director, 'has a respect for my written word that I've never seen a sign of
before', she told Diana Cooper. Enid was particularly thrilled with the performance of Stanley Ratcliffe, a thirty-eight-year-old osteopath who hoped
to become a professional actor, as Walker. 'He has a face that when he turned
it to you from the stage carried all the miseries of all of us.'

Roderick, Laurian and Richard all came up to Bradford for the opening
night. 'I simply yearn . . . for the time to come to have you here,' she wrote to
Roderick, 'you are absolutely in my bones (as well as my heart) – Darling,
Darling I do hope I can make you happier. I shall try so hard.'

However, *Poor Judas* was not the triumph she had hungered for. The play
received some unexciting notices in the local press. Towards the end of the
play, Jenny, Walker's daughter, says: 'I wonder what anyone wants to write
for when it costs so much to do it.' But Enid emerged from the war with her
passion for writing and fame, not only undimmed but magnified. The new
medium, the theatre, presented a greater challenge but louder accolades.
Binkie, 'the romantic Mount Everest of my theatrical struggles – its steepest
face', in refusing one of her plays, had added the tantalizing postscript that he
hoped she would, one day, write an original play for him. Now nearing sixty,
she was only too aware that time was crowding in on her.

With some regretful glances at the theatre she had failed to storm, in
January 1947, Enid, Roderick, Richard and Dominick set off on a three-month
trip to South Africa. On her mind during this holiday was a fantastic offer she
had just received from Carol Brandt, the wife of her New York book agent Carl.
Carol was a stunningly attractive executive of MGM, who came to stay with

Enid at North End House while on a talent-spotting tour. With her glamorous clothes, in drab post-war England, she was the proverbial breath of fresh air. Carol was always opposed to Enid's writing plays and wanted her to begin a novel, the subject of which had casually cropped up in conversation in Rottingdean. 'I only said it lightly, but she remembered it. She felt I was in an impasse spiritually when she was here and needed a whip of some sort or a ladder to climb out.'

The ladder Carol presented was in the form of a spectacular offer from MGM for Enid's proposed novel: $10,000 on signature of the contract and not returnable in any event; $25,000 on approval of the synopsis, and, upon this approval, they were 'absolutely obligated' to pay on delivery of the completed novel, $65,000 more, making a total of $100,000.

Naturally, the thought that MGM still believed her capable of earning that amount appealed to her vanity and, without Roderick's salary, the money was undeniably useful. She had, some years previously, considered making a diary out of her experiences of growing old, jottings which would accumulate over ten to fifteen years and which would not interrupt any other literary work. Carol's offer, although forcing her to discipline these vague intentions, might, she feared, become a millstone. It was a little too definite and, could have a rather 'chained down' effect on her. She told Carl, 'I don't like the idea that they part with $10,000 never to get it back no matter what I do.' It was not simply a question of honourable misgivings about accepting such a large sum, apparently for nothing. What if she could not produce that for which she had already been paid? But Carl remonstrated with her. Carol would be embarrassed with her employers if Enid did not take the advance. 'A deal with you was a fine and shining feather in her cap.' There was, Carl promised her, no reason to let the synopsis idea limit the subsequent development of her work. 'I am a coward about losing favour in the eyes of the Brandts,' she told Dominick. 'If I can't pull it off, Daddy will write to Carol and say, "I have grave fears of my wife's mental condition", and get me off like that – we'll see. Perhaps I can still do it.'

The inspiration was to 'catch' Diana Cooper as she approached old age. Increasingly, Diana became an indispensable element in Enid's life. Enid was uplifted by being within Diana's aura. 'It was a circle from which no one liked to be excluded. No one could afford to leave alone such a dispenser of life.' Some years previously the Joneses had been able to buy cheaply number 30, Hyde Park Gate and they then converted the pair of houses into ten flats. Enid and Roderick retained the Lutyens drawing-room in their own apartment, but there was another earmarked for Duff and Diana. 'Yours will be finished this year and first of all,' Enid promised her. The Coopers' flat did not materialize, but Enid poured all her feelings about Diana into her latest book. 'I don't want to embarrass you,' she explained. But she had been studying Diana and Duff, and each in relation to the other, while staying with them. 'When I say "study" that sounds a voluntary thing. But not at all, I mean you are a '*point du départ*' in my inner excitement, just as having babies was in *The Squire* and horses in *National Velvet*. The '*point du départ*' causes bells to ring, and the bells cause flashes and eventually (with luck) there's a proper bonfire.'

But the book widened into a fictional study of old age in general. The news that Enid herself was soon to be a grandmother was one factor impelling her towards a frank consideration of her own advancing years. On 23 January 1948, Timothy married seventeen-year-old Pandora Clifford, daughter of Sir Bede and Lady Clifford, a prominent Catholic family. The wedding was in Oxford and the honeymoon in Rottingdean. Pandora's parents were rigidly opposed to the match; they did everything they could to prevent it and refused to speak to their daughter afterwards. In this crisis, Enid was a stalwart support to the young couple. Bowled over by the romance of the affair, she was convinced that only in young love, like theirs, could be found true and equal passion. When journalists asked her whether she did not consider the bride rather young for marriage, she rounded on them: 'Throughout history girls have been getting married at this age.'

Enid took charge of the pregnant mother and, although Dr Waller was no longer practising, determined that Pandora be sent to his successor, Keith Vartan, who could expound to her the benefits of breastfeeding. When the baby, Annabel, was born on 14 August, the family was installed in North End House, where Enid could take charge of the nursery routine and ensure, once again, that it conformed to Waller principles. Enid adored Pandora; physical beauty in a woman always exercised a magnetic appeal on her. But, seeing in her new daughter-in-law an intelligent mind left uneducated, she assumed the responsibility for influencing such raw material by, among other things, directing her reading. There was no nurse for the baby yet. Enid, far from resenting the extra work, was pleased 'as it gives us more hold on the whole thing'. She told Cecil Beaton that she now felt 'more Queen-Bee-ish' than ever, and compared the newly enlarged Jones family to a sort of 'private club'.

But Enid was not preparing to sink into ever more lethargic grand-motherhood. Energetic not only in her writing, she was also highly active both in the garden and in the house. She was aware that she still had the power to attract, but photographs of her at this time reveal a buxom, heavy woman, her face gently folding into creases, with only her ankles and hair thinning. Never precisely vain, equally she always appreciated the value of good looks and the deterioration of her own body was not something she accepted easily. Pandora recalled that, when she first met her new mother-in-law, Enid had come in from milking the cow. Florabella was brought to London one winter and housed in a vacant stable next door. Enid was wearing an apron over a plain black but obviously expensive couture dress, her large rough hands indicating the peasant's work from which she had just emerged. But the quantity and quality of jewels she wore were just as sure an indication of the life-style she was used to.

At all events, in 1948 Enid decided to experiment with a health farm to see if, by fasting, she could shed some of the weight that had bothered her since childhood. Enid maintained that she was at Tring not just for obesity, but also for 'stupidity, pessimism of age and hay fever', as she explained to Antoine. 'To describe myself I am a person of great gusto, huge health, and driving energy. I am in middle age, even at the far edge of it, and spiritually I have begun to bind up, like a machine that has been run too fast. I am impacted: not worn out.' She quickly noticed that hunger was not discussed at the health farm 'because a careless word wakes it up', but her own thoughts were never far away from it. Enid considered that a meal 'is much more than the occasion for taking food. It is the climax to a period of time, which, if promised, is then too long. It makes the morning and the afternoon. It causes the evening to come.' She adored every aspect of food, from preparation to consumption. Few guests failed to remark on her singular concoctions. Diana Cooper warned Nancy Mitford before a visit to Rottingdean that she might get 'cows udders in marmelade' (*sic*). But Nancy considered it all delicious. She recounted to her mother: 'At tea Sir Roderick said, "Where's the loaf?" "Oh, it's hanging in a net in my bedroom – do fetch it." He came back with a literal stone, wholemeal, made by Enid from wheat that has never been manured or something. But the food is wonderful – best I had in England.'

Fifteen days of fasting was a torment which left Enid seventeen pounds lighter, but with a 'vast appetite for self-indulgence'. Needless to say, the weight was gained and lost again throughout the rest of her life. Although she went for further cures they were never successful; mostly because she would quietly consume surreptitious Scotches to calm her hunger pangs and nerves. She helped comfort herself with Vita's words that she preferred to see her well covered. 'It suits your general sumptuousness. I mean one's physique should match one's mental make-up and yours is so rich. Like a cornucopia.'

The rest also did little to alleviate Enid's other persistent health worry, growing insomnia. Many a night she lay awake until dawn, the image forming in her mind of herself as a boat needing to catch the tide to get away.

If she missed it, she would remain beached for the night. With many an opportunity to witness dawn on the Sussex Downs, she expressed her observations in a poem. She was thrilled when Cyril Connolly, of whom she was slightly in awe, accepted it for publication in March 1949 in the prestigious arts magazine, *Horizon*.* Cyril had been introduced to Enid by Gladwyn Jebb in the early 1930s, when he 'was very young and had no money and was a sponge'. He arrived one summer and stayed until autumn. Enid was riveted, but mildly intimidated by his genius. 'I fear the whip that flicks out in his talk.' From now on, Cyril took over Desmond's role in Enid's life as the brilliant talker and stimulant; but when would he review her books?

Carol Brandt negotiated frequent extensions to her MGM contract between 1946 and 1950, when she eventually delivered the finished novel. But, on reading the script, MGM rejected it after all and relinquished their option on film rights. Carol reassured her that they might be in the market for it again after it had been published.

Enid was, in any case, dissatisfied with her American publishers. She had already made clear to Thayer Hobson that, if Morrow published her new novel, she would expect a collected edition of her other works to accompany it. Hobson replied by quoting her the story of a man whose rope snaps while climbing down a sheer cliff face. As he hangs on with one hand, a huge eagle dives down to attack him. 'This is no time for an eagle fight,' the hero observed. Hobson added, 'So help me God! That is the line. That's just the way I feel about the idea of a collected edition of anyone just at the moment.' Enid was not sorry to give the book to Doubleday instead for an advance of $10,000. Roderick had also spent the post-war years writing and his autobiography was finished shortly before Enid's novel. But it was not having an easy time finding a publisher. Macmillan rejected it in England and in the United States Carol Brandt had to work hard to persuade Doubleday to take it. 'Which they knew and you and I knew would cost them money.' They agreed, 'after it had made the rounds of everyone else', only because of an 'implied promise' that Enid's next book would go to Doubleday. Enid was absolutely insistent that this deal be kept a total secret from Roderick.†

There followed the now familiar arguments about titles, covers and publication dates. Among the titles Enid suggested were: The Grand Climacteric,

---

* *Horizon*, edited by Cyril Connolly and, for a short time, by Stephen Spender, ran from Christmas 1939 to New Year 1950.

† When in 1967 Enid was deciding to whom she would offer her autobiography, Carol reminded her of the Doubleday arrangement. Enid considered this reminder 'disgraceful of her' and the autobiography was published in the United States by Atlantic Little Brown.

The Unknown Country, After Fifty, The Muzzle's Not Intact, and It's a
Shock to Get Old, before settling on the more rhythmical and elegant, *The
Loved and Envied*. But in October 1950, she received a copy of Doubleday's
proposed jacket which she complained was 'unimaginative, childishly drawn
... totally unworthy of my tense efforts over three years'. In a letter to
Doubleday's Lee Barker, she explained, 'I have just despatched you a boiling
telegram. It conveyed my deep disappointment; this filmy and vague young
woman standing and looking up the perspective of life to come ... has
everything in it I don't want.' But what had really riled her was the jacket
description of her as 'Enid Bagnold, the author of *National Velvet*'.
Mentioning only one of her books gave the impression she had managed only
one best-seller. 'I am not in that position and I cannot be presented like that.'
Finally she told Barker, 'Don't be offended at the savagery of my language. To
me it always seems quite mild. But I'm told it doesn't to other people.'
Doubleday quickly caved in and Cecil Beaton's design for the Heinemann
dust-jacket was rushed to New York. His image featured the dark-red curtains of a theatre box with the bust-line, gloved arms and turned-away profile
of a beautiful woman – a cover which Enid considered fascinating and very
bold, or perhaps she liked having his name associated with the book. Doubleday paid her the honour of making *The Loved and Envied* their leading book
of the new season and publishing it on 2 January, a date they reserved for
special books. Appearing three weeks later in England, it was selected as
Book of the Month and the *Daily Mail* choice; Hatchards bookshop in
Piccadilly recreated the cover for their entire window display over ten days.

The Loved and Envied is, yet again, a story without plot or, at any rate, the
flimsiest of plots. The narrative centres on a group of European aristocrats
bound together not only by the social level on which they all live, but by the
book's heroine and cynosure, Lady Maclean. The action takes place mostly in
an imaginary park outside Paris called Pouilly and based on Chantilly. The
Coopers had moved to the Château de St Firmin at Chantilly after Duff's
ambassadorship was over. In this fantasy atmosphere of ornamental fountains and lakes, formal lawns and informal follies Diana's gift for organizing
romantic picnics and receptions was given full rein. In *The Loved and Envied*
Lady Maclean's faithful admirers live at Pouilly in as close proximity to her as
possible. Although far removed from the domesticity of *The Squire*, the one
burning similarity is that both books reveal the power of the matriarchal type.
Ruby Maclean guides the lives of those who surround her just as the Squire
does her children. By clever use of flashbacks, Enid builds up a past for her
characters, but the reader never penetrates Ruby Maclean's mind. We know
that she is fifty-three, a famous beauty, and we learn about her through the

reactions of others – those who love or envy her – those whom she herself calls a 'wagonette of picnickers driving towards the edge of the world'.

The problem that gripped Enid was understanding how a woman of legendary beauty, such as Diana Cooper, could serenely grapple with the certainty of fading beauty in old age. She was fascinated by the effect on a woman's life of the fortunate accident of being born with a beautiful face. In *The Loved and Envied* this 'luck' was underscored by, on the one side, Ruby's Aunt Ursula, born with a savage facial deformity, who determines to launch Ruby on the world, and, on the other, by Ruby's daughter Miranda, whose jealousy of her mother manifests itself in shyness and obstinacy. Not that Enid believed beauty alone eased the passage through life; in fact, she concluded that in Diana's case it was almost an interference, preventing strangers from seeing qualities of mind beyond the face.

Diana Cooper may have been the book's mainspring, but Enid Bagnold was its mouthpiece. When a young man, almost half her age, proposes an affair, Lady Maclean is forced to define what is left to her in life: 'love, though it's not a perfect stranger to me, takes its place in the past with the other troubles. There's nothing now on those lines in front of me. I've had all I want. I don't mean I'm contented, nor do I understand how to face old age. But a last love won't solve that. It isn't that, with all its anxieties, that I want.'

There is, too, a stoicism in Ruby Maclean which is characteristic of Enid Bagnold. '"How unexpected that when it comes to the point one shouldn't mind!" she thought as she looked. "As though one had been led that way before. Like childbirth, getting older is only unpleasant if one resists!"'

The book's overall effect is somewhat rueful, melancholic even, as most of the characters dread, as did Enid, the onset of old age. But Ruby's unhappiness has a different root: it stems from the realization that she has failed to make happy either her husband, Sir Gynt, or her daughter, Miranda.

Miranda, overshadowed by her mother and forced back within herself, stands out as the book's most real character. Her portrait is sympathetically, but not uncritically drawn, and her dilemma in life is sharply and painfully demonstrated. Evidently, aspects of the taut relationship between Miranda and her mother had been experienced by Enid and Laurian. Miranda as a child did not go to school and was more at ease with animals, in this case dogs, than people. When she returns home, a young widow, after several years' 'exile' in Jamaica she is still 'sulky and struggling with herself'. She 'could not get through the first half-hour of welcome without an antagonism which hid her aching love.' At the same time, Lady Maclean experiences unadulterated joy. 'She had her child: she had a second chance to fulfil her task.' The final piece of advice Lady Maclean has for her unhappy daughter is pure Bagnold: the importance of gaiety and joy throughout life. Youth without these loses its point. 'If you haven't joy you have nothing better than I have,' she insists.

Two other characters in *The Loved and Envied* bore more than a passing resemblance to her friends. The Duca Alberti Marie-Innocence de Roccafergolo was almost a mirror image of Albrecht Bernstorff, or how she imagined Albrecht would have been at seventy and the role she thought he might have played in her life.

Alberti still had 'the fat which was the mild grief of his life' and 'the blond hair that clung round his temples as fine as a baby's'. The reader is told that a scandal in his youth had left him shy of women : 'a secret virgin forced to wear the scarlet cape of the seducer'. He loses this shyness in Ruby's presence.

The Duca Alberti had met Ruby during the 'gay, brilliant middle stretches of her career' and was 'at once bound to her side'. He now lived only for her. He tries to help Miranda by buying her expensive dresses only because the result might please her mother. It is of no consequence to Ruby that she and Alberti are not married. He offers her all she requires without this. 'I only care now for human beings who are as they are : not changed by wild and temporary feelings. . . . I like to be what I am. I like sober, solid relationship.' Finally, when the Duca knows he is dying, he leaves Ruby his vast fortune.

'You would have asked me to marry you if we had met early ?'
'Yes, of course.'
'Instead of which you want me to be your widow.'

There is also a not altogether flattering portrait of Princess Marthe Bibesco, barely veiled as the Duchess Alice. 'One of those people who, having given all the trouble necessary to get her own way, thinks no one has really noticed it.' Enid was prodded into caricaturing Marthe Bibesco partly because the Princess had recently been the unwitting cause of a further row between Enid and Violet Bonham Carter. At a cocktail party in the summer of 1949, Enid said lightly to Violet that Marthe was more trouble than Antoine, 'and who should know better than I who have several times had her and her maid to stay and had to make the oddest foods and trays and what-nots.' This brought 'a reproof of the highest order' from Violet until Enid was 'out of breath with indignation . . . and when I got a chance I really chose between a slap and being rude. . . . Mercifully I chose being rude.' Enid told Violet she talked too much and Violet stormed out of the house. However, Marthe continued to stay at Rottingdean, not only with her maid but, on occasions, with her grandson too. Writing about her in *The Loved and Envied* was Enid's idea of gentle revenge.

Reactions to the novel were mixed. Many reviewers praised Enid for writing a book full of wisdom and eloquence. She was 'a writer with a very special magic for she had made one woman in her fifties and men and women in their seventies and awaiting death, utterly fascinating.' But there were too many negative notices for Enid's comfort.

Duff and Diana Cooper both wrote Enid polite, congratulatory letters. Diana was 'much relieved and insanely happy that you should see me as you have, a beautiful, serene woman and unblemished, noble, interested, brave and good, instead of a raw, aged hypochondriac, fretted with panics and pains, funking the future with no pride or curiosity or enthusiasm.' Duff asked Enid to forgive him 'if I tell you frankly that I know Diana too well to recognize her . . . however the portrait that you have drawn is a gracious and beautiful one for which anyone would be grateful.' Desmond MacCarthy, in the *Sunday Times*, said he believed *The Loved and Envied* was a remarkable novel – Enid's best, but privately he bemoaned the name of the heroine – which made him think of 'Maclean your teeth'. Cecil Beaton, too, thought that Enid had overdone all the names in *The Loved and Envied*. Names had always caused Enid difficulty. She believed this was because of her habit of using the real people's names in early drafts and then changing them only at the last minute.

It was not simply that the names of the characters in *The Loved and Envied* had titles but that they lived aristocratic lives which brought Enid a shower of accusations of 'snobbery and sentimentality'. She was greatly aggrieved at what she saw as the critics' failure to look beyond the names ; to see that even people who were rich and titled were afflicted by the same problems of the human heart that beset everyone, sometimes she believed more so. One of her own constant plaints was : 'Dostoevsky could write poor and in prison ; please God help me to write rich.' Those reviewers who criticized her for the shallowness of the characters, for their lack of concern with the deeper and more sustaining values, such as religious philosophy, which might make old age bearable, in one sense missed the point. Enid was not trying to demonstrate any morals : she was, as always, simply a thoughtful observer of the human condition as she saw it, nothing more, nothing less.

Enid was more amused by a dozen or so letters from 'angry old women who said they still carried on a love life beyond their sixtieth year and that it was revolting and lacking in spirit on Miss Bagnold's part to write of the "cowardly" acceptance of the end of love.' Lewis Gannet in the *New York Herald Tribune* recognized Enid's courage in daring to write about old love – but considered that she failed to bring it off as a novel because 'most of her network of characters were vehicles for her ideas about love and age, rather than flesh and blood individuals.'

She was particularly hurt by *Time* magazine which considered her book 'an ambitious but brittle novel; a portrait of international nobility as it slowly succumbs to the ravages of death and taxes in post-war France. . . . Not all the wealthy fading beauties in novelist Bagnold's France are worthy of one little Velvet Brown.' In a radio discussion of the book, the critic Stephen Bone expressed the sentiments of the young, post-war world when he described the characters as

extraordinarily preoccupied with themselves and their own problems. None of them seems to love anything outside themselves. . . . It's an enormously wealthy book. They are all aristocrats, they've nearly all got titles, they have been totally unaffected by the War and public problems of any kind have never touched them. They are concerned entirely with the question of how they are going to grow old and growing old in all these cases seems to be just a matter of losing teeth, losing sight, getting feebler and finally getting into the grave. There is no suggestion old age might really bring an important new experience. But old age evidently does to some people.

In the climate of the 1950s, criticizing Enid Bagnold for her lack of social conscience could pass for serious artistic comment. It was a judgement that would not disappear, nor would she recognize its validity. 'You have no idea what it's like to be obstinate,' were words Enid put into Miranda's mouth. Enid never had, nor pretended to have, a social conscience and did not see it in any way as part of the artist's wardrobe. For her, the only way to understand human nature was to approach it through individuals, and through individuals whom she knew well. If these were rich or titled, then so be it. Enid always considered it 'the best book I ever wrote. I get a constant flow of letters from people of the calibre of Veronica Wedgwood* and others asking when the book is to be republished.' It was Enid's 'dearest wish' to see it in paperback. She knew publishers believed that the paperback-buying public was not interested in a titled set. Enid insisted they were wrong over this. 'They are as wrong as they were over Sir Osbert Sitwell's immortal descriptions of his aristocratic Great House in his novels.'

Sales figures were, however, disappointing in the youth-mad United States. In the first nine months it had sold only 27,000 copies against 50,000 in the UK. Doubleday 'went way beyond the normal advertising allowances on the book . . . and had to take in a good many returns.'

---

* Dame Veronica Wedgwood, the historian.

FIFTEEN

The Murmur of Delight So Madly Wanted

A FTER the full horrors of the concentration camps became known, the world-wide wave of sympathy towards Jews called for a readjustment in attitudes by Enid and her class. In 1946 Thayer Hobson told her of the unacceptability of the word 'Jew' in a new edition of *Serena Blandish*. 'What a state we have got into if we can't use the word "Jew",' she replied and proceeded to use it at will in a 1948 article about her visit to the health farm.

'The Jew', together with 'the Foreigner', had long been accepted as stereotypes in English fiction. Such literary anti-Semitism was, before World War II, perfectly respectable even in books issued by Jewish publishers. Compared with Dorothy L. Sayers or Agatha Christie, for example, Enid was by no means egregious. But increasingly, as she moved into the New York theatrical world, she became aware that her success was inextricably caught up with Jewish talent. That she accomplished the shift as smoothly as she did was a tribute to her charm. Her friends, if they knew her earlier convictions, forgave her.

In the spring of 1950, Enid went to Zurich, alone, to write a play. This time, Carol Brandt provided the inspiration for one of the protagonists. During her stay at Rottingdean with a friend, Stuart Rose of the *Saturday Evening Post*, she had read a novel written by twenty-eight-year-old Laurian, *Prince Leopold and Anna*.* Both Rose and Brandt admired it and the prospect of youthful fame for her daughter greatly stimulated Enid.

The play which resulted, *Gertie*, is the story of a motherless English family where everything depends on the father producing a long-awaited scientific book. Gertie is the younger daughter who is not prepared to wait for life to happen in this way and when Candida Kaufman, the rich and beautiful wife of her father's American publisher, Israel Kaufman, arrives with a male colleague, Rex, she seizes her chance. She re-enacts with her sister Sarah a play Sarah has written, trying to convince the Americans that she is simply telling the true story of Sarah's life. In addition, she persuades Rex to take a

---

* Published by Michael Joseph in 1948.

business gamble on her own future based on her looks and take her to New York to launch her. He, of course, has other ideas which Gertie, fiercely ambitious as she is, does not really mind. 'This is my talent and I'm going to use it. . . . He'll open the world for me.' The play ends with Candida and Rex fighting as to which one will have the rights to Sarah's play. Candida eventually gives in because her husband suddenly falls ill ; an exciting future in New York seems assured for the two girls. 'You've fallen on luck,' Candida tells them. 'When that happens in life, you need to be quick about it.' It was, in essence, a play about a young girl's desperate search for fame, much as its predecessor, *Lottie Dundass*, had been. Gertie, however, although she had no talent to offer but her face and personality, was in some ways a sharper picture of Enid in her youth. Praise, for Gertie, was an end in itself. She tells Rex, 'All pretty girls are adventuresses.' And again, 'Girls like I am are born to succeed if they can once get out into the world.' Towards the end, Gertie explains herself : 'Look at the fields ! I want to see what else there is, capitals and cities. Men whose eyes light when I walk into a restaurant. I want to be admired. I don't want to be in love. I want to be worn like a jewel on the forehead, to shine outward, not to warm inwards.' Enid was describing familiar emotions.

Enid sent the play to Carol and Carl in February 1951, well aware that it might be offensive. There was, for example, mention of Candida/Carol having no sex appeal. But Enid explained that this had nothing to do with Carol, who had plenty, but was 'necessary because [it] had a bearing on Candida's attraction and repulsion towards and from Sarah.' Luckily Carol reassured Enid she need have no concern about any personal reactions.

While waiting for a buyer for *Gertie*, Enid received an important theatrical boost. *Poor Judas* had been selected for presentation at the Arts Theatre, as part of the Festival of Britain. Enid gave a dinner-party after the special performance, where she sat herself next to Harold Waller, but was disappointed at being awarded third prize by the judges, Alec Clunes, Christopher Fry and Peter Ustinov. However, within a few months, a New York producer, Herman Shumlin – the first in a line who loved her work but found it broke apart in their hands – had bought *Gertie*.

Shumlin was in England in the winter of 1951. Enid invited him to Rottingdean for lunch. The meal was, according to Shumlin, wonderful, 'obviously concocted with great skill out of short rations'. After lunch they went into the garden and spoke of the play. While they were chatting Enid bent over her sleeping mastiff and asked for a paw. The dog did not stir. Enid repeated her request with no more response. Shumlin described what happened next : 'Then Enid spoke again, and I was electrified at the change in her voice. It did not seem to get any louder, but it was the voice of command. The authority not to be questioned. I straightened up and was ready to offer my own paw as the mastiff lumbered to its feet. . . . I had heard the voice of England.'

Shumlin had signed Glynis Johns in the title role and it was agreed that Enid should go to America for rehearsals. Being invited to New York was deemed an achievement in itself in her circle. 'Look at poor old Cecil and all the writers who have written hundreds of plays and have never been asked over there,' Oggie Lynn observed to Laurian. On 3 December 1951, Enid set off for the United States, travelling for the first time in an aeroplane. There was a photographer at the airport who asked her if she would be last on board so that she could turn around and wave for a picture. She complied but could barely manage a smile. In a memorable article after her trip, Enid wrote: 'There would have been an empty seat beside me but Death sat in it. Once or twice he tapped a forefinger on my knee. At Gander he turned sharply and looked at me. The descent seemed vertical. . . . But in the morning we arrived alive in New York.'

Shumlin, who had just emerged from two failures, was pinning many hopes on *Gertie* and Enid. He wanted 'a multitude of revisions' and, more difficult, for her to remove a suspicion that the English get the better of the Americans. But although he expected her to work hard, he was very generous. He put her up in a service flat on West 58th Street, a block away from Fifth Avenue, which she found riveting. 'He says I am to have my hair done and those sorts of things on him,' she told Roderick gleefully:

Tonight, I walked up to something called a SUPER market. Everything to eat in the world. You take a chromium pushcart (they fit into each other and there are dozens at the entrance to the store) and push it round yourself and fill it as you go with the things you want. Then when you've finished you arrive at a sort of parcelling desk and the pushcart is shoved from you. There are great treasure bins (frozen) all around and cartons of food covered with glacé paper already priced. People simply live off tinned and frozen food.

She was treated with great reverence, with several parties given in her honour. 'I am consulted, thought about, thought over, my meaning explained as though I were the Rosetta Stone and they the Egyptologists.' She was invited for Christmas lunch with Marcia Davenport, the writer friend of Jan Masaryk, and dined with Mina Curtiss, 'the friend of Antoine who wrote to me and who turns out to be a Jewish Highbrow'. She spent much time with Sam Behrman, 'who seems really fond of me. How can he be?' and his wife Else, and Harold Freedman and his wife, May. 'All my friends here seem Jews. Harold, Herman, Sam. They are very, very warm-hearted.' Sam and Harold she liked 'better than anyone I've ever met at all. Their whole atmosphere is civilized and witty and Desmondish but with much more life and less highbrow.'

Although she had corresponded with Harold Freedman for more than twenty years, meeting him was still a surprise. Born in Glasgow, Freedman had gone to the US with his family as a boy. She had not expected such quietness but she liked it. His advice was given calmly and without emphasis. It 'fell soft as dew. One hardly noticed it until the quality was gleaming.' He was a man with a mania for secrecy. Everyone told her he was 'wizard'; she knew she was lucky to have his support 'because if there is one human being whose praise I needed it was . . . Harold Freedman. He knew when one had dared to say those odd things that are so nearly crossed out. HIS was the murmur of delight so madly wanted, so musical to listen to, so exhaustedly happy making – at last.' Harold, in turn, thought highly of her talent and sympathized with her predicament. 'Oh God, I haven't got that long any more,' she would tell him. 'Speed, speed, speed, I am 60 and I want to hit the world.' Enid spent Christmas Eve drawing Harold in black ink, with his Homburg hat, white silk scarf flowing, black, too long overcoat hanging open and 'his bumpy forehead and total lack of eyes'. There were telephones and wires everywhere. She framed it herself the same day and presented it to him for Christmas.

As rehearsals progressed, the dramas thickened. Enid was appalled by the original set designs: 'The scenery is just what Americans think an impoverished English family lives in. It's what we think the Irish live in.' She wrote to Roderick: 'My powers of invective no longer end in tears as they do at home. They are *terrible*. But I'm not ashamed of myself. It's the only way to treat the dress designers, scenic designers and all. They are a pack of stupid self-willed, self-set-up people brought up in the gutter.' Such superiority was, of course, not always well received. Even her friend Cecil Beaton commented: 'America has done something quite curious to her in that she is so self-assured and convinced that she is miles above every American she meets.' The constant rows and disappointments, the tears and fights, were not improving the play's chances of success. Twice Glynis Johns threatened to pay back her fare to Shumlin and go home. 'She won't be directed at all and now hates him. It's naughty of her because, though I can see he's an idiot with her, if she could just pretend a bit all would be alright.' Enid appreciated Glynis's 'subtle brand of comedy' and wrote her 'sweet notes' saying how 'I admire her and how lucky I am to have her and how she is exactly Gertie. . . . But I just inserted a little plea for [Shumlin].'

Several of the actors were fired at the last minute but the play finally opened in New Haven, Connecticut, on 2 January 1952. Harold, unable to attend himself, begged Carol to go and try to keep the peace between Glynis, Shumlin and Enid. When the play moved to Boston, it was still being rewritten and everyone was pinning all hope on a miracle. With New York only weeks away, Enid was on edge. Sleepless for days, and aware that there was no such thing as a 'good run' in New York – it was either a smash hit or a failure – she kept going only with the aid of Dexedrine, which she had been taking since the dieting days of 1948. Her doctor, she confided to Diana Cooper, 'adores, as you know, drugging me in every way'. Carol Brandt was worried about the pills and managed to wean her off them in favour of 'a flock of sleeping pills' and tried to get her on to a proper sleeping schedule. Apart from that, she told Roderick, 'Enid was magnificent. Balanced, generous in her dealings with the people she must work with, firm but reasonable. Harold Freedman feels as we all do that she is a very great person in the truest sense of the word. We all adore her.' Such personal praise, however, was not enough to carry the play through. It lasted four days at New York's Plymouth Theater. Broadway theatre-goers missed many of the nuances and considered it too English. The *New York Times* said it lacked 'bounce and sparkle' and the *New York Herald Tribune* described it as 'almost entirely without theatrical vigour'. After the excitement of the flop was over, Enid had time to realize 'how disappointed and, in a way, ashamed YOU must be and the children. You must have built me up so . . . out of pride in me and now this is so difficult to explain. I do apologize so humbly and so from my heart for all the reverse gear you are now putting in . . . I couldn't do more than I did, as you know.'

Antoine was by 1951 a dying man. 'All my life I've carried him my little successes as a dog brings a stick,' Enid wrote to his daughter, Priscilla. Enid saw him for the last time in May after her return from America on the *Queen Mary*, and this time she told him of her humiliating flop. Although she telephoned and wrote to him several times during the next few months, he did not want to see or speak to her again.

The two had had a minor quarrel in 1948. Just as Enid was setting off for Dieppe, to stay with Diana, Antoine had descended on Rottingdean and asked her for a favour. It was to take a sack of food, cooking utensils and blankets with her to France and deliver them to 'a poor priest friend' of his. Of course, she agreed. 'I had never refused him anything.' Diana came down to the harbour to fetch Enid and her sack, but the following morning her intense curiosity made her inspect the contents. Both women were horrified to find

23 Timothy 'before he went to the war'

24 Enid's brother Ralph (*left*) on active service

25 Dominick when he left Eton

26 Enid mucking out the cow at her London home

27 Richard, Timothy and Laurian in wartime Rottingdean
28 Enid (*left*) with Duff and Diana Cooper at Chantilly, 1947

29 Elizabeth Taylor and Mickey Rooney
in the film *National Velvet*, 1944

30 Enid, her grand-daughter Annabel, Timothy's
wife Pandora and Prince Antoine Bibesco, 1948

31 Ann Todd and Sybil Thorndyke in *Lottie Dundass*, Vaudeville Theatre, London, 1943

32 Alan Napier, Polly Rowles and Glynis Johns in *Gertie*, Plymouth Theater, New York, 1952
33 Irene Selznick

34 A strange and cluttered place: the garden room at North End House
35 Edith Evans and Peggy Ashcroft in *The Chalk Garden*, Royal Haymarket, London, 1956

36 Anna Massey, Paul Curran, John Gielgud and Ralph Richardson
in *The Last Joke*, Phoenix Theatre, London, 1960

37 Roderick and Enid in the garden
at Rottingdean c. 1959

38 Charles Laughton in his favourite
armchair at North End House

39 Enid (*right*) and Lynn Fontanne at the Lunts' home in Wisconsin, 1962
40 Margaret Leighton, Alan Webb and John Williams in *The Chinese Prime Minister*, Royale Theater, New York, 1964
41 Deborah Kerr and Hayley Mills in the film of *The Chalk Garden*

42 Katharine Hepburn and Paul Harding
in *A Matter of Gravity*, New York, 1976

43 Working on the sofa

44 Enid Bagnold, 1980

it full of valuable antique silver which Enid had just smuggled out of the country for him. Enid, Diana and Nancy Mitford, who was another guest, decided to pay Antoine back by telling him that Enid had absent-mindedly left the sack on the quayside. When they heard of Antoine's frenzied panic, they knew their little joke had had its effect.

Of all Antoine's brutality which Enid might have resented, this incident near the end of his life rankled most. 'You did a most dangerous and alarming thing to me, that might have resulted in a scandal in the newspapers to Roderick, to Timothy, to all of us . . . to this very old friend who would have done anything for you at any time, you did something that might have been, if discovered, disastrous.'

Antoine died on 2 September 1951. Enid wrote in his obituary in *The Times* of 11 September that he was 'a specialist on his close friends, whom he tortured out of principle . . . whenever he suspected "promise", he was adamant, tyrannical; lashing where the will was soft, breaking off the flowery heads of excuses . . . his tenderness was so extreme that it had to be kept hidden.' Desmond MacCarthy told her she had 'done' Antoine very well, 'although only those who knew him could have seen the merit of what you wrote.' Within months Desmond himself was in a 'dilapidated condition'. He died on 7 June 1952.

W hile she had been in America, Roderick found himself, for the first time in his life, in the centre of the domestic crises that were normally Enid's lot. Enid had been unable since the war to find adequate domestic help. When some new neighbours with naval connections moved to Rottingdean, she asked if they could find her an ex-serviceman and his wife to live in. 'But it was impossible. Nobody would stay in that house long,' the neighbour commented. In 1951, Enid's host of servants had diminished to just three, who struggled to make the household run smoothly. Enid felt guilty at leaving Roderick to cope with the problems. One of the three 'has "the curse" every fortnight but I think everybody is hardened to that by now,' Roderick tried to reassure her. Shumlin was less sympathetic. 'I have never had your heavy burden of servant troubles but the whole institution, with its complicated personality problems, has always offended me. Wouldn't it be better if we were all taught as soon as we could walk to wash our own dirty dishes and make our own beds.' But of course it was not that simple.

Of deeper concern to Enid was her daughter's love life. Hitherto Enid had taken the closest interest in her daughter's affairs. When Laurian had gone to

Spain in 1949, Enid kept reminding her to 'be careful. Later one wants to marry someone and then one is so sorry that one isn't a virgin.' Had Enid really been sorry? Or was it simply a question of double standards? Laurian could accept advice from her mother because she had formed an unusually tight bond with her. 'As a child, I even disliked [Daddy],' she once wrote to her mother. '. . . I think for years I felt he interfered with the fun we had with you and he brought only disapproval.' But now, torn between the affections of two men, Laurian was forced to confide in her father. She knew that marriage to the Hon. Rowland Winn, son of Lord St Oswald, and the prospect of becoming mistress of Nostell Priory, one of England's finest stately homes, was immensely pleasing to her parents, but at the same time she was deeply in love with a Frenchman, whom they viewed as 'the enemy'. Pierre d'Harcourt, a former member of the French Resistance, had been betrayed and shot, and had spent most of the war in solitary confinement at Fresnes and at Buchenwald. Enid and Roderick did not favour his suit because he had been married already and belonged to a family so Catholic that civil divorce and marrying Laurian was not in prospect. While Enid was in New York she prayed for the marriage with Winn 'so that I think I would give my right arm away'. Enid did not need to tell her daughter what to do, they were close enough for her simply to will it. If her children were her greatest works of art, such a 'dazzling marriage' to Winn would crown Enid's achievement, she believed. But, much to her chagrin, Laurian broke off with him. After a year of great tension in the Jones household, Enid wrote to Pierre, begging him not to meet Laurian again. In March 1952, Laurian's engagement to Winn was announced; as she remarked sadly to Plankie, now her aunt, 'I suppose I shall do what everyone wants me to do.'

In a chilling note to her mother three weeks before her wedding, she stated plainly that she was 'marrying Rowland with the firm and overriding intention of never ceasing to love Pierre. If you think that to marry in such a frame of mind is disastrous, then I'd better not marry Rowland.' Apparently Enid did not and the wedding went ahead on 8 May 1952, with a grandiose reception afterwards at 29 Hyde Park Gate. If Enid could not foretell that her daughter's marriage was doomed to failure, the bouquet of white flowers that Pierre tossed into the bridal car as it drove off warned her more poetically.

SIXTEEN

High, High Drama Every Time

IN 1952, Enid was still tinkering about with old ideas hoping one of them would be transformed into a gigantically successful play. An American writer, Keith Winter, wanted to dramatize *The Loved and Envied*. Enid still hoped the main part in this would attract Edith Evans.

In spite of its American failure, Enid had not totally abandoned *Gertie*, and planned to write to Binkie again about an English staging. Freedman had heard from the New York producer, Irene Selznick, who was a close friend of Beaumont, that he always liked the play very much, and was apparently expecting only minor changes. Sam Behrman was working on a musical version of *Serena* and Enid had still not given up on *Heaven Only Knows*. She wrote to J. B. Priestley, whom she had met once at a dinner-party:

If a word from you can clear the way for me, I'll be so grateful. I hardly expect anything can but just to write may be a comfort.... I am so miserable, so boxed up, unable to think, helpless. I can't help thinking there ought to be a set of men (the kind of men who write detective stories, good ones) who formed a club for the advice of dramatists and who, with no pretensions to *writing* the plays, just sat in conclave for a high fee and knit their ready brains and say 'Why! Reverse your situation. *This* is the plot ... not *that*.'

Domestic conditions were, as always, far from perfect. Her three remaining Italian servants greeted her by handing in their notice on the day she returned home from America. 'They have had to be bribed after long negotiations including the whole of a "morning" to stay on until November,' she bemoaned to Harold. With Timothy, Pandora and three-year-old Annabel living at Rottingdean, household help was as important, but more difficult, than ever.

As she looked around for replacements, and, in particular, advertised for a nanny for Annabel, the grain of an idea struck her. By the summer of 1952 she had already a rough pearl in its shell. Because Enid had requested simply a 'lady', without qualifications, it seemed as if all the 'originals and castaways' of Hove and Brighton came out of their single rooms to present themselves at her door. Among them was one 'with a high Roman nose and white hair' whom Enid engaged. She lived, as Enid explained it later, in a sort of inner

silence into which she tried to enfold the child, never entering family conversation if she could help it. But one day, a judge friend, Sir James Cassels, came
to lunch. He told a story of a woman with a life sentence and what became of
her. The new nanny, at a separate table with the child, had her back to the
judge. But she showed a strange, almost trembling interest. 'She not only
turned round, she came right round as a ship turns and you see its bowsprit.'

From this strange action, Enid imagined what must have been occupying
her thoughts. Had she been someone whom he himself had condemned to
death but who had, on appeal, had her sentence commuted to imprisonment?
Enid was fascinated by the mind of a murderess: not a cold-blooded habitual
killer but 'a woman who committed a murder which could be remotely
sympathetic'. She wanted to write not a detective story in the usual sense –
she knew these were not deemed worthy of literary appreciation – but more a
study of psychology. She wrote to Sir James asking for all the details of a
judge at Assizes, attended court herself and devoured every book in the
'Notable Trials' series. From reading *Solitary Confinement* by Christopher
Burney, she learned 'when one is denied hobbies, work, reading, in fact
all the things with which we fill our day, that we are reduced and driven back
to the centre of life and must, for very desperation, deal with it.' Contemplating Pierre d'Harcourt's appalling wartime experiences drew her ideas in
the same direction. Thus, the more interesting character in Enid's new play
became, inevitably, the governess: she knew about life. She had been forced
to think. The lady of the house was only just discovering. When she was faced
with life and death problems, she 'crossed the room, she took down a book,
she polished a fork, she mended her amethyst chain, she asked someone to
lunch, she lifted the telephone so, like me . . . she had evaded God.' It was a
subtle acceptance of the Frenchman's worth.

At all events, by the autumn of 1953, Enid considered the manuscript
finished and, with high hopes, sent it off to Binkie. He read it, 'most carefully', over the weekend. 'A great deal of the play', he told her, 'has the
brilliant writing one expects from Enid Bagnold's pen, but I must confess I
found some of the symbolism confusing and muddling.' He was not 'really
clear as to whether the play has a deliberate state of madness'. He expounded
to Enid what he thought was the main theme 'but I feel that all this is terribly
obscure. . . . I am sorry to be so discouraging but I feel that in its present form
no ordinary theatre audience could disentangle so many cross-sections of life.'

Enid was, naturally, bitterly disappointed; as was Harold Freedman on
her behalf. But he urged her not to give up hopes of a production simply
because Binkie had turned her down. 'The play is a very fine piece of work
and by virtue of its quality and its not falling into the average theatrical mould

it takes on a special problem of its own. But problems are the essence of every successful theatrical venture.' Freedman knew that American managements in the early 1950s were much more receptive to fresh work than the English and that 'it may have to be introduced into England through an American management. . . . I wish I were in England to talk to you as I feel I could dispel some of those despairing vapours much more quickly than I can by writing.' Freedman decided to approach some of the actors directly, but in the meantime, was still working hard on Mrs Selznick. Much depended on which stars she could line up. Ruth Gordon was mentioned as a possible Miss Madrigal, the murderess turned governess, and Jean Simmons as the granddaughter. But negotiations had to be highly confidential because, once it was known that Binkie had rejected it, the play could be finished.

In February 1954 Harold was able to write to Enid : 'Actually Mrs Selznick is really very excited about the play. She has given it to Gladys Cooper who also is excited about it, and also to Jean Simmons, who is afraid of not being able to carry the part. But she is very much under Cukor's influence and I am hoping that out of this Mrs Selznick–Cukor thing something will emerge.'

Harold and Enid were soon pinning all hopes on Mrs Selznick. Daughter of the legendary Louis B. Mayer, Irene was brought up in Hollywood and married to David O. Selznick, the son of Mayer's former employer and rival. After the younger Selznick had established himself with *Gone With The Wind*, his marriage to Irene fell apart. When Irene came to New York she was determined to make a life and success story of her own. She had been highly praised for her production of Tennessee Williams' *Streetcar Named Desire* and followed this with John Van Druten's *Bell, Book and Candle*. Harold considered it was Irene's ability to secure Lilli Palmer and Rex Harrison which gave that play 'a value which it didn't really have and carried it to a great financial success here. . . . I am confident that she can even get Binkie to do the play with her if she could feel that you and she could work together. . . . She has tremendous influence over Binkie.' In March 1954, Harold decided to send Enid a five-page critique of the play which Irene had painstakingly prepared for him. In it she spoke of her misgivings – principally that the play was not focused – but concluded by saying : 'The more I read and examine the play, the more there seems to it – the more challenging, the more tantalizing. I am haunted by its gossamer flashes of poetry and beauty.'

Enid, in reply, accepted many of Irene's initial suggestions for improvement but warned, 'I shan't find anything easy . . . I chiefly remember your force of character and I welcome it. But you must remember how strong you are and pick up the eggshell with care.'

Irene Selznick came to London in July 1954 for six weeks' preliminary work on *The Chalk Garden*. The two women captivated each other but not uncritically. 'Enid was still flaming forward,' Irene wrote of her years later in her autobiography. 'Greedy for praise, affection and the last crumb on the plate, she was shamelessly stagestruck. I have known no one else in my life as eager for laurels as Enid still was at sixty-four ... in short she craved celebrity.'

Irene found Enid's conversation as stimulating as her written work except when it involved her. She was sharp enough to realize that Enid turned everyone who fascinated her into a 'character', and pre-empted her: 'The only covers you'll ever put me between are bed-covers.' Irene was quick to spot the process at work; the way she was served up as a trophy at mealtimes to the Jones children as proof of their mother's success. But Enid's gift for extrapolating the germ of truth and embellishing it was never given free rein with Irene. Eighteen years younger than Enid, with long shiny black hair and dark eyes, Irene had an exotic beauty that Enid appreciated and an undeniably fascinating past that she longed to know more about. In the absence of facts, Enid invented. Rifling through Irene's cupboards in her London hotel bedroom, she found racks of satin gowns and drawers full of jewels, the evidence she expected of a fabulously rich Hollywood Jewish princess. But Enid was offended that she did not bring these clothes to Rottingdean. 'When at work she always wore the same one.'

Irene complained about the cold in the Tower Room where they worked – only to be told that she was a 'thin-blooded American', but discovered later that Enid worked with a heated pad around her legs. At night she found her mattress unbearably lumpy and had to put up with a 15-watt bulb for reading – a serious matter since she worked in bed until the small hours. But she slept late which gave Enid time for her numerous rewrites.

A routine soon emerged. Irene would catch the Brighton Belle out of London every Friday, spend the weekend working at Rottingdean and then return after lunch on Monday to polish alone what they had worked on together. Irene realized that Enid had the whole gamut of emotional cards in her pack; she could be loving and grateful, resentful or guilty by turn. She could flatter, woo or charm, or she could blackmail on account of her age. Irene may have found the age factor disingenuous: the constant references to how little time she or Roderick had left, how difficult things were at her age, or how long she had worked on a play. But old age and fear of death were Enid's deepest anxieties. Nevertheless Irene admitted, 'I grew increasingly fond of her, she was so admirable and touching in her reach. I had taken no option on the play and had no obligation, but I got in deeper and deeper, and so did she.'

Not then a writer, Irene's talent was in seeing a theme and pulling it straight as one pulls a thread through a cloth. 'She never wrote one word of the play, and this was her pride. She pushed and poked me into rearrangements, into doing things I thought I couldn't do.' Enid had basketsful of *bon mots* called her 'plums', of which she was very proud. She took to stringing these up on a washing-line across the room. Irene could lighten the diet of 'plums', which were making many of the speeches indigestible.

Irene disciplined Enid out of her self-indulgence with words by forcing her to think about what she was trying to say and then say it in a way the audience understood. Enid loved the sound of various concoctions of words and if their meaning was hazy she would defend herself as being elliptical – a favourite Bagnold word. 'I don't know what it means but it falls so beautifully.' Irene told her she had to make every single line work if she was to have a successful play.

When Irene's six weeks were up, the play was far from ready. It was Enid's turn now to visit New York. Still frightened of flying, she sailed early in October on the *Queen Elizabeth*. Also on board, she was delighted to notice, was Lord Beaverbrook. Roderick was still smarting over his lack of a peerage and Enid decided to tackle Beaverbrook about it – 'which cost me a certain effort'. He told her, she reported home, that Roderick 'has never had a tythe of what he deserves . . . it ought to be got on with at once. Roderick deserves it. I've told Churchill so.' Roderick spent much of the time while Enid was away lobbying his friends among the press lords but to no avail.

On 13 October, Enid was back at Park Chambers, her old service apartment on West 58th Street, 'slogging away' as hard as ever. Seeing Irene ensconced in her 'magnificent suite' at the Pierre Hotel, 'the last word in luxury . . . impersonal and overloaded', led her to conclude, 'I think her interior taste must in some way have been rebuked by Rottingdean.' When Roderick heard that Enid had to scrimp and save on meals he was furious. 'Here you are the wife of a rich husband and yourself rich, struggling and making do as if you were some poor seamstress or an impoverished hack writer instead of a celebrated and best-selling author. . . . It is not in keeping with your position, especially compared with the luxury of Irene's suite at the Pierre.'

The constant rewritings and arguments were a great trauma for Enid. She was suffering from eye-strain and lumbago and sleeping never more than five hours. During one sleepless night, she wrote to Irene things she felt unable to say.

I have become like an elderly schoolgirl writing a difficult essay over whose shoulder the headmistress glances at every batch of sentences saying 'No good – my child! Start again!' I am not young enough to go through this – knowing that it is going to defeat us both. I am locked, at a standstill, tied – because I can't breathe under the continual rearrangement of small patches.

Laurian implored her mother to give up the Dexedrine. 'I feel so upset when I think of it. . . . If we should lose you through that play . . . rather us than the play.' But, in spite of her sixty-four years, she could call on amazing reserves of courage and energy. She told Cecil Beaton she was upset at the way photographs aged her. 'I get such shocks when I see pass in the mirror an old lady masking a sort of everlasting girl inside.' Nonetheless, Irene considered she 'insulted' her energy by the handful of Benzedrine she took every morning.

Enid was hoping to be able to return home within a few weeks as Dominick was about to be married. However,

I have the whole of Act Three to redo (according to Irene) and that will be a sweat and an agony. She hardly listens to what I do but just tears her hair. . . . But, in spite of her difficulties she does adore us both, especially you. I wish you could have heard her to me alone after dinner tonight. . . . She tore up and down the room, rather like Duse her hair down and her eyes burning. Not drunk. She'd had only water. That you were the most gallant man she'd ever met . . . 'because he is a *man* and I am not accustomed to men. Women here kinda castrate them. Roderick exhorts hard terms. But when they are fulfilled he gives everything. Look how he's managed you and I'll bet you were a handful. . . .' I think, as I've come all this way, I'd better stay the time she needs me. . . . Whatever she is or whatever her vices, faults or troubles she has . . . she is a fine, big, generous character in herself. She is the sort of woman who would die proudly I think.

Enid had, by now, fallen under Irene's sway. And she knew there was no chance of getting her play on without her.

When she returned in November, Enid was hopeful but not confident about the success she saw in store for her. Irene was aiming for an autumn 1955 opening. George Cukor had agreed to direct and Cecil Beaton, over-riding Irene's misgivings, had agreed to do the set designs. Beaton had encouraged Enid for months about this play; when Binkie turned it down he insisted that that only 'rebounds against him' and urged her to keep at it. He told her when he read the play that it gave him

such a glow of pleasure, admiration and excitement that . . . if the manuscript hadn't to be returned forthwith I would . . . re-read it to the exclusion of anything else, all the time. . . . It is a masterpiece. . . . It has a depth that shames most other plays into oblivion – I am really thrilled to the marrow. In any case I am sure someone very sensitive and imaginative must be given the responsibility of bring-ing this to life and if it's convenient and easily managed I'd love to help with the Chalk Garden and the interior.

Enid replied that she would 'be honoured if you would do the scenery if ever it gets done'.

Irene did not want to work with Cecil because of an incident in 1938. Cecil had illustrated an article for the February issue of *Vogue* about the sort of people now taking over Long Island society. The lettering in the drawing, which could only be read with a magnifying glass, included references to Mrs Mayer and Mrs Selznick, and the word 'kike'. The repercussions of this were severe as the New York press immediately picked up the scandal. *Vogue* was threatened with losing a vast amount of revenue as advertisers cancelled. Cecil left the country in disgrace. Only Enid's insistence made Irene think that, after seventeen years, it was time to forget. At all events, she recognized how important to Enid was Cecil's presence.

On 16 December, 29 Hyde Park Gate was again the setting for a big society wedding; Dominick, twenty-four, married Miss Joanna Grant, the daughter of Lady Tweedsmuir by her first marriage. Four weeks after the wedding Enid and Roderick went to Basutoland for a holiday. Enid was satisfied with her achievements in 1954. Doubleday had reprinted two of her novels in one volume, *The Happy Foreigner* and *The Squire*, which they called *The Girl's Journey* because 'men build their own lives, but no girl knows her journey', the publisher explained. This went but a little way towards the longed-for collected edition of her works but the glowing foreword by Arthur Calder-Marshall gave her some of the recognition she believed she deserved. Describing how all Enid Bagnold's work was rooted in experience, Calder-Marshall wrote: 'Yet, if the root is personal experience, the flower is universal. She has a curious ability of distilling from what she has thought and done and felt, an essence which is the meaning of life, not just her own life or those of other people, but the force of life itself.'

Enid had specifically requested that Calder-Marshall write the introduction because he had warmly praised her work already. But she was dismayed when she discovered what Heinemann intended to pay him. 'If my lifetime of slow work – not many books but I have put my very best in them – is only now worth a twenty guinea introduction I think you should have said so at the start. But you gave me to understand that in reissuing these two books everything would be of the best – including printing and set-up and binding.' Calder-Marshall learnt later that Enid paid Heinemann to send him a sum she believed more fitting.

Enid made considerable changes to *The Chalk Garden* during her holiday but it was never enough for Irene. 'Don't think I don't like and respect the old tyrant,' she admitted to Harold Freedman, 'she's fine. But she's bloody.... I have done a lot and a lot of work out here. And I think good work. But I never know with Irene.'

The pair corresponded at length in the spring of 1955 and then Irene came over again. Enid knew that she and Cecil were by now

what she calls hostell. I suppose by nature ... I want to get the best out of him because I believe in the best and admire him so much and I *know* he can do the play and understands it. What is maddening is not to be able to get over to him that knowledge because when I make an objection he associates it so much with Irene that he won't take it. ... It's a nuisance because I can see myself having such a time with them both in New York.

At one stage, Irene forbade Enid from mentioning his name and Enid resorted to 'making a poor little frail light joke in order to speak of him at all. ... It brought on such a paroxysm of screams that Richard (next door) said to me afterwards, "I didn't know whether to come in or not. I thought she was perhaps killing you. But as they were her screams, I comforted myself you were killing her."

Although adjustments were still being made to the script, the major roles in the play now had to be cast. For Mrs St Maugham, Enid had all along hoped for Edith Evans. 'Is she out of her mind? I wish we could get her, out of her mind or not,' Enid wrote to Harold. But again, Irene could not see this as a good idea. Gladys Cooper, still beautiful at sixty-seven, and a name to conjure with in England and America, had already cabled that she would be 'thrilled' to play the part. But even she began to have her doubts when she heard about the difficulties being encountered in casting the other parts.

Irene had originally been attracted to the play partly because she saw in her friend Katharine Hepburn the perfect Miss Madrigal. 'I had always longed to do a play with Kate.' But Hepburn never liked the play, did not 'react' to it and turned Irene down. Next they tried Wendy Hiller but she did not want to leave England. Enid even proposed Diana Cooper but Irene decided to 'withhold professional comment [on this] and instead say that no part is worth risking a long and beautiful friendship.'

Suddenly Irene hit upon the Irish actress, Siobhan McKenna. She loved the script but refused to be pinned down throughout that summer as she was hoping to act St Joan in New York. Finally Siobhan could not refuse Irene's generous offer to maintain her, her husband, governess and four-year-old son in New York for part of the time. 'She told me even the Oliviers didn't get that kind of money.'

On 11 July 1955 Laurian finally married Pierre, by then divorced. Enid, having long since realized her mistake, was now totally supportive of the couple. Delighted to see her only daughter happily settled, she hosted a small wedding lunch at Hyde Park Gate.

The following month Enid sailed for New York again on the *Queen Elizabeth*. She promised Irene that she would 'work like blazes' on the ship, but was distracted at leaving Roderick. 'I feel guilty and miserable and apprehensive, apprehensive all the time.' Enid never enjoyed goodbyes: 'I saw you walk away and *bore* it. Somehow I had rehearsed it so much it didn't have the terrible effect of last time!... It will only be bad when you go to bed and see my empty bedroom. Oh how fond we are of each other, aren't we.... It's just everything.'

But the worries and tribulations that had beset her while working with Irene in England were as nothing compared with the storms that broke loose the moment she arrived in New York. She went with Irene from the docks to her Fifth Avenue hotel, the Stanhope, and recounted to Roderick every detail of the saga that followed.

When she [Irene] got here immediately a phone call came through that something grave had gone wrong with George's [Cukor] release from MGM and that they reserved the right to call him back at any time ... so that one could easily be with no director at all. Then ensued, believe it or not, four hours telephoning.... She was going to have taken me out to dinner but she started lying on the other bed and my bags not even come up to the room and called California, one call after the other. First David Selznick for advice. Then her lawyer. Then another lawyer, then the present head of MGM, Dore Sherry. Then every sort of Jewish powerful name you can imagine, all the Ricklemeyers and Hubersteins and Finkeldiesels and threatening all the time to put her father on it.

However Enid told Roderick not to be 'depressed by the excesses of Irene – I tell them to you to amuse you with a sort of rueful, sour enjoyment that perhaps doesn't get through in a letter'.

George Cukor had great style and talent, but had not worked in the theatre for twenty-five years. He arrived in New York a week after Enid, barely familiar with the script. When Irene presented him with a scale model of the set to help him block his scenes, he asked her what it was for. At the first rehearsal George had insisted Enid read the play on the stage to the actors. She had adored doing this and performed extremely well; but Gladys, who considered herself as much an expert on the habits of the English upper classes as Enid, resented it. 'Before the reading she had called me Enid. After it, Miss Bagnold. Later, Lady Jones. As I ascended in social scale and went down in contempt, I realized she had classed me as a social character who by luck (and possibly ghosted) had got some fool to put on my play.' Gladys, wanting to play a beauty not a character part, loathed her entrance line: 'You can't fit false teeth to a woman of character,' and constantly muttered it inaudibly, complaining it was vulgar. Enid considered this ridiculous. 'Both Winston Churchill and I have them,' she retorted.* 'Well I don't!' Gladys snapped back. On opening night in New York Gladys got her own back: she simply did not say the line. Gladys constantly approximated her lines, which was not only a cruel anathema to Enid but which Irene, after two years' 'pitched battle' over the text, was not prepared to allow. She played it, Enid told Roderick, 'like a Wimbledon housekeeper's dated ill-bred idea of a great lady ... she gives the impression of a small, thin sarcastic woman instead of a rollicking furious almost restoration woman.' But George thought Gladys wonderful and seemed quite happy to accept her stage directions.

In the middle of rehearsals, George was recalled for retakes on his film, *Bhowani Junction*. And Enid, 'who not only had the courage, she had the urge as well', took over as director. She made several changes in his absence which did little to ease the mounting tension. But at least she found herself able to reply 'balls' to his 'shit' – 'so we are getting on'.

Irene and 'Miss' Beaton, as Enid referred to him in letters, were by this time at loggerheads almost every day over something; usually expenditure. Irene accused Cecil of trying to buy up half the antique furniture in New York for the play and asked Enid to supervise the purchases. She was to tell Cecil 'that this won't do and that won't do'. In addition, Irene brought in two of her friends, Laura Harding and Johnnie Johnstone, to oversee clothes and furniture respectively, both of which were Cecil's responsibilities. With his wings thus clipped, he was flapping around in a permanent 'white rage' and 'behaving like a child'. By 9 September, Enid considered Cecil and Irene were only *just* on speaking terms. 'She says he and George egg each other on ... both being homos. I manage to keep out of it but it's hard work skirting.' However, Enid, hoping to see her own Rottingdean garden-room on stage, thought Cecil had done well to reproduce 'the work-table, garden syringes, saw, shears, hats, baskets, catalogues, everything'.

For North End House was a strange, cluttered place, with none of the grandeur of a 'country house', but an undeniable atmosphere. The artefacts collected were not merely *from* her past, they *were* her past. A large wall-length mirror not only gave her garden-room the appearance of a stage set and one was indeed being constructed based upon her own home. This fusion of myth and reality was the zenith of Enid's adolescent dream-come-true. But the Rottingdean cobblestones, she complained, 'look like a gigantic skin eruption'.

* Enid had all her top teeth removed in November 1943. Although the initial relief from pain was 'heaven', she then underwent a long, extremely painful period when the gums felt as if they were 'boiling'.

On 21 September, the company moved to New Haven for the first performance. Enid was giving Fritz Weaver, playing Maitland, the butler, private
coaching in her hotel bedroom. 'He is desperate . . . because whenever I get the
right inflection into him George yells at him and destroys him.' At the same
time Gladys was sabotaging Siobhan, by stealing all her openings, saying something loud when expected soft or else giving a wrong cue. Irene was furious
with George for not standing up to Gladys and decided, in spite of all the
long-standing connections: '"This is where you take a flight, boy. . . ." The
things she said to him made my hair curl. Wonderful gangster Americanisms,'
Enid reported home. In New Haven Irene announced George's departure to
the company. Enid and she together were to direct until a replacement was
found. At the same time, Irene sacked Laurel, as she could not be heard;
Norah Gorson, an English actress, was sent back home in 'tears and hysteria'.
The understudy took over and performed magnificently. But then Betsy von
Furstenburg was engaged and the understudy demoted once again. Irene also
sacked a dog who would not do as he was bid on stage.

Not surprisingly, the New Haven notices were unexciting. 'British
drawing-room comedy that had fine words that couldn't be heard,' wrote
one. But Paramount offered for the film rights that week, and, highly uncertain
of the play's reception in New York, Enid decided instantly to take what she
could get now,

namely a sixtieth . . . of sixty-five thousand dollars and 10% of gross New York
takings on every week in New York that shows a profit. So that I get about 10 or 11
thousand pounds down anyway. And with a further possibility (Harold says) of
about a thousand pounds a week in N.Y. only. *They* take the world rights. I closed
for this because I think it wiser to be at least ten thousand pounds in hand. Rather
than have a vague chance of eighty thousand.

The company moved into Boston like a house of cards that would collapse
at the slightest breath of ill wind. Fritz Weaver, convinced it was now his turn
to be sacked, was to be seen staring at blank walls in passageways looking as if
he were rehearsing *Hamlet*. Irene was still making Enid rewrite large chunks
but the cast could not take any more. 'I said no at this point. The changes were
too late and not good,' Siobhan McKenna recalled. Quite suddenly Siobhan
fell ill from the tension. She was, briefly, almost comatose. Irene rushed her
own doctor to visit her and she recovered after a few days. George opened for
the company in Boston but then handed over to a new director, Albert Marre.

Irene had been relieved to get anybody, almost. Marre was just thirty, and
fresh from a big success in London with *Kismet*. According to Irene, he
damned himself at the outset by pronouncing the play 'too oblike'. But Marre
refutes this. 'At the first meeting I said everything was dreadful and needed

lots of changes . . . but I did appreciate the point of view, the way the lines had
to be said.' Marre recalled: 'I found the company in total anarchy, the
production in shambles and Gladys behaving appallingly, yelling everywhere. Enid was totally befuddled. . . . Irene was constantly trying to make
her redo scenes.' Marre remembered that the supply of Dexedrine was never
far away. Siobhan McKenna realized the impossibility of the young director's task. 'But he altered our positions, he brought the play down to earth
and let us perform.'

To straighten out some of the confusion Marre asked Enid questions about
the unwritten background. Was Madrigal guilty? What was her crime? To
which Enid replied, 'I really don't know. I can't write a play like this with
everyone driving me mad.' Marre then suggested looking at an earlier script.
'Maybe there are some good points there.' Enid, in desperation, showed him
'the original'. 'She did not tell me for several days what she had done,' Irene
recalled, 'but she hoped to persuade Marre to revert to some of her original
text.' When Enid confessed she 'wept tears of rage. She said "there's no fool
like an old fool. I've been disloyal and greedy. Please forgive me but he
appealed to my vanity."'

The Cecil trouble, which had been simmering since London, boiled over in
Boston. Marre considered Beaton an amateur in the theatre and demanded
some fundamental set changes. 'All the exits and entrances were up stage with
no reason for any of the cast to go down stage at all.' Irene, once she realized
that Cecil's chalky white set could not be lighted properly, and the actor's
faces disappeared against it, was also unhappy. She insisted on having it
resprayed in a shade of pale lavender. Cecil obliged but was in a fury over it.
Enid reminded him: 'It's the garden, not the house, that's chalk.'

Somehow, the play moved on to Philadelphia. Suddenly, the reviews were
good. But at the end of the month Roderick arrived. Irene had dreaded his
appearance, knowing only too well what effect this would have on Enid.
'What I couldn't bear was Enid telling me what Roderick thought about the
production. What a waste of time.' She had tried to persuade Enid to tell him
not to come. 'But she felt so guilty at leaving him. She felt he was entitled to
this.' Later, Roderick put all the arrangements for his trip in a large, manilla
envelope and wrote across it: 'RJ trip to USA for Chalk Garden. Practically
all paid very generously by EJ.' Her 1955 income from US book royalties
alone (before receiving any money from *The Chalk Garden*) was $2,382.

Carol Brandt was deputed to meet Roderick off the boat; Enid had insisted
on this, remembering both the travelling style to which he was accustomed
and that he was now nearly eighty. But Irene was right; Roderick was bored
while his wife was working at full tilt. On the night before opening, New

York was afflicted with a torrential rainstorm. Roderick, staying at the Century Club, wanted to go out but could not find a cab. He telephoned Enid at the theatre where everyone was in a state of panic and requested that she come and fetch him. It was the final dress rehearsal but, never questioning where her duty lay, she left the theatre instantly, stood out in the rain until, soaked through, she eventually hailed a cab. She collected Roderick and returned. She had been out of the theatre for a critical two and a half hours. Carol Brandt commented, 'She had very great love for him.'

The Chalk Garden opened at the Barrymore Theater on 26 October 1955, the day before Enid's sixty-sixth birthday. Wearing 'the most expensive dress I have bought since we used to be rich', Enid found it 'a balloon of a play. It rose in the warm air to the ceiling.'

'Oddly enough', as Enid remarked twice in her autobiography, there was no opening party. Irene guessed at Enid's disappointment. 'But no one was on very good terms and everyone was nervous. And there was Roderick. He never stayed up beyond 10.30 . . . but Enid couldn't leave him.' Irene went with Truman Capote and some of the cast to one restaurant, while Enid and Roderick had scrambled eggs and gin with Harold and May Freedman at a small bar near the theatre. Before the night was out they saw the reviews. Brooks Atkinson in the *New York Times* described *The Chalk Garden* as

a coruscating piece of work – witty in the literary tradition of Congreve, the lines carefully polished, the observations of character shrewd and hard-headed, the portrait of an upper-class world intimate and objective. . . . There is a stimulating mind at work in *The Chalk Garden*. It is courageous, subtle and detached. It is one of the keenest minds that have upset the complacence of Broadway for a long time.

Both Enid and Irene, geared for failure, wept on the telephone at such praise. Enid told her : 'It isn't so much the pleasure of success that I feel – as the glory of escape from humiliation.'

In the following months the play's success snowballed. All of New York's smart society went to see it. When Grace Kelly, escorted by Prince Rainier, saw the play, their visit made front-page news.

SEVENTEEN

Glued to History's Wall

WITHIN hours of the New York reviews, Binkie cabled: he wanted *The Chalk Garden* on in London as soon as possible. Sir John Gielgud was sent the script. If he liked it, he would recommend it to Edith Evans and Peggy Ashcroft; both would be happy to work under his direction. Enid also wrote to Peggy Ashcroft begging her 'to make my old age perfect' by playing Madrigal, a role which Enid told her owed a little to their mutual friend at the Babies Club, Nurse Raynham Smith. As Irene wrote to Beaumont there was no question of Gladys for the London production:

Neither Enid nor I would want to have Gladys. Although she is having a triumph in the part it is our feeling that a woman with a better ear and a bit more taste and intellect would fare even better. Her conduct has generally been quite unattractive and her manners atrocious. All I can say is that if we had not made the grade I would have attributed the margin of difference to Gladys' conduct and influence. On her behalf let me say that it was not entirely her fault, as she is a party who needs a very firm hand and in this case she had the director completely under her thumb, in fact completely intimidated.

Once again, however, the major problem was Cecil. By January 1956 Cecil knew he was not being asked to do the London production. Enid maintained that in addition to Irene being 'revengefully desirous' that Cecil be left out, Binkie did not want 'to have to pay your high fee or percentage. (He [Binkie] never told me that: Irene told me.) On top of that John came down here and saw pictures of the set and didn't want it. I think not that he *disliked* it but wanted ideas of his own, as Director.' John Gielgud refutes this: 'I had no part in the decision myself but was forbidden by Baumont and Mrs S. to go over and see the New York production.'

Gielgud believed that Beaumont's antipathy to Beaton was prompted mainly by a desire to protect his star, Edith Evans. She was already unwell when rehearsals began and 'Binkie was afraid of upsetting her if she had to work with Cecil again. During the war she had done *Heartbreak House* with him and they had rows over her dresses. One, a tea gown with a long train, she said got in her way whenever she entered.'

Whoever was to blame for Cecil's not being used, Enid attracted the full blast of his venomous tirades. In a fury built up over months of frustration and cemented with jealousy over Enid's great success, he savagely cut her out of his life. Throughout rehearsals in London, Enid was agonizing over the bitter rupture with Cecil. On 16 January he wrote to her that when he was told of the new designer for the London production, 'I felt once more that my friendship for you and my admiration for your work in general . . . had cost me dearly. . . . It is sad that so fragrant a blossom as your play should be surrounded by so much stink.' He warned her: 'If any part of my work, the ground plan, architecture, conception of the scene, the chalky colours, properties, flowers, etc., etc., are copied, then the Stage Designers' Union will have a strong case for compensation.' Irene commented: 'Scrubbing and hot baths have not succeeded in removing the stench of Cecil's letter.' Enid repeatedly tried to mend the rift. 'Let's forget about it,' she replied on 10 February. 'I am terribly sorry you aren't doing the décor here. It will be nothing like so distinguished. I am sorry about the whole thing, your experience in America and everything. But never sorry that I begged Irene to ask you to do it or that you agreed.' When this failed to soothe him Enid asked Diana Cooper for advice. 'Perhaps I was to blame for not fighting enough,' Enid admitted to her. 'The truth is, I have had to fight for him every inch of the way. Irene loathed him. She despised his lack of professionalism . . . she swore all through America she would never use him in London.' Diana, who was 'only concerned that my friends should be at odds', suggested Enid write a further letter.

Swallowing her pride, Enid once again attempted rapprochement. 'The thing that matters to me most . . . is that I have hurt you. Or that you think I have hurt you. . . . I am not only terribly sorry about everything (and it grows like a mountain of misunderstandings the more I look at it) but also terribly the loser. I have very, very few friends and you, to me, are one of the nearest.' Again Cecil came back with a 'one-sided wounding letter'. 'It isn't just that I am hurt,' he began, 'I am shocked and angry at such cowardice and underhandedness, to say nothing of the poor taste involved in this seedy business . . . the fact that you, who are not sufficiently of the theatre to have been contaminated by its lack of manners, should have proved yourself so weak and easily over-ridden is the real cause of such deep distress,' he told her. Having 'shot her bolt of sorrow', Enid tried finally to reconcile herself to the permanent loss of Cecil as a friend, but she mourned it as a death.

Despite all the criticism of Cecil's sets when *The Chalk Garden* was struggling in America, she now missed them. 'Yes I know the [London] décor . . . is beneath contempt,' she admitted to Diana Cooper. 'Binkie fobbed me off with a cheap little man with a beard from a garden city.' Gielgud knew of Enid's disappointment with the London set. 'She marched down the stalls and shouted "Good God no. You've had it painted Gingah!" when it was first put up. The poor designer [Reece Pemberton] had endless difficulties allowing for all the number of exits necessary and her wishes to put her Rottingdean garden room on to the stage.'

Enid took a close personal interest in the London production. She proposed at an early stage that her own daughter-in-law might play Laurel and told Irene she was having Pandora coached for the part. But the suggestion did not meet with general approval and gave rise to further adverse comments about Enid's amateurism. She was perturbed by Edith Evans's nervousness at rehearsals. 'Enid bullied her about getting words wrong,' Gielgud recalled. 'And I kept her away from the stage as much as possible. Once, after the opening night in Birmingham, I stood in front of Edith's dressing-room door to prevent Enid from going in.' But if Gielgud tried to keep her away she sent him pages of notes instead. 'Poor John . . . I can't keep it in. Banish me and I shoot my mouth on paper.' As a prelude to six pages of detailed instructions for her director, she explained:

I have been thinking why it is I attach so much importance to how each individual turn of speech is said. . . . It's because each flick or wrist-turn of dialogue . . . each pair of sentences – statement and riposte – has been studied off the life. So that in a way it can be said in that way or no other. . . . It's why, also, the play is a success on its dialogue though it's not very strong dramatically.

Gielgud, who came to know Enid well, found her 'a rewarding, appreciative friend'. In his view 'She *was* stagestruck but not really interested in the theatre, except as regards her own plays. A thwarted actress.' His abiding memory of her at this time was her 'personal vanity. She had a number of evening dress outfits in black satin, all alike, and would enter the hotel or theatre like a battleship.'

Before the British production was ready, the New York version was running into difficulties. 'Business has taken a tremendous tumble in New York this week. Not only with us but with every play,' Freedman wrote to Enid in March. He pressed Enid to accept a drop in her royalties, to $250 a week, so that the play could be kept going as 'a reigning success . . . for the sake of all the other rights, including the most important one of all – the British production.' But there were other plays 'pressing at the Shuberts' door' and the Shubert management did not have another theatre to offer them.

By return, Enid told him to do whatever he thought best. 'If I have to take less to keep the play going then you arrange that.' All the same she was, she told him, delighted at 'any snips that come my way. Amateur rights, German rights, television . . . all grist to the mill. Our own political situation suddenly seems grey from floor to ceiling and Roderick talks money depression – till I see all my good money going the way of the housekeeping like an old leaky boat with two broken oars each side. I long to *spend*. Just be careless and carefree. but it's not to be!'

With only days to the out-of-town opening Enid began to panic when she heard that Irene was planning to come over. She wrote to Harold explaining the situation. 'Binkie . . . tells me he recognizes symptoms in Edith like last year. . . . If Irene were to come too soon and fight to have Edith change her lines, we should have no play at all, for Edith would resign and Binkie says if she breaks down a second time it will be for ever. She is 67, very religious* and I think she would go straight into old age!'

There was another reason too. Enid had made some changes to the script which she knew Irene would not allow. 'I have not made many alterations but as it is that an English humorous play is being done in England I have "made bold" to put in a few things I have always wanted. . . . My "collaboration" with her is over. That was in America.'

On 21 March, the day *The Chalk Garden* opened in Birmingham, Harold had to write to Enid that the Shuberts had given their notice on the theatre and that 'last weeks' had been announced. Even that could not take away from Enid's glory over the thrilling reviews the play received in Birmingham and then Brighton. There was one more argument before the London opening. For some weeks Enid had been pestering Beaumont about opening-night seats, 'driving Binkie round the bend', according to Irene. 'At first she wanted the whole of the Jones family in the front row. Even when told that this was reserved for the critics she would not break it up into six and four. Then, when she heard that Binkie and I were sitting in a box, she wanted the Royal Box . . . she had lived all her life for this, she wanted to show off her triumph.'

On 11 April 1956 at the Theatre Royal, Haymarket, the atmosphere was electric, expectations were extremely high. Enid was not disappointed with the tremendous final applause. There were loud and long shouts for the author and the play became an instantaneous success. Surrounded by family and friends, Enid found the London triumph undoubtedly sweeter than New York's *succès d'estime*. One critic in particular, Kenneth Tynan, wrote an article in the *Observer* on Sunday 15 April from which she derived endless pleasure:

On Wednesday night, superbly caparisoned, the cavalry went into action and gave a display of theatrical equitation which silenced all grumblers. . . . The occasion of its

* As a convinced Christian Scientist, Edith would have been reluctant to call a doctor.

triumph was Enid Bagnold's *The Chalk Garden* (Haymarket) which may well be the finest artificial comedy to have flowed from an English (as opposed to an Irish) pen since the death of Congreve. . . . We eavesdrop on a group of thoroughbred minds, expressing themselves in a speech of exquisite candour, building ornamental bridges of metaphor, tiptoeing across frail causeways of simile, and vaulting over gorges impassable to the rational soul.

But he concluded by saying that *The Chalk Garden* probably marked 'the end of an era. Miss Stott's [Laurel] farewell to Dame Edith [Mrs St Maugham], as irrevocable as Nora's departure in "A Doll's House", represents the future taking leave of the past.'

The play ran for twenty-three months – a glorious but not entirely trouble-free run. Edith did fall ill and suffered from appalling constipation. A cure was eventually found which did not run counter to her religious beliefs, giving rise to the theatrical joke 'Edith's been'. Meanwhile, Gladys Cooper magnanimously agreed at very short notice to fly over and replace Edith in the part she had created. Peggy Ashcroft, pre-booked to appear in another play, had to leave after three months and was replaced first by Pamela Brown, who also fell ill, and then by Gwen Ffrangcon-Davies.

During this time Enid was awarded the American Academy of Arts and Letters Silver Medal and a cheque for $1,000 for distinguished achievement in the art of drama. 'Such praise,' Enid said in her written acceptance speech, gave her 'a sort of violence of delight . . . honour is a grace in life not unlike love. In old age it does instead of love.' She gave some thought as to how she would spend the $1,000. She was distinctly proud of her ability to earn money and had an unquenchable desire to give to her children. 'She enjoyed giving,' Timothy explained, 'like no one else I've known. She enjoyed it like one enjoys giving to a child on its first birthday; no expectation of thanks or anything, just to see the look of wonder.' She believed, as she wrote in *The Last Joke*, 'People must be suddenly enriched!'

But she had a habit of talking about her gross, pre-tax earnings, rarely considering her net-of-tax income, and she always maintained a fairly relaxed attitude to tax matters because they did not interest her greatly. Percy Popkin helped her save a little here and there on expenses which was gratifying. But against this was the irritation caused by Roderick's insistence that she contribute towards their joint tax assessment on the basis of her royalty income being treated as the top slice of their joint income.

From about 1950 onwards, she made various settlements of the copyrights in her books and plays not only as a result of John Foster, her barrister friend, persuading her that she was foolish to pay as much tax as she did, but also because it was such a pleasure to give.

Thus, having made all of *The Chalk Garden* proceeds over to her four children, 'so that I get none . . . the children said that I must spend the prize on myself. . . . I said, "a jewel", (not meaning it). The youngest son said, "You're too old for jewels!" But now I have decided. It's to be a canal. The garden here is too "downland" for a formal pool . . . I call it a canal but I fear it will look like a ditch.' And so, appropriately enough, she spent the money on her garden and had a small decorative canal with brick archways built. Then in the spring, she was also enjoying two new grandchildren. Dominick's son Romily was born on 18 February, followed on 21 April by Laurian's first child, Hattie.

As the production settled down to its nightly applause Enid worked on a published version of the play. She maintained that, in spite of two years 'fiddling' with Irene, the final script was not so different from her own original version. 'Did I ever tell you', she asked Harold Freedman, 'I turned up the original copy before she touched it and it wasn't so different! True the scene between the judge and Madrigal wasn't in it. That was about all. And it was never very well written – that scene. It was heavy and unreal.'

With the play established, Enid began to 'hate a certain subordination I feel to her [Irene] . . . (the result of so much bullying) and I hate bowing any sort of head towards her publicly over here because all my friends *so* resent her. Yet I can't but acknowledge that she has been determinedly loyal, persistently dogged, always at my side, fighting for me and the play.' Enid therefore could not bring herself to dedicate the play to Irene. 'Because I had at once a feeling that Irene wanted me to dedicate the play to her. I didn't want to do this. I was smarting over something or other from her as I so often am and have.' She considered Harold Freedman had been even more loyal. 'Cared for the play first . . . and bullied [Irene] into taking it.' At first Enid opted for a joint dedication, but at the last minute, changed her mind again. Harold was to have the dedication, alone, after all. But on the next page there was to be a foreword devoted entirely to Irene. 'She's done so much she must be placated,' Enid wrote to her publisher.

Enid always denied an awareness on her part of symbolism or allegory in *The Chalk Garden*. 'The equation of *The Chalk Garden* with dryness of the heart, which has been made by many critics did not occur to me while engaged on the play,' Enid told one interviewer. 'I see now that it is a reasonable interpretation but I was not consciously working out a parallel as I wrote. I had simply conceived Mrs St Maugham as making a muddle of everything, her garden and her grand-daughter.'

Similarly, Enid insisted there was no significance to the names, although it cannot be mere coincidence that Mrs St Maugham's daughter was, until Irene called for a change, Laura (in addition to the grand-daughter being Laurel) – neither very different from Laurian. An American study, 'Metaphor and Dramatic Structure in The Chalk Garden', points to a connection between Madrigal and the medieval Latin *Matricale*, meaning womb and the Italian *Madregal* with feverfew, a perennial herb noted for its febrifugal qualities. 'In addition to musical associations it appears that Madrigal's name has both material and botanical origins that Bagnold may have drawn upon.'

But the relationship between gardens and hearts was not as accidental as the author would have us believe. Enid herself was an expert and original gardener. Most afternoons she would wander down to her garden. It was because of this

personal, daily informed experience (of garden troubles) as it happens troubles with chalk soil and not at all allegorically, I made Miss Madrigal a gardener. I could 'feed' her expertly from myself. I (play-battle-wise) made Mrs St Maugham an idiot with a green thumb. . . . I had no idea myself of the allegorical significance until Madrigal herself lights on it, exclaims on it. It is her conclusion and discovery, not mine. When the play was a success and discussed, not one critic, not one person, would believe that, yet I know I make things. It's true.

Enid placed so much emphasis on how her words were delivered because she knew she had written a primarily verbal play. So often Enid was trying to express something intuitively felt, what she called 'lassoos . . . flings of written speech that seem nonsense but aren't nonsense and one has to trust them. But it's hard to uphold them in the face of opposition or doubt.' This insistence on trust when the words appeared nonsensical was the cause of much of Irene's frustration. 'A random line would start her off,' Irene explained, 'and then the piece would take off on a life of its own, a practice not conducive to structure.'

To a director putting on a revival of *The Chalk Garden* some years later, she advised:

The way to direct this play . . . is to use the strange and intricate language as though it was the everyday language of the actors. *Never* to seem as though one was saying something extraordinary. Emphasis ruins it. The language has to be tipped out as though one were saying 'please fetch the coal'. This language (my language) is their native air.

The Chalk Garden has been for many years an immensely popular play, both with critics and with audiences. In 1956, it toured throughout the United States with Gladys Cooper for a while, and also with Lillian and Dorothy Gish. Dame Sybil Thorndike played Mrs St Maugham in the first Australian production, with her husband Lewis Casson as the Judge. It is regularly re-vived and often performed by amateur companies.

In the mid-1950s, after the frequently 'silly' plays of the twenties and thirties, yet before audiences were accustomed to the kitchen-sink dramas of the late fifties and sixties, *The Chalk Garden* appeared both refreshing and provocative. With hindsight, it was possible to describe it as 'the most anachronistic' play of the year. But at the time the cast had a sense of being involved in something new and original.

When John Gielgud first showed Peggy Ashcroft a script, he warned her: 'I think you'll find it rather shocking.'

'Why?' she asked.

'Well, there's a girl in it who says she's been raped in Hyde Park,' he explained. In fact, the Lord Chamberlain found it rather shocking too and the word 'violate' had to be removed.

Three years later, after the first performance of *The Chalk Garden*, it was the subject of an academic treatise in the *Tulane Drama Review*. Professor Gerald Weales wrote that Bagnold's dialogue could be compared with Chekhov. 'The characters speak first to themselves and out of themselves. If occasionally they communicate, if their speeches sometimes land on listening ears, the effect is a lucky accident.' Weales realized that the lines lent themselves to interpretation possibly well beyond the author's intentions

because all of Miss Bagnold's lines demand attention. . . . It is a play about which one talks because it is evocative. But perhaps the most just reaction to *The Chalk Garden*, the one that Miss Bagnold most hopes for, is that one comes away from the theatre or the book saying, with Miss Madrigal, 'I shall continue to explore – the astonishment of living.

Reading the article made Enid feel 'as though plunged ahead into history. I feel I am dead and this has been written about me, glueing me to history's wall. I can't believe that I have really done what you say I have done.'

EIGHTEEN

They Are Furious with Me for Being Old

'THE important thing,' wrote Enid towards the end of *The Loved and Envied*, 'is to get reasonably exhausted by life, and avoid this hankering for repetition. What you've had, you've had.'

But Enid did hanker after the face she once had. In August 1956, she wrote to the renowned plastic surgeon, Sir Archibald McIndoe:

> I wish I could have a face lift
> Not for anybody else but for me.
> Or it might be for my husband (who loves me
> But thinks I still look as I used to be) . . .
>
> It's out of delicacy that I write to you in rhyme.
> Would it be unreasonable . . . would it be out of place . . .
> If I asked you to take a stitch in my face?
> It's tiresome to be immortalized
> By the last appearance.
> I should like a sort of clearance
> To antiquity.
> Before I go back into the ages varnished by Time.
>
> I don't want to be young again! I wouldn't undertake
> Two such risky journeys! But it would be agreeable
> In the foreseeable
> Fifteen years that's left me
> Not to look disagreeable . . .

He replied:

> Dear Lady Jones,
>
> In reply to your rhyme
> Re Old Father Time
> You've reached the Canal Turn in life;
> Just come and see me
> And your husband will see
> Mary Rose instead of his wife.

Enid was duly admitted to the London Clinic in Harley Street, and was pleased with the effect of the tucks. She claimed that, having sneaked some large scissors in with her, she cut through the bandages on the third morning after the operation. Immediately it was done she called for help. The nurse 'was as furious with me as I deserved ... but no harm was done.' She delighted in telling people about her facelift at a time when such operations were far from common and to talk of them rather shocking.

She longed, too, to repeat the triumph of her theatrical success. But redesigning her face was easier than reshaping her ideas. Enid had worked out a plot for another play. 'That's where I get done for. I can't decide. I have to twist and wrench the play story until it holds what I want it to hold, and then it's got muddled and complicated. I try never to abandon it for another for if I do I know I'm not going to better myself.'

The idea Enid was twisting and wrenching into shape began in 1954 as a short story entitled 'The Psalter'. She was prompted by the theft of Ann Boleyn's prayer-book from Hever Castle. But after sending it to the Brandts, Enid had second thoughts, believing she might be wasting too good an idea on a mere story. 'Even if it is not stage-worthy I think it is film-worthy,' she told Carl Brandt. 'If, therefore, I have written a story of value, do let us be careful what we do with it.' Carol, however, found the story 'incomprehensible' and, as Enid's energies were entirely taken up with *The Chalk Garden*, 'The Psalter' was put to one side.

In 1956, faced once more with the all too familiar blank white paper, Enid again broke out in a rash. 'It's very queer ... like hay fever, but it only comes on at the beginning of trying to get things straight. My poor forehead has two horns of red on it like a unicorn.'

She resurrected 'The Psalter' theme and tried to make a play of it, using a different object as the lost treasure. She wanted something 'small, precious, ancient, internationally famous', stolen for the gratification of a collector and kept locked away, rather than a jewel taken for the financial gain of a thief. Contained within the play were to be thoughts on death, old age and lost looks, her current preoccupation. The plot had to 'hold the daily secretion, the gum-droppings of life. And hold them transfixed.'

The play hinged on two big dramatic moments, a theft and a suicide. Interwoven with these was a love-affair. The action took place in a castle and the protagonists were two princely brothers, Ferdi and Hugo, based on the Bibescos. Ferdi, the elder of the two brothers, is a mathematician. He believes he has proved the existence of God scientifically and therefore wishes to commit suicide to check his theories. His younger brother, displaying something more than fraternal love, devotes his entire existence to preventing him. But first, Ferdi wants to recover a stolen portrait of his mother. He does this by means of an elaborate joke. Meanwhile, the daughter of the thief-art-collector has fallen in love with Hugo. Once Ferdi is convinced his younger brother has someone other than himself to live for, he kills himself.

Enid considered her task would have been made much easier if only she had 'someone to bounce the ball against. Oh what a thing to have ... to get reactions about your work,' she wrote to the American writer Maxwell Anderson. 'Roderick, my husband, would do it out of love. But he's not just exactly "in the trade" as regards unbaked scraps. You need to be knee-deep for that.'* She asked Harold : 'Is there no one you trust absolutely you could show it to without saying it's me ... and see if they are fearfully disappointed in the unravelling ?' Increasingly, she used Timothy, now an author himself as well as a barrister, as her sounding board.† He warned her tactfully : 'The only possible criticism from the commercial point of view is that it's about very out of the ordinary people and the situation is an unusual one.' But he made a number of suggestions and encouraged her to persevere.

It was not enough. Enid missed the creative input of Irene, yet wanted desperately to avoid her as 'people will think (perhaps it's me) I can't write without her'. In the summer of 1957 she felt further lowered by a bad attack of hay fever and underwent a painful treatment which involved burning the inside of her nostrils. She even contemplated scrapping the play and starting something entirely new. One year on, it had not yet been jettisoned when Charles Laughton arrived in Brighton.

The British-born Laughton was one of Hollywood's most talented actors. His reputation had been established by a string of successful pre-war films such as *Mutiny on the Bounty*, *Les Miserables*, and *Ruggles of Red Gap*. He had also made a notable Captain Hook in a British production of *Peter Pan*. He was, by instinct and training, a stage actor; only in the live theatre could his powerful, rich voice be projected to the full. Immediately after the war, Laughton had been proposed by Harold as a possibility for the main role in *Poor Judas*. Enid had been sorry not to land such a big fish. When he did return to the English stage after an absence of twenty-two years, it was to act in and direct a play by Jane Arden called *The Party*.

He and his wife, the actress Elsa Lanchester, decided that although the play was in London, they would prefer living in a suite at the Royal Crescent Hotel, Brighton, overlooking the sea front. By day they walked along the

---

* Roderick had by now almost entirely extricated himself from his wife's theatrical world. When Ruth Gordon and her husband Garson Kanin came to dinner, Roderick disappeared halfway through the meal. 'Presently, the butler pressed a telephone towards me and a voice said : "Miss Gordon, this is Sir Roderick. I just wanted to bid you goodnight. I had had enough of it".'

† *The Small Hours of the Night*, Barrie/Houghton Mifflin, 1950, and *Mr Twining and the God Pan*, Barrie/Knopf, 1953.

South Downs; at night they caught the Brighton Belle into London. A long-standing Brighton resident, Ernest Thornton Smith, made friends with the Laughtons casually and insisted they meet his friend, the writer Enid Bagnold.

Elsa described the day they met. 'I remember her floating towards us and wafting us into the living room – wearing the rather soft grey and beige chiffon that traditionally sits well on ladies who are getting along in years and have big busts.' Enid recalled how she had been in the middle of bathing her grand-daughter when the door-bell rang. 'I was immediately hooked with excitement, entranced; wanting Annabel disposed of in bed and simultaneously wanting to fetch ice cubes.' The two women did not get on. Elsa realized the boost Charles derived from the way Enid 'seemed to hang on his every word' and, powerless to alter a situation she did not like, stepped out of her husband's life for a season. Other than to deposit her husband, Elsa never went to North End House again. She found an alternative occupation in visiting her mother, who lived in another part of Brighton.

Laughton's was a complicated personality, damaged by his conviction that he was ugly, as well as fat, and overlaid with guilt about his homosexuality. For one summer, he lunched every week-day (except matinée days but including Sundays) at North End House. Every day his massive body sank deeply into the regency-striped armchair in the library; he made a similar indentation in Enid's life. She was mesmerized by the voice, the interest he took in her words and ideas, 'the whole machinery. . . . One was hypnotized at such a high level.' In the summer of 1958 Enid lived almost exclusively for Laughton. His combination of Albrecht's rotundity with Frank Harris's ugliness was a mixture that few women would find appealing. But Enid believed she had fallen in love again; something she had not thought possible at sixty-eight.* From now on she kept a photograph of him clipped into her dressing-table mirror.

There was a more sinister aspect to what she boasted of as her 'affair' with Laughton. Roderick, now eighty, was in decline and often remained upstairs, unwell. Enid guessed that Timothy resented Laughton's regular presence. He was 'full of unspoken criticism. . . . Charles whispered to me, "I feel a draught," when Timothy came in.' He perceived that Laughton had ensconced himself in North End House and the Joneses' life in a way that no other friend of his mother (or father) had ever done. 'He was behaving to us like a stepfather. Even Albrecht always behaved as a guest. But perhaps that was a question of

---

* Enid wrote in her autobiography: 'at sixty-eight, it was very like love. I leave this remark on the page as a gift to women – that the incandescence can appear again in winter like a hibernated moth.'

breeding.' Some of those who saw Enid and Charles together at this time believed Enid was even entertaining romantic notions of re-marriage to Laughton. This unlikely partnership was, however, hardly a realistic proposition as both had living spouses. But so immense was Laughton's power to affect that she found herself imagining the years ahead, spellbound by his voice and charm; above all, with him directing one of her plays. Her daughter-in-law, Pandora, summed up the situation: 'I did realize about Charles Laughton,' she told Enid years later, 'and was very impressed with your life forces ... your admiration for each other somehow seemed big enough to include Sir Roderick.'

Friends, too, were shown Enid's cold shoulder. Explaining to Cynthia Asquith why it was impossible to see her, Enid wrote: 'I am (I was going to say embedded, but hardly the word) with Charles Laughton. What I mean is, he jumped into my life ... I haven't a minute till he is gone. I could come over any day (afternoon) after that. He is a marvellous bundle of violent enthusiasms, great intelligence, and, oh so theatrically helpful.' Others noticed the change Laughton had wrought in Enid's behaviour. Michael Thornton, then a local journalist taken up by Enid, came to visit one day.

I arrived to find Charles Laughton sprawling in an armchair in the library. Enid was utterly infatuated by him and behaved in a skittish and girlish manner I had never seen before.... Laughton was plainly embarrassed by it and kept shifting about uncomfortably in his chair. I could never understand her interest in him, for he was repellently ugly and clearly homosexual. He greeted me with a sly, suggestive smile, and when I shook hands, his fat, moist fingers pressed themselves intimately against my palm.

When Laughton arrived, Enid believed she had a finished play. She had changed the title from 'The Psalter' to 'At The Top of His Form' (because of Emmanuel Bibesco's oft-repeated warnings that he would only kill himself in that mood) and then again to *The Last Joke* (because of the Bibesco penchant for jokes). 'Really one wants just very attractive words. It doesn't matter what they mean.' But Laughton convinced her it needed more radical revising than title changes. Promising Enid that he wanted to direct the play, he went straight to its heart and ripped it apart with her. 'We spend hours and hours undoing all the scenes ... pins all over the floor and now he is going to direct it.' Enid acquiesced in the destruction. When it was time for Laughton to go home, she was left 'trembling with the pieces in my hand and not much glue'.

He was due back the following year, however, as Glen Byam Shaw, the director of the Shakespeare Memorial Theatre, had invited him to play King Lear to mark the hundredth season at Stratford-upon-Avon. Until then the two corresponded at length about the play. 'I had gotten [*sic*] to lean on you so much,' Enid wrote to him that winter, 'that now I have to take a stick in either hand to get myself upright again. I am *thankful* you "think about me and the play". It is a help to think so.' A week later, she wrote again. 'I miss you so much that I've become housewifely and drab and depressed.' She missed, she explained, 'the sense of high theatre, high discoveries with you'. 'I had such extraordinary mental understanding with you that now I am spoilt for talking with anyone.' She wrote to him, only half-jokingly, 'I should like to buy a director, divorce him from ambition and keep him chained in a room here, waiting to read every page I write. If I were a Pharaoh . . . but then they wouldn't tell one the truth. Yet it's not truth one wants but admiration.'

Briefly, her energies were focused on the annual party that was given in the Lutyens drawing-room of her London flat for the Duff Cooper Memorial Prize. 'I do the arrangements and [Diana] waltzes in like a queen just as the party's starting. . . . It's the most dazzling party.' In 1958, Princess Margaret presented the prize to John Betjeman for his *Collected Poems*.

In the New Year, despondent about ever getting *The Last Joke* right, she decided to start another play, which Laughton himself had inspired. During the summer, Enid had driven him to Brighton station every evening to catch the 5 p.m. train for his performance in London. But when she tried to get him there a quarter of an hour earlier, so that she could do a little shopping on the way home, he protested wildly. He would be mobbed on the station. He could not bear coming face to face with his fame. Enid had only to watch such a scene once to know that it was true. Consumed by her own longing for fame and adulation, she had never before seen its claustrophobic effect, but it fascinated her. She began writing a play on the subject inspired by Laughton and in which she hoped he would take the main role.* But without his daily presence, Enid felt her isolation from the theatre acutely and was dejected at spending so much time on a play that appeared to have no prospect of being produced. Harold tried to encourage her but could not hide from her what she knew: the third act of *The Last Joke* was still far from satisfactory. In any case, he was angry with Enid for letting Laughton meddle in her writing to such a degree.

Laughton returned to England in late spring to prepare for his Stratford season as Lear, and Bottom in *A Midsummer Night's Dream*. Although he was without Elsa initially, he was completely wrapped up in his forthcoming performances. When he saw Enid again at Rottingdean, she feasted on his private performances; his Lear filled the library as 'his voice thundered

---

* This play called *The Monsters*, which Enid worked at intermittently until 1965, never materialized.

against the low ceiling'. She went to Stratford for the first night but, as much as Laughton's performance, she remembered a curious incident that occurred afterwards. During dinner with Laughton, she noticed John Osborne, the most fashionable of the modern playwrights. Enid would have enjoyed meeting him, but Laughton told her Osborne had refused to eat with them because he 'so hated *The Chalk Garden* and "all I stood for"'. Enid was hurt at the time, maintaining justifiably that she never 'stood' for anything. But Osborne believes Laughton's remarks, attributed to him, were fabrications. 'He seemed to me to be an extremely paranoid and mischievous character, also smarting from the tepid reception of his "Lear".'

As Laughton bowed out of her life, Enid reverted to *The Last Joke*, now in tatters.

It was not until the autumn of 1959 that Binkie was seriously discussing the play. But he was also 'wobbling, shilly-shallying, whether because he can't help it or because homosexuals stick together or for what real or merely convenient reason I don't know. Oh I feel so wild.' She told Irene she found Binkie's behaviour cruel. 'If he procrastinates with me he will really kill my talent and my next plays. . . . I have at most ten years left to write three more plays in. I can't write them if Binkie is weighing me up like a grocer selling a pound of tea. You and Harold have all the power. Get your lash around him, crack! Like they do in the circus when the white horse runs out.'

While Enid was 'striving like a demon' with major script revisions, Harold did his best to impress upon Binkie 'the urgency of getting ahead and getting a decision quickly'. Enid worked all over Christmas, sent 'no Christmas cards, presents snatched up in the evening. I didn't even buy the turkey.' To Harold she wrote unequivocally that Binkie had had 'a big success with me. Why can't he treat me with the respect that deserves and behave himself properly?' She threatened that, if Binkie's delays cost her what she wanted above all, 'for Roderick to be well enough and indeed to be alive, to see the play . . . I not only will never forgive Binkie, never speak to him, never put a play near him, but much worse than that, (for he won't care) my own powers will be broken.' Underscoring all her worries was concern for Roderick's declining health. He could 'no longer see my face very clearly . . . and it's so terrible'.

Before the year was out, Glen Byam Shaw, having completed his Stratford assignment, had agreed to direct Enid's play. He was working to convince John Gielgud to take the starring role. In the New Year, Binkie and Glen lunched Enid at Scott's in Piccadilly. Over the oysters Byam Shaw expounded on the play in a way that made even Enid blush. 'If he ever talks like that to

John G. he will have him in his hand.' Gielgud was soon committed; audition-ing for the other parts could then begin. For the role of Portal, the vulgar, Jewish tycoon art-collector, Enid favoured an unknown actor; the part could be 'made' by a good director. There was a 'new man' called Eric Porter, whom she recommended, but he was engaged all summer. Binkie and Gielgud both wanted Ralph Richardson, who would of course be a huge box-office attraction. But Enid, presciently, saw pitfalls. 'I would sooner have an unknown Portal than have Ralph Richardson and John get into a huddle together especially if Glen can't manage them.' Richardson, however, attracted by the huge success of *The Chalk Garden*, was determined to be in the next play by Enid Bagnold. 'I had to fight my way in . . . they couldn't keep me away.' But he wanted to fit in a holiday first as well as some lucrative film work. Enid struggled to resist anything which might cause further delay and, in any case, did not like him. When he visited her in February, he struck her as 'energetic, noisy and stupid. Kept insisting the play was about the beauties of lineage . . . and inventing titles. Cheek!' She found the manoeuvrings over stars agonizing. She was now seventy and convinced that Roderick could not live much longer. 'Oh these damned stars. I see them like prancing chess figures – forever on their hind legs (without any bodies).'

Harold understood the realities and tried to keep her steady. The English theatre had always, he told her, been run by actors and their managers. He suggested she read Bernard Shaw's letters about Ellen Terry and Henry Irving, 'when the situation was really worse'. He told Enid that once Irene's participation in the production had been arranged, things should be smoother. 'As you know, I welcome her involvement in the situation in England because she is the one bulwark against the cosy attempt of the British star system of doing plays to exploit themselves rather than to inter-pret the author. Irene is an author's producer; Binkie is an actor's one.'

While the role of Portal still hung in abeyance Enid turned her attention to casting his daughter Rose. She was bowled over by the young Vanessa Redgrave.

That is a wonderful, unusual girl [she wrote to Irene]. How can I describe what I mean about her . . . she has a sort of recklessness that Rose would have. She would think nothing of confessing to the lovers, and yet pulling it off that she was a great girl. There is nothing mingy or suburban or bitchy about her. Vanessa is a sort of young golden lion. . . . Will you not misunderstand me if I say that she reminds me also of myself (in youth)? I was a bit like that. So reckless and so gay.

But she was not available and Anna Massey took the part instead.

Meanwhile Enid had impetuously invited Glen's wife, the actress Angela Baddeley, to play Mrs Webster, Portal's mistress and the mother of Rose. Binkie was furious with her for interfering and Baddeley was vetoed by the rest of the company. Glen was disappointed and the episode created ill-feeling all round. Gielgud told Enid, 'I think Ralphie ought to choose his own Mrs Webster' – a remark which informed Enid that Sir Ralph Richardson had now definitely been offered the part. The role of Mrs Webster eventually went to Hazel Terry, a cousin of Gielgud's.

Enid also took a hand in the casting of Hugo. Having lunch one day in the Soho restaurant, Chez Victor, with Binkie and Glen she noticed a distinctive stranger at another table. 'That's the sort of man for Hugo,' she shouted, pointing at him. 'I must have him whoever he is.' By a coincidence her victim was an actor, Robert Flemyng. Enid had never seen him before.

Rehearsals began finally in the summer of 1960. But without Richardson. It was agreed that, as he did not appear in the first act, he could miss the initial weeks in order to complete work on the film, *Exodus*. When he did arrive he was 'tough as oak and looking like wood. While in Cyprus he had decided his movements and at what place on the stage he would say certain lines. . . . He walked over all Glen's planning.' Describing Richardson's performance eight years later, Enid said it made the flesh creep. 'It didn't creep because of the situation; it crept because of him.'

The rehearsals did not go smoothly. Enid was upset when many of the opening lines were cut from Ernest Thesiger's part as Old Toni because Glen believed he was too old to remember them. But, more fundamentally, she believed Ralph and John were approaching the play from separate standpoints and were in unison only in playing it 'too Macbethy' with not enough comedy. The two knights 'galloped in different directions, tearing the body apart as in the Middle Ages'. By the end, Enid considered that John 'is generous and a worker with humility. He's a child too. But a very bright one. Ralph Richardson, however, is an old bore. He plays Portal all sober and soft.' In addition to being 'ham-handed', he was giving Enid some of the old 'Gladys trouble'. 'He alters lines horribly and simply won't say certain things.'

By the middle of July the whole company was feeling uneasy about the third act. Enid had now written fourteen versions but it did not seem to be improving. One day at rehearsals, Gielgud, growing increasingly nervous, had been almost in tears. Finally he burst out, 'It simply doesn't work.' As she cut more of it away, she admitted to Harold: 'The Act seemed not to be there. To be a cloud.'

Flemyng was also miserable about the way things were going. He thought it might help if his part were cut completely out of the third act, a gesture which Enid thought 'very handsome' of him. Harold, too far away to prevent the change, was uneasy, though, seeing it as further proof of 'the way actors run the theatre in London'. The effect was disastrous. Audiences were deprived of the scene which should have revealed how Rose's wooing won Hugo round into a willing lover.* This was not, however, the only confusion which the play left unresolved. In Enid's original version the suicide was by poison. She wanted the suspense and dramatic irony of a drawn-out death from a cup of hemlock. Gielgud, or so Enid was told, wanted to shoot himself amid fireworks. She was given no choice in the matter. John apparently would not act in the play without this climax. She rewrote the end to accommodate the revolver. But without the words to explain his death wish, even Gielgud's genius could never make Ferdi's suicide – the play's central plank – a credible proposition. Whether the death was by poison or shooting was irrelevant to this flaw.†

Enid believed Glen was a director of great sensitivity and talent, but weak in the face of such strong-minded actors. 'His trouble is that he is unable to hold on to my lines when they want to change them,' she lamented to Harold. 'He is simply washed out. It must be his health. He could never have run Stratford like this.'

As Enid took the train home to Rottingdean one Friday afternoon, unable to throw off a cough and cold that she had had for ten days, she felt the play was collapsing about her. She was comforted only by the hope that it might be improved over the weekend as Glen and Angela were coming to stay. But later that evening Angela telephoned to say they would have to leave early on Sunday morning for a family christening. Enid was furious. She told Angela this was not long enough to sort out the third act trouble. '"You see, so much money is involved." – I meant money put into the play.' Angela was enraged at this remark and repeated her insistence that they would attend their grandson's christening. At this, Enid shouted down the telephone – 'I would never let a damn grandchild stand in the way of my work.' Glen, snatching the instrument, yelled back ('rather inconsequently', as Enid commented), 'I care for Angela a great deal more than I care for you!' and slammed down the receiver.

'I know it was rude,' Enid admitted as she relayed every detail of the row to

---

* Enid realized the error. Hugo is reinstated in the third act in the published version. *Four Plays*, Heinemann, 1970.

† John Gielgud denies that the shooting was his idea. After reading Enid's autobiography, he wrote to her: 'The revolver story is absolutely forgotten. I don't remember any discussion of the death – Binkie must have concocted it somehow. . . . No, no, I don't believe a word of it.'

Harold. 'I didn't mean it really.' She often used 'damn' and it meant no more than 'drat'. Of course she did not mean to damn the poor little grandchild. But the damage was done. Enid wrote immediately to 'Darling Angela', explaining how tired, fraught and full of despair she was. Would they not come anyway just for Saturday night?

Glen told her coldly he would come alone. But he considered Enid had done 'something utterly unforgivable' by putting everything in terms of money. In future, he would work only professionally with her. There was 'no spark of friendship left'. Angela, he added, never wished to see her again. He had informed Binkie of the row, which worried Enid intensely. 'I feel that he will couple it with the Cecil trouble. It may make Binkie think that I am difficult to deal with. But truly I'm not.'

In this morass, Enid longed for Irene. 'You dear old dynamo dragon,' she had written to her in January.

I can see you rear on hind legs, spouting fire and smoke, and the crest [dragon crest] rising in steel stalactites down the back of your neck – and the dragon tail threshing in those sharp twists – like a cat when it sees from the corner of the wainscotting – the mouse put out its nose. But – joking apart – I am *delighted* to be in the battle with you once more.

A few weeks later she pleaded, 'I am at your mercy. Do come. . . . Pull the threads straight but don't kill me.' Irene flew over in April but then Enid changed her mind: 'I suddenly wish to God I'd never let her come. Or asked her to. It was my fault. . . . Why, why didn't God give her tact and moderation as well as brains?' Harold reminded Enid that even though some of Irene's input might be painful, 'This is the first time that she has been involved in a second play with anyone and it speaks well of her devotion to you and deep recognition of your value.'

At the end of July, Irene paid a further visit to the troubled company. She persuaded Enid to try again with the third act. 'After having nearly killed me for ten days writing a new act (almost dictated) (and dictated from my own plums . . . which simply doesn't work) she has disappeared,' Enid told Harold. Is she 'in the sulks'? But Enid realized the problem. 'Having "promised me" to Binkie she has failed to deliver. And that has got her down. I would and can be sorry for her. But it's hard to be sorry when one is covered with wounds. When they form scabs I'll be sorry again, I expect.' Irene saw it differently. 'She got me to put in all the time and effort and then she never used my notes; she wanted this to be her own play.'

The play began its provincial tour with further revisions continually being attempted. Even at this late stage Irene was pressing Enid to go away to a hotel with her and rewrite for three uninterrupted days. Enid told Binkie she could not take much more: 'She wears me down so that my eyes stick out of my head. . . . I can't bear to be seen marching about with her everywhere, like two unpalatable power women!' After Newcastle Enid went back to Rottingdean, unable to face the rest of the tour. The play moved on to Leeds in early September, and then Irene, also deeply unhappy, flew home to New York.

By the end of the tour the actors were despondent. They could not fail to notice how audiences drifted out at the curtain in stupefied silence. Gielgud insisted on a meeting with Binkie at Brighton but this turned into a 'furious row'. Binkie had promised not to bring the play into London if the cast opposed it. They did. However, 'he had gone and booked the Phoenix behind our backs so we had to open – and I knew it wouldn't do.' He reminded Enid years later, 'I never went down to a first night with more conviction of impending disaster.'

Enid, slightly more hopeful, bought herself a pink taffeta dress from Norman Hartnell for the first night. She knew, as soon as she put it on, that it gave her a sort of 'success-expectant-look', when she should, instead, have been 'squaring her shoulders for failure'. But, even so, she was not prepared for 'the blackness of the disaster . . . the deluge'. The London critics, 'when they wrote "stinking play", "awful play", "commonplace mind bedecked with useless words",' etc., etc., made her feel she had 'been beaten about the head like a negro being lynched'.

There was, of course, an irony in the title which the critics were not slow to seize upon. 'The last joke and I hope it is', 'The Last Joke and a thin one', 'The Last Joke and not a chuckle', were three that Enid recalled (inaccurately) for Harold. She had meant a joke in the Proustian/Bibesco sense. And this was what she had been dealt. 'I think they sat up in some strange heaven and roared with wicked laughter at me and said, "How she *dares* put us in a wood, on Olympus, half-way to heaven! We'll put the wrong words in her head!" "Let's make everything Bagnoldish but meaningless."'

'What surprises me', Harold wrote to her, 'is that . . . there seems to be no indication or grasp of what the play was about.' He was right. The critics simply could not see what she was driving at. Milton Shulman, in the *Evening Standard*, wrote:

The speeches are not so much spoken as puffed out of some communal verbal hookah. . . . What they all think they are up to I would hate to guess. It is a long time since such a caravan of overblown nonsense has rolled into the West End masquerading as a serious vehicle for some of our best actors.

The Last Joke suffers chiefly from the fact that it is not obscure enough. One sees only too clearly the intellectual vacuum behind the teeming undergrowth of lush metaphors and exotic imagery.... One longs to hear just a simple, direct unadorned statement like 'Shut up' instead of 'Give me your silence, please.'

Bernard Levin asked: 'How shall we excuse Miss Enid Bagnold whose paper-thin, three-act, star-stuffed little play is smothered under bales of sham writing, mock-metaphor, nothing-over-sixpence aphorisms and poetry of a quality to set the teeth aching?'

Her erstwhile defender, Kenneth Tynan, declared: 'Alas for chivalry. Enid Bagnold has written a stinker. It is as if an architect had planned a towering folly and built instead a dilapidated ruin.' T.C.Worsley, in a more balanced piece for the *Financial Times*, saw the nub of her problem. 'Miss Bagnold is fashionably baffling,' he wrote. 'At least not so fashionably, for we are accustomed now to being baffled in low life. Here we are baffled in high.' But even he concluded: 'However interesting the parts, the play is badly out of focus, the impact almost totally blurred.'

There were a few crumbs of comfort. The *Glasgow Herald* reminded its readers that the play's 'unnecessarily waspish' reception by London critics 'is a sign that she has been accepted along with Noël Coward and Terence Rattigan as one of the established playwrights of the British stage.' Coward himself wrote her a warm letter from Switzerland: 'I am furious on your behalf. You have been treated with vulgarity and discourtesy far beyond the scope of criticism.' Only the sets, by Felix Kelly, were consistently praised for their elegance.

*T*he *Last Joke* had several themes, perhaps too many, but the dramatic clash was between Portal and Ferdi. 'Two men (one from hell and one from heaven) who come together at the last ditch because the beautiful "Greek" youth and atmosphere in youth of the one so affected the other that he turned the whole of his life – like a searchlight towards the ideal of just such a life.'

Portal explains to Ferdi that in his childhood,

I had never heard the charm of conversation. I had never heard gaiety before.... But what I want to explain to you is – that we did not use words – or only for shorthand communication.

My life was changed that afternoon. I followed you in the passages and in the garden. Once through an open door I heard you discussing love. I had never guessed that people allowed themselves to open the heart and turn it into talk.

It was as though we broke through a hedge – and heard old Greece talking!

This passage is, in some ways, the essence of the play as it was the essence of Jones family life. Having 'seen the stars' Portal sacrificed everything to obtain them, not only for himself but for his as yet unborn child. In this wild state he searched for a woman and found Mrs Webster. Once he had 'carved a daughter' he could not let the mother touch or contaminate Rose. Portal thought he could be mother and father, both. 'Portal's "drive to the stars" . . . was a tremendous thing. It was the great shining thing about him. He knew *he* could never be like the Cavanati gods and goddess. But he thought his daughter could be. And in a way she is. She is the great work of art.'

Enid defined Portal with some precision because his great drive in life mirrored her own : the Cavanatis influenced him as much as the Bibescos had touched her. The gracious life of leisure and sophistication, love of art, the subtle interchange of thought and talk, once this had surrounded her, almost fifty years earlier, life could never be the same again. If she was not quite up to their standard, she dreamt her child could be. Rose gets her Cavanati ; Enid never got her Bibesco. The play ran for six weeks in London. Enid, persistently optimistic, was even trying to persuade the actors to accept revisions once it transferred to the Phoenix. 'Always let's remember that a Phoenix is a bird that rises out of its own ashes,' she wrote to Irene. However, when it finally ended its tortured life, Enid felt almost relieved. 'At any rate it isn't there in the Charing Cross Road bleeding away. Its haemorrhage is complete.' All that remained was for her to compose letters to the cast, thanking them but regretting, etc. But the relief was tinged with sorrow ; for Roderick, in whose eyes she could not bear to be seen failing, and for Irene. 'I'm bloody sorry I've cost you a packet. I really, really am,' she wrote to her.

Her own finances were not in good shape after this fiasco. As she explained to Harold, she did not, at her age, write for money. But 'I am down the street financially ! I took on so much – thinking gaily "another fortune on the way !" I promised Roderick a two thousand pounds voyage to South Africa, children bigger allowances. . . .' Bearing in mind the success of *The Chalk Garden*, Enid had been persuaded into a sophisticated tax planning scheme for *The Last Joke*. It was designed to convert income into capital (as was possible in the 1960s) and so avoid tax completely. It was not without irony that she had written to Binkie in June 1960, thanking him for signing her contract at last, but now asking if *she* could delay. 'Timothy has a scheme', she explained, 'and it has involved taking counsel's advice and that always seems to take a bit of time'. But as the play flopped there was no income to convert.

Enid was not only hurt but bewildered by the critics. 'And to be bewildered is so bad for writing. Writing is sometimes like those wonderful

shots at tennis over the net and straight, that are only got by sheer confidence.' It was the first time in her life that her work had been so violently
attacked

so that I really began to have doubts as to whether I could write. . . . The personal
animosity shown me *personally* is extraordinary. They are furious because I am
old. Furious because of the Knights. Furious because of the complication and care
taken over the words. Furious because I am of my class. Because I don't have to
earn my living.

In her hour of failure she still turned to the (dead) Bibescos for advice. One
of Antoine's maxims was always to have some new work ready even before
the old was finished. '"That", he always said, "is a charm against the heart
being hurt by failure."' She now pulled out the play about fame inspired by
Charles Laughton. Antoine had been particularly in her thoughts that year
not only because her play was based on him and Emmanuel, but also because a
biography of Marcel Proust by George D. Painter*, which discussed them,
had recently appeared. It was 'an amazement to me', Enid wrote to the
author, who had then completed only Volume I. She offered her own remin-
iscences of the Bibescos for the second volume and held on to George Painter
as an important Bibesco relic. He sat next to Marthe Bibesco at the first night.
'You and Marthe are the two people who are both contemporary . . . nobody
but you two know that it was written springing from the brothers.'

Heinemann wrote to her that their decision about publishing the play
would depend on whether or not it was still running. 'Charlie Evans . . .
would never have written that.' Compounding her misery was a broken toe;
she was hobbling around with a stick. 'My sense of age is quite terrible', she
told Harold. But he held out to her the possibility that, if she were to get the
third act right, a New York production might yet be feasible. Only his faith
in her could 'light her with hope like sun does a landscape'.

---

* Published by Chatto & Windus.

NINETEEN

Bringing Old Clothes but a New Brain

A small cutting buried amongst the vitriolic reviews of *The Last Joke* recorded Sir Roderick Jones' eighty-third birthday on 31 October 1960. 'Much more important than all this tosh,' Enid scrawled across it. 'Darling, darling Roderick,' she had written to him that month, 'I don't say to you often enough (but I'm always thinking it) how much you have been to me over this play. Through you and your warmth and indignant belief I have hardly felt the pangs ... you have really and truly ... *deflected* pain completely from me over this.' She signed it, 'your loving, grateful, hard-working but protected wife'.

'If it's anything to know,' she wrote in a birthday letter to him, 'you have been the tree sheltering my whole life with you – the strongest man I ever knew – and the tenderest and the most loyal and undeviating. I woke up this morning full of love and gratitude and *admiration* at how you have put yourself aside and pressed me lovingly forward since we both have been what is supposed to be "old".

In their last few years together, Enid and Roderick continued to behave in a highly romantic fashion towards each other. Enid had planted hundreds of beautiful and rare roses in her Rottingdean gardens. Roderick often picked a single bloom to present to his wife. One Tuesday morning he carried in a perfect yellow rose in a simple vase to Enid's bedroom. Attached was a four-line 'Ode to a Rose' that he had, an hour earlier, composed in his room.

At the same time, the arguments did not entirely abate. 'He and I bicker so – in terrible love,' Enid confessed to Diana, the cause usually being something quite trivial. Enid's cooking, always imaginative, now became wildly so, with gin, vodka, cream or whatever was at hand, freely tipped in. One day, awash with cream, Enid served *oeufs en cocotte*, followed by a rich casserole of beef and vegetables. As she brought in the *crème brûlée* with a flourish, she saw Roderick exchange desperate glances with her guest, Mrs William (Tops) Vestey. 'Really, Enid darling, it looks wonderful but I simply can't,' Tops began. 'Nor I,' added Roderick. At this, Enid smashed the bowl to the floor and stormed off for the rest of the afternoon.

Once, Enid went to bed with the faint impression that she was 'in disgrace'.

This kept her awake much of the night. Then, on rising, she saw a sealed envelope slipped under her door 'and thought "This is *it*. What have I done?"' But in the letter, she found only consoling, caressing words from Roderick which left her 'radiant, relieved . . . and ready for anything all day'. But her day, in 1961, began and ended with Roderick. He was ill for most of the year and she, for the first time in her adult life, put her writing to one side to care for her husband. Dr John O'Hara, who had been Roderick's doctor for many years, had recently, rather reluctantly, taken Enid on his list as well. Suddenly he saw her in a different light. 'When he was ill, she gave up everything to comfort and help him and ease his final years,' Dr O'Hara commented. 'I began to appreciate that behind the façade was a very caring woman.'

Roderick staggered on throughout the year; more often than not bedridden, every day a little worse. In April, he fell victim to pleurisy and after that was barely strong enough to do anything for himself. The house was filled with nurses assisting at the lingering death. As Enid spent all her lonely meals with them, she was reminded of the red-caped sisters of The Royal Herbert Hospital, where she had worked, and how 'nurses have a genius for saying things that hurt. That undervalue life and death. They are corny with being used to illness.' Weak though Roderick was, the Joneses moved up to Hyde Park Gate for the winter. By Christmas 1961, Enid believed she was living a daily nightmare. 'On the one hand one gives the presents and there are the children. On the other there is Roderick lying in a half-sleep groaning. And when he is awake he is so miserable – it's a depression that is almost worse than pain.'

Each week he lost more weight. He was eating virtually nothing except, 'occasionally, crossly, a cup of soup'. It had been clear for some time that he was not going to be able to make the trip to South Africa in January, which he had booked on the *Windsor Castle*. It was the only entry which his rheumatic fingers managed to make in his 1962 diary. A new specialist came to see him on Boxing Day, but Roderick's death, it seemed, could not be delayed for many more days.

Enid watched him die, sleeping fitfully on a mattress beside his bed, reaching up to hold his hand if neither could sleep. If he was in great pain, she edged herself on to the side of his bed; 'but the wire cage and the tubes and things . . . it was like clinging to an aviary.' Enid had many lonely hours in which to observe her dying husband. 'The face on the pillow reflects but does not answer. . . . Oh to see life stop with the eyes of the living ! . . . Often both of us had spoken of it. But we had never known of that dividing, preoccupied silence before dying, when one is going and the other watches.'

As evening approached on 22 January, Enid knew it was to be Roderick's last night. His kidneys were failing rapidly. A transfusion had been proposed but the doctor warned them this would not be easy in his current state and the family, believing it would cause him unnecessary distress, decided against. That night, Enid climbed into his bed to cling to him. 'Roderick, darling, don't leave me,' she begged. He died at 4 a.m. Everyone was very calm. Nobody was in tears. 'In that stony silence I lost you though you were living. Then you were laid back and arranged for eternal lying ... and all night I looked at you, my heart bursting.'

As Sir Roderick's death came too late to make 'a proper showing' in *The Times* of 23 January, Dominick did not release an announcement until 9 a.m. In this way, he hoped, the following day's morning papers would have time to devote fuller coverage to Sir Roderick's life and achievements, not prejudiced by the evening papers having made the first announcement.

For Enid, the worst was now over. The funeral at Rottingdean village church was marked at Reuters by a thirty-second silence, during which no copy was transmitted nor any telephone used. Enid received hundreds of messages of sympathy and took great care in replying individually to each. The letter she felt best conveyed her own view of Sir Roderick was from the manager of the Standard Laundry. 'He was never an easy man to please and yet his praise was more generous and unstinted when we succeeded than his condemnation was severe when we failed.' She also sent, two days after his death, a short eulogy on Roderick to *The Times*, 'a letter which Sir William Haley, the Editor, said with regret, and perhaps rightly, that he could not use.' In it she wrote of the qualities she had most admired in Roderick: 'He had a lot to give, gifts special to a man. Clarity, common sense, temperance in negotiation, the wise word, the power to refrain. These were at the disposal of his sons and daughter. And especially of his wife.'

Dealing with the letters, funeral, memorial service and, in between, 'so many horrible words ... probate ... wills ... Inland Revenue', were all practical tasks which did not find Enid wanting. The night of the memorial service, craving links with the past, she went out to dinner with Mary Lutyens. She also sat down to write to Guen Bourke. 'It went off so well, so well,' she told her.

As Enid walked out of St Bride's Church, Fleet Street, on Timothy's arm, she realized she had carried it off: 'a thing I always thought I wouldn't. One of the things I thought I could never manage as he would want ... was the Memorial Service.' Enid felt relief not only because she had managed this first, most difficult step in her new life alone but also because Roderick had, days before his death, absolved her from brooding guiltily over the time her writing had taken from their togetherness. ''You've been a good wife,' he told her.

'Have I?'

Enid's courage did not desert her. Within weeks of Roderick's death she was hard at work again on her latest play. It was a short, one-act piece, written in under a month and then put to one side during Roderick's illness. She hoped, finally, that she could dispense with Binkie Beaumont. He had not been 'one hundred per cent enthusiastic' about this latest play. She complained to Harold that his influence

differs in no way from the Soviet influence on writers. He wishes to dictate 'uplift' and a palatable mixture he believes the public wants, and . . . that the playwright must serve as a sort of minor chef to dish up what is the appetite of the Stars. . . . The truth is he has no idea what I am after and, I suppose, takes advice. And what advice? A little group of homosexuals who change their minds and natter about and who have no idea either.

Harold responded by proposing that the Lunts – Alfred and his wife Lynn Fontanne – might be persuaded to make a stage come-back together in this play. An initial American production with such a popular double bill would also have the effect of circumventing Binkie. Enid was torn; on the one hand she thought she had had enough of stars, and the Lunts were exceptionally starry; on the other they would lend great weight to her tenuous construction. The central character was a famous actress on the eve of retirement. She has decided to dispense with husband (who has returned after abandoning her), home, career and children to embark on a new, independent life. She is looking for a wise man, a Chinese Prime Minister, to accompany her through what remains of her life. The theme was that new experiences can and must still happen in old age.

Lynn and Alfred had read the script but could not make up their minds. A major stumbling block was the inadequate role for Alfred. Enid contemplated rewriting and enlarging the husband's part but knew that that would destroy the play's balance. It was written for a woman and from a woman's point of view. 'I believe every ageing actress will give her eyes [*sic*] to act in it,' she told Harold. She undertook, none the less, minor revisions to tempt Alfred. But months passed without any definite response. Enid could not bear the indecision. 'Please, dear Harold,' she begged, 'without being angry with me, either make these Lunts pull their socks up or don't let's bother with them any more.'

However, in the early summer Enid received an enticing invitation to stay with the Lunts in the United States. The idea was that, in their presence, she might be able to make adjustments that would leave everybody satisfied. She accepted, as 'they must at least have a *leaning* towards doing the play', and was, she told them, 'TREMENDOUSLY excited. When I was nineteen I never guessed one could be so excited at seventy-two.' She tried, also like a nineteen-year-old, to lose some weight before they met her for the first time, and spent the summer 'having horrible lunches of yoghurt and half a grapefruit with no sugar. . . . I think writers get fat in the middle through sitting half their lives with their stomachs on their laps'. She offered to help with the cooking : 'I can make a *crème brûlée* and a *pain de Gênes* and walnut bread and tarragon chicken. . . . I am also willing to peal (no, peel) potatoes. . . . I sound like a cook at an interview.' Meanwhile she worried about her clothes, which were dirty and shapeless, but promised Lynn she would try and get them presentable before she left. Finding suitable clothes became one of the minor agonies of Enid's old age. Often she spoke of the advantages of a sort of uniform for the elderly and almost invented one for herself. She had several dresses made in the same style – a loose cross-over top with baggy sleeves – which she considered flattering for her large bust. But, she assured them, even if the clothes were old, the brain would be new.

The Lunts could not have extended a warmer welcome. They ascertained her favourite foods before she came, redecorated a bedroom in her honour and Alfred drove the hundred miles or so to meet her from Chicago's O'Hare airport. (Enid insisted on pronouncing this O'Hara, believing it was a good omen for flying as her doctor was called O'Hara.)

The Lunts lived in a beautiful old farmhouse buried in the wooded countryside of Genessee Depot, Wisconsin. The house sat above an apple orchard, looking out over meadows, lakes, scrub and forest. Cathleen Nesbitt was also staying at the time, which delighted Enid. As girls in pre-war Chelsea, they had moved in overlapping circles : Rupert Brooke was in love with Cathleen, when Enid was going about with Lovat Fraser, but the two had never met.

It was a warm evening when Enid arrived. Cathleen and Lynn were sitting by the swimming-pool chatting. They were 'dressed as for a First Night at the Opera. . . . The impression of two women kept aside from wear and tear in some age where there was no age, has never left me.' Alfred and Lynn, their devotion to each other and the completeness of their lives, consumed Enid. 'Youth has nothing to do with it. . . . They have exhausted fame. They don't want it any more,' she wrote later. This Enid did not immediately appreciate. For the first days were spent relaxing. There was talk of the theatre, food and clothes. Lynn was a most accomplished dressmaker and Alfred a cordon bleu chef. There were lively discussions, too, about old age and prolonged youthfulness. As they all indulged in admiration of each other, Enid found favour for her energy and zest for life. But there was no mention of the play. Enid dared not refer to it. She began to wonder whether the invitation had been a ghastly misunderstanding, a scheme of Binkie's to relax the pressure on him. After three days, she decided impetuously to ask them what they thought. Hesitantly, they told her to read it to them. 'Looking back on it now,' she wrote in her autobiography, 'I understand perfectly that they didn't deal in yes or no. But they liked me. And I adored them. We talked of my play but bit by bit I let the subject drop.'

The realization that it would be impossible to accommodate both the Lunts and herself with this play did not depress Enid. She wandered happily around their rambling house for several days more, exploring the long-grassed meadows in her bare feet, enchanted by Cathleen as much as by Lynn.

Shortly after she returned to England, she went on holiday again, this time with Richard to Ischia. It was an opportunity to reappraise her future relationship with Richard, now the only one of her four children still living at home. She recognized she did not treat him as the grown man he was and felt ashamed. 'It's partly because I've been in at the fight of all the painful growing up . . . only it gives me a sort of guilt that prevents me as yet getting that holiday looseness of setting.' She had made all the arrangements for the holiday herself and just expected him to fall in. 'I keep wondering if Richard is happy . . . I treat him wrong. I have known his difficulties too long and I make too much allowance for him,' she admitted. The holiday provided a change of scenery but she hated 'Italian poverty and dirt and vices and greed'.

A visit from Diana Cooper with her friend, Iris Tree, provided the next welcome break in her Rottingdean routine. In expectation of their stay Enid straightened the house a little and managed to get some new curtains up. As a widow herself for some eight years, Diana well understood Enid's pain and that her own presence alleviated it. The friendship between Diana and Enid cemented. In October, Enid drove over to France to stay with Laurian's in-laws near Rheims. She always adored driving, especially at night, coming home over the deserted downs and in spite of a sobering near-miss that summer. Lynn Fontanne had given Enid some false eyelashes, but whilst she was driving one day in Sussex, one of them had come off and fallen into her eye, making her sneeze furiously and swerve all over the road.

Constant holidays were not, however, a cure for Enid's 'period of upsetness'. 'I am not good at taking a holiday, my only holiday is writing and writing successfully.' Nor did she, any longer, feel the need to escape Rottingdean as she once had. Mrs St Maugham had faithfully reflected Enid in declaiming: 'In a village one is down to the bones of things. When I was at my height – though I lived here – I never knew them! They were waiting for my old age like wolves it seems!' Suddenly, when she could have moved away from Rottingdean, remaining there took on a new appeal for her. Roderick had bequeathed The Elms to Enid, who in turn gave the house to Laurian and, shortly after Roderick's death, she and her family began making plans to leave London and move back to Rottingdean. The idea of Laurian living across the road was 'heaven' for Enid. Also, in her seventy-second year, Enid found herself suddenly amid a crowd of 'intoxicating' new friends who were mostly based in Brighton.

Cyril Connolly had introduced Enid to the drama critic of the *Financial Times*, T.C. (Cuthbert) Worsley. His review of *The Last Joke* had been one of the more moderate. Worsley was then living in a flat in Brighton with his friend, Johnny Luscombe. But Worsley's emphysema made this flat, arrived at after many stairs, increasingly unsuitable. Over dinner, Enid immediately offered the pair the 'ravishing little cottage' next to her house. The Joneses had always had difficulties in letting Dale Cottage. Desmond MacCarthy, who used to sleep in it when he came to stay, maintained it was because there was nothing wrong with it but everything right, which made people suspicious. Enid told Cuthbert she thought it was because she had furnished it too well 'that I couldn't bear anyone to have it. When people came over it I always said "no".' 'And so', Worsley recalled later, 'I was put in the way of another treasured friendship. Cyril was childishly delighted with having achieved this.'

Enid told the Lunts about her new life. 'Lots of men around me mad about the theatre. Cuthbert Worsley ... Terry Rattigan and through them lots of actors, critics and the whole thing is something I have never had before and now it expands my nostrils like a hunting horse who hears the horn.' From now on Enid saw Cuthbert every day. Usually he would come over for a drink before supper. He gave her all the theatrical encouragement he could muster but warned her that both she and Rattigan were 'out of fashion. . . . He says that well-to-do people hardly go to the theatre any more (TV, parking difficulties, dinner difficulties and a preference for a certain amount of party-going) whereas the people who swarm into the theatre are the Wesker crowd.' Cuthbert, Johnny and Terry were new friends 'yet curiously old ones. The first friends since Roderick died. That's what makes you all so dear to me.'

Enid was still wildly ambitious, 'like a child with the world before it'. She reflected that: 'Being seventy-two doesn't mean that I shan't be ninety-two. But it puts a sort of pressure on. . . . I feel that I have done nothing, cut no ice, accomplished nothing.' In November, eleven months after Roderick's death, she sent her new play, now enlarged, to Peter Hall, Director of the Royal Shakespeare Theatre. But he 'reacted against' it. The trouble, he thought, was that 'the wit and observation is so brilliant that the underlying life is not deep enough ... it sometimes makes me feel that it's flippant and sometimes pretentious because the inner life is not strong enough.'

Hall's imputations of flippancy, pretension and lack of feeling confounded her. 'It's a method of writing, a fan held up to mask feeling.' As she saw it, this was irony. What she had written in the play about being a mother at seventy was, she believed, 'stuffed' full of feeling. She conceded, however, that Hall had also made some positive comments and decided to do further work on it.

Hall offered to send the play to Michael Codron. But he, too, turned it down. 'I feel it's such a rebuff at my age for these refusals to happen to me.' Before the year was out, Enid had a flicker of interest from Edith Evans. She had once asked Enid to write just such a play and now wanted to read this one for a second time. But, again, she turned it down. Notwithstanding, Enid invited her to a dinner-party at Hyde Park Gate, in honour of the Lunts, and there Edith explained: 'Oh, I can't be bothered with a play about people's inner lives or their hearts or their selfishnesses. *Think* what is happening to the world, to Cuba, to us. The atom bomb etcetera.' Whereupon Enid replied: 'Then get someone to write you a play about Cuba and the Bomb and see how it goes. Nobody will come to see it. The human heart and its idiosyncrasies will outlive it all – if the world survives.' Later on, 'effect of alcohol, I dare say', Enid took Edith to one side to tell her, 'You are a very stupid woman for a genius!'

Harold tried to bolster Enid's sagging confidence. There was a chance, he reminded her, that Ina Claire might play *The Chinese Prime Minister*. And Ruth Gordon, who had taken the lead in *Serena Blandish* thirty-three years previously, had expressed interest. Reiterating his conviction that it was in Enid's best interests to secure a star first and then line up the management for the play, he counselled yet more patience. But, with so many rejections from directors and stars alike, Enid believed 'even the village institute would refuse it'.

In the New Year Lynn Fontanne invited her to go and stay with them once more, this time in their New York apartment. Enid doubted there was anything further to be discussed about the play and worried that she might feel a gooseberry, but, she promised: 'I would be (for a large woman) practically non-existent ... so discreet ... you see I am slipping and sliding nearer and nearer this happiness.' Just after she accepted, however, Harold telephoned with news that the director Joseph Anthony loved her play and would shortly be in London to meet her. When Enid explained about the Lunt invitation, Harold reprimanded her, 'quite cross, saying that it was frivolous to go to New York just when he'd put me on the map with Joe Anthony.'

Joseph Anthony was a mild-mannered, former actor from Wisconsin, trained in the Lee Strasberg method school. He was, Harold told her, 'a very sensitive fellow . . . brought up in the theatre.' He was in London to direct *Mary, Mary*. 'Wildly impressed', after reading Enid's play, he took time off from rehearsals to talk about it with her. 'The first encounter was fabulous,' Anthony recalled. 'She made a doorway that was ordinarily magnificent dwarf into a cabin-like hole as she flung it open. Once closed, then she was transformed. She became kittenish with a light patter to her voice, infinitely seductive, enchanted by the possibility of my doing what she called "my little play".' Anthony told her over lunch that he was stunned by the quality of her cooking and writing equally. But he did not feel it appropriate to discuss substantive matters at the first meeting.

By the end of January Enid thought Anthony was sufficiently involved to justify her taking a room on the top floor of the Hyde Park Hotel in Knightsbridge for two weeks' uninterrupted work. Every night she despatched a wad of work to the nearby Park Lane Hotel, where he was staying. He telephoned her in the morning to discuss it. Occasionally she worried that there was still no contract with Anthony, but she enjoyed working with him at this early stage. 'He doesn't suddenly come along like old Irene with a bulldozer and say, "All that out!" . . . He guides it into a better position and suggests places where strengthening is needed.'

After *Mary, Mary* opened, Anthony returned to the United States. Contracts had by then been drawn up although no star had yet been found. Enid was to follow a few weeks later with a view to an autumn staging of *The Chinese Prime Minister*.

Before she left, Enid felt despondent and apprehensive. The *Evening Standard* had just published a series on Elizabeth Taylor, 'very gaily and well done and attracted attention'. But in the section on her childhood and role in the film *National Velvet*, there was no mention of Enid. Two days later, the *Daily Mail* featured another child actress, Hayley Mills, then starring as Laurel in the film of *The Chalk Garden*, 'and again, not a word about me'. Enid had had virtually nothing to do with the film but had written to 'that damned old Edith', again playing Mrs St Maugham, to ask if she could come down to watch a day's shooting. 'She had the nerve to ring me up and say "Yes, dear, if you keep quiet in your corner." Who does she owe the play to anyway?'

Enid was worried about leaving Richard alone in the house, a new problem, and was hastily interviewing a variety of cooks, cleaners and gardeners. And she was concerned about her dog. Henry, a miniature black and tan terrier, had very particular requirements, including an insistence on being tucked up in his basket at night, otherwise he would whine until the ritual had been satisfactorily performed. Fortunately Johnny Luscombe agreed to look after him.

Above all, she was worried about her relationship with Joseph Anthony, which was already showing signs of deterioration. She felt the play was being 'cheapened' by many of Anthony's proposals. The main character – originally called 'Mrs Forrest' but now 'She' to give her the same universality as 'the Squire' – he wanted softened, humanized, less arrogant and less confident. 'But I had that out with him! Not a touch of womanliness.'

In April, Enid went to stay with Anthony and his wife, Perry, at their home in up-state New York. This was a low-built, clapboard house with a swimming pool and wild garden, half an hour from the city. Enid worked hard all day, attempting modifications to the plot, but not to the characterizations. 'Oh the damn frustration of the world,' she moaned to Cuthbert: a world where directors flattered her words and then insisted on changing them. She found her hosts extremely kind but complained about the diet they offered her: 'Toast sandwiches for lunch with glasses of milk and tea and thick soup and then cookies. All starch. And grits for breakfast . . . so one is rushing to the loo all afternoon.'

While there, the Lunts invited her again to stay with them. She loved their company but resented the delaying effect of their indecisiveness. She wanted to tell them 'to go to hell. . . . But my "advisors" won't let me. I think they think the stake is too big, (not for me but for them).' So crucial was the possibility of their appearance, that this time the management was to pay Enid's fare and expenses to Wisconsin. Enid herself had paid £400 for her first 'Lunthunting' trip.

By the time she joined them in May, she knew definitely they were not going to act in her play. 'What Harold thinks happened is that, in her noble, wifely way, she has taken its refusal on *her* shoulders when it's really Alfred's petty annoyance all the time that his part isn't as long as hers, a new view with which Enid concurred.

Enid returned to Rottingdean, as always, for the summer. Knowing the play would dissolve without a star, she wrote to Margaret Leighton 'a begging letter' and asked Cuthbert, who knew her, 'to put in a word for the worth of the play'. Maggie, although only forty-one, was finally persuaded that her lack of years was no obstacle. Once she had agreed, everything else fell into place. Alan Webb was engaged as Bent, the butler who 'dies' and recovers on stage. Even Binkie, once he grasped the imminence of an American production, was suddenly 'in love' with the play, having ignored both it and Enid for months previously.

Enid sailed to the United States again in the late summer of 1963. She had not made all the script changes Anthony required. 'Oh Joe, I've worked so hard,' she wailed. 'I simply can't do any more. This is the play I want to write,' she told him.

Anthony was furious. But, in an attempt to show solidarity between author and director, he invited Enid on stage at the first rehearsal to talk about the play. She explained how she saw life for a woman as 'a perpetual engagement list: from seventeen to fifty it gets fuller and fuller and always in a more petty way. Looking beyond the minute to the next one wasting the minute itself . . . the Chinese Prime Minister represents an adventure in age. What can we do with it to stop life being a reiteration?'

Anthony thanked her and told her, 'Now *our* work begins.' Trying to be gracious, he advised her to leave the company alone for three weeks before returning to listen. 'Oh so I'm being driven from the theatre, am I?' she asked. Eventually, he agreed to let her stay but not on the stage. Nor could she whisper to him. 'I think he could feel the radiations of despair running from my body to his.'

The arguments were mostly about how much the actors were to move about on stage. When Anthony told her the play was not a musical recital, she replied, 'It's not a skaters' rink either.' Anthony believed that Enid's attempts to get the actors to remain motionless on stage, so that the audience could appreciate her words, stemmed from jealousy of the actor's role. The accusation was, in part, justifiable. Enid had a long-standing belief in the inferiority of the intelligence of actors. John Gielgud and Edith Evans might both have genius but it was an innate sort of genius which did not understand at any deeper level. Some years previously, at a Rottingdean village fête, when a young boy distinguished himself in a children's pantomime, the then Miss Cicely Courtneidge, who had opened the proceedings, commented:

'That boy will be an actor.'

'Indeed he will not!' interjected Enid, who knew him. 'He's far too intelligent.'

This attitude also led to trouble with Oliver Smith, one of New York's most experienced set designers. He wrote to her in September, 'I cannot tell you how much I adore your beautiful, elliptical play (that explains the presence of ellipses in the plan and elevation).' But such a majestic, busy set was not what Enid had in mind and she wasted no time in criticizing it when she met Smith for the first time. 'He didn't mind,' she assured Cuthbert. 'What a nice man. . . . Thank God I know what I'm talking about when I talk about drawing. . . . I realize now that – as it's an *oral* play we ought to have done it merely with screens instead of a realistic set so as to give the message to the audience as the curtain goes up – to *listen* and *not look.*'

Enid was almost as meticulous over actions as she was over words. She demonstrated to Alan Webb how to sharpen the carving knife, telling him precisely to the inch where to put the blade on the steel. Distraught, Anthony went to Albert Marre for advice on how to deal with Enid. Marre suggested locking her out of the theatre. But when Anthony complained to Roger Stevens, the producer, he was told she might take her play away if they did this. From now on, Anthony kept her further back in the bowels of the auditorium, but he could not prevent her mouthing the words, semi-silently, shaking her head in horror, or writing a constant stream of notes. Some days she drove Anthony almost to breaking point as she ran up and down the aisle with 'suggestions'. 'I get some of them down his throat,' she told Cuthbert. The actors were deluged by her notes, usually pushed furtively under their dressing-room doors.

But Anthony was adept at spotting whenever Enid had intervened and this unleashed further fury. Margaret Leighton was in an awkward position. Frequently she rang Enid at her hotel late at night to ask for advice. She was worried about what both she and Enid perceived as Joe's 'misdirection' of Oliver, her stage son. 'He is', Enid relayed to Cuthbert, 'a short, stocky red-faced emotional lad and Joe is making him more emotional. I DON'T want a mother's boy in a play of mine.'

Although this actor was eventually changed, here was the root of the problem. Not only was the central character of the play frankly autobiographical – the Squire grown up, as Enid had initially expounded to the actors – but the rest of Enid's family had been recreated for the play too. It would be simplistic to maintain that this part was pure Timothy, than Dominick. But, as spring-boards for her imagination, her sons and their wives were particularly important for this play. In *The Chinese Prime Minister* Enid was revealingly honest about her shortcomings as a mother-in-law as she saw them. 'What is the terrible truth about me (which I face up to innerly) is that I so love my children and feel they are so remarkable and have such a language of their own that I recognize I bear with a bad grace any interference of that "community language" or feeling by those that they marry. . . . I was chiefly thinking of what a bad mother-in-law I am.' Given the personal background to the play, she could not have her family played any old way – only she knew what they were really like.

Enid considered all the actors (apart from the British duo, Maggie and Alan) miscast. 'Very brash and American and no idea of "intimacy" in speech, and always churning up Freudian entrails of why they must do this or that. . . . Is it the umbilical cord? etc. etc. . . . I hear them arguing and asking Joe the most extraordinary questions about psychology.' This, of course, ran counter to Enid's philosophy of life, which was to delight in things as they were. Just as she had no desire to improve or crusade, equally she did not seek to establish complex motives for what to her seemed natural behaviour. She believed in an uncomplicated enjoyment of life and friends and people, 'of whatever is the extreme opposite of angst'. This made her and Joe natural enemies. Enid recognized that 'no director is ever good enough for an author', but she had hoped that she would be allowed to say just a few things to point up the meanings more subtly.

On 24 November, Enid was being interviewed in a sumptuous restaurant by a journalist from the *New York Times*. Suddenly the *maître d'hôtel* tiptoed up to the journalist and said, 'The President's been shot.' The journalist quickly seized a telephone to find out the latest news. Enid was appalled at what she considered excessive grief and emotion over Kennedy's assassination. 'It's not that I'm not aware of the full nature of the tragedy, but they all seem to be buying black handkerchiefs to swell out their hearts.'

In early December the company 'hauled in' to Toronto. Enid poured out her frustrations to Cuthbert, now her sole confidant. 'Joe has turned into a stiff-necked tyrant with no give and take. "Points" are being lost every day by the handful and my wretched play is constructed on "points". Really I ought to have directed it myself if it weren't for all those other things like lighting etc. I really could have.'

By the time they opened in Toronto's Royal Alexandra Theatre on 7 December, Anthony was no longer speaking to Enid because of her latest 'suggestions' letter to Margaret Leighton. Enid wanted more authority and less charm from her leading lady. She required the lines to be said straight, not recited as poetry. She wanted a style that she began to think only Edith Evans could convey. 'Edith's voice and manner are so tremendously needed. It's so terrible to hear it in my mind and then *not* to hear it.' Maggie, tormented by the strains, threatened to leave the play before New York. She was angry and upset and, as she frankly admitted, did not understand her part. Sometimes she forgot her words, at other times her extreme nervousness was evident from a catch in her throat. Enid realized, eventually, that Maggie could not take all the badgering. 'I do see now that Maggie is someone far more fragile than I had supposed.'

In Boston, the cast was not helped by appalling snowstorms. One night, a mere twenty-seven people spread themselves out thinly in the stalls. As Enid took a cab to the theatre, the driver asked her, 'You bin to that? Kinda tacky show, they say.'

The reviews in Toronto and Boston were not good. One Canadian critic commented that Margaret Leighton was 'terribly tortured by nerves and driven to accept audible prompting by the end of the evening.' Others called it 'a thin-blooded evening', 'disappointing' or 'baffling'.

Although Enid hoped that the play might have been pulled together somewhere along the road, she foresaw failure in New York and braced herself. She paid for Dominick to fly over and be with her for the first night at New York's Royale Theater. 'I wonder if he can ever know the extreme of delight it gave me.' She was as concerned to pull off a success in front of her own son as she was with the public. But Dominick, in the fifth row with his mother, was unable to sit through the play. Soon after the curtain went up, he disturbed an already anxious audience to go and vomit as a lunch-time dish of shark wreaked its revenge. Afterwards, Roger Stevens gave a first-night party at Sardi's at which Enid waited for the reviews, calm only because she had swallowed large quantities of a potent cough mixture. Walter Kerr's influential report in the New York *Herald Tribune* was more than she had dared hope for. He was, he wrote, touched by the play,

I think because I have seen one whole play in which there is not a single careless line.... For playwright Enid Bagnold never does anything merely because she cannot think of anything better to do. Whatever she does, she does on impulse, inspiration, with a jump and with a dagger in her hand, eyes gleaming. The gleam, the mad glint of her inspiration may indeed flash out of the untidiest of corners. But in itself it's marvellously pure.

He concluded: 'It shimmers on the stage – and wavers there like a vast insubstantial spider's web, strung with bits of real rain. It is not conventional and it is not altogether secure. But it is written. And what a blessing that is.'

Others were similarly effusive. *Time* magazine called it a 'triumph of style not substance ... in the present semi-illiterate state of the US stage, pure English makes an irresistible lever for an audience.'

Before the party broke up, Joseph Anthony presented all the company with white china rosebuds. 'Mine had a small card tied to it: "To a monster",' Enid recalled in her autobiography. She was not being entirely fair with this misquote. Anthony had actually written: 'I suppose it was in the cards that I should come to find you a monster as well as magnificent. No matter the outcome of the plot, the essence will always be chiefly admiration and wishes that you are rewarded, and love too will persist.'

Enid returned to Sardi's the night before she was due to sail home, as Lyn Austin, Roger Stevens's deputy manager, gave a farewell party for her. By now the play had established itself as a major hit, with long queues at the Royale box office. However, Enid arrived in frosty mood, furious at having had to struggle through blizzards along Seventh Avenue to get there; months before her arrival she stated that the only luxury she required was a car to get her about New York. Nevertheless, when she saw Anthony, she stretched out her arms in a forgiving gesture, expecting him to fall into her embrace. But Anthony had hardened by now. 'When I did not,' he recalled, 'she put out her hand and I pretended not to see it. "What! You do not shake my hand when we're a success and you used to kiss it?" Enid asked me. "I had other plans for this play,"' he told her bitterly. Love had not persisted and they never spoke again.

Before she left England, Enid had typed out a memo for herself. 'DO NOT WISH TO PLEASE", twice in capitals, headed the list. In that, at least she had succeeded.

TWENTY

Money Doesn't Matter Any More : Get The Plays On

THE immediate problem facing Enid on her return was loneliness. To Diana she admitted how she missed Roderick, how she would wander round the garden thinking of him, wishing him back, and then pondering the mysteries of life itself. Cuthbert, who had been Enid's lifeline to the theatre, was in difficulty too. His health had deteriorated so that he could no longer chase up to London for theatre reviews. In this crisis Enid immediately and indefinitely waived all rent. Meanwhile, the *Financial Times* offered him a less demanding post, that of television critic. But Enid needed more than Cuthbert. She placed a severe advertisement in *The Times* : 'Badly needed but not wanted : self-contained person (not "as family") two rooms, bathroom, TV. Salary. Maid. Assist savage old woman playwright . . . no tact required ; taciturnity valued.'

Not surprisingly, this produced few suitable servants. 'How damnable (yet unmentionable) domestic troubles are,' she grumbled to Diana. 'I got one [cook] and she ran away. Another schizo. Austrian. Took night train to Vienna. Since then hopeless. And Italians down at Rott. – spoiled all winter.' She felt as if she lived permanently among the pots and pans, with onion under her fingernails. There was as yet little diminution in her energy but her own health was now causing her some problems. She began to suffer bouts of frequent pain in the pit of her spine and needed household help as much as ever. Eventually in 1964, she found a married couple of Polish origin, Mr and Mrs Michalovsky, always known as The Micks. In spite of many confrontations, they stayed for thirteen years.

To cheer herself up, she wrote a 'crowing' letter to Peter Hall about the success of *The Chinese Prime Minister* in New York. He replied modestly that he was 'delighted . . . you could crow. There's nothing better than being proved wrong about a play : the more success the merrier.'

As she viewed the years that might lie ahead, she began seriously to contemplate writing her autobiography. She was encouraged by Laurian, who never tired of hearing about her mother's life, by Irene Selznick who saw it as a way of preventing more theatrical fiascos, and by Carol Brandt, who always regretted Enid's abandonment of novel-writing. Enid herself believed it would be an opportunity to say in public 'that stars are old fashioned . . . stars hanker after well-knit drama plays. And in making them all the fragility and good cobwebs are squeezed out.'

There were other reasons too, not least of which was the growing interest amongst a new generation in her pre-World War I contemporaries. She found herself frequently being asked for her memories of people like Horace Brodzky, Lovat Fraser, Gaudier-Brzeska and the rest. Her growing awareness that Enid Bagnold had survived as a fresco-figure of Edwardian Chelsea developed into a desire to determine her own place in that corner of history.

She had made little more than odd notes, vignettes, when she was summoned to a meeting with Binkie and Edith at the Globe Theatre in February. Enid could not believe that Edith would not take the part of She in the English production of *The Chinese Prime Minister*, 'Everyone says her voice rings out in every line.' Yet Edith appalled her on this occasion. 'Silly old venal creature . . . she horrified me. She has only one gift. Her gift. All the rest is bogus. Bogus goodness, bogus unselfishness, bogus nobility. Only her talent is real.' However, Enid still wanted her and Binkie assured her, if script alterations were made, she could have her. Rehearsals could begin in the late summer for an autumn opening. Only the hope that Dame Edith Evans would infuse her play with life kept her struggling with further re-writes (some of which caused major linking problems), fretfully and for long hours. As she constantly pointed out to Harold, she could get on with nothing else while it hung over her and she was now in her seventy-fifth year.

In spite of its New York *réclame*, the play was not proving a major commercial success and could not be prolonged beyond April. Naturally Enid wanted a New York hit to strengthen her hand with Binkie, but he was unimpressed with the American production when he saw it in the spring. 'Maggie, of course, was darling,' he told Enid, but 'looking a glamorous thirty-five, not seventy'. He said he was 'still enormously enthusiastic' about the play for London, but she well knew that his enthusiasm started and ended with Edith Evans.

Just as Binkie was about to commit himself to the play, Edith Evans was invited to star in Laurence Olivier's forthcoming production of *Hay Fever* at the National Theatre. Enid was distraught at what she called the abduction of Edith. 'I know it seems to you', she wrote to Olivier, 'that for me to wait nine months for Edith – till March – is a small thing. I would like you to know what it humanly means to me.' Olivier replied at length, telling Enid to accept that Edith was not in any case going to open in her play tomorrow as she was filming in August. 'As I would only be allowed to have her till March . . . that brings down the time that you now consider I am pinching her off you for, to just about half that which you are telling yourself it is.' But, he added mischievously, 'I gather from both Edith and Binkie that they are no longer absolutely happy about the play and that is the reason for the present situation.'

Neither did Olivier shirk telling Enid that his life too was shrouded with difficulties – a serious illness, no holidays for two years, three new ventures collapsing. This was a revelation to her. Her old stoicism returned:

I believe I have been making a martyr of myself *to* myself. I suppose I have been saying to myself, 'seventy-four ... seventy-four ... you'll soon be dead', when the likelihood is that I'll write a splendid play at ninety and on my ninetieth birthday I shall be put on by you at Chichester and, chewing on two sticks of hickory, I will hobble in with a laurel wreath on my white hair. I am sorry I made such a fuss.

Accepting the inevitable, she prepared to wait.

During the spring and summer of 1964, in addition to making script changes, she looked at new tax-saving schemes. The hope was that the money from *The Chinese Prime Minister* would be sufficient over a couple of years or more to maintain North End House. Roderick had always been most careful about preserving the fabric of the house, patching up here, decorating a room there. Enid did not really care and, increasingly, it all but fell apart.

Irene Selznick had a different proposal for making money. She was, she told Enid, 'delighted to find the movie grosses on *Chalk Garden* are absolutely wonderful throughout the country. That being the case ... you are "hot" and this would be the ideal time to get back to that notion of mine about a film treatment of *The Last Joke*.' She promised not to mention a word as yet to Binkie 'who would truly breathe down our necks as he would love to wash out the red ink on that production. Speaking for myself, I, too, would like to retrieve the investment as it is the largest financial loss I personally have ever sustained on a production.'

Enid was enraged. Only a few weeks ago, Irene had tried to persuade her to devote all her time to an autobiography. 'Now you want me to do a money-maker! To recoup you and Binkie? I didn't actually know that you yourself had an investment in *The Last Joke** and I'm dreadfully sorry you should be the loser.' In any case, Enid was sceptical of success for a film of *The Last Joke*. It had been 'hashed up by butchers, trampled upon by buffaloes. And you think the bloody pieces might stink attractively in the nostrils of the film industry?' she asked Irene. Nor could she, any longer, be motivated merely by money. 'I shall be giving up a slice of my precious evaporating life

---

* Compare with Enid's letter to Irene quoted Chapter 18 on page 213.

if I do this. But I would do it for the children. . . . They have so married themselves that nobody supports them. Even *The Chalk Garden* won't keep them all, I think. And endless boys to go to Eton !'

In October, however, her theatrical plans were rebuilt and the film idea demolished. Edith Evans was, after all, to play She; Alan Webb agreed to recreate his highly praised New York role of Bent. And a new director had been found. 'He is called Vivian Matalon,' she wrote to Webb, 'and he is a Syrian Jew from Jamaica by origin.' Enid had invited him down to Rottingdean to stay the night so that Cuthbert could be summoned over for his verdict 'and Cuthbert said he was all right. "Intelligent, but not too intelligent". . . . Of course he wants alterations. When was there ever a director who didn't ?'

Enid was touched by Matalon's gallantry, especially when he paid her taxi fares. 'But I am going', she insisted, 'to settle everything according to your pocket and mine! I am much better off than you are. . . . Don't be offended. . . . If you were my grandson I would tip you, wouldn't I ?' she asked in a letter enclosing a £20 cheque.

Having secured Edith, the rest of her 'family' then had to be cast. Finding the right son was, as in America, a matter of delicacy. Otherwise 'it alters what I really mean about the relationship', Enid insisted to Matalon. 'Oliver isn't *dominated* by her. The fact that she says he is a "woman's son" means (in my mind) that they are very intimate : more intimate than if he had been sent away to school too early as Tarver had been. . . .'

Enid was, from the outset, unhappy with Brian Aherne as Sir Gregory. She believed he had 'got the fundamental idea of Sir Gregory wrong', and wanted to write and tell him so. As Matalon advised against a letter, she tried instead to persuade him to lower his voice in places, to give a different slant to the words.

'That's too subtle, dear !' he told her.

'My play is subtle, only you don't seem to see it,' she replied.

But for both Enid and Matalon, Edith Evans was the major problem. When rehearsals began, Enid had already started work on a new play. This helped deflect her natural instinct for daily attendance. But in addition, travelling was now a considerable effort for her. Matalon found collaboration with Enid a stimulant but working with Edith a great tribulation. 'She was', he explained, 'simply, too old for the part. She would often drop off to sleep in mid-sentence. Usually I would send her home early in a taxi and continue the rehearsal with her understudy and the rest of the cast.' Enid sympathized with Matalon having to deal with two old women. 'Not that I don't think of myself a hundred years younger than Edith ! In fact – immortal.' Enid was critical not simply of her heroine's failing memory : 'Edith looks like a turnip anyway – won't make up eyes or face,' she wrote. Mary Lynn, the stage manager, considered Enid was bullying Evans and refused to let her near the dressing-room. 'She handed me piles and piles of notes for Edith. If I had read them all to her we would never have opened in London,' Miss Lynn commented.

At least two weeks before opening, Matalon realized that Edith 'was patently never going to get there. She wouldn't play the part except as a glamorous, loving woman, which had nothing to do with the play.' In addition, Edith's attitude towards death, based on deep-seated religious beliefs, was at variance with Enid's rather irreverent attitude in the play. 'Every cold and ironic shaft of mine, especially on death, was turned and plastered with treacle.' Days before opening, Enid was still trying to overturn Edith's sentimentalizing and handed Matalon a further wadge of notes. 'Enid, please stop,' he told her. 'I can't listen to any more. You know I can't get any of this done.' Then, overwhelmed by his perception of having failed Enid Bagnold, Matalon broke down. Enid wept too. That night the two of them stayed at North End House drinking gin until the small hours.

When the play opened at the Globe Theatre on 20 May 1965, Edith, in her magnificent Hardy Amies creations, looked every inch the great actress she was playing. 'But she destroyed the play,' Matalon asserted. One night she simply dropped three pages of script because a scene on the telephone which she hated doing was approaching.

Enid did not expect kind treatment from the London critics. But they were less vituperative than she feared. Bernard Levin calling it a 'civilized, eloquent and attractive play' was a particularly unexpected prize. 'Never mind that the sentence ends, "never quite lives up to the promise of the first act",' she told him in a thank-you letter. Levin also talked of 'the play's warmth, grace and intelligence and language that serves the half-forgotten purpose of delineating human beings. . . .' Alan Webb apologized to Matalon 'for not having made your task exactly easier . . . to say the least. . . . You can't imagine what a bore it is to repeat a play in London which has already failed in New York.' He should, he realized, have refused the London production 'which, in any case, I have only done . . . out of admiration for [Enid's] age and tenacity.' John Perry, Binkie's deputy, could not entirely accept that Edith had been a mistake. He admitted,

The memory and the power are failing. The genius is beginning to dim *but*, and it's an important *but*, you are still getting a great personality and a quality of acting which to my mind is memorable. I am truly sorry you are hurt and disappointed but that's the trouble about writing for the theatre. . . . You want the knife's edge of acting and directing and one rarely gets that.

Her spirits were lifted briefly by one or two fan letters. Robert Helpmann told her he was 'thrilled with such beauty of writing'. Vivien Leigh had been 'enchanted, amused, touched and surprised throughout an evening'. But the summer ended on a note of deep disappointment for Enid. Edith Evans, the supreme Bagnoldian interpreter, for whom she had waited so long and so patiently, had joined forces with her too late. The play proved a disaster and closed after three months.

'I have thought and thought,' she wrote to Mr Abbot Van Nostrand, of Samuel French in New York, 'about this terrible problem ... of how to maintain the taste of one's own talent (the only thing one has to offer) amid the battles and malcastings and, especially the vanity of directors.' She suggested to Timothy, 'Perhaps I'll have a toy theatre made and play it just to myself, dangling cardboard puppets. It might make a nice story about a playwright going mad.' A more realistic solution was to get her plays published before looking for a management. 'I don't intend to go out a-wooing any more after these directors who are mostly failed writers, failed ballet dancers, failed actors and who have discovered this method of wearing a plume of self-satisfaction on their heads.' She felt warmly towards Samuel French who had just had a copy of *The Chinese Prime Minister* especially printed and bound for her in dark-green leather with handmade end-papers. This gesture left Enid 'gloriously astonished, gloriously taken aback, profoundly pleased'. When she read in French's play parade that 'there are few writers working today in the theatre who are able to write in a manner as witty and civilized as Enid Bagnold', her mind was made up. The next play would go to Samuel French for publication before anyone could change a single word or stage direction.

The play in question, *Call Me Jacky*, of which only the first two acts were written, 'is a comedy of course'. It concerned 'a lady who seems behind the times but is in front of them'. While wrestling with her usual 'hump', the third act, Enid received an invitation to stay with one of her oldest friends, the former Dolly Tylden, now Mrs Violet Henson, who lived in Tunisia. The two women had corresponded fitfully over the past forty-five years or so; now, a potent mixture of curiosity, loneliness and an ambition to get the third act right, which she might do in a new setting, led her to accept. In October, after wearisome train and boat rides, she arrived in Hammamet.

Enid was not prepared for such a depressing experience. Although seventy-six, she refused to consider herself old. 'But they are so OLD. I've never been shut up with people (nice people) who have got so emptied by age. One taps and there's only an old hollow sound.' Violet she found 'sad and crumpled and trying to smile'. Jean, her second husband, 'is a bit indescribable.

Nothing perks them up. I can't talk because she can't hear and *he* doesn't want to.' The realities of decrepitude left Enid faintly disgusted. 'Everything is very dirty, napery, spoons etcetera and smells because eyes can't see and noses apparently can't smell.' She was sad for what Violet had been: 'clever, perceptive . . . a most particular person. This girl, so outrageous and daring, so "right" (in judgements) such a leader. . . . I don't say there's nothing left but what's left is so sad.'

Enid tried to work but found the atmosphere less than conducive. 'Of course I can look at the trees. I can look at the ten camels that take tourists along the fringe of the sea; I can pick a blue lotus. But it needs fountains of spiritual life from me to make that last all day.'

Violet had suffered badly during the war as her husband had been imprisoned by the Germans while she and two dogs had been confined to one room in the house. Ten Germans occupied the rest. 'I don't mind her hating the Germans. She went through a lot from them. But I mind it being said on and on at every chance. A button – and out comes the tune.'

It was, in short, a relief to return home before the year was out, albeit to find Cuthbert and Johnny grappling with a major domestic crisis. Johnny's married sister, Daphne Webb, in a state of shock and grief, had been forced to leave home with her three young sons. She did not want the boys to live with their uncle in a homosexual *ménage*, yet had no money and nowhere else to go.

Enid immediately made a small flat at the back of North End House available to them. She rushed to get the heating going, have it cleaned and furnished adequately and then filled it with as many fresh flowers as she could find in winter. 'Without her help I cannot imagine what would have become of my sons and myself,' Daphne recalled later. Enid's thoughtfulness towards Cuthbert and Johnny did not end there. A few months previously Enid had given them £1,000 'because I had made up my mind long ago that if ever I got this play on in London I would do what I am doing now . . . it has nothing whatever to do with the play money I may, or may not be making. It is . . . infinite gratitude for your extraordinary belief in this play in the face of all odds.' Now she capped this with a further small sum at monthly intervals, to help ease Cuthbert's 'immediate anxieties and money-pressures' over Daphne and her sons. 'It does seem to me that if I can help I ought to. Rather – let's put it – I want to.'

The crisis averted, Enid returned to *Call Me Jacky*. Yet 'the moment I altered it, it went out of shape like a top hat that has been sat on.' Harold continually wrote, encouragingly, asking when he could see it. But on 16 February his son Bob telephoned with the news that his father had died in his sleep.

Freedman's premature death at sixty-nine was one of the sharpest blows to

Enid's old age. 'I didn't think he would ever die. I thought he was immortal.' In an obituary composed the next day she wrote: 'This marvellous man, this prince of Jews, deeply religious, humble, courageous, immensely experienced – wily, hard and tender, fell out of my life last night like the centrestone of an arch.'

'I have a play nearly ready for him now and he will never read it. I shall never get that praise – if it deserves it.' Without praise, Enid always maintained she could not write. But without Roderick or Harold who was to supply it?

In April she went again to 'one of those country starvation-clinics where you pay an awful lot for grapefruit juice'. On her return, she finally sent *Call Me Jacky* to Samuel French. But their reaction was disappointing. 'Don't say "With gratitude for being allowed to read it." You must know I was hoping for a different letter. I don't care about gratitude. I want praise,' she admitted to Noel Woolf. 'Alas does one never grow out of that desire?' For the rest of the year a rather flattened Enid found herself living 'on an old wheel of routine. Writing. Waiting . . . trying, trying.'

The summer was punctuated by an extended visit from Dominick now separated from his wife, Jo. 'He is coming with his paramoor [*sic*] and her five children and his one,' she wrote to Lynn Fontanne, explaining why she could not stay with them. 'Not that that is an unmixed blessing. I am not keen on her five! Poor things – they are but children. But still . . . how would you like five unrelated paramoor's children all over the garden. . . . But then I so love Tucker.'

Enid was greatly pained by the realities of Dominick's marriage. Jo was in need of constant psychiatric supervision and the inevitable strain on her son was an agony for her. She was therefore happy that he had found in Cecilia Cussans a new love and hoped that a plan for rebuilding the North End House interior, to accommodate Dominick and his new family, might succeed. 'I had grown rather strangely used to my lonely life in the decaying house. I ought *not* to grow used to it,' she wrote to her youngest son before the visit. She was not in the slightest perturbed by her son living with a woman who was not his wife. In fact she had advised 'setting up house together. I don't believe these days it matters so very much.' Of greater concern to Enid was that Dominick should not, in addition to his own commitments, have to support his stepchildren as well, as 'then no love or happiness could eventually survive'.

It was not an easy summer. Enid realized that she preferred her independence to other people's children and the rebuilding scheme was dropped. In spite of difficulties and arguments, Enid and Richard had worked out a tolerable means of co-existence. Richard, increasingly self-sufficient, was often irritated by his mother's demands on him: for example, to run to the post office or to fetch a particular herb from the garden. Then he would go, with a flourish and 'Yes, sir' on his lips. At the same time, Enid tried, as ever, to do what she could, and often prepared four cooked meals a day, including cake, for him. Although they kept to themselves as much as possible, Richard frankly admitting he was bored by her literary chats with Cuthbert, visitors could not but be struck by her tender treatment of her grown son. 'Thank God for that darling Richard. How you must love him,' Lynn Fontanne commented after a visit to Rottingdean. 'I wonder if you know how I love him and ache over him?' she asked Diana. 'Always have. He is deeply good. Loyal – never sees the worst, always the best in anyone.'

Diana Cooper also proved a most loyal friend to Enid at this time, sometimes motoring down to Rottingdean for lunch, which gave Enid immense pleasure. Once Diana brought a young actress friend of hers, a Bagnold fan desperately keen to meet her idol. Enid was often inspiring to younger women, grasping at an opportunity to share her books with a fresh mind. Georgina Ward was not only beautiful and intelligent but responsive. After just one meeting, she was able to write: 'Don't alter a line of *Call Me Jacky*. You've said what you intended to say and you've said it exactly. It's all there – precisely and beautifully laid out. Stick to it.'

Georgina offered to return to Rottingdean, armed with a tape recorder, and talk Enid through the opening stages of her autobiography as Enid had complained of the difficulty she was having in getting started. Georgina was neither journalist nor historian but the truly interested listener Enid craved. Although Enid had believed she was only at ease creating sentences on a typewriter, together they made a beginning which Georgina was determined not to let drop.

There were other beneficiaries at this time of Enid's diffuse gift for friendship. Several actresses who had heard of Enid Bagnold or who knew her slightly telephoned her if they were playing at Brighton's Theatre Royal. She almost always invited them to North End House for a meal. Among them were Julia Foster, Hayley Mills and Irene Worth, who were all aware of a lasting effect from meeting her. She met, at a party given by Asa Briggs, then Professor of History at Sussex University, the young American writer, Janet Burroway. Enid made it clear she was not interested in Janet's husband, Walter Eyselink, the director of the Gardner Centre for the Arts at the University, when she invited Janet to visit her alone at Rottingdean. On these occasions, Enid offered advice for living as well as writing. She impressed upon Burroway the importance of being able to cope. 'She was always hardest on those she felt had not managed their lives,' Burroway recalled. 'And yet Enid herself, although she appeared tough and coping externally, was really very badly disappointed inwardly as a writer. In her own eyes she was not successful. The later failures had wiped out the past glories. She felt she was ending her life in a down spiral.' The inner misery was so well shielded that even her own daughter sometimes failed to see it. 'Can't you understand that I am vulnerable and sad and *not* triumphant?' she wrote to Laurian. 'If I have the habit of triumph it is only like my face powder.'

Her eagerness to see a successful production of *Call Me Jacky* was, there-fore, overwhelming. She had asked Vivian Matalon to send it to James Roose Evans at the Hampstead Theatre Club and Peggy Ashcroft, who she hoped might like it enough to play the lead, to show it to the director, Frank Hauser. Hauser was interested in it for the Oxford Playhouse but flinched when told of Enid's demands for control of casting and daily supervision of production.

Enid had, by this time, decided to find herself a new agent. Leaving Harold's son Bob was distressing but she felt he could never be as good as his father. Eventually she settled on Margaret (Peggy) Ramsay for England and Robert Lantz in New York. Miss Ramsay soon grew alarmed by Enid's panics and apparent desperation over *Call Me Jacky*. 'You are allowing yourself to be neurotic and nervy about something for no reason at all,' she told her in a most un-Haroldish letter. 'You must keep an inner calm and an inner life and not allow your nerves to become wayward – it's unnecessary and unhelpful to you. . . . NO self-indulgence of nerves.'

'Yes, I'm often frantic,' Enid replied by return. 'But very seldom depressed . . . I'm *not* a bit neurotic. I only suffer from what everyone suffers who doesn't know where the words and thoughts come from and doesn't know why or when the source might dry.' However, she promised her new agent that: 'Now I've got you I've never felt so cosseted and ready to be kicked into shape and – oh dear me – looked after. . . . I'll be calm, I'll be obedient.'

By midsummer, once contracts had been signed with Donald Albery for Frank Hauser to direct, Enid felt able to spend a few weeks with the Lunts. This time Lynn decided it was time to recreate her friend's appearance and Enid, without a murmur, acquiesced. For some years now, to hide her mean and thinning hair, Enid had taken to wearing expensive but ill-fitting wigs. Lynn did not think they looked attractive and organized her own hairdresser to chop Enid's remaining hair very short and curl it tight 'like a negress'. 'After four hours and twenty minutes I was done. I was apparently a triumph . . . I had a net put over tiny short hair that would never move again.' As always, Enid enjoyed her visit to Lynn and Alfred. The small-town friendliness of Genessee Depot delighted her in a way Rottingdean, even now, never had. 'Everyone knew everyone and everyone was kind. . . . But in between the apple pies they mostly talked of cancer.'

*C*all Me Jacky opened at the Oxford Playhouse for a two-week run on 27 February 1968. Enid had had her 'West End treatment' and was optimistic that her plays might thrive in the more intimate atmosphere of a small, out-of-town theatre. She had a good team assembled, too. Dame Sybil Thorndike, intrigued by the play, had needed no persuasion to act Mrs Basil. Paul Eddington played Herbert; Georgina Ward, with heavy brown make-up, the black girl, Elizabeth; and Edward Fox, the grandson, Niggie. The caricature part of Shatov* was played by Sheila Burrell.

But the play was her most disastrous failure yet. The audience, many of whom were left-wing intellectual undergraduates, hissed and booed and were at one with the critics in reviling both the play and its author for, at best, being behind the times and, at worst, being 'anti-black, anti-left, a sorry old bitch sitting in a castle'. There was no question of transferring to London. 'It lay upside down at Oxford like a dog with its paws in the air,' Enid wrote later.

Blinded by the Bagnold idiom and the richness of setting, the critics could not see that the real message of the play was 'a sort of astonishment that young people think that the generation behind them hasn't experienced the same thing.'

Blasting out her own modernity, she wrote to Vivian Matalon, 'Oh *Fuck* them all . . . they got more bitter, wounding, flinch-making every day. How *could* they think the play was an old Tory muck up grinding at the lefts? How could they – and even Cuthbert has ratted a bit. He said smoothly, "Well dear it wasn't Tory when we read it together, but it comes out Tory" . . . I am on the bitter side but recovering.'

She had not recovered enough to give her protégé, Michael Thornton, an interview. 'It wouldn't now do you any good to interview me. Nobody thinks I'm important, anyway. . . .' Enid was aggrieved that whereas Harold Pinter, whom she greatly admired, could write themeless plays and refuse to explain them, she should be attacked for the very same fault. But the critics, determined to extract a theme, found the wrong one. Ronald Bryden's report in the *Observer* was, for Enid, the most 'wickedly cruel' and she wrote to him

* Even the name here is unoriginal: Dostoevsky's terrorist in *The Possessed* is also called Shatov.

about the 'pain you caused me. . . . It was more stupefaction,' she went on. 'The play is dead, anyway, killed by all of you.' Of *Call Me Jacky* Ronald Bryden said he could not bring himself 'to write temperately. . . . A Tory attempt to rewrite *Heartbreak House*, it obviously intends to exasperate people like myself beyond speech and succeeds totally.' But even this was as nothing compared with the 'marvellous deathblow' delivered by *The Times*, 'on the lines of . . . "I wonder that a lady of seventy-eight who has already had two such flops has the toughness to try yet another play . . ." something like that. . . . But writing's writing and you can't stop it because of a flop,' she retorted. Equally, she did not believe in making a fuss about things, but got on with the next idea.

Writing had become a torment for Enid. But the pain of not writing was overwhelming. Knowing no other life, having exhausted novels and plays, she was finally ready to complete the autobiography which she had first attempted almost sixty years before.

TWENTY-ONE

I Am Much Disappointed To Be A Cripple

FOR almost ten years, Enid had been making occasional attempts to write her autobiography. If she did not tackle it soon, she feared, all the best stories about her would be stale from use in other people's biographies. A major stumbling-block was dealing with Roderick and their life together. 'Do write about our marriage,' he had often exhorted her, 'it's so extraordinary.' But to Guen Bourke, she admitted, 'I somehow can't talk of Roderick. . . . Don't know how to put him in focus if I ever do write the autobiography. And it may stop me writing it.'

The biggest spur was a searing desire to refute the critics of her plays. One, she felt, was especially worthy of rebuke.

My dear Penelope Gilliatt [Enid wrote in an early draft of an introductory chapter], You are to me particularly an arbiter. You and what you represent are what has undone my courage. . . . To write plays has been the love and agony of my late middle and now old age. You have been consistently spiteful about me, even to the length of bringing in my name with aspish comment when reviewing another play – not mine. . . . I am not ashamed of being so affected by a critic. Keats died of much the same thing. One is tender in one's parts when these are genital.

There followed several lines crossed out. She then continued:

Have you chosen me because I am Lady Jones? Is it because you think I am a successful social woman – shouting under the smallest of titles (earned by my husband and worn by me because it is his) who has somehow had the luck to get a success with a play?

Laying my hands about idly attempting to find some pretext to open an autobiography I may as well choose you to make my explanation to as anyone else. Particularly as I don't know you. Well, I am not what you think I am.

This introduction, Enid planned, would lead naturally into an account of how Enid saw herself, daughter of a Royal Engineer, sprung from a solid, middle-class, English family background.

In fact, Enid *had* met Penelope Gilliatt. In 1956, as a novice journalist for *Vogue*, Miss Gilliatt had taken Enid out for lunch to commission her to write a piece on any subject she liked. Enid chose 'Servants and Success'. Eight years later, Enid took exception to a series of articles written by Miss Gilliatt (then married to John Osborne) as the newly-appointed theatre critic for the *Observer*. Enid kept these, clipped together, with red circles around the most hurtful passages. Miss Gilliatt declared in her first piece:

People behave now as if . . . the battle over the garden-trug kind of play had long ago been won and forgotten. But I am not so sure they are right. . . . An admired piece like James Saunders' *A Scent of Flowers* seems to me to lie bang in the tradition; it is irredeemably mandarin and precious and takes us right back to the days of *The Chalk Garden*.

In a review of *Any Wednesday* by Muriel Resnik, Miss Gilliatt commented:

The reason why the admission is not made is the same as the reason why the heroines of Enid Bagnold's plays are not declared to be grim and mandarin old bags. . . . Because it makes the unflattering calculation that the audience is full of people with characters just like hers, married to men who have put the theatre tickets against tax and who would like to hang their business symbol, worked in diamonds, around someone else's neck.

There were others in similar vein. Had Enid's fame as a dramatist reached the levels of Shaw or Wilde, taking a play ten years old and standing it in odious comparison with a current work, might have been justified. Without that fame, such uncomplimentary references to her work appeared to Enid merely gratuitously offensive. Twenty years later, Penelope Gilliatt maintained she 'admired and loved' Enid Bagnold. 'I was one of her most fervent admirers . . . her repressed wit was brilliant and very rare for a woman – I can't conceive she could think this of me.'

In the event, Enid scrapped the open letter to Gilliatt as a method of introduction to the autobiography, but from the words, flailed down upon the page, there remained the chaff of bitterness which was sprinkled throughout the later pages of the book.

Once she settled down, she wrote quickly. Establishing and maintaining the correct tone was difficult, and she no longer relied on Cuthbert's sharp pedantry to help discipline her thoughts. Uneasy at permanently living off Enid's charity, he and Johnny decided to buy a small property of their own in Brighton. They still visited North End House, where his growing melancholia, so alien to Enid's nature, became a disturbing influence. The intellectual intimacy evaporated. In the early chapters, Enid's task was lightened by her father's devotion to collecting Bagnoldiana which, of course, influenced the focus of the project. She sorted through all the letters and papers and half-finished manuscripts which she or her parents had so meticulously kept since her childhood, annotating where necessary. She asked old friends to return her letters and mostly they complied. Where gaps remained, her creative memory occasionally came to the rescue. But a decision to say almost nothing about her children, a radical reversal of her approach to fiction, meant that it would, inevitably, never be a complete picture. There was, too, a certain reticence in relation to herself. Although always the central figure in the landscape, Enid was far more revealing of herself in her plays and novels than in her autobiography. This gave the book a certain patchiness, of which Enid was unhappily aware. She had difficulty, too, over the ending because, 'I haven't died! Looking at other people's "Lives" I see that's how they end up, though they hadn't meant to.'

The autobiography was all but finished by January 1969. She had done her best to be honest and thought that her audacious revelations about Frank Harris were perhaps more truthful than wise. She was excited to see what reaction such a bombshell would bring, but told Carol Brandt, who read it in advance, not to breathe a word to anyone. 'It's a pity it should get smeared about beforehand.'

As soon as the manuscript was completed, Enid made up her mind to try and relieve the pains and aches which had persisted throughout the writing of the book. Arthritis in her hip and knee, as well as sciatica, had grown rapidly worse so that she could no longer climb up to her Tower Room, but lay instead on a sofa in the mellow garden-room, surrounded by tables of books and papers and with baskets of work by her side. The only solution, it appeared, was to have her hip joint replaced, at that time a relatively new operation. She wrote to the surgeon, Sir Henry Osmond-Clarke, in the hope that he would operate at the beginning of May. 'It is a three and a half hour operation and of course at seventy-nine I may die,' she told Carol. 'I don't think I shall but I must behave as though I might.'

The problem she wished resolved in case she died was how to ensure the publication of her plays. She decided therefore that no publisher could have her autobiography without agreeing to produce simultaneously a companion volume of four of her plays. 'It is very important to me that the volumes come out bound the same and on the same day. Just as though they were two volumes of my life, (which they are).' Of course Enid knew that this was not an enticing prospect – plays do not generally make money; even less so failed plays – but on this point she was adamant.

The operation was performed at the Fitzroy Nuffield Hospital on 6 May, and Enid remained there for three weeks. She was not a good patient and the pain was more severe than she had anticipated. Morphia was prescribed, as she had requested by letter in advance. 'By giving me plenty of morphia you can't turn me into an addict. I am too much in charge of myself. But like everyone else, I don't much like pain.' She had often been given morphia before, for minor operations as well as childbirth, and enjoyed the sensation. 'All these fancy things now with fancy names never seem to act like a good old third of morphian.' The doctors believed that the operation had gone smoothly. Yet by the time she was declared fit enough to return home for the summer, she was still not feeling well and was still reliant on the morphia. Waves of nausea regularly overcame her and she felt unable to tackle the list of corrections and changes awaiting her on the autobiography. She was soon back in bed with a high fever caused by a secondary bladder infection. 'More pills to go down the throat,' Enid commented wryly. Depressed by her slow recovery, Enid began to fear she might be bed-ridden for the rest of her life.

In addition to her poor physical health, her spirits had been dragged down by a rejection of her autobiography in America. 'A less meandering book without asides and parenthetical remarks and stray thoughts that simply have popped into her head at the moment of writing would make a volume that would be better received critically and commercially,' was the official view of the publishers, Random House. Such a resounding refusal might, a few years previously, have devastated her. But the accumulation of negative reaction to her plays had so knocked her confidence that she was strangely prepared for failure. Fortunately, Edward (Ted) Weeks, senior editor at the Atlantic Monthly Press, soon pronounced it 'honest, sincere and unique; a book of power'. Weeks's enthusiasm for her plays was, however, in doubt and less than a fortnight after her operation, pepped up by some secret Dexedrine she had sneaked into the nursing home, she reprimanded him. 'You know that I wrote the Auto in order, like a spread-eagle, it might carry the plays. I may be misguided but I can but be what I am . . . and what I am believes as fiercely in the future of my plays as Chekhov did . . . if there is any doubt about the plays, you can't have the book.'

After the Random House rejection, Enid lost some faith in Carol Brandt's ability to negotiate on her behalf. To Dwye Evans at Heinemann she wrote, 'She simply scolds me when she writes to me. She always has.' Increasingly, she turned to him for advice. She admitted in a long letter one day, as the nausea lifted briefly:

I have often been rude (and arrogant) to you, and you have always replied with patience. I have forgotten the things I have said (better so but I am *sorry for them*). You have been so kind to me . . . now more than ever when you take on your shoulders so much work and negotiation. . . . I can see by what you say that you understand that I feel (and rightly) humiliated by the lack of chivalry towards literature, the lack of chivalry towards a woman of eighty who has quietly done her best with words all her life.

By the middle of the summer, she felt well enough to deal with some of the problems that had arisen, such as dates not always tallying with the record. More seriously, it was clear that some of her attempts to be honest were potentially libellous. For example, in the first draft, Enid had described Edith Evans as 'arrogant, unapproachable and wrong'. This had to be dropped. She also deleted a reference to her father's pain from piles, well imagining his anger at such public indiscretion.

Heinemann rushed to get *Enid Bagnold's Autobiography* out in time for her eightieth birthday on 27 October 1969. Like a newly discovered relic, Enid found herself fêted by journalists and reviewers. Praise flooded in from friends as well and only one or two took issue with her version of events. Peggy Ashcroft told her it was a 'masterpiece in its truest meaning and you must feel very, very happy in it'. At the same time, she recognized the sadness 'that my monster-master, the theatre, has seemed so cruel to you'. Enid was upset, as of old, that her friend Cyril Connolly had not written about it. 'You seemed, very sweetly, by talking to me about my book, to want to make up to me in that neither you nor Raymond [Mortimer] reviewed it,' she wrote to Cyril. 'Of course I minded, because I have such a venerating opinion of you both and to be in your good graces was worth all the other pleasures I have had.' But Cyril was easily forgiven. And as he and his wife Deirdre lived nearby, she bombarded them with invitations and, almost as often, with 'incredible generosity'. To Cyril, she gave several valuable first editions, 'because you show such pleasure . . . like a pleased child'. When Deirdre was expecting her fourth child at the age of thirty-nine (and after the cross words about the review), Enid paid for a maternity nurse for her for three months.

Enid had been noticeably reserved in her comments on Cecil Beaton. Just before she finished the book, Worsley had effected a reconciliation by persuading Beaton to come over from Brighton, where he was working, to Rottingdean. Enid and Cecil had not spoken for twelve years but Cecil had sent her a note the year before from Australia wishing her success with *Call Me Jacky*, and Worsley well knew Enid still craved Cecil's friendship. 'Dear Cecil – I have missed you like a great chunk of my life,' she told him.

The two proceeded warily with this second attempt at friendship but Enid was soon sending Cecil a warmly inscribed copy of her autobiography and invitations to stay. 'I'll be so sad if I don't see you,' she told him. Cecil wrote to her, after reading the autobiography, that he was 'touched and pleased by the nice things you say about me. I can't quite recognize myself as being the wonderful person you make me out to be, but I not only give you a Dickensian bow for the bouquet, but a kiss on each cheek.' In his diaries, however, published in 1978, he wrote, 'In the afternoon I read Enid Bagnold's excellent autobiography. In the book all her qualities are apparent; also her dislike-ableness; she is *not* a nice person. But her honesty and strength of character are amazing, and I feel sorry that she should have spent so much time writing so few good plays.'

The American edition of the autobiography was not due until August 1970 and, meanwhile, Ted Weeks was beginning to irritate her with his attempts to edit the book. She was 'angry because I have never been "edited" before'. She rigidly refused to Americanize her vocabulary in any way. 'Each country has the charm of its own language and England may have gone a long way under but not that far.' Moreover, she would not entertain any change of title, for which he was strongly pressing. 'Nothing you can suggest connected with peacocks, ravens, clouds, memoirs etc. will move me.' Weeks wanted several passages in the book expanded, and Enid agreed that 'some of your letter I will think about'. But, she told him, she did not really care if she were not published at all in America. 'I am about to be eighty and that is a powerful age because I am indifferent.'

She was not indifferent, however, to the reaction of Irene Selznick, and by April 1970 Irene's silence told her something she had written must have wounded her. 'I think it is the intrusion into your private (so private) life when I describe how Roderick came back to Philadelphia and you cried. I hesitated a long time when I wrote that but in the end I thought it made up the picture of you and gave the "heart" side to the rest of the build-up.' Although insisting that her version of events was true; and although she had already corrected the proofs in galley, Enid told Irene she could, if she wanted, telephone Weeks and ask him to delete whatever had hurt her. Irene did so immediately and the offending passage was cut from the American edition. There had never been any tears at Philadelphia, Irene maintained; only once, earlier, had she cried and that was at Rottingdean when her mother died. Enid had to foot the bill for making changes so late in the day.

Having made her peace with Irene, Enid pondered her next move. 'I have written my autobiography and happily proclaimed myself eighty. And now where, standing on that foolish mountain top, am I to move next?' As she came from a long-lived family, there was every chance she might live until ninety but another ten years would only be bearable if she were occupied with writing. 'I can't write,' she told Irene. 'It's partly the morphia they've given me. ... What a difficult thing it is to explain drugs,' she went on, perhaps imagining Irene's disapproval. 'It's not the pleasure of the pill. It's the depriva-tion when the gaps get too long in between having it. I am very unhappy just now. ... I'm unhappy because I can't write.'

Enid never was 'demorphiaized'. And the pain from her hip never went away. Within a few months of the operation, an abscess developed, and she never fully recovered from that setback. From then on, she had to use a crutch all the time and she grieved over her lack of mobility. She went to see the surgeon again, where she learned that 'ninety-two per cent of patients who have the operation are extremely satisfied'. It was scant comfort to Enid to be part of the other eight per cent.

In spite of the morphia, the pain was often insupportable and getting worse; she was also suffering other ills, such as numbness in both hands, which she believed resulted from constant use of the crutch. Her debilitating health had meant there was little point in maintaining Hyde Park Gate, which was therefore sold. 'It hurts me so,' she told Diana, reflecting on no longer being able to host the Duff Cooper Memorial Prize party there. 'My one social evening (one left of all the many, many over the years) – the one night when I meet the people, old now, whom I so wanted to know when young. And not only that. I am so vain, so proud of all the things I collected, but more too of the house itself. To me there never was such a house green with fig leaves ... and love affairs in the garden – Albrecht Bernstorff, Donald Strathcona and telling Roderick after a suitable bit, and him laughing. He never minded. . . . Come down soon,' she finished, 'and let's cripple around.'

In addition to Hyde Park Gate, she decided after the operation to give up Lucy, the mastiff bitch she described with such frustration at the end of her autobiography. Lucy was intended as a guard dog and a friend, a silent alternative to the woman companion she was encouraged to find. She had never been without a dog before but, although lonely, she preferred her own company to the obstinacy, depression and regular morning messes of her latest animal.

In the early days of her addiction, Enid read every page of de Quincey's *Confessions of an Opium Eater* and discussed the possibility of a cure in great detail with her children. She knew her current condition 'can't be right or sound or healthy. Certainly not happy. Also it makes me useless.' In moments of deepest anguish, she questioned if this state of mind had anything to do with the morphia. Was it possible that she had slowly developed a power of writing that had outstripped her powers of invention? 'In other words, I am sick of my style.' But slowly, she settled into a highly disciplined routine with the morphia, injecting herself (in 1971) with half a grain twice a day, and accepting she would never be able to give it up. The reality of withdrawal pains during a cure terrified her and, quite possibly, the morphia was making her old age tolerable. 'If I take no notice of my inner (and Puritan) feelings, *and if I never increase* (the most important) I don't suppose it much matters ... staying how I am.' She had consulted a doctor, 'a psychoanalyst,

I think. . . . He told me that by keeping me asleep for a fortnight through the means of two drugs . . . he thought he could cure it.' But it was feared she might become addicted to one of those drugs instead. 'Also, at my age, eighty-two, it was dangerous for me to go through the torture (as it would be, they said) of curing the habit.'

From 9 a.m. until about 2 p.m., always her most creative hours, Enid felt more or less her former self and tried, occasionally, to write. She started a sequel to *The Loved and Envied*. 'I did twenty thousand words but then I stopped; and can't go on. It is nauseating. I have had to hide it from my sight. It's not that I think it bad. I just feel I can't end my life on fiction.' Starved of ideas, she resorted to a diary: how an octogenarian coped with the minutiae of daily existence. Called 'Quotidienne', it occupied her on and off for some months as she lay on the sofa staring at the cracks in the ceiling, which was increasingly kept together with sticky tape, at the buckets in the corners to catch the drips that the tape could not hold, or at the faded, time-ravaged but still heavy curtains.

Salvation, however, came indirectly from Margaret Ramsay. She had introduced Enid to the Director of Drama at Yorkshire Television, Peter Willes, with the intention that he should coax a new, short play out of her. Willes had been to Rottingdean to meet her in 1968, but, although Enid liked him, she was unwilling to commit herself while she was in such distress from her hip and with the autobiography unfinished. Willes was enchanted by Enid, 'caught in her powerful web', and agreed to wait. In 1970, once her condition stabilized, he began regularly commuting from Leeds to Rottingdean, staying the night and helping her create a one-hour television play. A completely new plot was, by now, beyond her powers and so they decided to adapt *The Chinese Prime Minister*. It was not an easy task. But he worked devotedly and patiently, convinced that she could still produce good drama.*

There followed almost a year of collaboration during which 'every word in a line is weighed and if there is one too many through an alteration not done by me . . . it will surely stick out like a sore thumb when it comes to be read out or played.' Willes sometimes felt Enid's insistence on 'a hidden rhythm of remark and response' was a ploy to avoid having to change things. 'After all, it was not a verse play,' he pointed out. In spite of this obstinacy, Willes considered that Enid, at eighty-two, was 'still brilliant and original'. Both he and Enid had hoped Peggy Ashcroft might take the leading role. However,

* This meant Margaret Ramsay, whose idea the television play had been, had nothing to do with the subsequent contract as the rights to *The Chinese Prime Minister* belonged to Robert Freedman. Enid thus found herself temporarily back under his wing.

she turned it down and the part of She went to Judy Campbell, under Christopher Morahan's direction. Enid came up to London for rehearsals and was not inhibited from castigating Miss Campbell for pouring the milk into the cup before the tea, 'an old snobbishness about the tea going in first that she couldn't throw off', Willes commented. On another occasion, she brought Diana Cooper to rehearsals; the cast were terrified of the two old ladies' opinions.

The play went out on 2 November 1971. Enid approved and so did most of the reviewers. A few weeks before, when Peter Willes had interviewed her for the *TV Times*, she spoke of having forgotten the books she had written.

They have flown away. Nothing makes one happy that is done and finished. All the same it is a help in age if you have pulled a little success out of life, from which there might be results and revivals – it flares up an old fever. To totter from time to time to some high table has its sad side, but it's better than not tottering there at all.

The publication of the autobiography had brought Enid Bagnold to a new, younger audience, many of whom thought they detected in her a soulmate. But she was exasperated by the fan mail which resulted. 'They had read my book and had enjoyed it, but when they wrote to me they got into the wrong train. I had to answer and I grudged it. . . . And if I don't know or respect them, why do they think their admiration pleases? Isn't it enough that I wrote the book?'

The wider awareness of Enid Bagnold created a suitable climate for revivals of her plays and, in May 1971, *The Chalk Garden* returned to the Theatre Royal, Haymarket. Gladys Cooper, now eighty-two herself, once again triumped as Mrs St Maugham, with Joan Greenwood as Madrigal. Now that Enid was again friends with Beaton, there were no difficulties about using his costumes. Cecil could not resist praising Gladys to Enid, 'though no doubt she is greatly helped by her dresses'.

There was some praise from critics too. J.C.Trewin, a long-standing Bagnold admirer, hailed *The Chalk Garden* as 'one of the century's genuine gifts to posterity'. However, Milton Shulman attacked 'the play's tight-vowelled inhabitants tinkling epigrams over the tea-cups'.

Gladys Cooper was due to go with the play to Canada, but in October she was suddenly taken ill with pneumonia and Cathleen Nesbitt stepped in at the last moment. 'I am terribly disappointed, especially about Toronto,' Gladys told Enid, 'but I am relieved and happy for the company's sake that it is going to be all right. . . . *Our* Mrs St M. . . . has been one of the most satisfying parts I have played (how awful, I may never play her again) and through her, dear Enid, with love I am your buddy, Gladys.' Gladys Cooper died on 17

November. Also in 1971, *The Chinese Prime Minister* was revived in America. Franklyn Lenthall, producer at the small Boothbay Playhouse, Maine, ran the play briefly in August and told Enid: 'Our audiences were almost unanimous in their liking of the play and many thought our production superior to the Broadway one.'

Before the year was out, Enid had been interviewed by John Higgins of *The Times* and made an appearance on a new television chat show in conversation with Esther Rantzen and Harriet Crawley. Enid had not wanted to discuss the programme in advance, which made her appear cantankerous and nervous. She had consulted Diana beforehand about her clothes, but the three-quarter-length gloves which she wore throughout looked, at best, anachronistic. Nerves, however, did not prevent her snapping at Miss Rantzen, 'Evidently, you haven't read all my books, have you?' They covered a wide range of subjects, from Frank Harris to Edith Evans, and many of Enid's remarks appeared superficially to give comfort to feminists. She asserted that 'Marriage distorts a woman's life ... because it reinstates man as leader, woman as led.' Although the woman may be happy (as, mostly, Enid had been) to have her life thus distorted, 'eventually she reinstates herself as a woman. Marriage twists, but not necessarily badly.' But Enid was no feminist. Stridently, she told the young interviewers how important it was to give authority to men. 'If you run down a man's authority, I don't think he has as much left as a woman might have.'

Enid was now sure of nothing except her continued dependence on drugs and her loneliness. Her grandchildren, as they developed into individuals, were a source of great pleasure to her. As she watched them play, the knowledge that they were part of the 'bloodstream thing', that they would perpetuate Bagnold traits such as courage, was both fascinating and comforting. And, after Roderick's death, she grudgingly began to take some small part in the life of the village. She became Patron of the Rottingdean Drama Society in July 1967 and also President of the Rottingdean Preservation Society, always attending the AGM and, occasionally, speaking.

In 1972, however, she embroiled herself in parish politics. Michael Thornton, who had returned to live in Rottingdean and was helping to edit the parish magazine, invited Enid to write a 'Guest of the Month' feature. It was the sort of charitable time-waster that Enid loathed. But as a refusal would have meant loss of face for Thornton, she accepted. In a piece entitled 'Behind the Mute White Front', Enid described the unexciting routine of her old age. Every day she rose at twenty past seven, awoken by the alarm clock.

From a quarter to ten until twenty to one, is 'a lucky dip in the brain, a dip to find what will shake out of the corners? What speck of gold or gilt? Have I talent?' But the highlight of every day was an afternoon visit from Laurian. 'She keeps me on tenterhooks, but she comes. If anyone else calls during her precious hour then I am monstrously odious to them.'

It was not well received. Rottingdean villagers were not interested in such introspective reflections. 'I really don't think Enid need have bothered,' one local lady commented. Enid had long been isolated within the community and she knew it. Although her loneliness had become a subject for local gossip, one parishioner voiced the thoughts of many: 'Well, I'm afraid it serves her right. She never wanted to know any of us or make friends when Roderick was alive and now it's really too late.' Few people in Rottingdean realized or understood her importance as a writer and were in any case unimpressed by the claims of fame, notoriety or rank. Such an attitude was typical of many an English village, but was especially strong in Rottingdean. Even Rudyard Kipling, to an extent, suffered from the same ostracism during his years there.

Some months after Enid's article, Thornton invited Miss Jessie Seymour, who had lived in the village for forty years and worked hard for the Preservation Society, to be 'Guest of the Month'. Within minutes of the magazine being delivered to North End House, Enid was on the telephone to Thornton 'in a white hot fury. In twenty-five years I had never heard her quite as angry as that.' The cause of Enid's indignation was that Miss Seymour's article on 'The Preservation of Rottingdean' carried no reference to Roderick 'after all he had done and spent, running into hundreds of thousands of pounds – to ensure the unspoiled survival of the village.'

Enid also wrote to the vicar, Canon Ivor Walters. 'I am simply flattened with surprise. . . . How could she write that article without a mention of what I can only describe as her backbone?' She enclosed a long letter extolling Roderick's work for the village, which she demanded should be published in the parish magazine immediately. If extra pages were required she offered to pay for them. Walters tried to defuse the controversy. He proposed that Enid's comments should be used as a feature, not a letter, and should appear in the following January's issue to coincide with the fiftieth anniversary of the Joneses' arrival in the village. Enid was temporarily mollified. But then she changed her mind. 'No, Ivor, no. . . . It won't do. While you were here I wanted to please – as every woman wants to please. I'm left now sitting in a mountain of indignation.'

The 'Great Vicar–Me Row' (Enid's description of the episode) was still simmering in September when Enid went away 'driving myself slowly and gently all over France to Laurian's new house'. On her return, Diana Cooper came down to stay. Then, in November, Enid chose new ground on which to pitch battle with the vicar. She objected, belatedly, to his plan to build an extension, consisting of two lavatories and two changing rooms, to the eleventh-century St Margaret's Church, directly facing North End House. He was, she told him, 'distorting and ironing out of balance the primitive façade of an ancient monument. . . . Don't say,' she pre-empted him, '"But you never come to church." It is not that. It is the lack of respect for the past, for antiquity that I mind.' Walters responded by reminding her that the drawings had been on display for ages. 'You really have not a leg to stand on.' The phrase was a gift to Enid. 'Yes, I've got a leg or two to stand on (though one is a bit proppy up on a stick). But both are propped up by disagreement.' Not satisfied with this, Enid also raised the matter in *The Times*' correspondence columns and decided once again to tackle Canon Walters about the proposed feature on Roderick. She asked him to come round so she could vet the article before publication. Obligingly, the vicar called the following evening, but was stunned by Enid's continued belligerence. Towards the end of the acrimonious meeting, he riposted, 'Fifty years you've been here and never given a penny to the church.'

'The only duty I can think of is the pew rent and as I don't go to church and don't use the pew, I didn't think of continuing it,' she replied. 'I would rather (and do) give to charities of my own knowledge – mostly individuals. To say that I ought to give to the church when I suppose I am of no specific religion seems to make me subject (in that case) to the synagogue or the baptist chapel or any other building representing a faith. I am not a mean person and I was . . . well, as I say, taken aback.'

In the January 1974 issue of the Rottingdean Church and Parish News, there appeared an 'overdue acknowledgement of our debt' to Sir Roderick Jones. The piece was signed D.M.I.Walters. Enid wrote to thank him for his compromise, but complained that the final sentence of the article ('And debts must be honoured') was, 'I thought . . . a little snappy.'

TWENTY-TWO

The Last Attachment

BY 1972, Enid was virtually unable to write. 'I am so used to writing that to live without it is lonely and a waste of time. I have plenty of thoughts to put down but I am so sick of myself and my own mind that I don't put them down.'

Georgina Ward never gave up her valiant attempts to lift Enid above her morphia-induced malaise. 'Our link is that she drives me to write and, on my side, I try to watch over her life and, as much as is possible, try to guide her... I am very, very fond of her.' Georgina, who lived intermittently at Dale Cottage, would send Enid lists of subject headings, often Enid's own quotes, insisting that she write a thousand words on each, just for the practice. Enid, fifty-one years older than Georgina, respected the efforts, but could not respond.

'And then I gave her Noel Willman,' Georgina recalled later. 'I waited for about a month, but when he started reorganizing the kitchen, I thought the time had come....' Noel Willman was fifty-three when he met Enid; although trained as an actor, he had worked for many years as a director. 'I was reluctant at first to enter into her world because I am anti-social by nature. But one day I saw a copy of *Call Me Jacky* lying around and said, "This play is absolutely not right, but is so full of interesting things".' Willman's spark of interest immediately reactivated Enid's drive to write, but she had to be sure of him: 'If I did try to get it right, would you help me – Oh, I know you could.'

For the next three years, Willman spent two days each week at Rottingdean. He was both collaborator and potential director. Sometimes there would be terrible rows if Enid was worried over a phrase she could not get right. But the two grew very close, in some ways uncomfortably so. 'Enid was a most fascinating woman, but occasionally I would get tired of the play and feel almost trapped with her. She was very possessive, wanting to control everything around her and to entangle me in her family life.'

But Enid's family life was evaporating at this time. Laurian was living in France on her husband's family estate – a loss which her mother likened to an amputation; Timothy had moved to the west country and Dominick now lived on a boat in France. Richard, too, had bought his own flat in London and had finally fled the nest in the autumn of 1974. Letting Richard go was a sorrowful but courageous decision for Enid. 'Very likely she was sad,' Richard said, 'but she didn't try to make me stay.'

Bereft of her children, Enid became more demanding and dependent on Noel Willman. He in turn recoiled. 'I was sometimes awful to her. I have a cruel streak in me and can make myself mean to people close to me because I simply can't bear enveloping feeling.' Diana dubbed him Enid's 'Last Attachment', but the alliance was less than binding.

Meanwhile, the revised play was slowly emerging as an original entity. The stereotypes of *Call Me Jacky* had been odd, unenticing characters. Enid now rounded them out as well as making their usefulness in the play more apparent. One day she told Noel that she had a new idea, but was frightened to tell him about it. 'I've thought about what Jacky should be. . . . I'd like her to levitate.' Noel's positive response thrilled her and some of her old vitality returned. She read every book she could find on the subject and also asked friends such as Cyril Connolly to supply her with information.

This new, central theme for *Call Me Jacky* galvanized the playwright as much as the play. It gave the work a spring, to make a woman who believed in nothing believe in something, and had a propitiating effect on Enid by tempting her to believe that death, which still terrified her, was *not* the final end. She would regularly tell Noel that, preoccupied by dying, she had been unable to sleep. 'What do you think happens?' she would beseech him. 'It frightens me so. It seems to be the end of me. I'll be no more.' Noel's answer, that she would always live on through her words, sometimes pacified her. Having always scorned religion, she now envied those who were comforted by it, such as her Catholic son-in-law, Pierre. 'I'd like you to hold my hand on my death-bed,' she used to tell him. She was especially tortured by the thought that she might be cremated alive since her drugs tended to induce a death-like state.

The reworked version of the play, now called *A Matter of Gravity*, was a high-style piece of eccentricity with no pretensions towards realism. In it, Mrs Basil voices some of Enid's reflections on senility and death. When Elizabeth, her daughter-in-law, returns from Jamaica, intent once more on taking over the family house, Mrs Basil finally agrees. 'There are things to which I am tied – that need loosening . . . I can do without them. . . . Dispossess me of my house and I can raise the bricks again with my divine eyes! Dispossess me! I'm moving on.'

Mrs Basil then summons an ambulance to take her to a suite at the local asylum and everyone is dumbfounded by what they see as a 'wild goose chase'. 'Is that what you call a search for God?' Mrs Basil asks. She will come back, she declares, 'I'm only going to train myself a little – for eternity …'. Although Mrs Basil, like Enid, found it hard to believe in God, she now admitted the possibility that He might exist. 'Then I must trust Him not to be careless. I am good material!'

After almost three years of revisions, Noel was still not sanguine about the possibility of a production. Then he had to go to America for several weeks and Enid dreaded managing without him. She advertised in the local papers for companions, but was unlucky. Of greater comfort was Noel's promise to show her script around in New York. At the back of her mind throughout the rewriting, she had an image of Katharine Hepburn as the perfect Mrs Basil. Hepburn, then in her mid-sixties and enjoying legendary status as the major American screen actress, had been dangled before her by Irene Selznick for as long as she could remember. But the early plays had not fired her. However, Miss Hepburn had been in England in the spring of 1968 and had visited Enid at Rottingdean. The two women, eighteen years apart yet alike in so many ways, took to each other instantly. 'What a joy finally to meet you,' Hepburn wrote to her. 'You were a sort of fantasy because Irene talks a great, great deal about you. … The reality is much more thrilling.' Enid hoped that, now they had met, this play might evoke a different response.

Noel showed *A Matter of Gravity* to Roger Stevens (producer of *The Chinese Prime Minister* on Broadway) and his partner, Robert Whitehead, who both liked it. They discussed the likelihood of actresses such as Judith Anderson, Celia Johnson and Helen Hayes being interested in the starring role, but each knew that Katharine Hepburn's appearance would be the magic ingredient.

Hepburn loved it. 'It was a delicious play. It had a quality. … I didn't care what it was about.' In spite of this enthusiasm, she was 'vacillating … usual theatre anxiety', for almost a year. But in the spring of 1975, Enid reported proudly to friends: 'The great heroine has arrived – Katharine Hepburn. I've taken a suite for her at the Royal Crescent [hotel].' Once Hepburn was committed, it was a question of pinning Enid down to finish the outstanding rewrites. Whitehead, Hepburn and her secretary, Phyllis Wilbourn, would arrive every day at North End House with picnic baskets full of crisp salads and fruit for lunch to ensure that Enid had no excuse to disappear into the kitchen preparing meals. Hepburn, being in no doubt that she was re-creating Bagnold on stage, thought it important to study the original at first hand. She said later: 'It has been a real treat pretending to be you all these months. Very rewarding.'

In the summer, Noel set about casting and engaged, amongst others,

Christopher Reeve as the grandson. In Noel's absence, Enid suffered the first of several slight strokes. Although she recovered her strength, from then on there were times when she could not work on the play at all and, with the onset of senility, she often lapsed into miserable confusion.

Once rehearsals began, Noel sent Enid regular progress reports. She yearned to see her play performed, especially in America where she always felt she was accorded more respect than in England. However, she was now a registered morphia addict with a dosage of 60 mg five times daily. United States' drugs legislation prohibited her from bringing morphia into the country and would not recognize her own doctor's right to prescribe there. A protracted correspondence with the Home Office followed, during which Enid asked the chief Medical Officer whether he had read *National Velvet* 'when he was a little boy'. Finally it was agreed that she would be permitted to enter the United States with enough morphia and other drugs for the journey and, if accompanied by a fully trained nurse, sufficient reserves in case of delay. To ensure a trouble-free arrival, an American lawyer was sent to Philadelphia airport but, in the event, nothing went wrong.

Noel took her to a rehearsal and she was thrilled by the company's veneration for her. Zoë Whitehead, actress wife of the co-producer, examined Enid's suite at the Barclay Hotel and decided it was not clean enough. So, getting down on all fours, she scrubbed it herself and was thus employed when Enid walked in. Assuming she was the maid, Enid thanked and then dismissed her. But Noel noticed a sharp deterioration in her mental state. When he left her for an hour or so in the hotel she could not remember his name. 'Is it Leon?'* she asked when he returned.' 'It must be a great strain having the author on your hands,' Peggy Ramsay remarked knowingly to Willman.

When Enid, wearing a vivid floral caftan, walked barefoot down the aisle of the Forrest Theater on the first night, she looked distinguished and glamorous. She was never happy with the ending of the play, to the point where it became an obsession with her, and was still proposing changes two years later. But she was enraptured by Hepburn's performance. Irene was right: Hepburn was a natural Bagnold heroine. She was able to convey the stoicism characteristic of all Enid's work because it was part of her own armoury. She had, too, a great respect for age and, therefore, for Enid. 'I think Enid's virtue was her amateurism,' Hepburn said. 'Because of her independence of spirit, her work had an individuality in the way that the work of an untrained painter has. . . . Above all we liked each other.' Talking about why she had

---

* 'Noel' spelt backwards.

been attracted to the play, Hepburn explained how she found some contemporary drama 'degenerate and offensive and ridiculous.... It's a peculiar bunch of writing that's being done today. It doesn't interest me one whit.' *A Matter of Gravity* was a real discovery for her: 'a play about people'.

The Philadelphia notices were mixed; mostly good for Hepburn, but less so for the eighty-six-year-old playwright. William B. Collins in the *Philadelphia Inquirer* was an exception: 'Katharine Hepburn returned to the stage last night with a superbly commanding performance in a new play worthy of nothing less.... *A Matter of Gravity* deals with love and death and the upward mobility of the human spirit in witty and almost dauntingly literate terms.' Enid sent this review to Diana, scrawling across the top: 'Money rolling in and rolling out on "suites", barrack-loads of furniture and carnations. Kate and Last Attachment and sweet nurse my only friends.' The play moved on to Washington, whence Enid flew home.

She went directly to stay with Laurian in France, where suddenly she fell gravely ill and, for a while, was in a coma. 'I can't think for what reason. I'm never ill. I had seven falls almost like cannon-balls but afterwards more like having been kicked by a horse. Then I got pneumonia and all but died. I can only remember a sort of soft floating. There have been four nurses and, as you can imagine, it has eaten up all the money I had been so proudly making.' Enid believed she had suffered a further 'very slight stroke, which I can't bear to speak of because they won't let me drive. It's terrible not to drive. It gives me claustrophobia.'

In December she was considered fit enough to return home by ambulance, but a long period of convalescence followed. For weeks she could barely manage more than a dozen steps from her bed and even five months later Willman reported that she was 'hallucinating. I talk to her on the 'phone. But she doesn't make much sense.'

Enid's one great remaining ambition was to become a Dame of the British Empire. Although she had been made a Fellow of the Royal Society of Literature in 1970, she felt this was inadequate recognition of her services to the Arts. Michael Thornton had taken it upon himself, before Enid's first major illness, to send a long report on her to the Honours Committee. He showed it to Enid for her comments, 'not daring NOT to do so'. 'You've done it wonderfully,' she told him. 'Pointing out those mediocre dame-ships ... is very good.' Laurian, knowing how much a title in her own right would mean to her mother, exhorted Thornton: 'Yes, we must get that honour. I have hammered away at Nora Beloff [the journalist and a personal friend] who promises she is doing ditto to Kenneth Tynan, who she says has the ear of Lady Falkender. But don't let's let up!' On 10 December

1975, Enid was notified by Downing Street that she was being recommended for appointment as a Commander of the Order of the British Empire (CBE). She was extremely disappointed, to the point of regarding it as an insult. 'I am not very pleased,' she informed Thornton by telephone. 'I rang up Diana Cooper and she rang up Mrs Wilson [the Prime Minister's wife, now Lady Wilson] who said it's really like the toss of a coin whether one gets the OBE or CBE. At first I thought I would turn it down but now I've more or less decided to accept it.'

Within a week, Enid came to terms with her award and thanked Thornton for all his efforts. 'I'm too ill to write a proper [*sic*]. I don't know quite why I'm ill, I think it's the play. . . . You've done so much I don't know how to thank you as much.' Her CBE was duly announced in the New Year's Honours List on 1 January 1976 and on 10 February, in a wheel chair, Enid received her award at Buckingham Palace. She was accompanied by Laurian, Timothy and Richard.

One week earlier, *A Matter of Gravity* had opened at New York's Broadhurst Theater. Katharine Hepburn, on stage throughout, was undeniably a crowd-puller, but for all its oddity, the play had by now acquired its own momentum and become a fashionable talking point. None the less, the Broadway critics were scathing. Rex Reed, in the *Daily News*, called it 'a nightmare . . . an idiotic monstrosity'. Clive Barnes wrote: 'The mysteries and pseudo epigrams of Miss Bagnold seem to fade away.' But friends offered encouragement. The writer, Sumner Locke Elliott, praised Enid for having written 'perhaps the last play of ideas, illuminated, beautiful, luminous. A rhythm of ideas, metaphysics and wisdom. A thrilling experience . . . and last night's audience so dominated by young people in their twenties, not just the old Broadway fossils who can afford the hideous prices.'

The play closed on Broadway after ten weeks, but reopened in Denver on 29 September 1976 for a tour of nine cities with Katharine Hepburn still in the lead. Even breaking her ankle in Los Angeles could not persuade the redoubtable actress to leave the play. With a heavy cast on her leg, she took to a wheel chair on stage, thereby adding a new dimension to Mrs Basil. 'You would be amused to see the wheel chair version,' she wrote to Enid. 'What a bore that we're so far away. . . . I think of you so often through the play, dear Enid.'

A Matter or Gravity appealed to middle America. By this time, quite unexpectedly, the money was 'rolling in'. Early on in her relationship with Willman, Enid had suggested giving him ten per cent of the author's royalties. 'You've spent two years working on this play and you've been so wonderful for me,' she told him. Willman refused at first, pointing out that he would be getting director's royalties in any case, but she insisted. 'Finally I asked

Laurian who said, "You must let her because she really enjoys giving."' By September 1977, the gross box-office takings were just over £3½ million. For a time, Enid was netting £1,000 a week. She had never earned at such a high rate before.

Enid was sorry not to be part of the tour: 'A few years ago, how I should have enjoyed going with it, but now I don't care.' She went instead to stay with Laurian, where once again she fell ill. 'But I am a bit in love again (at eighty-seven yesterday)* and that's perhaps a good sign against illness. It's the Last Attachment and I've made him rich (and wanted as a director). But the result is I never see him as they want him in America.'

Once back at Rottingdean, Enid felt old, muddled and a failure as she watched all the money she had made being spent on nurses for her. This time, the film director Bryan Forbes, then working on a film sequel to *National Velvet*, came to her rescue. 'He seems to me a nice man, who could understand that I need work. I think perhaps I'll write and tell him. And it will be all the easier since I don't want or need money,' she confided to Diana. She cabled to him: 'Have ideas National Velvet don't want money. Trust you Enid.'

Forbes went to some trouble to get Enid writing again. He promised he would find time to work with her and exchange ideas. 'You must not despair. You must not lose heart. You must not stop believing in your own genius. . . .' Although Forbes persuaded MGM to pay her £1,000 as the author of the original story, there could be no collaboration on the new screenplay. In July, anticipating many criticisms, he sent her his first draft of *International Velvet*. 'If it doesn't totally distress you, I would obviously love to know what you think.'

Enid was distraught beyond reason as she read Forbes's story. In order to have an American child of British parentage, he had made her an orphan. The girl goes to live with her Aunt Velvet, who now resides in America, after her father, Donald in the original book, is killed. But since Donald was based on Dominick, Enid was convinced that some terrible accident must have befallen her own son. She had just been to stay with Dominick on his schooner off Marseilles, and, in spite of the difficulties in climbing on and off board, loved being with him. Once she was reassured that Dominick continued to flourish, she accepted the rest of the story.

As Christmas loomed, she became intensely aware of her loneliness. She had recently sacked the Micks, her domestic help of thirteen years' standing, but was terrified by the resulting isolation. 'Whatever shall I do? I've become

* Neither eighty-seven, nor yesterday. Enid was eighty-eight on 27 October 1977.

unbrave since I've become old and can't bear living in a house alone.' She began thinking about selling North End House and buying a flat in London, but the house was almost crumbling apart and she knew it would not be easy. 'Only an Arab would buy it. Do you know a nice rich one?' she asked Diana.

Enid wanted to spend Christmas 1977 in France with Laurian's family, but believed that her recurrent illnesses there resulted from the quality of the French morphia. She tried again to negotiate with the Home Office to take her own supplies with her, but was devastated when told this was against the rules. 'Rules that would divide me from the thing I love most, my children. My daughter, oh so unfortunately for me, married a Frenchman . . . my two grandchildren are very dear to me. This Christmas is special,' she begged the medical officer to understand, 'because my youngest son is also coming. . . . Being eighty-eight next week I haven't so long to see him.'

In spite of her unease about French morphine, Enid arrived in France in brighter mood than of late. She was quickly irritated by the typewriter Laurian lent her, complaining that its letters needed picking out and 'I've only got my injection needle to do it.' But she was looking forward to the publication of *A Matter of Gravity* by Heinemann in 1978. 'And then there are bits and hopes and beginnings of a new book. . . .'

John Randle, a publisher who had set up a private printing press in Gloucestershire, had been to visit Enid in the autumn to discuss the possibility of publishing some of her poetry. 'I'm really so happy you like my poems. I've never dared dream of publication before.'

While sifting through her manuscripts, he came upon a big old journal. Across the front was written: 'If I die I want this sent to Miss Schuster.'* Inside was a mixture of handwritten pages and typed letters pasted in. When Randle confronted her with it, she told him it was always referred to as 'The Death Journal' and its contents were love-letters to Frank Harris. 'Take it away and have a jolly good read.' She herself had not read it for years. 'I couldn't be bothered to decipher all that handwriting so I don't know what horrors are coming to me.'

Randle was amazed by the diary and eager to publish it; an idea which thrilled Enid. She thought this might occupy her as 'I've *nothing* to write ahead of me except if the "Death Book" might provide it.' When he sent her an early draft she could not bring herself to read it through. 'All that ancient love for that ancient ruffian . . . it's like looking at one's face in a pond when one is dead. Is it indelicate or indecent? And his horrible face.' Later, when she had digested it all, she worried it was not as good as she had thought it.

* Adela Schuster and her brother Frank were older friends introduced to Enid by Frank Harris.

Enid was pleased to see the selection of her poems in print:* 'They look tremendously well bound and the glitter is fabulous,' she complimented Randle and his wife, Rosalind. The Randles now found themselves at the core of Enid's existence and recipients therefore of her frequent invitations and often nonsensical missives. Sometimes she would write several notes to the same person each day, perhaps forgetting to sign them or putting them in the wrong envelopes. If staying with Laurian, her daughter would collect her letters to send in one envelope, 'otherwise the post never stops'. Often she knew she was not making sense. 'Excuse me if I talk nonsense,' she asked John Randle. 'I often talk myself to sleep.' Her keen mind, sharp for so many years, was finally losing its edge. But there were, in this twilight world, still moments of lucidity, as when she constantly praised Laurian's kindness and goodness towards her: 'Laurian was absolutely sweet to me ... Lorni (my daughter) was very, *very* sweet to me.'

In this state, constant supervision by a nurse was a necessity and, in 1978, Pat Brown arrived. For two years, Nurse Brown ran Enid's life, even deciding when she could or could not have a glass of water. The two women battled daily. Enid's physical strength might have been failing, but her will, including her will to live, remained indomitable. Nor did Diana Cooper forsake her friend. When she visited, Enid would try to look her best, stopping at the mirror on the stairs and, after a long look at herself, pronouncing, 'Enid, you look beautiful today.'

She made one final effort to host a lunch on 25 July 1980, a gloriously sunny Friday. John Randle was coming and also a young photographer, Tara Heinemann. In their honour, Enid, who now weighed just over seven stone, had put on a smart black and white silk dress, curled her white hair and wore make-up and earrings. Then, just before lunch, Diana Cooper arrived with a friend, the writer Hugo Vickers. Pat Brown was not expecting these two and was most put out. But eventually they all sat down to lunch, slightly later than planned. After half an hour or so Enid looked up from her food and said wistfully, 'I am *so* enjoying this party.'

But it was Enid's last. In a few weeks' time, she was to be moved to London. North End House, both in size and dilapidation, had become a ridiculous proposition for one old lady and her nurse. Enid had few friends who could visit her regularly from London and almost none locally, but, although the possibility of her moving had frequently been aired, abandoning 'this drunken palace' was difficult because it meant giving up a part of herself. Timothy recognized that North End House

* *Poems by Enid Bagnold*, Whittington Press, 1978.

was as much a work of art – perhaps more – than anything you've written. Imagine what it must have felt like to be brought up actually within a work of art while it was being made. . . . Like Leonardo's workshop, while he was there, having been one's nursery. And I don't exaggerate, by the comparison with Leonardo because above a certain level . . . the process of creation which I grew up watching – is I think always much the same.

'Precious letter', Enid jotted across it.

Enid insisted, whenever the matter was discussed, that, if she were to move to London, it must be to Hamilton Terrace in St John's Wood. Both her grandfather and father had lived in houses there, and the sense of continuity, if she were to die there, had great appeal for her. In addition, Richard now had a flat at 17A Hamilton Terrace, which Enid coveted, and Diana was but a short walk away in Little Venice. In 1977 Enid had even advertised in *The Times* : 'Hamilton Terrace. Will anybody sell me a basement flat with access to garden (uneven number) ?' When she heard that Dame Anna Neagle, whose husband, the film producer Herbert Wilcox had just died, might be selling her ground-floor apartment in the road, she contacted her immediately. But Dame Anna's flat was not for sale.

By 1980, the move had acquired some urgency because of Enid's costly nursing requirements. Her heavy drugs intake meant that she could never be without at least one fully trained nurse, day and night. As a suitable flat could not be found quickly, it was agreed with Richard that Enid would move to his flat. In February 1980 he bought a new flat, also in Hamilton Terrace, enabling her to have his.

Enid was aware of little that was happening to her now. She moved to London in September, before the packers arrived in early October with instructions that nothing be thrown away ; even scraps of paper, if they bore Enid's words, were to be preserved in tea-chests. On 16 and 17 October Christie's organized a sale of all her possessions at the house. A marquee was erected in the garden, but the grim weather, as well as a bigger sale nearby, depressed prices. Barely a hundred people attended, many of them out of curiosity. Interest centred mainly on the books and paintings that faithfully represented each segment of her life. The Sickert portrait was sold for £750. A Beaton painting fetched the same and a self-portrait by Katharine Hepburn reached £420. The two-day auction realized a total of £72,321.

Once ensconced in the road of her forefathers, Enid did little more than sleep, eat and sit in an armchair waiting for occasional visitors. A new nurse, Mrs Marie Hughes, was in overall charge of a team of nurses. Nurse Hughes dealt gently with Enid. She also transferred to a new doctor, David Davidson, recommended by the Paddington Drug Dependency Clinic. He was shocked to discover his patient required 375 mg of morphia daily in addition to high dosages of other drugs.*

It was the highest dose he had ever been called upon to prescribe. While realizing that to take her off morphia would be 'cruel and pointless', supplying her with the amounts to which she was now accustomed was not easy. The prescriptions were provided by the Drug Dependency Clinic but the drugs were collected from a chemist. Chemists were reluctant to keep such large stocks for fear of burglary. Eventually it was decided to substitute methadone, which could be given orally, for some of the morphia, and Enid appeared unaware of the difference.

She was unaware, too, that her children 'were getting to the financial point when a nursing home was looming', and were examining suitable ones. However, when Dr Davidson advised against further upheaval, the idea was dropped. She was overjoyed when Dominick, 'her Benjamin', visited her for the last time in February 1981. They had not seen each other for over three years. Death, which until a year before had been a daily preoccupation, now hardly entered her thoughts as she began sliding out of the world. 'Mummy is rather less "present" than she was,' Laurian told Thornton. Pierre, whom Enid thought might have comforted her in her dying days, was now too ill himself to be near her. By the end of February Enid was taking no food and barely speaking above a mumble. On 30 March the family was notified that she was unlikely to last the night.

Enid died at 7.45 a.m. on 31 March 1981; the official cause of death was listed as bronchopneumonia. Only the nurse was there. Laurian flew over to be with her mother, but arrived too late. 'I don't think she would have been aware if I had been there. But I wish I had, all the same. . . . She died very peacefully – she who had doubted death. In the end it came stealing in quietly and just snuffed out her candle.'

Dr Davidson was summoned. Timothy had already discussed with him Enid's wish that a vein be slit. The doctor was extremely reluctant to carry out this bizarre procedure, fearing that a deep cut on a drug addict could raise questions from the coroner. But Timothy told him he had solemnly promised his mother that this would be done as a way of ensuring she was actually dead.† Accordingly, having cleared it with the coroner, Dr Davidson made a small nick in her leg. No blood appeared.

The death was announced, amongst other places, on the BBC World

---

* A usual dose of morphia for a cancer patient in some pain might be 50–60 mg daily, and often less for the elderly.

† Cutting the veins of a dead person will not cause bleeding as the blood will have clotted.

Service and by Dan Rather of NBC in the United States. Those who had loved her saw the end not as a sadness but as a release. 'For her sake I'm glad she's out of it,' Georgina Ward told Timothy. 'The morphine hell cheated her of *being* – up to the hilt.'

'I think of her now at last,' Laurian wrote a month later, 'not as the poor prisoner I felt she was over these last years (a state so utterly alien to her) but as the mother I always knew, triumphant, a marvellous companion, and always a support and comforter.'

Enid was cremated at Golders Green and the interment of ashes took place at St Margaret's, Rottingdean, at 2 p.m. on 11 April. It was a 'very joyous' occasion, according to Laurian. 'Sun out just for it and in again, and two ducks waddling across the graveyard.' 'She'd have liked that,' commented the new vicar, the Reverend Noel Staines.

After the service, Laurian, Timothy and Richard wanted to hug their memories for a few moments longer; but with The Elms gone and North End House almost sold, the descendants of Sir Roderick Jones and Enid Bagnold had nowhere to meet but in a tea-shop in the village high street.

Laurian bravely went ahead with arrangements for a memorial service on 2 November, although her husband Pierre was now dying. As Enid had wished, the service was held at St Paul's, Covent Garden. Richard chose the hymns, John Gielgud read the lesson and Nigel Nicolson, son of her old friend Vita Sackville-West, gave the address. He spoke of how she saw herself 'in the image of her own children'; for they, more than anything else, she considered her true memorial.

She had, several years earlier, contemplated donating her papers, including letters from H.G. Wells, Antoine Bibesco, Vita Sackville-West and Virginia Woolf and others, to a university, thereby establishing a Bagnold Collection. But, daunted by the preliminary sorting required for such a quantity, and faced with a 'collective lack of enthusiasm from us children', she had the papers auctioned by Sotheby's in March 1979. They raised over £10,000. She had also toyed with the idea of presenting her Gaudier-Brzeska head to the Tate. She had not done so, she always maintained, because, when she approached Sir John Rothenstein at a party to discuss it, he had cold-shouldered her. "Excuse me", he said with the waspish irritation of an interrupted man, "but I am talking to my director".' So I didn't give it to the Tate.' Thus both tentative steps towards Bagnold posterity had foundered.

Before dementia set in, Enid had formed an image of herself as having 'slowly turned into a snail leaving a shining track. Yes it shines, but I'm sick of the shine.' She was, at the time she wrote this, sick of her style, sicker of her failures and sickest of the praise she received only for the same old things.

Enid Bagnold never doubted that she was born with talent, but her gift for humour, human observation and communication enmeshed itself with an early insecurity. As soon as she could, she moved into rich and aristocratic circles which gave her the feelings of warmth, ease and security she needed in order to explore life. But when she also wrote about these circles, it muddied her talent. Many critics failed to see beyond the dirty water of distinction to the clear understanding of relationships below. By refusing to shun either social delights or the pleasures of sharing her children's lives, she failed to concentrate fully on intellectual pursuits. By refusing, as she did, to put her writing first, to the exclusion of all else, she laid herself open to charges of amateurism, irrespective of how hard she might have worked. Thus was she deprived of the help and support she might have received from fellow writers and intellectuals. Slowly, and with great sadness, she came to realize that her own experience was perhaps not an inexhaustible source from which to create books and plays. Moreover, it was perhaps no longer relevant to the contemporary generation. She remained sure of her talent, but had never found the key.

As she climbed courageously above the professional vicissitudes of her late middle and old age, she believed that her progeny were not only her most enduring memorial – 'the Pharaohs built the Pyramids for the same reason' – but also her most creative work. Her resignation in 1979 as a Fellow of the Royal Society of Literature was symbolic of the disillusionment she felt towards the claims of her profession. Yet she overflowed with love for her children. 'I could never love you less whatever you do,' she told Timothy. She exuded pride in their achievements, especially if these owed anything to her. Timothy inscribed in his first book: 'if ever I become anything near as good a writer as you are, it will be due to all you've taught me and all the help you've given me.' 'Well, that's not quite true,' she responded, 'but it's balm for a mother to hear.' She told Dominick never to feel remorse after her death 'on the lines of "I might have been nicer . . . or I might have seen more of . . . or I might have told her . . .".' He was to remember instead that he 'gratified my deepest sense of motherhood'.

National Velvet and *The Squire, Lottie Dundass* and *The Chalk Garden* had generated the success which Antoine Bibesco had taught her to prize above everything. Ultimately, she found it empty and sought lasting gratification from her children. In return she would have given them everything. 'I've had a good life . . . my greatest luck is to have been born with a happy nature. . . . My own children are less happy than I am. . . . I wish and wish that I had given more of my ability-to-be-happy to them.'

APPENDIX

In Germany Today

Hitler's New Form of Democracy

By Enid Bagnold

During the last fortnight I have driven myself in a Ford car 2,200 miles through Belgium, Germany, Sudetenland, Czechoslovakia, a corner of Austria, back into Germany, through part of France, and so home. Over two-thirds of the journey lay in Germany, starting at Aachen – Cologne, Coblenz, Magdeburg, Berlin, Leipzig (with a divagation of two days into Sudetenland and Czechoslovakia), Passau, Berchtesgaden, Munich, Ravensburg, Ueberlingen, and out of Germany into Strasbourg.

In the big towns I did no more than stop the night at an hotel, eat my breakfast, and be gone. I met no single person of importance, or even of the upper classes. I received no propaganda into my mind because I had not the means to receive it. I cannot read the newspapers and, though I speak a little German for the common uses of the day, when I am replied to in German it immediately gets beyond me.

At petrol-pumps, garages, in little inns, in shops in the morning and the evening I talked as best I could, and often, even in the country, was answered in a limited way in English. I had no particular opportunity of talking to young people, but could observe their ways, health, appearance and manners. Most of the men I talked to in garages and other places were men of Hitler's age, ex-prisoners of war, and ex-soldiers. Women also, peasants, owners of small cafés where I stopped for coffee, I was able to talk to in simple sentences.

Vital Germany

To begin with, I will get right down to the hard knocks I am going to receive by saying that to drive from any of the countries I have named over the frontier into Germany is like driving from the Whitechapel Road into, say, a County Town just before Christmas. Immediately you are in Germany you are aware of a blaze and bustle of activity and gaiety. Children run about, or wobble on their bicycles, shouting to each other. There is vigour and expectancy on the faces, and friendliness, a look as though to-day was an occasion, and not, as in the paintless depressed streets across the neighbouring frontiers, one of an endless sequence of anxious days driving you on into old age.

The impact of this vitality was so violent, so immediate, so on the threshold of entry, that its impression never left me as a source of wonderment and preoccupation. I kept returning to it in my mind. 'This vital life, this health and strength, and look of happiness, there is nothing like it in Europe.' And often I thought of America. America, but without strikes.

From one end of Germany to the other, spending two days among the young troops crowding Karlsbad, in the country villages, or passing literally miles of workmen engaged in road-making, everywhere the manner and manners of the people were alike, the manner of happy people, helpful, open, frank, without depression or suspicion.

After Six Years

During days and days of driving a certain essence of humanity arises from the roadsides and villages to one who passes lightly, impersonally as a bird, unregarded, and inhabited by a stream of commentating, half-conscious thought. Something is drawn up into the mind out of the life of the anonymous working people in fields and towns which becomes knowledge without words.

Once absorbed into the stream of this activity, I began to travel in it and with it in the order of the cities and towns I have named, continually receiving in a manner which is perfectly open to criticism (because very little was done by direct conversation) an infiltration of pictures and impressions which hardened slowly into definite lines of thought.

Six years old, and a giant, Germany stands out of focus among the shaken nations around her – Germany, this mysterious page written on Europe, its inner policy so shunned and unexplored, drifted under my wheels. I felt that even an amateur, an unspecialized citizen of another country, has an equal chance with anyone to attempt an understanding and an exploration for himself.

The *need* to understand is evident to anyone who does not believe in counter-attack.

Gulliver in Europe

As I went deeper into the humming countryside and felt the steady strength of the life, I thought with wonderment and horror of that week in September, and through what blind misunderstandings we might have found ourselves at war with what I saw. On all sides was the hand of Gulliver in Europe – giant roads, giant traffic, giant buildings, and behind them and working in them a steady, disciplined people, adoring its leader.

How could a pinched, suspicious, and quarrelling Europe hope to fight unity and discipline like this? Why should they not rather examine it and find out how it is that in six years a policy has been devised and carried out which has penetrated eighty million people with a new attitude towards life.

Are we, then, to condone the persecutions? We shall have to accept them as we have had to accept Abyssinia. So violent an evolution is like an operation. Cutting is done. For Germany is Luther again, breaking away from the Catholic Church; and when has a wave of puritanism come without persecution? Hitler had decided that the Jews were to be no more than the touch of yeast in the bread. The proportion of yeast in the Continental loaf is too old and too strange a problem for English minds. But with the persecution came also self-severity, severity toward the Aryan, sacrifice, discipline, coupled with the old recurring fight for freedom from dogma. That is the reason for the war with the two churches. *Gott Glaub Ich*, and that alone is the name of the new religion.

A Turning Point

Sir Samuel Hoare said at Clacton that September, 1938, was a clear turning-point in his life. He made then a very brave step forward which may be just ahead of a turning-point in Europe. He defended, not only the policy of friendly relations with this new Germany, but he defended Hitler himself. Hitler the spearhead of Hitler's new democracy. For that I believe is to be the strange future and transformation of democracy in Europe.

Born in wrath, born in despair at the impotent callousness of our old democracies (so unwieldy that from the surface of their faces they were losing mouth to speak, ear to hear, eye to see), has sprung with the flames of a harsh puritanism the unrecognized Phoenix of a new form of democracy, a spear-point democracy tapering through a small group to one man; something tightly controlled yet infinitely flexible to suit the incalculable expansions and re-adjustments of our age.

Sunday Times, 6 November 1938

Works by Enid Bagnold

A Diary Without Dates, Heinemann 1918. Virago, in association with Heinemann, 1978.
The Sailing Ships and other poems, Heinemann 1918.
The Happy Foreigner, Heinemann 1920.
Serena Blandish or The Difficulty of Getting Married, Heinemann 1924, Morrow 1946.
Alice and Thomas and Jane, Heinemann 1930.
Alexander of Asia, Heinemann 1935 (translation of *Alexandre asiatique* by Marthe Bibesco).
National Velvet, Heinemann 1935, Morrow 1935.
The Squire, Heinemann 1938, Morrow 1938.
The Loved and Envied, Doubleday 1950, Heinemann 1951, Chatto and Windus 1970.
Two Plays (*Lottie Dundass* and *Poor Judas*), Heinemann 1951.
Gertie (play performed 1952).
The Girl's Journey (reprint of *The Happy Foreigner* and *The Squire*), Heinemann 1954.
The Chalk Garden, Heinemann 1956.
National Velvet (play), Dramatists' Play Service Inc. 1961.
The Chinese Prime Minister, Random House 1964.
Call Me Jacky included in *Plays of the Year* No. 34, Elek Books 1968.
Enid Bagnold's Autobiography, Heinemann 1969, Atlantic Little Brown 1970.
Four Plays (*The Chalk Garden, The Last Joke, The Chinese Prime Minister, Call Me Jacky*), Heinemann 1970, Atlantic Little Brown 1971.
A Matter of Gravity, Heinemann 1978.
Letters to Frank Harris and others, Whittington Press in association with Heinemann 1980.
Poems, Whittington Press 1978.

Source Notes

Direct quotations and some other passages in the text are identified here by page number and the last few words. Obvious quotations and those whose source is implied in the text are not further explained. The place of publication is London unless otherwise stated. Where a work by Enid Bagnold is quoted, only the title is given.

This book is principally based on the letters, manuscripts, diaries, cuttings and books preserved by Enid throughout her life – The Bagnold Papers. At time of writing these were in the possession of her family. I have also referred to private letters and documents written by Enid Bagnold which are now the property of the recipients or their literary executors, as well as those owned by universities and other libraries. Some correspondence between Enid Bagnold and Antoine, Emmanuel and Marthe Bibesco is owned by Hugo Vickers.

The following abbreviations have been used:

EB	Enid Bagnold
EBA	*Enid Bagnold's Autobiography*, Heinemann 1969
RJ	Sir Roderick Jones
1916 AM	Enid Bagnold's unpublished Autobiographical Memoir, 1916
Berg	The Henry W. and Albert A. Berg Collection of English and American Literature in the New York Public Library
BRBML	The Beinecke Rare Book and Manuscript Library, Yale University, Connecticut
HRC	The Humanities Research Center, University of Texas at Austin
McFL	The McFarlin Library, University of Tulsa, Oklahoma
RA	Roderick Jones Archive, Reuters
UCLA	Department of Special Collections, The University of California in Los Angeles

ONE
Born a Writer

p1 see her again,' Michael Thornton to author, 14 Dec 1984

p2 natural communicator.' Jeanne Heal, *You and Your Handwriting*, Pelham Books 1973

p2 they are old. They can.' *EBA*, p. 254

p2 always of me.' EB to Gerald Weales, 8 Mar 1959

p3 see my own name.' EB to Col. Bagnold, 27 Oct 1934

p3 can't forget it.' *EBA*, p. 41

p3 little ancestor worship.' unpublished notes

p3 arrive at me.' *EBA*, p. 41

p4 bodies of the dead.' Edward Dix to T. Bagnold, 9 Feb 1811

p4 history of injustice'. unpublished papers

p5 his elder brother' unpublished notes

p6 heard yer voice.' family tradition

p8 seen such luxury,' Nellie Ravenhill to EB, undated

p9 go without him.' Ethel Bagnold Diary, 17 Sep 1888

p9 part of the writer.' Col. Bagnold to EB, 25 Aug 1933

p9 its high traditions.' Obituary supplied by Plymouth Library : Source unknown

TWO
I Don't Regret the Little One Being a Girl

p10 temperament and upbringing.' Nellie Ravenhill to EB, undated

p10 pleased with her,' Col. Bagnold to William Alger, 31 Oct 1889

p10 girl a bit.' *ibid.*

p10 little thing every day.' Ethel Bagnold to William Alger, 1 Nov 1889

p11 He was an earl.' *EBA*, p. 7

p11 him in Hell.' *ibid.*

p11 near the top one' *EBA*, p. 6

p11 born a boy.' *EBA*, p. 5

p12 my young ones.' Notes sent by Ethel Bagnold to Mrs William Alger, 2 Feb 1896

p12 why haven't I? *ibid.*

p13 obedient in future.' Lines copied by EB, 17 Aug 1902

p14 She was dead.' *EBA*, p. 13

p14 had Picasso's eyes.' *EBA*, p. 14

p14 growing all round,' EB to Noel Coward, 26 Feb 1965

p14 summit was completely enveloped.' *Memoirs of William Hickey*, Vol. II, Ed. Peter Quennell, Routledge, Kegan Paul, 1975

p15 alive in the memory?' EB to Noel Coward, 26 Feb 1965

p15 books for her,' quoted in *EBA*, p. 18

p16 all that myself,' EB to (Aunt) Edie Daniel, 30 Oct 1901

p16 nails are filthy' *EBA*, p. 21

p16 live without loves,' *ibid*

p16 a little drug-taker ...' Extract from *The Loved and Envied* quoted in *EBA*, p. 22

p17 Nor it did,' *EBA*, p. 20

p17 before I've done,' EB to Harold Alger, 8 Jan 1901

p17 frivolity and selfishness,' William Alger to EB, 10 Oct 1901

p18 accompany it, danger comes.' Harold Alger to EB, 15 Dec 1902

p19 word was law,' Victoire Fairclough quoted in *Aldous Huxley* by Sybille Bedford, Collins and Chatto and Windus 1973

p19 into Married Quarters.' Unpublished notes

p19 before I spoke,' *ibid.*

p19 be my heaven,' Priors Field School Magazine, No 81 1971

p20 a dazzling enlightenment,' 1916 AM

p20 DID occur to me.' EB in Priors Field Jubilee Magazine 1902–1952

p20 sash with hope.' *EBA*, p. 31

p20 never come again.' Priors Field Jubilee Magazine

p21 'O god give me fame.' This phrase, with minor variations, was often quoted by EB

p21 bearable though insipid.' EB to Mrs Bagnold, 13 Sep 1906

p21 name of Switzerland,' EB to Mrs Bagnold, 11 Nov 1906

p21 real and only life,' Diary, 4 Sep 1906

p22 awfully chic.' EB to Mrs Bagnold, 17 Feb 1907

p22 failures are frequent.' *ibid.*

p22 vague on it.' EB to Winifred Bright, 3 Mar 1907

THREE

An Artistic and Bohemian Milieu

p23 rabble don't go' EB to Mrs B, 2 Oct 1909

p25 unless you make it,' 1916 AM

p25 them as they are.' *ibid.*

p25 like a father,' *EBA*, p. 62

p26 and Bohemian milieu ...' EB to Ralph Bagnold, 8 July 1909

p28 as he had seen them.' Haldane Macfall, *The Art Chronicle*, 17 Nov 1911

p28 I could be "taken".' EB to Cathleen Nesbitt, 22 Jan 1972

p28 my father's advice.' EB to Raymond Mortimer, 8 June 1973

p28 only way out.' 1916 AM

p29 with an umbrella.' 1916 AM

p29 unique physic phenomena.' *ibid*

p30 muffled in the glass.' *EBA*, p. 73

p30 of unpolished light.' *ibid.*

p30 shaking with dread.' EB to Raymond Mortimer, 8 May 1973

p30 and then it went.' *ibid.*

p30 it's for nuns.' quoted in *EBA*, p. 75

p30 continue to thirst ...' Walter Sickert to EB, undated

p31 like a man' *EBA*, p. 64

p31 getting your letters,' EB to Mrs Bagnold, 2 Mar 1912

p31 more to me ...' EB to Mrs Bagnold, undated

p31 full of servants.' EB to Mrs Bagnold, 13 Oct 1912

p32 a budding marvel,' EB to Mrs Bagnold, 28 Feb, no year

p32 and be reasonable.' Haldane Macfall, *The Book of Claud Lovat Fraser*, J.M.Dent and Sons 1923

p32 very beautiful girl' *ibid.*

p32 not an artist' quoted in H.S.Ede, *Savage Messiah*, Heinemann 1931

p32 ceaseless quiet noise,' EB in taped interview with Michael Parkin 1971

p32 can use itself.' *ibid*

p32 leaving him behind.' *ibid*

p33 promised to give you.' Henri Gaudier Brzeska to EB, 6 Mar 1912

p33 extraordinary, exactly like.' EB to Mrs Bagnold, ? May 1912

p33 Oh that's nice,' Gaudier to Sophie Brzeska, 30 Nov 1912

p33 urbanely fat.' EB in taped interview with Michael Parkin 1971

p33 being a bore.' Diaries of Harold Nicolson, 29 April 1931, unpublished entry

p33 cast of her head.' Gaudier Brzeska to Sophie Brzeska, 30 Nov 1912

p33 disgusting to look at.' Gaudier Brzeska to Haldane Macfall, 26 Feb 1912, Victoria and Albert Archive

p34 so drawn out.' H.S.Ede letters to author, 27 Oct 1984 and 8 Nov 1984

p34 would not like it.' *ibid*

p34 bag on the wall.' H.S.Ede, *Savage Messiah*, 1931

p35 saying a word.' Gaudier Brzeska to Sophie Brzeska, 3 Dec 1912

p35 was then 10.30.' *ibid*

p35 touch with things.' *ibid*

p35 kind of harbour.' EB to Jacob Epstein, 12 May 1930

FOUR
Sliding into Madness

p36 like garden pests,' Myfanwy Thomas to EB, 9 Jan 1970

p37 by the ocean.' Death Journal, 2 Apr 1918

p37 power of Garrick.' *Sunday Times*, 8 Feb 1959

p37 rings and grey nails.' EB to Mrs Bagnold, 26 Sept 1912

p37 he's rather spotty.' EB to Mrs Bagnold, undated

p37 paper of my own.' EB to Mrs Bagnold, 13 Oct 1912

p37 I've ever seen.' Frank Harris annotation above article in *Hearth* and *Home*, 29 Aug 1912

p38 arrangement of the universe ...' quoted by EB to Mrs Bagnold, 26 Sept 1912

p38 crystal of her own words.' *EBA*, p. 86

p38 not at all important.' EB to Mrs Bagnold, 6 Nov 1912

p38 Into the grass.' Extracted from 'Eve' by Ralph Hodgson 1913, annotated by EB 'written about Enid Bagnold and Frank Harris'.

p39 friend but lazy.' unpublished notes

p39 sliding into madness.' *EBA*, p. 91

p39 room in the Cafe Royal.' *EBA*, p. 92

p39 would be an inelegance.' Phillipa Pullar,*Frank Harris*, Hamish Hamilton 1975

p40 of the session,' *EBA*, p. 92

p40 corporal made sergeant.' *ibid*

p40 little natural affection.' quoted by Philippa Pullar, *Frank Harris*

p40 original in their dispositions.' Hugh Kingsmill, *The Will to Love*, Chapman and Hall 1919

p40 dreamed love to be. *ibid*

p41 fettered by circumstances.' quoted by EB to Antoine Bibesco, undated

p41 gentlewomen, poor things.' *ibid*

p41 maintained and respected.' Col. Bagnold to EB, 5 Apr 1914

p41 dirt in other ways.' *ibid*

p41 down each month.' Cecilia Cussans Conversation with author, 14–15 Apr 1984

p42 the martyred leader.' EB quoted in *Max*, a Biography by Lord David Cecil, Constable 1964

p42 hatch hens' eggs', quoted in *EBA*, p. 95 ('Harris took the postcard from me afterwards.')

p42 out of his difficulties. 'George Bernard Shaw to Max Beerbohm, 12 Feb 1914

p42 portraitist to Modern Society.' Max Beerbohm to Enid Bagnold, undated

p43 faces of other visitors.' David Cecil, *Max*

p43 but doesn't hear. 'Death Journal, 28 Mar 1918

p43 could have, I expect.' Death Journal, undated

five
What a Soldier of Fortune is Every Unmarried Girl

p44 out to be dust,' EB to Mrs Bagnold, undated

p44 forget and come.' EB to Mrs Bagnold, undated

p44 they hate me.' EB to Mrs Bagnold, undated

p44 woman ought to live.' EB to Charles Evans, 'about 1918'

p44 instead of Frank Harris.' *EBA*, p. 100

p45 mad with intest' *EBA*, p. 102

p45 that did instead.' unpublished notes

p45 each other or alone.' *EBA*, p. 106

p46 new electric sea.' unpublished notes

p46 others doing things.' Michael Parkin Interview 1971

p46 rebecome a virgin.' *EBA*, p. 109

p47 and yet wonderful.' unpublished notes

p47 makes a lot of noise.' EB to Mrs Bagnold, undated

p47 soaked in blood.' *EBA*, p. 112

p47 provocative nothing suggestive.' Death Journal, 4 Nov 1914

p48 use the medium.' Death Journal, 4 Apr 1914

p48 a little poet.' Death Journal, undated

p48 first to me,' EB to FH, 14 Dec 1916

p48 life and love together.' EB to Frank Harris, 15 Nov 1915 *p48* relation to each other,' *ibid.*

p48 other's written word,' *ibid.*

p49 intimacy and tenderness.' *ibid.*

p49 purses of the gold coin,' *ibid.*

p49 insist on it firmly.' EB to Frank Harris, 11 Dec 1915

p49 It's all over.' EB to Frank Harris, 18 Oct 1916

p49 for common fare,' quoted by EB to Frank Harris, 26 May 1915

p50 a pity I can't,' EB to Frank Harris, 11 Dec 1915

p50 be more extrovert.' *EBA*, p. 85

p50 were the pioneers,' unpublished notes

p50 awfully "la chose".' quoted by EB in letter to Ralph Bagnold, 1 Oct 1915

p50 that kind of thing.' *ibid*

p51 Antoine marry me.' Death Journal and EB letter to Antoine Bibesco, 14 Aug 1928

p51 may be so again.' Emmanuel Bibesco to EB undated – pinned to Death Journal

p51 like him, dead.' Death Journal, 22 Nov 1915

p51 and the Sorbonne.' EB to George Painter, 31 Jan 1960

p51 Something witty please,' unpublished story

p52 art of (the Bibescos)' *George D. Painter, Marcel Proust*, Chatto and Windus 1959

p52 friends was gossip.' *ibid*

p52 and hardly slept.' Death Journal, 24 Jan 1916

p52 nervous and unhappy.' *ibid*

p52 beautiful for you to see.' Phrase often quoted by EB

p52 out of sight?' 'To Emmanuel Bibesco', by EB, first published in *The Sailing Ships*, Heinemann 1918; reprinted, Poems, Whittington Press 1978

p53 equivalent of Lavinia.' George Painter to author, 15 Oct 1985

p53 from the ruins.' Extract from Walter Marsden, *Lincolnshire*, Batsford 1977

p53 like Ivy Low.' Death Journal, undated

p53 he retires, beckoning.' *ibid*

p53 regrets ... for years.' *ibid*

p54 were going to,' *ibid*

p54 sure of nothing.' *ibid*

p54 education through you.' Mrs Bagnold to Emmanuel Bibesco, 10 Aug 1916

p54 the ground floor.' *EBA*, p. 121

p54 Tell me ...' EB to Frank Harris, 24 Feb 1916

p54 ambience of a Goddess.' Christabel Aberconway to EB, 10 Sept 1952

p55 reasons, my dear.' Death Journal, undated

p55 to be taken.' *ibid*

p55 inside her house,' *EBA*, p. 118

p55 gave me any.' EB to Frank Harris, 14 Dec 1916

p55 have the picture.' EB to Frank Harris, 18 Oct 1916

p55 weren't in America.' EB to Frank Harris, 18 May 1917

SIX
The Letters I Might Have Written You

p56 for the right,' EB to Ronald Clark, ? Aug 1974

p56 and "admired" me.' *EBA*, p. 109

p56 to get hurt,' EB to Irene Cooper Willis, 12 Aug 1915

p57 respond at all.' Vita Sackville-West to EB, undated

p57 woman's job now.' EB to Frank Harris, 18 May 1917

p57 friendships and combinations;' *A Diary Without Dates*

p57 is the last straw;' *A Diary Without Dates*

p57 stick it out,' *A Diary Without Dates*

p57 something for yourself,' *EBA*, p. 128

p58 have left them.' *A Diary Without Dates*

p58 love his Pot?' *EBA*, p. 117

p58 from getting married?' Antoine Bibesco to EB, undated

p58 you one day.' Antoine Bibesco to EB, undated

p58 steady, continuous work.' Antoine Bibesco to EB, undated

p58 moved me least.' *A Diary Without Dates*

p59 reason to be.' EB to Frank Harris, undated

p59 fickle continuously,' Emmanuel Bibesco to Gwynaeth Cooper Willis, undated

p59 is your partner,' Emmanuel Bibesco to EB, undated

p59 memory of you.' Emmanuel Bibesco to Gwynaeth Cooper Willis, undated. This and other undated letters above are in a series to Gwynaeth Cooper Willie and EB from Emmanuel Bibesco. Batch annotated by EB: 'Letters sent back to me by Antoine.'

p59 angry with Virgilia,' *EBA*, p. 125

p60 silence about it,' Antoine Bibesco to EB, undated

p60 back a flower,' Desmond MacCarthy to EB, 20 July 1917

p60 some more "potting",' EB to Desmond MacCarthy, 30 Jan 1918

p60 hang on to you?' Quoted by EB to Leonard Woolf, 8 May 1967. University of Sussex Library, Manuscript Section

p60 review this book!' *Letters of Virginia Woolf* Vol. 2, 1912–22, p. 213 *Berg*

p60 Bagnold paints too.' *ibid*

p60 is before me,' EB to Frank Harris, 12 Mar 1918

p61 a good deal' *ibid*

p62 opulent on it.' EB to Frank Harris, 12 Mar 1918

p62 has been received,' Ettie Desborough to EB, 16 Mar 1918

p62 bar Siegfried Sassooon.' *Lady Cynthia Asquith Diaries 1915–1918*, 28 Mar 1918, Hutchinson 1968

p62 appreciative, stimulating listener.' Lady Cynthia Asquith *op. cit.* 24 May 1918

p62 talked to someone else.' Quoted by EB to Leonard Woolf, 8 May 1967

p62 is so scarce.' Philip Sassoon to EB, 25 Apr no year

p62 I want .. is that.' Death Journal, 10 June 1981

p62 in my silly cap.' EB to Professor Mackenzie, 17 Oct 1971, *BRBML*

p62 life and a flower.' Death Journal, 10 June 1918

p63 no love-responsibility.' *EBA*, p. 132

p63 facts were quite different,' Rebecca West to J. and N. MacKenzie: comments on typescript of their book on H. G. Wells

p63 the all-time low.' *ibid*

p63 and meant nothing.' *ibid*

p63 the easiest of all.' Foreword to *The Sailing Ships*, Heinemann 1918

p63 a clever creature.' H. H. Asquith to unnamed, 29 Oct 1919

p63 bright and eager.' 1916 AM

SEVEN

My Dear Virgilia, You Have Wrinkles Under Your Eyes

p64 chique [sic] to go.' Antoine Bibesco to EB, undated

p64 startling psychological effect.' An impression of Enid Bagnold by Vera Denis-Earle, *Queen* Magazine, 17 Apr 1946

p64 wear her clothes.' *ibid*

p65 anyone would know.' EB to Col. and Mrs Bagnold, 28 Nov 1918

p65 bombs all night.' EB to Mrs Bagnold, 8 Dec 1918

p65 water in turns.' EB to Mrs Bagnold, 12 Jan 1919

p65 give me flowers.' EB to Mrs Bagnold, 18 Jan 1919

p65 as the prettiest.' EB to Mrs Bagnold, 22 Jan 1919

p65 a minute at parties.' EB to Col. Bagnold, 1 Jan 1919

p65 he was married. EB to RJ, 14 Feb 1924

p66 father-in-law, dear Virgilia.' *EBA*, p. 127

p66 awfully suited.' EB to Mrs Bagnold, 15 Feb 1919

p66 so in love.' EB to Desmond MacCarthy, undated

p66 new and wonderful.' *ibid.*

p66 are so ugly.' EB to Col. Bagnold, 27 Mar 1919

p66 off army rations.' EB to RJ, 14 Feb 1924

p66 lighting upon Aldebrande.' *The Happy Foreigner*

p66 the only choice.' EB to Mrs Bagnold, 27 Mar 1919

p67 out in January.' EB to Frank Harris, 5 June 1918

p67 engaged to people.' EB *EBA*, p. 134

p67 go in a second.' EB to Col. Bagnold, 12 Sept no year

p68 It was zoological.' unpublished notes

p69 My father's death.' Sir Roderick Jones, *A Life in Reuters*, Hodder and Stoughton 1951, p. 26

p69 of Government House,' Pamela Glenconner conversation with author, 25 Feb 1984

p70 a going concern.' *A Life in Reuters*, p. 166

p70 to Napier and me.' *A Life in Reuters*, p. 196

p70 Bank of Scotland.' *ibid.*

p70 most relentlessly': Lawrenson and Barber, The Price of Truth, Mainstream 1985

p70 else at Reuters.' RJ to John Buchan, 21 Jan 1918 RA

p71 to escape from.' *A Life in Reuters*, p. 227

p71 five pounds.' *EBA*, p. 136

p71 in a month.' *ibid*
p71 all I have.' *ibid*
p71 twenty years or so.' Col. Bagnold to EB, 28 Apr 1920
p71 under your eyes,' quoted by EB to Marthe Bibesco, 3 Feb 1962 HRC (and elsewhere)
p71 last burning kiss.' RJ to EB, 21 Apr 1920
p71 to get married.' EB to Mrs Bagnold, 18 Apr 1920
p71 from other slums.' EB to Mrs Bagnold, 26 Apr 1920
p71 for your writing.' RJ to EB, 27 Apr 1920
p71 ever went on.' EB to Mrs Bagnold, 29 Apr 1920
p71 my returning immediately.' EB to RJ, 30 Apr 1920
p71 be summoned back.' RJ to EB, 30 Apr 1920
p71 he made me.' *EBA*, p. 137
p71 before the wedding.' *EBA*, p. 136
p71 out in Paris.' *EBA*, p. 137
p72 one up to me ...' EB to Mrs Bagnold, 4 May 1920
p72 get a peerage,' EB to Col. Bagnold, 4 May 1920
p74 serve two masters.' Ethel Smyth to EB, 16 Jan 1920
p74 hard little letter.' Harold Nicolson to Vita Sackville-West, 19 Mar 1920
p74 and vicarious pleasure.' Walter Sickert to EB, undated
p74 part of an institution.' *A Diary Without Dates*
p74 four observant friends.' *A Diary Without Dates*
p74 perilous with you.' EB to RJ, undated (first page lost)
p74 happiness will last.' Col. Bagnold to EB, 28 Apr 1920
p74 do very well.' Mrs Bagnold to EB, 4 Apr 1920
p75 do anything first,' EB to RJ, undated, written Sunday before wedding
p75 The Times altogether,' EB to Mrs Bagnold, 9 July 1920
p75 function like yours.' Harold Alger to Mrs Bagnold, 13 July 1920
p76 do about it?' RJ to Mrs Bagnold, undated (July 1920)
p76 war-ravaged areas.' Rebecca West, *New Statesman*, 10 July 1920
p76 sap of life.' Katherine Mansfield, *Athenaeum*, 16 July 1920
p76 easily the nicest.' EB to Mrs Bagnold, 20 July 1920

EIGHT
We'll be Such a Success at a Marriage

p77 who made them.' EB to Mrs Bagnold, 4 Aug 1920
p77 occasionally something else.' EB to Mrs Bagnold, 10 Aug 1920
p77 a pulling horse.' RJ to Mrs Bagnold, 29 July 1920
p77 hurried, busy exercise.' EB to Mrs Bagnold, 29 July 1920
p78 used to it.' EB to Mrs Faulkner, 23 Aug 1920
p78 are down here.' Mrs Bagnold to EB, 3 Oct 1920
p78 round the towns.' EB to Mrs Bagnold, 14 Aug 1920
p79 your literary reputation.' Century Editor to EB, 18 Oct 1920
p79 I think, obvious.' Col. Bagnold to EB, ? July 1920

p79 domestic I am.' EB to Antoine Bibesco, 9 Dec 1920

p79 as Lady Smith,' *ibid*

p79 Jones and blushed.' *ibid*

p79 up half Revillon.' *ibid*

p80 then they giggle.' *ibid*

p80 blood and a bone . .' 'Enid Bagnold "The Chalk Garden",' first published in
British *Vogue*, May 1956

p81 popularity and acclaim.' EB to Ralph Bagnold, 14 Oct 1921

p81 not fail you.' Quoted by EB to RJ, 17 Oct 1921

p81 been a baby.' *ibid*

p81 more with wonder.' RJ to EB, 17 Oct 1921

p82 you into eternity.' RJ to EB, 19 Oct 1921

p82 success at a marriage.' EB to RJ, 17 Oct 1921

p82 slept with me?' *EBA*, p. 138

p82 I'm so ashamed.' EB to RJ, 14 Dec 1921

p82 this filthy simile.' EB to Cynthia Asquith, 29 Oct 1936

p83 could be terrible.' James Lees-Milne, *Another Self*, Hamish Hamilton 1970

p83 anchor of my existence.' RJ to EB, undated

p84 Ford towards Chelsea.' Harold Waller to EB, 12 Dec 1923

p84 answers by typewriter.' Quoted by EB to RJ, 21 Dec 1923, RA

p84 appreciative back again.' *ibid*

p85 chic of my squalor.' EB to RJ, 11 Jan 1924, RA

p85 out of the blue.' EB to RJ, 1 Feb 1924, RA

p85 not even immaculately.' *ibid*

p85 not like it.' EB to RJ, 1 Apr 1924, RA

p85 Have Desmond down.' RJ to EB, undated

p86 merchandise in the Bible.' EB to RJ, 24 Mar 1924, RA

p86 what operatic tinsel.' *ibid*

p86 or Barbusse's le Feu.' H. G. Wells, The Dream 1924

p86 of married life.' EB to RJ, 23 Mar 1924, RA

p87 son of a negress.' *Serena Blandish*

p87 stream began to flow.' unpublished notes

p87 rather like Antoine.' EB to RJ, undated (1924), RA

p87 a fresh dilemma.' *ibid*

p87 finger in every pie.' *Serena Blandish*

p87 handle my character,' *ibid*

p87 upon genuine duchesses.' *ibid*

p87 the end of (the book).' EB to Antoine Bibesco, undated

p87 marry her himself.' *Serena Blandish*

p88 as her husband.' Col. Bagnold to RJ, 16 May 1924

p88 of society life.' Mrs Bagnold to EB, 15 May 1924

p88 and Roderick's too.' *ibid*

p89 on your condition.' Mrs Bagnold to EB, 18 May 1924

p89 under a pseudonym.' Charles Evans to EB, 21 May 1924

p89 marvellous as Martin.' Rebecca West to EB, undated

p90 same nine months,' EB in Baby Book

p90 Lady Buckingham together.' EB to RJ, ? Jan 1925

NINE
The Beauty of a Young Man

p91 of one individual.' Official Reuter/Press Association statement, 3 Dec 1925, quoted by Roderick Jones, *A Life in Reuters*, p. 340

p91 of one individual.' Official Reuter/Press Association statement, 3 Dec 1925, quoted by Roderick Jones, *A Life in Reuters*, p. 340

p91 cold, English soil.' EB to RJ, 9 Apr 1926

p91 consultation and argument.' *A life in Reuters*, p. 355

p91 as a husband.' EB to RJ, undated 1924

p92 ideas for children.' EB to Desmond MacCarthy, 4 Mar 1926

p92 but she could do?' (and above Danesforth sketch), unpublished papers

p93 front of us.' EB to RJ, 21 May 1925

p93 away in Dorset.' EB to RJ, 26 July 1926

p93 reading your note ...' Harold Waller to EB, 14 Aug 1928

p93 leave out wilfully.' *ibid.*

p93 await her summons.' Harold Waller to EB, 17 Aug 1928

p94 I was sick.' EB to RJ, 11 Aug 1926

p94 idea at all.' *ibid.*

p94 flip of the mind.' EB to RJ, 6 Sept 1926

p94 in my hands.' EB to RJ, ? June 1926

p94 such a task.' EB to Cynthia Asquith, 12 July 1926

p95 wretched jewellery behind?' EB to Moira Tillie, 27 Oct 1928

p95 cheapness and heavenliness.' *ibid*

p95 still within me.' Geneva Journal, undated

p96 you are thin.' EB to Antoine Bibesco, 31 Aug 1927

p96 him in a play.' EB to Moira Tillie, 12 Oct 1927

p96 just as good.' EB to Antoine Bibesco, 31 Aug 1927

p96 write about him.' *ibid*

p96 of the mind, none.' EB to Moira Tillie, 12 Oct 1927

p98 has done before,' EB to Antoine Bibesco, 14 Aug 1928

p98 specialist in bathing)' *ibid*

p98 dressing for dinner.' *ibid*

p98 association with Krishna,' Mary Lutyens, Edwin Lutyens, John Murray 1980

p99 marriage was unique.' Mary Lutyens to EB, 22 Apr 1974

p99 to believe it.' Geneva Journal, updated

p99 in your house,' Mary Lutyens to EB, 11 Nov (1969?)

p99 to mount me.' *ibid*

p99 love with you ...' *ibid*

p100 in my house.' unpublished notes, Geneva Journal

p100 for such situations.' *ibid*

p100 moment for love.' *ibid*

p100 through the night.' *ibid*

p100 *ce fut merveilleux*' Randall Neale to EB, 19 July 1928

p101 all around me.' EB to Randall Neale, 20 July 1928

p101 Lady Jones' visit,' Reuter Memorandum, 17 July 1928

p101 being paid for.' EB to RJ, 16 July, no year

p101 servant, Roderick Jones.' RJ to EB, 24 July 1928

p101 you at all,' Randall Neale to EB, 18 Aug and 25 July 1928

p102 he worshipped you.' Mary Lutyens to EB, 11 Nov (1969?)

p102 stick to it.' Antoine Bibesco to EB, 27 Sept 1928

p102 to dance with.' EB to RJ, ? Aug 1928, Geneva Journal

p102 things on it.' *ibid*

p102 of bad instinct.' EB to RJ, ? Nov 1928

p103 being a mother.' quoted by EB to RJ, ? June 1926, RA

p103 not fed properly.' *ibid*

p103 thrust at visitors.' Nigel Nicolson conversation with author, 27 Jan 1984

p103 pleasure to her.' Timothy Jones to author, 17 Mar 1986

p103 spartan nursery. Mary Lutyens conversation with author, 30 Nov 1983

p103 unsatisfied desires.' EB to Miss A. Schuster, 21 Jan 1927

p103 for long enough.' *ibid*

p104 its legs about.' *ibid*

p104 a domestic philanthropist.' EB to Harold Waller, 28 Feb 1928

p104 easier to draw' words printed on cover

p104 Waller ... inspired me.' EB to Harold Waller, 14 Apr 1934

p104 moment of my own.' EB to Babies Club Committee, 18 July 1929

p104 facts of life.' S. N. Behrman, *Tribulations and Laughter*, Hamish Hamilton 1972

p104 the wrong sort,' EB quoted in *Evening News*, 27 Feb 1929

p105 a poor weakling.' *ibid*

p105 if we did that.' Ruth Gordon interviewed by Garson Kanin about Enid Bagnold for author, 31 Oct 1984

p105 lifelong enmities.' S. N. Behrman *op. cit.*

p105 plural, dear boy?' Ruth Gordon interview, 31 Oct 1984

p106 see it again.' Quoted by Ruth Gordon, 31 Oct 1984

p106 have finished it.' Harold Freedman to EB, 25 Jan 1929

p106 cut about it.' EB to Harold Freedman, 9 Feb 1929

p106 out in the pram.' EB to RJ, undated

p106 understand some day.' Mary Lutyens conversation with author, 30 Nov 1983

TEN
I Feel a Dictatorship Longing Coming Over Me

p107 does it once.' EB to Janet Burroway, 27 Sept 1972

p107 openings and stratagems,' RJ to EB, undated 1961

p107 and more houses.' *Alice and Thomas and Jane*, Heinemann 1930

p107 children sat still.' *ibid*

p108 Downs are Roman.' *ibid*

p108 over the sky.' *ibid*

p109 extremely rare quality?' Naomi Mitchison, *Time and Tide*, 18 Oct 1930

p109 way things happen.' Desmond MacCarthy, *Life and Letters*, 1930

p109 like the wind.' EB to (Aunt) Edie Daniel, 28 July 1931

p109 went for her.' ibid.

p109 to do anything?' EB to unnamed, 28 July 1931

p109 a doctor ordered me.' EB to Marthe Bibesco, 21 Oct 1931, HRC

p109 danger of rape.' *ibid*

p110 governed by sex.' EB unpublished story: 'Kiki Travels with a Donkey'

p110 described it well.' Timothy Jones to EB, 13 Sept 1965

p110 want to write' EB to Col. Bagnold, 13 Nov 1931

p110 you never know) Enid.' EB to RJ, undated (Nov 1931) RA

p111 when I do.' EB to Col. Bagnold, 13 Nov 1931

p111 one was seventeen.' 'Kiki' *op. cit.*

p111 who really know.' *ibid*

p111 of the windy stars.' poem by Vita Sackville-West, *Collected Poems*, Vol. 1, Hogarth Press 1933

p111 I'm so proud,' EB to Vita Sackville-West, 7 Nov 1931

p112 above his ear.' *EBA*, p. 180

p112 inherit the earth,' Handbook for German Rhodes Scholars at Oxford by Albrecht Bernstorff

p113 removed from the room.' Peter Ustinov conversation with author, 20 Apr 1984

p113 offended the German Government.' Peter Ustinov, *Dear Me*, Heinemann 1977, and interview with author, 20 Apr 1984

p114 will bring peace.' EB to J.I. Garvin, undated HRC

p114 of our willpower.' Albrecht Bernstorff to EB, undated (12.15 p.m.)

p114 influence on me.' EB to Albrecht Bernstorff, undated

p114 filled with impressions,' EB to Col. Lawson, 28 Apr 1933

p114 divine of him,' *ibid*

p114 my dear dear.' EB to RJ, 24 May 1933, RA

p115 unraped Saturday evening'. EB to RJ, May 1933 ('no idea of the date'), RA

p115 in your wife.' *ibid*

p115 Liberals, like Violet [Bonham Carter].' EB to RJ, Friday ... 1933, RA

p115 did with Mary.' EB to RJ, Sat morning 1933, RA

p115 sore all day.' RJ to EB, 22 May 1933

p115 against the outer world.' *The Times*, 2 June 1933

p116 heels in love,' Albrecht Bernstorff to EB, 9 July 1933

p116 and the parting kiss!' Albrecht Bernstorff to EB, 21 Apr, no year

p116 and will be,' Albrecht Bernstorff to EB, undated

p116 queerly clever.' EB in Baby Book

p116 I can't think.' EB report on Nurse Brighty, 31 Dec 1933

p116 be Richard's salvation.' *ibid*

p117 *was* the German."' undated, unpublished notes

p117 desire – snobbery – kindness.' *ibid*

p117 it will come.' EB to RJ, 15 June 1933, RA

p117 lonely beyond words.' EB to RJ, dated by him 10/11 July 1933, RA

p118 go to bed.' EB to RJ, 31 July 1933, RA

p118 a Mary over again.' EB to RJ, undated 1933, RA

p118 like him very much.' Harold Waller to EB, 3 Dec 1932

p118 can do to me.' 14 Apr 1934, EB to Harold Waller, 14 Apr 14

p118 straight – bless you!' *ibid*

p118 night with ichthyol' EB to RJ, dated by him 17 Oct 1933, RA

p118 by your concern,' EB to RJ, 2 Nov 1933, RA

p118 and have children.' EB to RJ, 12 Oct 1933, RA

p119 muddle of both.' EB to RJ, 9 Oct 1933, RA

p119 veiled on society.' EB to RJ, 2 Nov 1933, RA

p119 back of my mind,' EB to Vernon Bartlett, 6 Nov 1933

p119 hunting for God.' *ibid*

p119 be the thing . . .' EB to RJ, 24 Apr 1934, RA

p119 riling for Wells,' *ibid*

p119 at the circus.' EB to Professor Ryle, 30 Nov 1935

p119 Begum of Bhopal.' Harold Nicolson to Vita Sackville-West, 7 Nov 1933, published in Harold Nicolson's *Diaries and Letters*, Vol. 1, 1930–39, Collins 1966

p119 of your face.' Albrecht Bernstorff to EB, undated

p119 in a fuller sense.' Albrecht Bernstorff to EB, undated

p120 not inelegant parcel.' The Last Will and Testament of Enid Algerine Jones, 2 Feb 1934

p120 on her letters.' Minutes of Boasting Party, 8 Mar 1934

p120 dull old dog.' Donald Strathcona to EB, 11 July 19?

p120 was a party' *EBA*, p. 189

p120 doubtful rainbow colours.' *EBA*, p. 145

ELEVEN

The Absolute First-Hand Vision of Things

p121 Recording Angel': *EBA*, p. 107

p121 hands in pockets': EB to Mrs Susan Faulkner, 19 Dec 1930

p122 on a cement floor.' *EBA*, p. 147

p122 On to our stage.' *ibid*

p122 horses are concerned.' Sue Boothby conversation with author, 22 May 1984

p122 than a mother.' *EBA*, p. 148

p123 girlhood for me.' EB to Marthe Bibesco, 11 Feb 1938, HRC

p123 in her bath.' Mrs Ralph BAgnold conversation with author, 25 Jan 1985

p123 the strongest exception.' Quoted by Mrs William Vestey, conversation with author, 24 Sept 1984

p123 shall be sorry.' EB to Bett Asquith, 17 Nov 1930

p123 without the interest.' *EBA*, p. 148

p123 as a collaboration.' EB to Bett Asquith, 2 Sept 1934

p124 win the Grand National.' Timothy Jones conversation with author, 12 Sept 1983

p124 capital out of it.' South African radio broadcast, 13 Feb 1947

p124 to her next adventures.' *National Velvet*

p124 mouthful of metal.' *ibid*

p125 standard of the family.' *ibid*

p126 intensely for ourselves.' South African radio broadcast, 13 Feb 1947

p126 contracts with Heinemann.' EB in Baby Book.

p126 without a struggle.' EB to H.B.Carter, 28 Feb 1935

p126 agent I know.' *ibid*
p127 bit of writing.' *EBA*, p. 171
p127 the most fastidious.' Raymond Mortimer, *New Statesman and Nation*, 6 Apr 1935
p127 vision of things.' Hugh Walpole, *Book Society News*, Apr 1935
p127 village gossip.' EB interview with magazine, unidentified
p127 dig in the field.' EB to Col. Bagnold, 30 Sept 1935
p128 meat from them.' Mrs Winnie Maxwell conversation with author, 25 Sept 1984
p128 arrangements at home.' Lord Monk Bretton conversation with author, 4 Dec 1984
p128 mid-day train today.' EB to RJ, ? 1935, RA
p128 I feel protected.' EB to RJ, 23 Oct 1935, RA
p128 a new face.' EB to RJ, ? Oct 1935, RA
p129 in saying tedious.' EB to RJ, 11.20 p.m., ? Oct 1935, RA
p129 in your bedroom.' *ibid*
p129 loving you are.' *ibid*
p129 because I'm jealous.' EB to RJ, ? May 1936, RA
p129 life without you.' RJ to EB, 21 June 1933
p129 I love you.' EB to RJ, undated 10.35 p.m., RA
p129 with exquisite mitigations.' EB to RJ, 31 Dec 1935, RA
p129 in a teashop.' Unpublished play notes
p129 in my daily life.' *ibid*
p129 lovely English landscape.' Albrecht Bernstorff to EB, 3 June 193?
p130 head-writers also did.' Albrecht Bernstorff to EB, 6 May 193?
p130 upset Herr von Ribbentrop.' Sir Roderick Jones, *A Life in Reuters*, Hodder and Stoughton 1951, p. 396
p130 was highly embarrassed.' Lord Freyberg letters to author, 6 and 14 Jan 1985
p131 and my position.' unsigned, undated typed submission
p131 stand in his way.' J. Bryan and C. J. Murphy, *The Windsor Story*, Granada 1979

TWELVE

Birth with its Horrors and its Beauties

p132 house this is.' EB to Laurian and Timothy Jones, 6 Oct 1937
p132 sense of sex.' EB to Marthe Bibesco, 15 Feb 1937, HRC
p132 approaching the gates.' *ibid*
p132 am having four,' EB to Marthe Bibesco, undated, HRC
p133 way of parties.' EB to Marthe Bibesco, 22 June 1937, HRC
p133 overpowering strength.' EB, undated synopsis to Carl Brandt
p133 nearer than that.' *ibid*
p133 herself as ruler.' *ibid*
p133 old and free.' *The Squire*
p133 honest, female males.' *ibid*
p133 a third sex.' *ibid*
p133 not a lesbian.' EB to Diana Cooper, 3 Dec 1965
p134 hum of death,' The Squire

p134 chestnut Romney loveliness,' *EBA*, p. 120

p134 love-woman in The Squire.' EB to Cynthia Asquith, 8 Nov 1943

p134 is my youth.' EB to Cynthia Asquith, 8 Nov 1943

p134 such childish things.' EB undated synopsis for Carl Brandt

p134 had the key.' *The Squire*

p135 am his gardener,' *ibid*

p135 more healthy race,' Laurian Jones to Ethel Raynham Smith, undated

p135 never have been.' Ethel Raynham Smith to EB, 24 Feb 1943

p135 entered my house.' EB speech on Ethel Raynham Smith's retirement, 1949

p135 won't bankrupt us,' Thayer Hobson to EB, 1 Dec 1937

p136 saintliness of motherhood.' EB to Thayer Hobson, 8 Mar 1938

p136 in great detail.' EB to Thayer Hobson, 3 Jan 1938

p136 get it right,' EB notes for a foreword to later edition of *The Squire*, 5 Jan 1953

p136 exist that pain!' *The Squire*

p137 the ordinary sense.' EB to Thayer Hobson, 3 Jan 1938

p137 sort of thing,' Thayer Hobson to EB, 17 May 1938

p137 road in life.' EB to Ethel Raynham Smith, undated

p137 daring of Birth.' Advance publicity by *Ladies' Home Journal*

p137 their gymnastic paces.' *Time and Tide*, 22 Oct 1938

p137 any other art.' *Spectator*, 28 Oct 1938

p137 spoken or written.' Antoine Bibesco to EB, undated

p137 used nursery napkins.' H. G. Wells to EB, 21 Oct 1938

p138 in its cradle.' Vita Sackville-West to EB, 26 Oct 1938

p138 you've brought forth.' Harold Waller to EB, 10 Oct 1938

p138 men never taste.' Logan Pearsall Smith to EB, 4 Aug 1942

p138 one unlucky child?' unpublished notes

p138 have missed a birth!' unpublished notes

p138 fear of death,' EB to Antoine Bibesco, 20 Mar 1938

p138 and ride together.' EB to Col. Bagnold, 20 Oct 1938

p139 that are good.' EB to Laurian Jones, 17 Nov 1938

p139 to receive it,' 'In Germany Today', *Sunday Times*, 6 Nov 1938 (see appendix for full article)

p139 the upper classes.' *ibid*

p139 for English minds.' *ibid*

p139 moveless and dumb.' EB to Miss Bentley, 26 June 1961

p139 passion for truth.' Edmund Blunden, *The Fortnightly*, June 1939

p140 the concentration camp,' Dame Ethel Smyth, *Sunday Times*, 13 Nov 1938

p140 Bagnold is both.' Commander R. Fletcher, *Time and Tide*, 17 Dec 1938

p140 head of the firm.' *ibid*

p140 to my husband.' EB, *Time and Tide*, 31 Dec 1938

p140 this great Agency,' *ibid*

p140 particular mistrusted her. Olivier Bell to author, 26 July 1984

p141 The Emperor's New Clothes.' Maurice Baring to EB 15 May 1939

p141 shipped off alone.' Violet Bonham Carter to EB, 10 Nov 1938

p141 be treated seriously.' *ibid*

p141 understand one's position.' Albrecht Bernstorff to EB, undated Monday morning *p141* than we have.' EB to Albrecht Bernstorff, undated

p141 if you can.' *ibid*

p142 not the courage.' RJ to Laurian Jones, 18 Oct 1938

p142 over the world.' RJ to Ribbentrop, 9 June 1938, RA

p142 'appropriate' he said. Ribbentrop to RJ, 29 June 1938, RA

p142 any other 'ism.' RJ, *A Life in Reuters*, p. 398

p142 sickness and tedium.' EB to Laurian Jones, 8 Nov 1938

p142 thing in life.' EB to Laurian Jones, 3 Nov 1938

p142 anti-climax here.' *ibid*

p143 with their aims.' EB to PEN Club, 24 Feb 1939

THIRTEEN

It's a Privilege To Live in These Times

p144 stopped their milk,' Laurian d'Harcourt to author, 4 Sept 1985

p145 wished her dead!' EB in Baby Book

p146 in my intelligence.' EB to Miss Bentley, 26 June 1961

p146 to the coast.' EB to Editor of *The Times*, 23 June 1940

p146 points of view.' EB to Edward Weeks, 16 May 1969, HRC

p147 from the start,' EB undated annotation on letter from Ethel Raynham Smith to EB

p147 of cramped virginity.' Harold Waller to EB, 23 Apr 1940

p147 will hurt you.' Ethel Raynham Smith to EB, 23 Apr 1940

p147 for each other.' Laurian Jones to Ethel Raynsham Smith, undated

p147 cold of riding.' EB to Ralph Bagnold, 23 Nov 1940

p147 much as that,' Virginia Woolf to EB, 28 Oct 1928

p147 "secondrate" women friends,' *The Diary of Virginia Woolf*, Vol. 3, 1925–1930, Friday, 21 Feb 1930, edited by Anne Olivier Bell, The Hogarth Press 1980

p147 never yet worn' *EBA*, p. 183

p148 off were unimportant.' Trekkie Parsons conversation with author, 19 Sept 1985

p148 the "smart set".' *ibid*

p148 and leave you.' *Virginia Woolf to Vita Sackville-West, 26 Dec 1940, Berg*

p148 always has been.' Vita Sackville-West to Virginia Woolf, 2 Jan 1941, Berg

p148 full of regret.' EB to Cynthia Asquith, 4 Apr 1941

p149 their war work.' 'On Being Sent a Joint of Beef at Christmas', *Harper's* Magazine, New York, Aug 1952

p149 remains of mine.' 'Robinson Crusoe', or, The Farmer from Scratch, BBC Radio Talk Series, 1 Feb 1942

p149 hence butter-making.' Timothy Jones to author, 17 Mar 1986

p149 bit of muslin.' Talk No. 2 in 'Robinson Crusoe' series

p149 a good poem.' *ibid*

p150 our obstreperous merchandise.' Diana Cooper, *Trumpet from the Steep*, Rupert Hart Davis 1960

p150 as an ornament.' EB prose synopsis of play, undated

p151 acting experience needed.' C.B. Cochran to EB, 12 Sept 1941

p151 I could have.' EB to Cynthia Asquith, 7 Sept 1944

p151 for the stage.' Desmond MacCarthy, *New Statesman and Nation*, 31 July 1943

p151 the family fortunes.' Vita Sackville-West to Virgina Woolf, 27 Feb 1941, Berg

p152 live without you.' EB to RJ, dated in red by RJ, 19 Dec 1940 RA

p152 loyalty to you.' RJ to EB, 26 Nov 1940

p153 and his country,' George C. Scott, *Reporter Anonymous* ch. 13 'A Mysterious Resignation', Hutchinson 1968

p153 the whole thing.' EB to RJ, 2 Feb 1941

p153 task is heartbreaking.' RJ to Alexander McLean Ewing, 12 Oct 1941, RA

p153 liable to tax.' Arthur Balfour to RJ, ? Mar 1942, RA

p154 some special event.' Dominick Jones to author, 20 Jan 1986

p154 held-back valedictory' EB to Mr Barrington Ward, 29 Oct 1941

p154 future of Reuters.' *ibid*

p154 former important job.' *Chips: The Diaries of Sir Henry Channon*, 10 Oct 1942, Weidenfeld and Nicolson 1967

p154 a Roman matron,' EB to Cecil Beaton, 4 Mar 1942

p154 of loving gratitude.' EB to Cecil Beaton, 15 May 1943

p155 first nights Ha ...!' EB to Cecil Beaton, 8 Mar 1943

p155 ... frantic temper.' unpublished notes

p155 on the stage.' Cecil Beaton to EB, undated

p155 for our living.' EB to Edith Evans, 23 Nov 1942, quoted by Bryan Forbes, *Ned's Girl*, Elm Tree Books 1977

p156 in the village.' EB to Cynthia Asquith, 19 Apr 1945

p156 and resolutely unsurprised.' *The Times*, 20 Dec 1943

p156 rabid sister-in-law,' Albrecht Bernstorff to EB, undated

p156 would-be escapees.' Albrecht Bernstorff, undated letters to EB, Peter Ustinov conversation with author, 20 Apr 1984; *see also* Graham Greene, *A Sort of Life*, p. 136

p156 must be dead.' EB to Mary Lutyens, 14 Nov 1944

p156 a great comfort.' EB to Diana Cooper, 1 Sep 1944

p156 of the Time.' Claud Cockburn, *Bestseller: The Books that Everyone Read 1900–1939*, Sidgwick and Jackson 1972

p157 pounds every year.' Vita Sackville-West to EB, 14 Feb 1939

p157 from non-residents.' Percy Popkin to EB, 13 Aug 1940

p158 as you'll find.' Bosley Crowther, *New York Times*, 15 Dec 1944

p158 how to jump.' Elizabeth Taylor conversation with author, 23 May 1984

p158 a different medium.' South African radio broadcast, 13 Feb 1947

p158 on a stocking ...' *ibid.*

p159 sticking to films' quoted by Dominick Jones conversation with author, 16 Apl 1984

p159 poor huge neck.' EB to Diana Cooper, 25 Aug 1945

FOURTEEN

The Pessimism of Age

p160 in a nunnery.' EB to Antoine Bibesco, 11 Dec 1945

p160 shell under her.' *ibid*

p160 I hope, dramatic.' *ibid*
p160 he has to do.' *Poor Judas*, Act III
p160 dumbdounded.' EB to Joan Ling, 27 Aug 1945
p160 really read it.' EB to Joan Ling, 15 Feb 1946
p160 confidence-making name.' EB to Diana Cooper, 25 Aug 1945
p161 the managements' heads.' Joan Ling to EB, 8 May 1946
p161 to play Walker.' Michael Redgrave to EB, 14 Feb 1946
p161 to Tyrone Guthrie.' Robert Morley to EB, undated
p161 publish your books.' Hamish Hamilton to EB, 17 Jan 1946
p161 reputation nor money.' Harold Macmillan to EB, 6 June 1946
p161 could not write.' EB to Harold Macmillan, 21 June 1946
p162 a second chance.' Philip Ziegler, *Diana Cooper*, Hamish Hamilton 1981
p162 a sign of before,' EB to Diana Cooper, 23 Nov 1946
p162 all of us,' EB to Diana Cooper, 23 Nov 1946
p162 try so hard.' EB to RJ, 17 Nov 1946
p162 it's steepest face,' EB Obituary of Binkie Beaumont, *The Times*, 29 Mar 1973
p163 to climb out.' EB to Joan Ling, 28 Nov 1946
p163 what I do.' EB to Carl Brandt, 23 Nov 1946
p163 in her cap.' Carl Brandt to EB, 3 Dec 1946
p163 of the Brandts,' EB to Dominick Jones, ? Mar 1947
p163 still do it.' *ibid*
p163 dispenser of life.' *The Loved and Envied*
p163 first of all,' EB to Diana Cooper, 13 May 1948
p164 to embarrass you,' EB to Diana Cooper, 16 July 1946
p164 a proper bonfire.' EB to Diana Cooper, 16 July 1946
p164 at this age.' EB quoted in newspaper reports
p164 the whole thing.' EB to Diana Cooper, 31 Aug 1948
p164 Queen Bee-ish ... private club.' EB to Cecil Beaton, 11 Sept 1948
p165 age and hayfever,' EB to Antoine, 11 May 1948
p165 not worn out.' *ibid*
p165 evening to come.' *Good Living*, Contact Books, No. 13, Dec 1948
p165 had in England,' Nancy Mitford to Lady Redesdale, 27 Sept 1950
p165 for self-indulgence.' *Good Living*, op. cit.
p165 pangs and nerves.' Interview with Mrs William Vestey, 24 Sept 1984
p165 like a cornucopia.' Vita Sackville-West to EB, 19 June 1948
p166 in his talk,' *EBA*, p. 286
p166 at the moment.' Thayer Hobson to EB,, 17 Oct 1947
p166 cost them money.' Carol Brandt to EB, 19 Jan 1967
p166 of everyone else.' Lee Barker to EB, 12 Dec 1955
p167 over three years,' EB to Doubleday, 3 Oct 1950
p167 I don't want.' EB to Lee Barker, 3 Oct 1950
p167 presented like that.' *ibid*
p167 to other people.' *ibid*
p168 edge of the world.' *The Loved and Envied*
p168 that I want.' *ibid*
p168 if one resists!' *ibid*
p168 her aching love.' *ibid*

p168 fulfil her task.' *ibid*
p169 than I have,' *ibid*
p169 fine as a baby's.' *ibid*
p169 of the seducer.' *ibid*
p169 be your widow.' *ibid*
p169 really noticed it.' *ibid*
p169 and what-nots.' EB to Maurice Bonham Carter, 9 Sept 1949
p169 highest order,' *ibid*
p169 chose being rude.' *ibid*
p170 utterly fascinating.' Fanny Butcher, *Chicago Sunday Tribune*, 14 Jan 1951
p170 curiosity or enthusiasm.' Diana Cooper to EB, 26 Jan 1951
p170 would be grateful.' Duff Cooper to EB, 21 Jan 1951
p170 'Maclean your teeth.' Desmond MacCarthy to EB, 6 Jan 1951
p170 snobbery and sentimentality.' *The Times*, 26 Jan 1951
p170 end of love.' EB in World Books Broadsheet, April 1953
p170 and blood individuals.' Lewis Gannet, *New York Herald Tribune*, 1 Jan 1951
p171 little Velvet Brown.' *Time* Magazine, 30 Dec 1950
p171 to some people.' Stephen Bone, BBC Radio, The Critics, 1951
p171 to be obstinate,' *The Loved and Envied*
p171 to be republished.' EB to Dale? 11 Feb 1962
p171 good many returns.' Lee Barker to EB, 12 Dec 1955

FIFTEEN

The Murmur of Delight So Madly Wanted

p172 the word "Jew",' EB to Thayer Hobson, 4 Mar 1946
p173 world for me.' *Gertie*
p173 quick about it.' *ibid*
p173 into the world.' *ibid*
p173 to warm inwards.' *ibid*
p173 and from Sarah.' EB to Carol Brandt, 28 Feb 1951
p174 voice of England.' Herman Shumlin, *Boston Suunday Post*, 13 Jan 1952
p174 asked over there,' quoted by Laurian Jones to EB, 16 Jan 1952
p174 alive in New York,' EB, *The Flop, Atlantic Monthly*, Oct 1952
p174 things on him,' EB to RJ, 5 Dec 1951
p174 and frozen food.' EB to RJ, 11 Dec 1951
p174 they the Egyptologists.' EB to RJ, 18 Dec 1951
p174 a Jewish highbrow.' EB to RJ, 17 Dec 1951
p174 can he be?' EB to RJ, 18 Dec 1951
p174 very warm-hearted.' *ibid*
p175 and less highbrow.' EB to RJ, 25 Dec 1951
p175 quality was gleaming.' *Atlantic Monthly, op. cit.*
p175 happy-making – at last.' EB in *Dramatists' Guild Quarterly*, Spring 1966
p175 hit the world.' EB to Harold Freedman, 17 Feb 1951
p175 lack of eyes.' EB to RJ, 25 Dec 1951
p175 Irish live in.' EB to RJ, 11 Jan 1952

p175 in the gutter.' EB to RJ, 9 Jan 1952

p175 American she meets.' Cecil Beaton to Lady Juliet Duff, 7 Feb 1952

p175 would be all right.' EB to RJ, 3 January 1952

p175 plea for (Shumlin).' *ibid*

p176 in every way.' EB to Diana Cooper, 8 June 1944

p176 sleeping pills.' Carol Brandt to RJ, 16 Jan 1952

p176 all adore her.' *ibid*

p176 theatrical vigour.' *New York Herald Tribune*, 31 Jan 1952

p176 as you know.' EB to RJ, 4 Feb 1952

p176 brings a stick.' EB to Priscilla Hodgson, 4 Sept 1951

p176 to her again.' Priscilla Hodgson conversation with author, 8 June 1984

p176 refused him anything.' *EBA*, p. 203

p177 if discovered, disastrous.' EB to Antoine Bibesco, 29 July 1948

p177 be kept hidden.' EB obituary of Antoine Bibesco, *The Times*, 11 Sept 1951

p177 what you wrote.' Desmond MacCarthy to EB, 25 Sept 1951

p177 dilapidated condition.' Desmond MacCarthy to EB, 18 Mar 1952

p177 that house long.' Private information

p177 that by now.' RJ to EB, 18 Dec 1951

p177 our own beds.' Herman Shumlin to EB, 28 Feb 1952

p178 isn't a virgin.' Quoted by Laurian Jones to EB, 2 July 1949

p178 brought only disapproval.' Laurian d'Harcourt to EB, 1 Sept 1977

p178 as "the enemy".' EB to Pierre d'Harcourt, 13 Mar 1952

p178 right arm away.' EB to Rowland Winn, 5 Mar 1952

p178 dazzling marriage.' EB to RJ, 31 Dec 1951

p178 wants me to do.' Mrs Ralph Bagnold conversation with author 25 Jan 1985

p178 not marry Rowland.' Laurian Jones to EB, 14 Apr

SIXTEEN

High, High Drama Every Time

p179 . . . not that.' EB to J.B.Priestly, 14 May 1952

p179 on until November.' EB to Harold Freedman, undated

p180 see its bowsprit.' unpublished notes

p180 be remotely sympathetic.' EB to Mr Musgrave, 18 Aug 1952, Pattee Library, Penn State University, Pennsylvania

p180 deal with it.' unpublished notes

p180 evaded God.' *ibid*

p180 confusing and muddling.' Binkie Beaumont to EB, 13 Oct 1953

p180 state of madness.' *ibid*

p180 cross-sections of life.' *ibid*

p181 successful theatrical venture.' Harold Freedman to EB, 31 Oct 1953

p181 can by writing.' *ibid*

p181 something will emerge.' Harold Freedman to EB, 19 Feb 1954

p181 influence over Binkie.' Harold Freeman to EB, 18 mar 1954

p181 poetry and beauty.' Irene Selznick to Harold Freedman, 16 Mar 1954 *p181* eggshell with care.' EB to Irene Selznick, 4 Apr 1954

p182 she craved celebrity.' Irene M. Selznick, *A Private View*, Knopf/Weidenfeld and Nicolson 1983

p182 are bed-covers.' Irene Selznick conversation with author, 13 and 21 Apr 1984

p182 mother's success.' *A Private View, op. cit.*

p182 the same one.' *EBA*, p. 223

p182 so did she.' *A Private View, op. cit.*

p183 I couldn't do.' *EBA*, p. 224

p183 a certain effort.' EB to RJ, 9 Oct 1954

p183 told Churchill so.' *ibid*

p183 rebuked by Rottingdean.' EB to RJ, 13 Oct 1954

p183 at the Pierre.' RJ to EB, 16 Oct 1954

p184 of small patches.' EB to Irene Selznick, 22 Oct 1954

p184 than the play.' Laurian Jones to EB, 30 June 1954

p184 everlasting girl inside.' EB to Cecil Beaton, 25 Nov 1954

p184 took every morning.' *A Private View, op. cit.*

p184 proudly I think.' EB to RJ, 15 Oct 1954

p184 rebounds against him.' Cecil Beaton to EB, undated

p184 and the interior.' Cecil Beaton to EB, undated (Dec 1953)

p185 it gets done.' EB to Cecil Beaton, 26 Dec 1953

p185 knows her journey.' Doubleday publicity handout

p185 of life itself.' Arthur Calder-Marshall foreword to *The Girl's Journey*, 1954

p185 set-up and binding.' EB to Dwye Evans, 20 June 1953

p186 But she's bloody.' EB to Harold Freedman, 29 Mar 1955

p186 know with Irene.' *ibid*

p186 both in New York.' EB to unnamed, June 1955

p186 you were killing her.' EB to Harold Freedman, 27 June 1955

p186 mind or not.' *ibid*

p186 play with Kate.' *A Private View, op. cit.*

p186 long and beautiful friendship.' Irene Selznick to EB, 29 Mar 1955

p186 kind of money.' Siobhan McKenna conversation with author, 21 Aug 1985

p187 all the time.' EB to RJ, 11 Aug 1955

p187 It's just everything.' *ibid*

p187 father on it.' EB to RJ, 16 Aug 1955

p187 through in a letter.' *ibid*

p187 on my play.' *EBA*, p. 229

p188 well I don't.' quoted by EB to RJ, Sept 1955

p188 almost restoration woman.' EB to RJ, undated (Sept 1955)

p188 urge as well,' *A Private View, op. cit.*

p188 we are getting on.' EB to RJ, 19 Sept 1955

p188 that won't do.' EB to RJ, 19 Sept 1955

p188 like a child.' EB to RJ, 27 Aug 1955

p188 hard work skirting.' EB to RJ, 9 Sept 1955

p188 baskets, catalogues, everything.' EB to RJ, 19 Sept 1955

p188 gigantic skin eruption.' *ibid*

p189 and destroys him.' *ibid*

p189 a wrong cue.' EB to RJ, 26 Sept 1955

p189 Wonderful gangster Americanisms,' EB to RJ, 9 Sept 1955

p189 tears and hysteria.' EB to RJ, 17 Sept 1955

p189 bid on stage.' Siobhan McKenna conversation with author

p189 of eighty thousand.' EB to RJ, 22 Sept 1955

p189 rehearsing Hamlet.' Siobhan McKenna conversation with author

p189 late and not good.' *ibid*

p190 make her redo scenes.' Albert Marre conversation with author, 20 Apr 1984

p190 let us perform.' Siobhan McKenna conversation with author

p190 driving me mad.' *ibid*

p190 appealed to my vanity.' Irene Selznick conversation with author, 13 and 17 Apr 1984

p190 down stage at all.' Albert Marre conversation with author

p190 that's chalk.' Siobhan McKenna conversation with author

p190 waste of time.' Irene Selzick conversation with author

p190 entitled to this.' *ibid*

p191 great love for him.' Carol Brandt conversation with author

p191 used to be rich.' 'EB and "The Chalk Garden"', first published in British *Vogue*, May 1956

p191 to the ceiling.' *EBA*, p. 234

p191 couldn't leave him.' Irene Selznick conversation with author

p191 for a long time.' Brooks Atkinson, *New York Times*, 13 Nov 1955

p191 escape from humiliation.' *New York Times*, 1 Jan 1956

SEVENTEEN

Glued to History's Wall

p192 old age perfect,' EB to Peggy Ashcroft, 9 Dec 1955

p192 completely intimidated.' Irene Selznick to Binkie Beaumont, 3 Nov 1955

p192 own, as Director.' EB to Cecil Beaton, 23 May 1956

p192 New York production.' John Gielgud to author, 19 June 1984

p192 whenever she entered.' *ibid*

p192 so much stink.' Cecil Beaton to EB, 16 Jan 1956

p193 case for compensation.' Cecil Beaton to EB, 16 Jan 1956

p193 of Cecil's letter.' Irene Selznick to EB, 18 Feb 1956

p193 that you agreed.' EB to Cecil Beaton, 10 Feb 1956

p193 not fighting enough,' EB to Diana Cooper, 23 May 1956

p193 use him in London.' *ibid*

p193 be at odds,' Diana Cooper to EB, undated

p193 of the nearest.' EB to Cecil Beaton, 23 May 1956

p193 one-sided wounding letter.' EB to Cecil Beaton, 31 May 1956

p193 such deep distress,' Cecil Beaton to EB, 30 May 1956

p193 bolt of sorrow,' EB to Cecil Beaton, 31 May 1956

p193 is beneath contempt,' EB to Diana Cooper, 23 May 1956

p194 a garden city.' *ibid*

p194 to the stage.' John Gielgud to author, 19 June and 3 Feb 1984

p194 for the part. EB to Irene Selznick, 17 Jan 1956

p194 from going in.' John Gielgud to author, 3 Feb 1984

p194 mouth on paper.' EB to John Gielgud, 3 Mar 1956

p194 very strong dramatically.' EB to John Gielgud, 3 Mar 1956

p194 a thwarted actress.' John Gielgud to author, 3 Feb 1984

p194 like a battleship.' John Gielgud to author, 15 Feb 1984

p194 with every play,' Harold Freedman to EB, 2 Mar 1956

p194 you arrange that.' EB to Harold Freedman, 6 Mar 1956

p195 it's not to be!' *ibid*

p195 into old age!' EB to Harold Freedman, 11 Mar 1956

p195 That was in America.' *ibid*

p195 round the bend.' Irene Selznick conversation with author, 13 and 17 Apr 1984

p195 off her triumph.' *ibid*

p195 leave of the past.' Kenneth Tynan, *Observer*, 15 Apr 1956

p196 Edith's been.' John Perry conversation with author, 19 June 1984 and others

p196 Instead of love.' EB acceptance speech for American Academy of Arts and Letters Silver Medal Award, 16 May 1956

p196 look of wonder,' Timothy Jones to author, 19 Dec 1984

p196 be suddenly enriched!' *The Last Joke*, Act 1

p197 prize on myself.' EB to Maxwell Anderson, 24 June 1956

p197 like a ditch.' *ibid*

p197 heavy and unreal.' EB to Harold Freedman, 21 Feb 1961

p197 and the play.' EB to Harold Freedman, 23 Apr 1956

p197 am and have.' *ibid*

p197 must be placated,' EB to Dwye Evans, 30 May 1956

p197 on the play,' EB quoted in Windsor Repertory Theatre magazine, June 1958

p197 and her granddaughter.' *ibid*

p198 have drawn upon.' Cynthia S. Matlack, Associate Professor of English, University of Pittsburg Quarterly Journal of Speech, 1973

p198 things. It's true.' unpublished notes

p198 opposition or doubt.' EB to Gerald Weales, 8 Mar 1959

p198 not conductive to structure.' *A Private View, op. cit.*

p198 their native air.' EB to Director of Ostrave State Theatre, undated

p199 the most anachronistic.' John Russell Taylor, *Anger and After*, Methuen 1962

p199 in Hyde Park,' quoted by Peggy Ashcroft conversation with author, 26 June 1984

p199 a lucky accident.' Professor Gerald Weales, *Tulane Drama Review*, Vol. 111, 11 Dec 1958

p199 the astonishment of living.' *ibid*

p199 I have done.' EB to Gerald Weales, 8 Mar 1959

EIGHTEEN
They Are Furious with Me for Being Old

p200 you've had, you've had.' *The Loved and Envied*
p200 Not to look disagreeable .. EB to Sir Archibald McIndoe, 5 Aug 1956
p200 instead of his wife.' Sir Archibald McIndoe to EB, 17 Sept 1956
p201 harm was done.' *EBA*, p. 238
p201 to better myself.' EB to Maxwell Anderson, 4 July 1956
p201 is film-worthy,' EB to Carl Brandt, 31 Jan 1954
p201 do with it.' *ibid*
p201 incomprehensible.' quoted by Timothy Jones to EB, 22 July 1956
p201 like a unicorn.' EB to Maxwell Anderson, 24 June 1956
p201 internationally famous,' EB to James Laver, 8 July 1956
p201 hold them tranfixed.' EB to Maxwell Anderson, 4 July 1956
p202 about your work,' *ibid*
p202 knee-deep for that.' *ibid*
p202 in the unravelling?' EB to Harold Freedman, 2 Nov 1957
p202 an unusual one.' Timothy Jones to EB, 22 July 1956
p202 write without her.' EB to Harold Freedman, 29 Nov 1957
p202 enough of it.' Ruth Gordon to author, 31 Oct 1984
p203 have big busts.' *Elsa Lanchester Herself*, Michael Joseph 1983
p203 fetch ice cubes.' *EBA*, p. 239
p203 his every word.' *Elsa Lanchester Herself, op. cit*
p203 a high level.' *EBA*, p. 240
p203 a hibernated moth.' *EBA*, p. 239
p203 more sinister aspect.' Carol Brandt conversation with author, 18 Apr 1984
p203 feel a draught,' *EBA*, p. 240
p204 question of breeding.' Timothy Jones conversation with author, 25 Mar 1984
p204 Enid of re-marriage.' Private information
p204 so theatrically helpful.' EB to Cynthia Asquith, undated
p204 against my palm.' Michael Thornton to author, 14 Dec 1984
p204 what they mean.' EB to Harold Freedman, 9 Nov 1957
p204 to direct it,' EB to Cynthia Asquith, undated
p204 not much glue.' *ibid*
p205 to think so.' EB to Charles Laughton, 2 Dec 1958, UCLA
p205 drab and depressed.' EB to Charles Laughton, 11 Dec 1958, UCLA
p205 discoveries with you.' EB to Charles Laughton, 14 Mar 1959, UCLA
p205 talking with anyone.' undated
p205 wants but admiration.' EB to Charles Laughton, 30 Jan 1959, UCLA
p205 most dazzling party.' EB to Charles Laughton, 11 Dec 1948, UCLA
p205 such a degree.' EB to Robert Freedman, 26 Feb 1967
p206 the low ceiling.' *EBA*, p. 240
p206 all I stood for.' EB to John Oborne, 21 May 1968
p206 of his Lear.' John Osborne to author, 12 Nov 1984
p206 feel to wild.' EB to Harold Freedman, 25 Nov 1959
p206 horse runs out.' EB to Irene Selznick, 22 Nov 1959

p206 a decision quickly.' Harold Freedman to EB, 22 Dec 1959

p206 buy the turkey.' EB to Harold Freedman, 28 Dec 1959

p206 behave himself properly ?' EB to Harold Freedman, undated

p206 will be broken.' *ibid*

p206 it's so terrible.' EB to Harold Freedman, 25 Nov 1959

p207 in his hand.' EB to Harold Freedman, 2 Jan 1960

p207 can't manage them.' EB to Irene Selznick, 30 Jan 1960

p207 keep me away.' Ralph Richardson quoted in *Daily Express*, 5 Oct 1960

p207 inventing titles. Cheek!' EB to Irene Selznick, 4 Feb 1960

p207 (without any bodies).' EB to Harold Freedman, 8 Feb 1960

p207 was really worse.' Harold Freedman to EB, 5 Feb 1960

p207 an actor's one.' *ibid*

p207 and so gay.' EB to Irene Selznick, 4 Feb 1960

p208 own Mrs Webster.' quoted by EB to Glen Byam Shaw, 2 Feb 1960

p208 whoever he is.' Robert Flemyng conversation with author, 3 Apr 1984

p208 all Glen's planning.' *EBA*, p. 244

p208 because of him.' *ibid*

p208 in the Middle Ages.' *EBA*, p. 245

p208 sober and soft.' EB to Harold Freedman, 24 July 1960

p208 say certain things.' *ibid*

p208 To be a cloud.' EB to Harold Freedman, 18 July 1960

p209 theatre in London.' Harold Freedman to EB, 9 Nov 1960

p209 word of it.' John Gielgud to EB 3 Nov 1969

p208 To change them,' EB to Harold Freedman, 24 July 1960

p209 Stratford like this.' EB to Irene Selznick, 13 Sept 1960

p209 into the play.' EB to Harold Freedman, 18 July 1960

p209 of my work.' *ibid*

p209 care for you!' *ibid*

p210 mean it really.' *ibid*

p210 utterly unforgiveable.' *ibid*

p210 truly I'm not.' *ibid*

p210 you once more.' EB to Irene Selznick, 30 Jan 1960

p210 don't kill me.' EB to Irene Selznick, 24 Mar 1960

p210 well as brains ?' EB to Harold Freedman, 11 Apr 1960

p210 of your value . . .' Harold Freedman to EB, 4 Apr 1960

p210 in the sulks ?' EB to Harold Freedman, 15 Sept 1960

p210 again, I expect.' *ibid*

p210 her own play.' Irene Selznick conversation with author, 13 and 17 Apr 1984

p211 unpalatable power women!' EB to Binkie Beaumont, 14 Aug 1960

p211 a "furious row".' John Gielgud to EB, 3 Nov 1969

p211 it wouldn't do.' *ibid*

p211 of impending disaster.' John Gielgud to author, 3 Feb 1984

p211 shoulders for failure.' EB to Irene Selznick, 13 Sept 1960

p211 disaster . . . the deluge..' EB to William Kimber, 7 Oct 1960

p211 a negro being lynched.' EB to Jack Minster, 19 Oct 1960

p211 in her head!' *ibid*

p211 Bagnoldish but meaningless.' EB to George Painter, 19 Oct 1960

p211 play was about.' Harold Freedman to EB, 5 Oct 1960
p212 your silence, please.' Milton Shulman, *Evening Standard*, 29 Sept 1960
p212 the teeth aching?' Bernard Levin, *Daily Express*, 29 Sept 1960
p212 a dilapidated ruin.' Kenneth Tynan, *Observer*, 2 Oct 1960
p212 fashionably baffling,' T.C.Worsley, 29 Sept 1960
p212 totally blurred.' *ibid*
p212 the British stage.' *Glasgow Herald*, 1 Oct 1960
p212 scope of criticism.' Noel Coward to EB, undated
p212 such a life.' EB to Irene Selznick, 29 Feb 1960
p212 old Greece talking!' *The Last Joke*, Act III
p213 work of art.' EB to Irene Selznick, 29 Feb 1960
p213 its own ashes,' EB to Irene Selznick, 10 Oct 1960
p213 haemorrage is complete.' EB to Irene Selznick, 21 Nov 1960
p213 really, really am,' EB to Irene Selznick, 15 Nov 1960
p213 children bigger allowances ...' EB to Harold Freedman, 9 Oct 1960
p213 bit of time.' EB to Binkie Beaumont, 27 June 1960
p214 sheer confidence.' EB to John Gielgud, undated
p214 each my living.' EB to Harold Freedman, 15 Nov 1960
p214 hurt by failure,' EB to William Kimber, 7 Oct 1960
p214 from the brothers.' EB to George Painter, 19 Oct 1960
p214 have written that.' EB to William Kimber, 10 Nov 1960
p214 is quite terrible.' EB to Harold Freedman, 15 Nov 1960
p214 does a landscape.' *ibid*

NINETEEN
Bringing Old Clothes but a New Brain

p215 but protected wife.' EB to RJ, 6 Oct 1960, RA
p215 to be "old".' EB to RJ, 31 Oct 1960, RA
p215 in terrible love,' EB to Diana Cooper, 31 Dec 1960
p215 rest of the afternoon.' Mrs William Vestey conservation with author, 24 Sept 1984
p215 in disgrace.' EB to RJ, 19 Jan 1961
p215 have I done?' *ibid*
p216 anything all day.' *ibid*
p216 very caring woman.' Dr John O'Hara conversation with author, 20 Nov 1983
p216 used to illness.' EB to Harold Freedman, 26 Dec 1961
p216 worse than pain.' EB to Harold Freedman, 26 Dec 1961
p216 cup of soup.' *ibid*.
p216 to an aviary.' EB to Diana Cooper, undated
p216 the other watches.' EB unpublished notes, Nov 1962
p217 decided against. Dominick Jones conversation with author, 1 Apr 1984
p217 leave me,' she begged. Carol Brandt conversation with author, 18 Apr 1984, quoting conversation with EB
p217 my heart bursting.' unpublished notes
p217 a proper showing.' Dominick Jones to author, 20 Feb 1984

p217 when we failed.' Manager of Standard Laundry, Woolwich to EB, 24 Jan 1962
p217 could not use.' undated annotation by EB typed below copy of letter, 25 Jan 1962
p217 Inland Revenue,' EB to Harold Freedman, 22 Feb 1962
p217 so well, so well,' EB to Guen Bourke, 14 Feb 1962
p217 the memorial Service.' *ibid*
p218 no idea either.' EB to Harold Freedman, 12 Aug 1961
p218 to act in it.' EB to Harold Freedman, 14 Jan 1962
p218 them any more.' EB to Harold Freedman, 30 May 1962
p219 doing the play,' EB to Harold Freedman, 8 May 1962
p219 excited at seventy-two.' EB to Lynn Fontanne, 26 June 1962
p219 on their laps.' EB to Lynn Fontanne, 28 June 1962
p219 at an interview.' EB to Lynn Fontanne, 26 June 1962
p219 never left me.' *EBA*, p. 253
p219 it any more,' *ibid*
p220 the subject drop.' EBA, p. 255
p220 looseness of setting.' EB to Cuthbert Worsley, 20 Sept 1962
p220 allowance for him.' *ibid*
p220 vices and greed.' *ibid*
p220 period of upsetness.' EB to Harold Freedman, 22 Feb 1962
p220 and writing successfully.' EB to Cuthbert Worsley, 20 Sept 1962
p220 wolves it seems!' *The Chalk Garden*, Act 1
p221 always said "no".' EB to Cuthbert Worsley, 28 Sept 1962
p221 having achieved this.' T.C.Worsley for *Adam Historical Review*, 1974/5, tribute to Cyril Connolly
p221 hears the horn.' EB to Lynne Fontanne, 30 Oct 1962
p221 the Wesker crowd.' EB to Harold Freedman, 15 Oct 1962
p221 so dear to me.' EB to Cuthbert Worsley, 3 June 1963
p221 world before it.' EB to Cuthbert Worsley, ? Sept 1962
p221 accomplished nothing.' *ibid*
p221 reacted againt' it. Peter Hall to EB, 6 Nov 1962
p222 not strong enough.' *ibid*
p222 to mask feeling.' EB annotation on Peter Hall letter, 8 Nov 1962
p222 happen to me.' EB to Harold Freedman, 5 Dec 1962
p222 for a genius!' Quoted by EB to Harold Freedman, 23 Nov 1962
p222 would refuse it.' EB to Harold Freedman, 19 Nov 1962
p222 nearer this happiness.' *ibid*
p222 with Joseph Anthony.' EB to Lynne Fontanne, 22 Jan 1963
p223 in the theatre.' Harold Freedman to EB, 10 Dec 1962
p223 "My little play".' Joseph Anthony conversation with author, 16 Apr 1984
p223 strengthening is needed.' EB to Harold Freedman, 5 Feb 1963
p223 attracted attention.' EB to Harold Freedman, 29 Mar 1963
p223 word about me.' *ibid*
p223 play to anyway?' *ibid*
p224 cheapened.' EB to Harold Freedman, 25 May 1963
p224 touch of womanliness.' EB to Cuthbert Worsley, 30 Jan 1963
p224 of the world,' EB to Cuthbert Worsley, 8 May 1963

p224 loo all afternoon.' EB to Johnny Luscombe, 11 May 1963
p224 but for them).' EB to Cuthbert Worsley, 8 May 1963
p224 "Lunthunting".' *ibid*
p224 long as hers.' EB to Cuthbert Worsley, 15 May 1963
p224 worth of the play.' EB to Cuthbert Worsley, 23 May 1963
p225 want to write,' Joseph Anthony conversation with author, 16 Apr 1984
p225 being a reiteration?' unpublished notes
p225 *our* work begins.' Joseph Anthony conversation with author, 16 Apr 1984
p225 theatre, am I?' *ibid*
p225 body to his.' EB to Johny Luscombe, 19 Nov 1963
p225 skaters' rink either.' Joseph Anthony conversation with author
p225 far too intelligent.' Michael Thornton to author, 14 Dec 1984
p225 plan and elevation).' Oliver Smith to EB, 30 Sept (1963?)
p225 What a nice man.' EB to Cuthbert Worsley, 2 Nov 1963
p226 and *not look.*' *ibid*
p226 of the theatre.' Joseph Anthony conversation with author, 16 Apr 1984
p226 down his throat,' EB to Cuthbert Worsley, 2 Nov 1963
p226 play of mine.' EB to Cuthbert Worsley, 15 Nov 1963
p226 bad mother-in-law I am.' EB to Timothy Jones, 28 June 1960
p227 questions about psychology.' EB to Cuthbert Worsley, 30 Nov 1963
p227 opposite of angst'. Timothy Jones to author, 27 Nov 1984
p227 for an author.' EB to Cuthbert Worsley, 30 Nov 1963
p227 out their hearts.' EB to Cuthbert Worsley, 24 Nov 1963
p227 really could have.' EB to Cuthbert Worsley, 30 Nov 1963
p227 to hear it.' EB to Cuthbert Worsley, 15 Dec 1963
p227 I had supposed.' EB to Cuthbert Worsley, 15 Dec 1963
p227 show, they say.' *EBA*, p. 261
p228 of the evening.' Brad Evans, *Telegram*, 10 Dec 1963
p228 it gave me.' *EBA*, p. 262
p228 blessing that is.' Walter Kerr, *New York Herald Tribune*, 3 Jan 1964
p228 for an audience.' *Time* Magazine, 10 Jan 1964
p228 too will persist.' Joseph Anthony to EB, 2 Jan 1964
p229 for this play,' Joseph Anthony conservation with author, 16 Apr 1984

TWENTY
Money Doesn't Matter Any More: Get The Plays On

taciturnity valued.' EB, *The Times*, 13 Feb 1964
p230 spoiled all winter.' EB to Diana Cooper, undated
p230 success the merrier.' Peter Hall to EB, 20 Jan 1964
p231 are squeezed out.' EB to Diana Cooper, 15 Aug 1962
p231 in every line.' EB to Binkie Beaumont, 16 Feb 1964
p231 talent is real.' EB to Harold Freedman, 25 Feb 1964
p231 was darling,' Binkie Beaumont to EB, 1 Apr 1964
p231 still enormously enthusiastic.' *ibid*
p231 means to me.' EB to Laurence Olivier, 30 June 1964

p232 yourself it is.' Laurence Olivier to EB, 1 July 1964
p232 the present situation.' *ibid*
p232 such a fuss.' EB to Laurence Olivier, 2 July 1964
p232 of The Last Joke.' Irene Selznick to EB, 24 June 1964
p232 on a production.' *ibid*
p232 be the loser.' EB to Irene Selznick, 27 June 1964
p232 of the film industry?' *ibid*
p233 go to Eton!' *ibid*
p233 a director who didn't?' EB to Alan Webb, 16 Oct 1964
p233 you, wouldn't I?' EB to Vivian Matalon, 16 Feb 1965
p233 about the relationship,' EB to Vivian Matalon, 5 Feb 1965
p233 Tarver had been ...' *ibid*
p233 Sir Gregory wrong,' EB to Brain Ahcrne, 11 Apr 1965
p233 rest of the cast.' Vivian Matalon conversation with author, 30 Sept 1984
p233 In fact – immortal.' EB to Vivian Matalon, 31 Dec 1964
p234 up eyes or face,' EB to unnamed, 12 May 1965
p234 opened in London,' Mary Lynn conversation with author, 14 Mar 1984
p234 with the play.' Vivian Matalon conversation with author, 30 Sept 1984
p234 plastered with treacle.' EB to Noel Woolf, 24 Oct 1965
p234 the small hours.' Vivian Matalon conversation with author, 30 Sept 1984
p234 destroyed the play,' *ibid*
p234 and attractive play.' Bernard Levin, *Daily Mail*, 21 May 1965
p234 of the first act.' EB to Bernard Levin, 26 May 1965
p234 delineating human beings,' Bernard Levin, *Daily Maily*, 21 May 1965
p234 failed in New York.' Alan Webb to Vivian Matalon, 11 Nov 1965
p234 age and tenacity.' *ibid*
p234 rarely gets that.' John Perry to EB, undated 1965
p235 beauty of writing.' EB to Robert Helpmann, 2 June 1965
p235 throughout an evening.' Vivian Leigh to EB, 3 June 1965
p235 vanity of directors.' EB to M. Abbot Van Nostrand, 24 Dec 1965
p235 playwright going mad.' EB to Timothy Jones, 26 May 1965
p235 on their heads.' *ibid*
p235 profoundly pleased.' EB to Noel Woolf, 24 Oct 1965
p235 as Enid Bagnold,' French's *Play Parade*, Autumn 1965
p235 front of them.' EB to Noel Woolf, 24 Oct 1965
p235 old hollow sound.' EB to Cuthbert Worsley, 14 Oct 1965
p236 doesn't want to.' *ibid*
p236 can't smell,' *ibid*
p236 is so sad.' *ibid*
p236 last all day.' *ibid*
p236 comes the tune.' *ibid*
p236 sons and myself.' Daphne Webb to author, undated 1985
p236 face of all odds.' EB to Cuthbert Worsley, 23 May 1965
p236 and money pressures.' EB to Cuthbert Worsley, 4 Feb 1965
p236 I want to.' *ibid*
p236 been sat on.' EB to Vivian Matalon, 2 Mar 1966
p237 he was immortal.' EB to Walter Kerr, 17 Feb 1966

p237 if it deserves it.' EB in *Dramatists' Guild Quarterly*, Spring 1966
p237 for grapefruit juice.' EB to Jean Kerr, 13 Apr 1966
p237 of that desire?' EB to Noel Woolf, 19 June 1966
p237 Waiting ... trying, trying.' EB to Vivian Matalon, 2 Mar 1966
p237 so love Tucker.' EB to Lynn Fontanne, 16 May 1966
p237 grow used to it,' EB to Dominick Jones, 13 Jan 1966
p237 so very much.' EB to Dominick Jones, 18 Sept 1964
p237 could eventually survive.' *ibid*
p238 must love him,' Lynn Fontanne to EB, undated
p238 best in anyone.' EB to Diana Cooper, 8 Nov 1969
p238 Stick to it.' Georgina Ward to EB, undated
p239 in a down spiral.' Janet Burroway conversation with author, 2 July 1985
p239 my face powder.' EB to Laurian d'Harcourt, 20 Feb 1967
p239 indulgence of nerves.' Peggy Ramsay to EB, 3 May 1967
p239 source might dry.' EB to Peggy Ramsay, 4 May 1967
p239 I'll be obedient.' *ibid*
p239 like a negress.' EB circular letter to family, 22 Aug 1967
p239 never move again.' *ibid*
p240 talked of cancer.' *ibid*
p240 sitting in a castle.' EB to Frank Hauser, 12 Mar 1968
p240 paws in the air,' Preface to *Call Me Jacky*, Elek Books, Plays of the Year, 1968
p240 the same thing.' EB to Ronald Bryden, 13 Mar 1968
p240 side but recovering.' EB to Vivian Matalon, undated
p240 I'm important anyway ...' EB to Michael Thornton, 10 Mar 1968
p240 to explain them. EB Preface to *Call Me Jacky*, op. cit.
p241 wickedly cruel.' EB to Frank Hauser, 12 Mar 1968
p241 by all of you.' EB to Ronald Bryden, 13 Mar 1968
p241 and succeeds totally.' Ronald Bryden, *The Observer*, 10 Mar 1968
p241 because of a flop,' EB to Ronald Bryden, 13 Mar 1968

TWENTY-ONE

I Am Much Disappointed To Be a Cripple

p242 me writing it.' EB to Guen Bourke, 4 May 1964
p242 these are genital.' unpublished notes, draft for introduction to autobiography
p242 success with a play? *ibid*
p242 think I am? *ibid*
p243 days of The Chalk Garden.' Penelope Gilliatt, *Observer*, 18 Oct 1964
p243 someone else's neck.' Penelope Gilliatt, *Observer*, 9 Aug 1965
p243 this of me.' Penelope Gilliatt conversation with author, 25 Sept 1984
p243 was unhappily aware. Timothy Jones conversation with author, 12 Sept 1984
p243 hadn't meant to.' EB to Carol Brandt, 1 Jan 1969
p243 smeared about beforehand.' EB to Carol Brandt, 11 Jan 1969
p243 though I might.' EB to Carol Brandt, 1 Jan 1969
p243 (which they are).' EB to Carol Brandt, 2 Jan 1969
p245 much like pain.' EB to Sir Henry Osmond-Clarke, 1 Jan 1969

p245 third of morphian,' *ibid*

p245 down the throat,' EB to Dwye Evans, 20 June 1969

p245 critically and commercially,' Random House report, 14 Apr 1969

p245 a book of power.' EB to Edward Weeks, 16 May 1969, HRC

p245 have the book.' *ibid*

p245 she always has.' EB to Dwye Evans, 20 June 1969

p245 all her life.' EB to Dwye Evans, 15 June 1969

p246 unapproachable and wrong.' EB to Michael Thornton, 10 Nov 1969

p246 very happy in it.' Peggy Ashcroft to EB, undated

p246 so cruel to you.' *ibid*

p246 I have had.' EB to Cyril Connolly, 6 Apr 1970, *McFL*

p246 incredible generosity.' Deirdre Levi to author, 26 Jan 1984

p246 like a pleased child.' EB to Cyril Connolly, 9 Apr 1970, *McFL*

p246 chunk of my life,' EB to Cecil Beaton, 21 Feb 1968

p246 don't see you,' EB to Cecil Beaton, 6 Mar 1969

p246 on each cheek.' Cecil Beaton to EB, 27 Dec 1969

p247 few good plays.' Cecil Beaton's Diaries: 1963–1974, *The Parting Years*, Weidenfeld and Nicolson 1978

p247 been "edited" before.' EB to Edward Weeks, 21 July 1969, HRC

p247 not that far.' *ibid*

p247 will move me.' *ibid*

p247 will think about. *ibid*

p247 I am indifferent.' *ibid*

p247 of the build-up.' EB to Irene Selznick, 10 Apr 1970

p247 to move next? EB to Irene Selznick, 5 May 1970

p247 I can't write.' *ibid*

p248 are extremely satisfied.' Sir Henry Osmond-Clarke to EB 5 Nov 1970

p248 let's cripple around.' EB to Diana Cooper, 7 June 1969

p248 makes me useless.' EB to Dominick Jones, 31 Dec 1971

p248 sick of my style.' EB to Dr Ed Bigg, 7 Jan 1972

p249 staying how I am.' EB to Dr Ed Bigg, 4 Jan 1972

p249 could cure it.' EB to Dr Ed Bigg, 13 Dec 1971

p249 curing the habit.' *ibid*

p249 life on fiction.' EB to Hilary Spurling, 21 Mar 1971

p249 her powerful web,' Peter Willes conversation with author, 17 July 1984

p249 out or played.' EB to Robert Freedman, 11 Aug 1970

p249 remark and response,' *ibid*

p249 not a verse play,' Peter Willes conversation with author

p250 couldn't throw off,' *ibid*

p250 tottering there at all.' EB interviewed by Peter Willes, *TV Times*, 2 Nov 1971

p250 wrote the book?' *ibid*

p250 by her dresses.' Cecil Beaton to EB, 29 Aug 1971

p250 gifts to posterity.' J.C. Trewin, *Lady*, 13 May 1971

p250 over the tea-cups.' Milton Shulman, *Evening Standard*, 28 Apr 1971

p250 especially about Toronto,' Gladys Cooper to EB, 5 Oct 1971

p251 your buddy, Gladys.' *ibid*

p251 the Broadway one.' Franklyn Lenthall to EB, 22 Aug 1971

p251 books, have you?' EB in conversation, 'She And She', BBC, TV, 22 Aug 1971
p251 woman as led.' *ibid*
p251 not necessarily badly.' *ibid*
p251 woman might have.' *ibid*
p251 "bloodstream thing".' EB to Timothy Jones, 6 July 1967
p252 Have I talent?' Rottingdean Parish Magazine, 1 Mar 1973
p252 odious to them.' *ibid*
p252 need have bothered.' Private information
p252 really too late.' *ibid*
p252 angry as that.' Michael Thornton to author, 14 Dec 1984
p252 survival of the village.' *ibid*
p252 as her backbone?' EB to Canon Ivor Walters, 9 Aug 1973
p252 mountain of indignation.' EB to Canon Ivor Walters, 16 Aug 1973
p252 Laurian's new house.' EB to Michael Thornton, 29 Oct 1973
p253 antiquity that I mind.' EB to Canon Ivor Walters, 14 Nov 1973
p253 leg to stand on.' Canon Ivor Walters to EB, 6 Nov 1973
p253 up by disagreement.' EB to Canon Ivor Walters, 21 Nov 1973
p253 penny to the church.' quoted by EB to Canon Ivor Walters, 9 Dec 1973
p253 say, taken aback.' *ibid*
p253 ... a little snappy.' EB to Canon Ivor Walters, 14 Jan 1974

TWENTY-TWO
The Last Attachment

p254 put them down.' EB to Dominick Jones, 31 Dec 1971
p254 very fond of her.' EB unsent letter to Lord Ward of Witley, 7 Jan 1972
p254 time had come ...' Georgina Ward to Timothy Jones, 24 Apr 1981
p254 of interesting things.' Noel Willman conversation with author, 18 April 1984
p254 know you could.' *ibid*
p254 her family life.' *ibid*
p255 make me stay.' Richard Jones to author, 28 May 1985
p255 bear enveloping feeling.' Noel Willman conversation with author, 18 Apr 1984
p255 her to levitate.' *ibid*
p255 be no more.' *ibid*
p255 on my deathbed,' Laurian d'Harcourt to author, 29 July 1984
p255 I'm moving on.' *A Matter of Gravity*, Act iii
p256 I am good material".' *ibid*
p256 much more thrilling.' Katharine Hepburn to EB, 13 Nov 1968
p256 it was about.' Katharine Hepburn conversation with author, 19 Apr 1984
p256 usual theatre anxiety,' EB to Michael Thornton , 19 Sept 1974
p256 Royal Crescent [Hotel]. EB to Michael Thornton, 24 Apr 1975
p256 Very rewarding.' Katharine Hepburn to EB, 11 May 1977
p257 was a little boy.' Quoted by Home Office to EB, 17 Oct 1974
p257 Is it Leon?' Noel Willman conversation with author, 18 Apr 1984
p257 on your hands,' Peggy Ramsay to Noel Willman, 4 Nov 1975

p257 liked each other.' Katharine Hepburn conversation with author, 19 Apr 1984

p258 me one whit.' Katharine Hepburn quoted in *New York Times*, 16 Jan 1976

p258 play about people.' *ibid*

p258 dauntingly literate terms.' William B. Collins, *Philadelphia Inquirer*, 28 Oct 1975

p258 my only friends.' EB undated annotation above review

p258 so proudly making.' EB to Michael Thornton, 15 May 1976

p258 gives me claustrophobia.' EB to Michael Thornton, 26 Aug 1976

p258 make much sense.' Noel Willman to Peggy Ramsay, 29 Apr 1976

p258 NOT to do so.' Michael Thornton to author, 14 Dec 1984

p258 is very good.' EB to Michael Thornton, 23 June 1974

p258 let's let up!' Laurian d'Harcourt to Michael Thornton, 27 Oct 1975

p259 to accept it.' Michael Thornton to author, 14 Dec 1984

p259 you as much.' EB to Michael Thornton, 22 Dec 1975

p259 idiotic monstrosity.' Rex Reed, *Daily News*, 6 Feb 1976

p259 to fade away.' Clive Barnes, *The Times*, 7 Feb 1976

p259 the hideous prices.' Sumner Locke Elliott to EB, 27 Feb 1976

p259 play, dear Enid.' Katharine Hepburn to EB, 23 Nov 1976

p259 wonderful for me,' quoted by Noel Willman conversation with author, 18 Apr 1984

p260 really enjoys giving.' *ibid*

p260 I don't care.' EB to Diana Cooper, 4 Nov 1977

p260 him in America.' *ibid*

p260 or need money,' EB to Diana Cooper, 13 Feb 1977

p260 Trust you Enid.' quoted by EB to Diana Cooper, 13 Feb 1977

p260 your own genius ...' Bryan Forbes to EB, 30 Jan 1977

p260 what you think.' Bryan Forbes to EB, 5 July 1977

p261 a house alone.' EB to Diana Cooper, 6 May 1977

p261 nice rich one?' *ibid*

p261 to see him.' EB to Home Office, 22 Oct 1977

p261 needle to do it.' EB to Michael Thornton, 21 Dec 1977

p261 of a new book ...' EB to Michael Thornton, 21 Dec 1977

p261 of publication before.' EB to John Randle, 12 Nov 1977

p261 jolly good read.' quoted by John Randle, conversation with author, 5 Aug 1984

p261 coming to me.' EB to Michael Thornton, 21 Dec 1977

p261 might provide it.' EB to John Randle, 8 Dec 1977

p261 his horrible face.' EB to John Randle, 28 Dec 1977

p262 glitter is fabulous,' EB to John Randle, 28 Mar 1979

p262 post never stops.' Laurian d'Harcourt to Michael Thornton, 25 Oct 1979

p262 myself to sleep.' EB to John Randle, 1 Dec 1979

p262 sweet to me.' EB to John Randle, 7 Nov 1979

p262 look beautiful today.' quoted by Pat Brown, conversation with author, 8 May 1984

p262 enjoying this party.' Tara Heinemann diary, 25 July 1980

p262 this drunken palace,' EB to John Randle, 3 Nov 1977

p263 to garden? (uneven number)' *The Times*, 29 June 1977

p263 upon to prescribe.' Dr David Davidson conversation with author, 10 Feb 1986 *p264* "cruel and pointless".' *ibid*

p264 home was looming,' Laurian d'Harcourt to Michael Thornton, 5 May 1981

p264 "her Benjamin",' *ibid*

p264 than she was,' Laurian d'Harcourt to Michael Thornton, 7 Jan 1981

p264 snuffed out her candle.' Laurian d'Harcourt to Michael Thornton, 5 May 1981

p265 up to the hilt.' Georgina Ward to Timothy Jones, 24 Apr 1981

p265 support and comforter.' Laurian d'Harcourt to Michael Thornton, 5 May 1981

p265 have liked that,' Rev Noel Staines to author, 17 Feb 1986

p265 her own children;' Nigel Nicolson Memorial Address for Enid Bagnold, 2 Nov 1981

p265 from us children,' Timothy Jones to author, 29 Nov 1984

p265 to the Tate.' *EBA*, p. 70

p265 sick of the shine.' EB to Sumner Locke Elliott, 21 Nov 1971

p266 the same reason.' Quoted by Irene Selznick to EB, 4–7 May 1954

p266 whatever you do,' EB to Timothy Jones, 16 May 1977

p266 mother to hear.' quoted by EB to Timothy Jones, 18 Sept 1964

p266 sense of motherhood.' EB to Dominick Jones, 26 Aug 1964

p266 ability-to-be-happy to them.' EB to Michael Thornton, 21 Dec 1977

Index